ALSO BY WILLIAM SOUDER
A Plague of Frogs

UNDER A
WILD SKY

UNDER A WILD SKY

JOHN JAMES AUDUBON AND THE

MAKING OF *THE BIRDS OF AMERICA*

WILLIAM SOUDER

NORTH POINT PRESS

A DIVISION OF FARRAR, STRAUS AND GIROUX

NEW YORK

North Point Press
A division of Farrar, Straus and Giroux
19 Union Square West, New York 10003

Distributed in Canada by Douglas & McIntyre Ltd.
Printed in the United States of America
First edition, 2004

Grateful acknowledgment is made to the following for permission to reprint previously published and unpublished material:
Lines from "Sleepless Night" by Octavio Paz, translated by Eliot Weinberger, from *Collected Poems 1957–1987*, copyright © 1986 by Octavio Paz and Eliot Weinberger. Reprinted by permission of New Directions Corp.
The author also wishes to thank the American Philosophical Society for permission to quote from various unpublished manuscripts, and from *The Life and Letters of Alexander Wilson* by Clark Hunter, copyright © 1983 by the American Philosophical Society for its *Memoirs* series, volume 154.

Library of Congress Cataloging-in-Publication Data
Souder, William, 1949–
    Under a wild sky : John James Audubon and the making of the Birds of America / William Souder.— 1st ed.
        p. cm.
Includes bibliographical references (p.   ).
    ISBN 0-86547-671-3 (hc : alk. paper)
    1. Audubon, John James, 1785–1851. 2. Ornithologists—United States—Biography. 3. Audubon, John James, 1785–1851. Birds of America. I. Title.

QL31.A9 S68 2004
598'.092—dc22

                                                                                2003026141

EAN: 978-0-86547-671-4

Designed by Jonathan D. Lippincott

www.fsgbooks.com

10   9   8   7   6   5   4   3   2   1

For Joe, Martha, Tom, and Elizabeth

The living are alive
walking flying ripening bursting
the dead are alive
oh bones still hot
wind shakes and scatters them

—Octavio Paz

CONTENTS

I

AUDUBON AND WILSON

1

PHILADELPHIA

Tanagra rubra: The Scarlet Tanager
You have now before you representations of one of the most richly coloured of our birds, and one whose history is in some degree peculiar.   —*Ornithological Biography*

On a fine spring afternoon in 1824, the daily coach from Pittsburgh swayed down the turnpike toward Philadelphia, the team moving easily on the smooth, macadamized lane. The road ran beneath forested hillsides, dropping steadily as it came alongside the Schuylkill River near the city. The woods were green and alive with birds, which flushed at the oncoming hoofbeats and sped off through tunnels of sunlight and shadow. From far away came the bleat of geese flying in wedges high above the horizon, and closer by was the hissing of cupped wings as flocks of ducks coasted in to land on the river. Peering out from the carriage, John James Audubon watched the birds intently, though his thoughts traveled on to the days ahead in the city. Unlike the birds, which came back every year, Audubon had been away a long time.

The stage rumbled over a wooden bridge and rolled through the city, halting near the Delaware waterfront and its bustling taverns and inns. Audubon climbed down and swept a hand through the mane of hair that hung past his shoulders. He was an imposing figure, rangy and athletic, and, according to many women who knew him, dashingly handsome. Dressed in buckskin pantaloons and a dirty greatcoat, Audubon blinked at the city's broad, cobbled streets and immaculate plank sidewalks. It was the fifth of April—his wedding anniversary. Audubon was just shy of thirty-nine years old.

Streetlamps were being lighted. A waxing moon hung low in the western sky. Audubon had lived beneath that sky for seventeen years, moving from place to place, acquiring a family while making and losing a fortune in a string of business failures. The carefree life he'd known as a young man on his father's estate outside of Philadelphia was a distant memory. Partnerships in enterprises from Kentucky to New Orleans had gone to dust, several in ugly confrontations. In one dispute, Audubon had lost several thousand dollars he could ill afford when the owner of a steamboat Audubon held as collateral made off with the vessel in Henderson, Kentucky, taking it down the Ohio River, then the Mississippi, all the way to New Orleans. Enraged, Audubon chased the man to Louisiana and back. He got neither the boat nor his money. On returning to Henderson the man threatened Audubon's life—but bided his time. He finally took Audubon by surprise one morning, clubbing him over the head in the middle of a city street. Audubon, who'd recently injured his right arm and had it in a sling, appeared defenseless. But as blood poured down his face, Audubon used his good hand to draw a dagger from his belt and stab his attacker in the chest. A mob that included many of Audubon's creditors later had to be dispersed from in front of his house. But while the man's wound was grave, he recovered. Charges against Audubon were later dismissed on grounds of self-defense. Shortly afterward Audubon was insolvent and was forced into bankruptcy after being arrested and briefly jailed in Louisville over outstanding debts.

So it had gone, from one river town to another, always heading downstream, always riding a little lower in life. Moving west and south through Kentucky, then down to Mississippi and Louisiana, Audubon had tried his hand at shopkeeping, lumber milling, real estate development, and teaching. He'd worked as a dance instructor, fiddler, and taxidermist. He'd taught fencing and art, drawn portraits, sold landscape paintings and urban sketches on the street. Lucy, his wife, found occasional work as a governess. But the one thing that held Audubon's interest—and the thing he was best at—was hunting and studying birds.

Keen-eyed, and with a tolerance for the rigors of the outdoors, Audubon had wandered widely across the American frontier, honing his woodcraft. He disappeared into the wilderness often, turning up days or weeks or even months later, laden with trophies: animals of every kind—most dead, sometimes a few still living—plus eggs, nests, plants, and a myriad of brilliantly hued skins of birds both known and unknown to science. And there were his paintings. Audubon had begun drawing birds as a child. He had talent, but more important, he had a rare feeling for his subjects. He was as interested in how birds lived as he was in their appearance. Over time, as he refined his technique, Audubon's paintings had begun to merge the beauty of the birds with their wildness in a way no previous naturalist had managed. As his fortunes dwindled, Audubon's collection of paintings grew thick.

By 1823, Audubon felt his time and his prospects running out. He and Lucy were living near New Orleans with their two nearly adolescent sons. Two daughters had died in infancy. Despite his frequent absences, Audubon was devoted to his family and weary of their precarious circumstances. At the urging of friends who admired his paintings but were doubtful of their value on the frontier, where anyone curious about birds and nature had only to look around, Audubon came East in search of an agent or publisher. He may have envisioned some kind of book—illustrated volumes on natural history were popular, though shockingly expensive—or, more likely, he thought only of finding someone who might tell him how to sell his work.

He left New Orleans that fall, taking along his elder son, Victor, who was fourteen. Initially they rode comfortably up the Mississippi aboard the steamship *Magnet*, turning east into the Ohio River on October 15—where unexpected low water prevented further progress by boat. Audubon, impatient to proceed, arranged to have his belongings forwarded and set off with Victor toward Louisville on foot, accompanied by two other passengers. One of them, a big man named Rose, warned Audubon that he was in a great hurry and would not wait for a young boy unable to keep up.

Audubon worried about Victor as well. He knew this stretch of low, swampy country, having walked through it some years previously when ice had forced him from the river. At another time he had hiked along the Ohio farther ahead, after lightning killed a horse literally from underneath him. Beyond the river confluence stretched an endless wood, both pretty and daunting. The land was sparsely settled, with few roads. Narrow trails, which had to be walked single file, sometimes petered out in thickets or vanished in burned-out forests snarled with deadfall. The distance upriver to Henderson, Kentucky, where Audubon hoped to find transportation, was more than two hundred miles.

In the end, it was Audubon and Victor who outpaced the other travelers, and later Audubon would recall the episode as a happy adventure, though it was, he admitted, "a tough walk for a youth." Victor at times appeared near exhaustion. On one occasion he grew faint and collapsed sobbing—only to be roused by a smiling Audubon who pointed out a large turkey strutting through the woods close by. Somehow, Victor woke restored each morning. He was a pleasant, intelligent boy, with his father's high forehead and large eyes, and, evidently, some of his sturdy constitution.

Audubon, as usual, strode over even the most difficult terrain without complaint, repeatedly leading the party out of trouble, encouraging everyone on, breaking trail or slogging ahead through the rocky shallows when they were forced down to the river's edge. He caught fish to eat and kept a watchful eye on their bearings. Well versed in the customs of backcountry travel, Audubon unerringly found houses where the group could put up at night. His powers of observation operated continually, and he found their various hosts as interesting and as colorful as the many birds in the area. They met a man who kept a large black wolf that was "tame and gentle." At another place where they stopped, Audubon was disgusted by the man of the house, who was lazy. The man's industrious wife was uncommonly attractive and seemed slightly out of place. She had delicate hands, lovely blue eyes, and a manner that suggested "her right to belong to a much higher class." The memory of the morning feast she served the travelers—ground corn, freshly killed chicken, and coffee—remained with Audubon. It was, he said, the best breakfast he had ever eaten. Upon leaving, he gave a dollar to one of the children and said a tender goodbye to the woman as she nursed a baby. The husband, Audubon noticed, stood by sullenly, smoking his pipe.

After three days' walking, the group topped a hill early in the morning and saw a vast forest spread out before them. The rising sun lit the frost on the trees. Mile by mile, Audubon coaxed the party onward while thinking to himself that this must be among the most beautiful places on earth. The season was turning. They found ripe peaches in an orchard and saw wood ducks fattening themselves on the acorns collecting in the river bottoms. At the end of an arduous day, Audubon took Victor for a swim in the wide Ohio. As the sun went down, they lazed in the glassy current and watched as robins flying south filled the sky overhead.

They had marched six days, the fifth in a driving rain, when they came at last to a decent road, where the others in the group decided they must

slow down. Two hours after reluctantly leaving the rest of the party behind, Audubon and his son reached the Green River ferry, just above
Henderson, where they hired a wagon to take them on to Louisville. On
the crossing, they dangled their feet in the cool water as the river slipped
quietly by on its way into the heart of the untamed country.

Audubon and Victor stopped a few days later at Shippingport, a trading community on the south bank of the Ohio, just below the falls at
Louisville. Audubon had barely enough money remaining—$13—to
rent a room. They called on old friends, and as Audubon and Lucy had
hoped, Victor was placed as an apprentice in their family's counting
house. Audubon spent the winter saving for the remainder of his trip. He
occupied himself dodging old creditors and painting portraits, signs, and
even murals on the interiors of steamboats. In March he had booked passage for Pittsburgh. He brought with him only a few possessions, including a kit of watercolors and an unusually handsome double shotgun with
fine engravings on its breech. Firmly clutched under one arm was an
oversized portfolio tied with string.

In Philadelphia Audubon found lodging in one of the inns on tavern row.
The noise and activity was disorienting. Rooms were cramped but cheap—
$10 a week, which included two heavy meals a day featuring slabs of
meat, eggs, fowl, and cheese, accompanied in the evenings by wine and
ale. In his small room with its rough bed and whitewashed walls echoing
with the woozy laughter of taverngoers until late at night, Audubon made
his plans. Within a few days he had bought a suit of clothes, and readied
himself for introductions to some of the city's influential citizens. He decided against cutting his hair or even buttoning his shirt collar. He hoped
his rough style marked him as a true backwoodsman—an image Audubon
was convinced would lend credibility to his claim as a naturalist. He also
felt his curling locks recalled the city's foremost figure, Benjamin Franklin, in an appealing way.

Audubon called first on Dr. James Mease. Mease was a prominent
physician and part of Philadelphia's growing community of intellectuals,
many of them doctors, who had developed an interest in their young
nation's natural history. And Mease was an acquaintance. He'd known
Audubon as an adventurous, undisciplined teenager who once lived close

to his friends the Bakewells, in the country outside Philadelphia near Valley Forge.

The Audubon who appeared at Mease's doorstep in a prosperous section of Chestnut Street had changed considerably. He was now a middle-aged man, rough-looking and obviously nervous. His English—muddled when Mease had known him as a recent immigrant from Europe—was improved, despite a still noticeable French accent. Mease, taken aback at seeing Audubon after such a long absence, was even more surprised when Audubon came inside, loosened his inexpensive new coat, and untied his portfolio. Awed by Audubon's paintings, Mease suggested they get the opinion of a knowledgeable ornithologist. And he had one in mind—a young visitor to the city named Charles-Lucien Bonaparte, who was himself engaged in the study of American birds.

Only twenty-one years old, Bonaparte was already an accomplished naturalist. Aboard ship to the New World—a trip that lasted fifty-one nervous days, during which the ship encountered several terrible storms en route from Plymouth to New York—Bonaparte had collected an assortment of fishes and turtles, and had shot and studied many birds, including several unknown species of petrels. Upon landing in America, Bonaparte was immediately smitten with the young republic, which he declared "the most perfect of all those that have ever existed, without excepting those of Athens, Sparta, and Rome." He set about investigating the many strange animals new to his experience. Like all European newcomers, he was fascinated by the American rattlesnake. He was at the same time naïve about certain New World fauna, like the small black-and-white quadruped he encountered one day while out riding. Dismounting, Bonaparte chased the animal hoping to catch and examine it. He got close enough to the skunk to learn what it was.

Bonaparte had been welcomed into Philadelphia's scientific and social circles after arriving there in the fall of 1823, about the same time that Audubon had left New Orleans. At first, he stayed at Point Breeze, his relatives' New Jersey estate on the Delaware River, about twenty-five miles north of Philadelphia. That winter Bonaparte and his pregnant wife moved to the city not far from Dr. Mease and Bonaparte began corresponding with the Academy of Natural Sciences. The academy, formed only eleven years earlier by a handful of amateur naturalists who met weekly above an apothecary, had become one of the country's leading learned institutions. Its monthly *Journal*, first published in 1817, was an important scholarly publication. In 1819, four members of the academy had been chosen for Stephen Harriman Long's expedition to the Rocky Mountains—the first scientists to accompany such a government-sponsored endeavor. Meetings now took place every Saturday evening in the academy's own building, which also housed a large library, as well as an overflowing collection of natural specimens.

In January 1824, Bonaparte submitted a paper on his new petrels to the academy, where it was read to the members and later accepted for publication. On February 24, while Audubon was shivering on the docks and saving his pennies in Shippingport, the academy elected Bonaparte as a member. He was received warmly a week later at his first meeting. Bonaparte's new colleagues doubtless respected his ornithological work, but they were probably influenced by his glamorous connection with Europe as well. Born in France and raised in Italy, Bonaparte had wealth and a title of sorts. He was the prince of Musignano, which was neither a country nor even a locality, but merely his father's house on a hill overlooking the Italian town of Canino, not far from Rome. Still, Bonaparte was an aristocrat, even if he wasn't a very impressive one physically. He had dark hair and eyes, and he was short and plump. Everyone agreed he was the spitting image of his late uncle Napoleon, the emperor of France.

When Mease took Audubon to meet Bonaparte a few days later, the two naturalists saw at once that they were quite different, though they had much in common. Audubon, obviously, was French. But he was poor and only marginally educated, and seemed uncomfortable in his surroundings after years away from civil society. For his part, Audubon regarded the little man before him as scarcely more than a boy—though he was literate and precocious and displayed the easy assurance of the upper class. Both men must have found their meeting in this way the kind of odd circumstance that could only happen in America.

Bonaparte brushed aside the awkwardness of the moment. Like most naturalists, he was insatiably curious. Bonaparte invited Audubon to show him his drawings and made space on a table where the portfolio, which seemed unusually large, could be opened. As Audubon fumbled with the string, Bonaparte may have allowed himself to hope the portfolio contained a bird or two he could add to a list he was making of undescribed or misidentified North American species. The New World was full of tax-

onomic opportunity. Bonaparte, who'd pored over rare illustrated texts
and investigated European specimen collections of birds from around
the world, expected that he knew more about these matters than almost
anyone alive. And Bonaparte had a good idea of what Audubon's paintings might look like. With luck, they would be proper scientific renderings—clean, two-dimensional studies of the birds in static profile, wings
demurely folded alongside their bodies, the plumages neatly colored
against a white background. Such work required not only skill, but also
discipline and a patient attention to detail—not exactly qualities that
Audubon projected.

Bonaparte stepped nearer the table. Audubon opened his portfolio.

It is unclear at which meeting of the Academy of Natural Sciences
Audubon first appeared after that. But word of everything else that happened in Philadelphia that summer traveled far and for a long time, as is
usually the case with bad news.

Bonaparte had been amazed by Audubon's drawings. In his brief time
in the city, Audubon had met a few painters Mease knew, and they had
praised his work. But Bonaparte was the first person who truly understood the significance of what Audubon had brought out of the wilderness—and also the first to share Audubon's passion for his subjects. The
paintings were unlike anything the young prince had seen, though they
depicted something he loved deeply—the terrible life-and-death struggle that is nature itself. Aububon's birds were breathtakingly beautiful.
And huge—even the largest were painted to full life-size, some filling
Audubon's enormous sheets of paper from edge to edge. But it was the
aliveness of the images that startled and delighted Bonaparte. Instead of
showing only what the birds looked like, Audubon had captured how
they lived. Wheeling beneath storm-wracked skies, clamoring in bushes
and trees, recoiling from attacking animals, or ripping flesh in bloody
gobbets from freshly killed prey, Audubon's ferocious birds looked as if
they might fly screeching off the page. This was not good form, not the
accepted style at all. It was something totally new. To Bonaparte, the birds
looked truly wild, much like the strange, nervous man standing next to
him.

With Bonaparte as his patron, Audubon rushed through the city over
the next several weeks, being introduced to artists and scientists. Mean-

while, his new acquaintances developed a fascination with the artist— an inquisitiveness Audubon met with a Kentucky storyteller's penchant for exaggeration. Audubon was quite a piece of work—shy and awkward one minute, a blustery braggart the next. Everyone wanted to know who he was and where he came from. His account of himself, even alongside the slight support Dr. Mease could offer, was difficult to swallow. Audubon claimed to have been born in the territory of Louisiana. His father, he said, served as an admiral in the French navy and had also been a hero in the American war of independence. His mother was a Creole of Spanish extraction, who was courted and married by his father at her sprawling plantation near New Orleans. After her untimely death, Audubon was taken to France, where he was adopted by his father's second wife and developed an interest in nature and painting. One of his teachers there, Audubon boasted, was the great portraitist Jacques-Louis David. At eighteen, Audubon had come to America to manage his father's property, a large farm called Mill Grove, just west of Philadelphia. From there, he said, he had traveled far, seeing much of the country while devoting himself to the study of birds, acquiring a knowledge of their ways and appearance that he felt sure was unequaled by any other ornithologist.

And that is how the real trouble started.

Audubon was on safe ground in his airy dismissal of European naturalists as "cabinet ornithologists" who studied American birds by looking at moth-eaten stuffed specimens, never setting foot in America. Beginning with Thomas Jefferson—who had identified more than one hundred new bird species and who feuded with scientists in France over the vigor and uniqueness of New World fauna—American naturalists had been eager to gain authority in their own country. In Philadelphia, especially among members of the academy, any informed opinion against European views of American natural history was enthusiastically received.

But Audubon threatened the legacy of Alexander Wilson, America's preeminent ornithologist and a hero in the cause of New World scientific independence. Wilson, who had come to Pennsylvania from Scotland in 1794, was a poet and naturalist. A lonely man, Wilson was repeatedly troubled by political and romantic intrigues. He supported himself as a weaver and peddler, and later by teaching school and working as a book editor. Wilson discovered an interest in birds after he was befriended by William Bartram, an eminent botanist whose well-stocked library in

Philadelphia became Wilson's favorite retreat. In 1804, the year he was granted citizenship, Wilson had set out to draw and write about all the birds of North America. He was advised against it. He had limited artistic ability and the large, lavishly illustrated book he had in mind—what we would today think of as a coffee-table book—made little financial sense. It was almost sure to cost him more to publish than he could ever hope to earn back.

Wilson never did get rich. But he did publish *American Ornithology*. When he died suddenly in 1813 at the age of forty-seven, he had completed seven volumes and was working on the eighth. By any measure, it was the most handsome, the most expensive, and one of the most important works yet published about America. At the Academy of Natural Sciences, Wilson was revered as the "father of American ornithology"— a true giant in American natural history—and *American Ornithology* was regarded as an almost sacred text, the first major scientific publication produced in America by an American.

Audubon failed to be suitably impressed. He may have mentioned what he believed were mistakes in Wilson's taxonomy and drawings. He may have alluded to his later claim that he had actually met Wilson—in Kentucky. As Audubon recalled, Wilson had shown up in Louisville some years back, selling subscriptions to his book and looking for new birds. According to Audubon, Wilson had been flustered and then dismayed when Audubon, who seemed ready to purchase *American Ornithology*, instead got out his own bird drawings, which on comparison were decidedly superior to Wilson's. In an attempt to make his visitor feel better, Audubon said, he took Wilson hunting the next day and even helped him locate and bring down a new species of warbler—a bird Audubon now claimed Wilson had included in *American Ornithology* without acknowledgment.

All of this—the sketchy story of where he was from, the frontiersman posturing, and especially the casual disparagements of Wilson—was in the air when Audubon at last made his way to the Academy of Natural Sciences on a Saturday evening sometime between May and the middle of July. He arrived with Bonaparte in the prince's carriage, stopping before a narrow, two-story brick building with high, arched windows. They walked down a sidewalk that skirted a courtyard and mounted a steep flight of stairs. Audubon, portfolio pressed to his side, was naïvely convinced that he stood on the threshold of acclaim.

Although the members of the academy were in the end divided in their feelings about Audubon and his birds—a few were enthusiastic about the drawings—the mood at the academy would swing against him. It was not entirely his fault, since there was little Audubon might have done differently that would have prevented the opposition of the long-faced man presiding over that evening's session.

The son of a rich ship chandler and rope maker, George Ord was only four years older than Audubon. He was a doughy, sharp-tongued man who had spent more time tending the family business and going to academy meetings than he had tramping the woods. His only serious attempt at field research was an abbreviated expedition to Florida with several academy colleagues in 1817. The explorers got as far as St. Augustine, where rumors of Indian unrest forced them to retreat. What Ord had that Audubon didn't was a reputation as a zoologist. Ord was also an influential promoter of American science—in particular the science of Alexander Wilson. Ord had been a close friend of Wilson's and was the executor of Wilson's estate—not that it amounted to much. Wilson died with many more liabilities than assets, but Ord construed his responsibility in larger terms. He'd completed Wilson's unfinished eighth volume of *American Ornithology* and had started on the ninth and final installment. Ord was protective not only of *American Ornithology* but also of Wilson's role in earning respect for American science, and he took an instantaneous dislike to Audubon that would congeal into lifelong hatred.

Ord dismissed Audubon's drawings, which he found gaudy and ridiculous. They were simply too, too much. Audubon, he said, had twisted his subjects into attitudes never seen in nature. The images were too big and too busy with extraneous elements like trees and flowers—Audubon had commingled zoology with botany! Ord did not limit his observations to Audubon's art and science. In the weeks following Audubon's appearance before the academy, Ord denounced him as a man without honor—an imposter and a liar who misrepresented himself and traduced the reputation of Alexander Wilson. Ord was delighted when he learned that a young artist named Joseph Mason, now working in Philadelphia, claimed to have collaborated with Audubon in Louisiana, painting background plants and flowers under the false impression that he was to be given credit for these contributions.

Audubon, who could well have wondered why he was set up for this abuse, evidently didn't. He never questioned Bonaparte's motivations, which must have been complex, in bringing him to the academy. Bonaparte, who didn't have the same investment in "American" science as other members of the academy—and who did not share their reverence for Wilson—may have been insensitive to the politics of the situation. More likely, he wanted to see what would happen when Audubon's brash new interpretation of North American birds came up against Wilson's. Bonaparte hinted at a future partnership with Audubon. But he was already engaged in a delicate business of collaborating with Ord on the continuation of *American Ornithology* while at the same time drafting a series of papers for the academy disputing many entries in the Wilson classic. His loyalties divided, Bonaparte sided with nobody, steering a middle course that Audubon—hungry for the prince's approval—went along with.

Bonaparte was circumspect as well, carefully avoiding asking Audubon too many questions. But he could easily have checked out his new friend's story. Jacques-Louis David, Audubon's supposed teacher, had recently painted portraits of Bonaparte's wife and sister-in-law. And Louisiana was not the faraway place to Bonaparte that Audubon assumed it was in claiming it as home. Bonaparte's father had negotiated the 1801 treaty with Spain that ceded the territory to France—two years before his uncle Napoleon sold it to Thomas Jefferson.

Audubon's company stole some of the luster from Bonaparte's reputation around Philadelphia. They seemed an odd, guileless pair—one compact and neat, the other a hulk fresh out of the woods, both of them so animated and eager, so *French*. Their manners were foreign and their instincts for doing the wrong thing infallible. After the disastrous visit to the academy, Bonaparte had another idea. He took Audubon to see Philadelphia's most accomplished engraver, a man named Alexander Lawson. Lawson, who had engraved the plates for *American Ornithology* and who had stood by Wilson during the arduous years of its production, had already heard all about Audubon from George Ord. Bonaparte and Audubon called at Lawson's shop one morning early enough to wake him up.

Lawson could not believe that Bonaparte took Audubon seriously. Flipping through Audubon's portfolio, Lawson repeated Ord's complaints about the drawings. They were too big. The images were mushy and in some cases wrong. The birds looked unnatural. He told Audubon he could understand why some people liked his work—it really wasn't bad for a self-taught amateur. But ornithology, Lawson said, was about "truth" and "correct lines." When Audubon mentioned his training under David, Lawson was incredulous. He was even more put out when Bonaparte suggested that he wanted to publish some of Audubon's drawings. "You may buy them," Lawson said, "but I will not engrave them."

Audubon was not without supporters. Charles-Alexandre Lesueur, a fellow French expatriate and illustrator who had discovered more than two thousand new species of fish on a daring expedition to the South Pacific, considered Audubon's drawings brilliant. But he suggested that Audubon would be more likely to find a publisher for them in Europe. Lesueur cosponsored Audubon's nomination to the academy. Although the bylaws stipulated that election of a new member required a unanimous vote, this was not normally a great obstacle. Admission to the academy after being nominated was almost automatic. So the vote on Audubon, in the face of stiff opposition to his election, was an unusual one. Members cast their votes by dropping either a white (yes) or a black (no) marble into a small wooden box. Ord, though he could have blocked Audubon's election by himself, lobbied against Audubon's suitability and expected support from his colleagues. He got it. When the vote for Audubon was counted on August 31 he had been officially blackballed.

Audubon was, by then, long gone. Sensing that the situation in Philadelphia was hopeless, he decided not to wait out his rejection at the academy and instead left for New York at the start of August. He found the city empty in the heat of late summer—and learned that word of his failure in Philadelphia was already spreading. Facing dim prospects of finding a publisher for his drawings, Audubon visited the Lyceum, New York's version of Philadelphia's Academy of Natural Sciences. His work was so admired there that he was invited to deliver a paper and was hastily elected a member. But he continued to feel uncomfortable in these gatherings, and grew increasingly "cloudy and depressed" in the city. Audubon entertained the contradictory thought, reflecting his doubt and ambition all at once, that he had wasted his life and might "die unknown." After a few weeks he decided to return to Louisiana. He took his time, traveling through upstate New York, earning a few dollars sketching landscapes as he went. He idled for weeks watching the waterfowl massing ahead of their migrations before making his way to Pittsburgh, where he managed to buy a skiff and head downriver. Unshaven and wearing moccasins, he visited Victor at Shippingport, where he endured the stares of townsfolk appalled at his appearance. By the time he got home it was late fall. He had been gone for more than a year.

On the long way back, Audubon had weighed his options. He would have to find the means to go to Europe to publish his work. That seemed certain. Audubon was less sure how to deal with the most widely shared criticism of his drawings—their size. It had never occurred to him to scale down his birds from their natural dimensions. He had invented his own technique for posing freshly killed specimens against a grid so that he could copy them exactly. To accommodate larger birds like turkeys and eagles, Audubon used the largest available papers—a size called "double elephant" that measured nearly forty by twenty-seven inches—and even then long-necked birds like cranes or swans had to be bent into somewhat contrived positions to make them fit. Publishing these large color images would be, Audubon had been assured, utterly impractical. It would cost a fortune to produce, and even if it could be managed who would want to buy such a huge and expensive book?

Floating downriver under the stars, traveling by day with the birds once again going in his direction, Audubon decided there was no answer to those questions other than to try anyway. Audubon had many gifts, but perhaps none was more valuable than his short memory for hardships and reversals. He forgot about his critics in Philadelphia and reflected instead on his luck at having met there a few people who were more encouraging. Thinking about his drawings, Audubon had a sudden insight. He didn't want to change their scale—but he could put them in a more appealing order. There were large birds, medium birds, small birds—a crude visual phylogeny. Audubon began to imagine his drawings produced in groups, each composed of one large image accompanied by several smaller ones.

While Audubon drifted back into the wilds of America, in Philadelphia George Ord sniffled back into his work on *American Ornithology*, hoarding new species and descriptions, feeling himself well rid of a would-be usurper of Alexander Wilson's legacy. It had been a nasty job, but a necessary one. Ord was not about to let American science lose the ground it had gained in recent years by endorsing Audubon's substandard work. Besides, the man was obviously a fraud—as dishonest as his drawings were worthless. Audubon, he was sure, was headed back to the swamps of Louisiana where he belonged, unlikely to be heard from again.

As it turned out, Ord was right about a few things. Audubon was not exactly who he claimed to be. His father was not an admiral. He had not been born in Louisiana. He never studied with Jacques-Louis David. John James Audubon, in fact, was not even his real name.

2

COMING ACROSS

Troglodytes hyemalis: The Winter Wren
The extent of the migratory movements of this diminutive bird, is certainly the most
remarkable fact connected with its history.   —*Ornithological Biography*

At the end of the eighteenth century, the coastal settlement of Les Cayes looked out over a busy Caribbean harbor on the southwestern arm of Saint-Domingue—the island known today as Haiti. It is a poor country now, but in those days it was not. After Columbus landed there, the island was plundered and its native Indian population destroyed. For more than two centuries Saint-Domingue was home to wild cattle and pigs and an equally unruly assortment of English, Spanish, and French colonists and freebooters. By the late 1700s, the western portion of the island was under French control and had grown far richer than the Spanish part to the east. Sugar and coffee plantations, built on the blood and sweat of African slaves, prospered. At night, a ribbon of lights from towns and sugar mills along the coast traced the line of the sea, and Saint-Domingue was known throughout Europe as a thriving and bountiful colony, ripe with opportunity.

On April 26, 1785, a twenty-seven-year-old chambermaid named Jeanne Rabin, recently arrived from France, delivered a baby boy after a difficult two days of labor at a plantation just outside of Les Cayes. Rabin, already weak from the effects of unremitting tropical illnesses, never fully recovered after the baby arrived. Despite frequent medical attention brought to her by the baby's father, a French sea captain from Nantes named Jean Audubon, Rabin died a few months later.

Audubon's mulatto housekeeper Sanitte, with whom he already had two children and would soon have another, took charge of the infant. This tangled domestic arrangement—Audubon also had a legal wife back in France—relied on unstated conventions between whites and people of color, but it was a relatively uncomplicated situation in the loose social climate of the island. Audubon and Rabin had met on board ship from France. Sanitte stepped aside when the captain's new love showed up at the plantation—and then resumed her position as lady of the house after Rabin died.

They called the little boy Jean Rabin. His early childhood was happy. Saint-Domingue was lush and mountainous, with thick forests and a warm, hypnotic sea close by. The abundant wildlife delighted Jean, who showed a curiosity about nature as soon as he could talk. Though his father was often absent and his mother had died before he knew her, the boy had the run of the plantation and several half-siblings to play with. Yellow fever and malaria were epidemic on the island, and European settlers complained of Saint-Domingue's oppressive heat and torrential rains. But the climate suited Audubon's children. Young Jean's eyes were often turned upward, looking to the trees and across the wide tropical sky for birds, which were everywhere in dizzying profusion. Pelicans, sand-pipers, frigate birds, herons, parrots, cuckoos, trogons, gulls, terns, plo-vers, and owls were common. In winter months they were joined by eagles, swallows, warblers, shearwaters, grosbeaks, and hosts of other species from the north.

Jean Audubon continued a hard life at sea. He first sailed at the age of thirteen, and at fifteen was wounded and captured when his ship was at-tacked by the British. After a year and a half in an English prison, Audubon returned to France and again went to sea, eventually gaining command of his own merchant ship. Seeking his fortune in the New World, Audubon acquired the plantation at Les Cayes and was soon trading in cargoes of sugar, coffee, tobacco, and slaves. In 1779, with the American Revolution in progress, he was again captured at sea by British forces and this time im-prisoned in New York. After his release, he briefly commanded a French naval corvette just as the war was ending.

In the spring of 1789, with another revolution brewing in France, Audubon looked to diversify his assets. He sailed to America with a ship-load of sugar, which he traded for a farm called Mill Grove, twenty miles outside of Philadelphia. But the deal was no sooner done than Audubon had a new worry. The colonists in Saint-Domingue had become alarmed at mounting unrest among the slaves—unrest being the simmering final stage before open rebellion. With only 35,000 French colonists on the island and close to a half-million black slaves, the civil order of Saint-Domingue was balanced on a knife's edge of colonial privilege and racial oppression. Nervous authorities there declared white control "in imminent peril." They blamed the sudden instability on whites who were, in the words of one official communiqué, "drunk with liberty" and sympathetic to blacks demanding enfranchisement. In fact, Saint-Domingue was on the brink of a fifteen-year struggle toward independence that would produce a general evacuation of the French colonists. Those who didn't leave were eventually massacred.

For a time Audubon believed his family in Les Cayes was more or less safe, as long as he stayed away. But as the situation deteriorated he worried about six-year-old Jean, who was white, as well as his younger mixed-blood half-sister, Rose, who was unusually fair. Finally, he arranged passage to France for the two children. They arrived in June of 1791, eyes wide open at this strange country an ocean away from their home, and thrilled at being reunited with their father and at meeting his wife Anne. Three years later, the Audubons corrected the children's ambiguous status by adopting them.

Jean Rabin became Jean Audubon. He was sent to school, where he showed an interest in making pencil sketches of birds, but was otherwise an indifferent student. At the age of eleven, he was enrolled at the naval academy at Rochefort. There he became an accomplished musician—he played the flute and the violin—and learned to dance and fence. He was also known for his swimming prowess. All of which was somewhat beside the point. Young Audubon did miserably in his military training, and also demonstrated a propensity for seasickness. After three years, he was dismissed for failing several classes. His disappointed father, who was about to retire after reaching the mid-level rank of commander in the French Navy, began to think his son needed a change of scenery and occupation.

In March 1803, the elder Audubon received unexpected news from America. The tenant farmer living at Mill Grove had discovered lead ore on the property. Lead, with its many uses in munitions and paints, was a valuable commodity. Audubon dispatched an agent from Nantes to open a mine at Mill Grove, and turned his attention to his now-eighteen-year-old son. Napoleon was conscripting an army on the eve of declaring himself emperor. The Audubons were not eager to see their son drafted and thought his prospects would be brighter in America. In August, they put young Jean on a ship bound for New York—but not before extracting a promise from him that he would never reveal his illegitimate birth. When he walked down the gangway at the piers on the East River in Manhattan a few weeks later, Jean carried documents stating that he was from Louisiana—the sprawling western territory the United States had just acquired from France. The papers gave his name as John James Audubon.

While Audubon was a toddler being dandled in the gentle surf at Les Cayes, a book of poetry was causing a sensation on the other side of the world, in Scotland. Its author, a peasant farmer named Robert Burns, had gained overnight celebrity for a slim volume of earthy verse treating everyday subjects. Despite a modest first printing of six hundred copies, *Poems, Chiefly in the Scottish Dialect* stirred readers of every kind, from the literati in Edinburgh to field hands and tradesmen who saw their own lives and passions reflected in Burns's lines about love and work. Imitators appeared across the country. One of them was a twenty-year-old weaver named Alexander Wilson, who lived in the town of Paisley. It seemed that everyone in Paisley was either a weaver or a poet. Many fancied themselves both.

Now a suburb of Glasgow, Paisley was then the fastest-growing city in Scotland. Situated on the pretty White Cart River in a region known as "the Seedhills," the town was a model of the new industrial and trading prosperity. It was also a hub on the smuggling routes from America and the Far East. Goods moving between the beaches on the Firth of Clyde and Glasgow regularly passed through Paisley. Sugar and tobacco were smuggled, as was a large quantity of tea, all in avoidance of British taxes. As much as half the tea consumed in England entered the country illegally, principally by way of Scotland.

But it was cloth making—in particular its trademark patterned silk gauzes—for which Paisley was better known, and to which its comfortable middle class was indebted. Weavers endured tedious, physically exhausting hours at their looms but earned good money. Many of them belonged to after-hours clubs, associations of fellow workers who shared pastimes such as fishing, hunting, political debate, and especially golf. In the summer, when twilight lingered late in western Scotland, the weavers of Paisley could be seen heading out for rounds of golf long after their workdays and dinners were done.

As a boy, Wilson was called Sandy—short for Alexander—a gentle, fair nickname for a child who was neither. Wilson had dark hair and eyes. He was thin, but grew tall and passably handsome, with sharp, solemn features. The Wilson family fortunes were up and down. His father traded smuggling for weaving and respectability when he married, and for a time the family's prospects were sunny. Young Sandy, who was bright and bookish, was sent to school in preparation for joining the clergy. But his mother's death when he was only ten changed everything. His father quickly remarried, and Wilson's stern new stepmother ended his studies and sent him to work as a cowherd on the windswept moors between Paisley and the coast. The solitude and the countryside appealed to him, but Wilson was not good at this work. He much preferred reading and contemplating nature to tending the herd, which often strayed.

At thirteen, Wilson accepted a three-year apprenticeship as a weaver. When his father renewed his smuggling activities, the family moved about ten miles west of Paisley, to an ancient, half-ruined castle called the Tower of Auchinbathie, leaving Wilson behind to learn his trade. Nobody knew for sure how old the tower was, but local legend held that it had once been owned by the father of William Wallace, the national hero of Scottish independence, in the thirteenth century. Wilson visited his family there on weekends. He took up hunting and was often out with his gun, chasing grouse across the fields near a well-known hilltop called Misty Law, the highest place in the county.

Wilson was a distractible young man. He developed a love of poetry, memorizing the mock epic poems of Alexander Pope, and often reciting verse or composing his own while he worked at his loom. He took a job in a weaving shop near Edinburgh, and began spending part of his time on the road peddling the cloth he helped to make. He traveled from one end of Scotland to another on foot, calling at farmhouses and in towns. When business was good, he stayed in inns and wrote to his friends from fashionable addresses. His letters often included poems or fragments of poems. Sometimes the whole letter was in verse. Wilson was moody, and he walked through a land of moods. With midnight approaching on New Year's Eve in 1788, Wilson wrote to a friend back in Edinburgh from

St. Andrews, on the dark threshold of the North Sea, reflecting on the universal human failure to take advantage of a short life on Earth:

> *Respected Sir,*
> *Far distant, in an inn's third storey rear'd,*
> *The sheet beneath a glimmering taper spread,*
> *Along the shadowy walls no sound is heard,*
> *Save Time's slow, constant, momentary tread.*
>
> *Here lone I sit; and will you, sir, excuse*
> *My midnight theme, while (feebly as she can)*
> *Inspiring silence bids the serious Muse*
> *Survey the transient bliss pursued by Man.*
>
> *Deluded Man, for him Spring paints the fields:*
> *For him, warm Summer rears the rip'ning grain;*
> *He grasps the bounty that rich Autumn yields,*
> *And counts those trifles as essential gain.*
>
> *For him, yes, sure, for him those mercies flow!*
> *Yet, why so passing, why so fleet their stay?*
> *To teach blind mortals what they first should know,*
> *That all is transient as the fleeting day.*

When Wilson was broke, he slept in the open or in barns and wrote to no one. The travel proved agreeable. Wilson was an eager sightseer, visiting historic locations, archeological curiosities, old golf courses. He made frequent detours on private pilgrimages to the homes of well-known writers. Wilson was also always on the lookout for graveyards, where he stopped to add to his collection of epitaphs copied from headstones.

Wilson's idol, Robert Burns, who lived only a short distance from the Tower of Auchinbathie, found his subjects all around him. Burns wrote about farms and churches and country life. Poetry seemed to abide, waiting to be born, in the gray airs over Scotland. And nothing was outside the realm of literature, no subject was too mundane for a poet's consideration. Burns wrote an ode to a field mouse he'd accidentally run over with a plough, and told the tale of a hardworking farmer's Saturday night.

His poems were frequently crowded with descriptions of the natural world:

> The Wintry West extends his blast,
>   And hail and rain does blaw;
> Or, the stormy North sends driving forth,
>   The blinding sleet and snaw:
> While, tumbling brown, the Burn comes
>   down,
>   And roars frae bank to brae;
> And bird and beast, in covert, rest,
>   And pass the heartless day.

Many heartless days were in Alexander Wilson's future, but the power to describe them as Burns did would mainly elude him. Like Burns, Wilson was attuned to his surroundings. Unlike Burns, his vocabulary and his imagery were mostly uninspired borrowings. The cleverness and sensitivity friends detected in Wilson himself rarely materialized in his writing. He wrote a poem about his hunting spaniel. When he abruptly ended a flirtation with a girl working for his family and she poisoned the dog out of spite, he wrote a poem about that, too. Wilson wrote poems about his life on the road that inspected every particular of his experience. A lost pack. A rainy night. The way a drop of water would form at the end of his nose on a cold winter day, "dangling, limpid as the brain it leaves." Wilson's eyes were open to the world around him, but what he saw came across as trivial and dull in his poetry.

Wilson began to chafe under a growing burden of unrealized ambitions. He barely scraped by on the money he made weaving and peddling. He fell in love with a woman named Martha McLean. Martha was beautiful, literate—and just out of Wilson's reach. Her family was proper, and they viewed Wilson, who was poor and aimless and worryingly artistic, as unsuitable. But the two met often, and talked of poetry as they walked in the evenings beside the Cart. In Wilson's mind at least, an erotic attraction formed between them. He wrote poems about Martha's ravishing beauty, describing in panting verse improbable late-night assignations on the moonlit moors.

But Wilson's fascination with Martha stalled. In addition to the social chasm between them, Wilson's attentions were often elsewhere. And so was he. Encouraged to publish his poetry—not everyone thought him without talent—he found a printer who agreed to bring out a book if Wilson would sell subscriptions to it in advance. He succeeded in selling a few hundred copies on a peddling tour, but it was far less than he had hoped. Wilson had to beg forgiveness from the cloth supplier whose goods he had neglected on the trip, and only a last-minute subscription and promise of help from a local nobleman allowed publication of his book to go forward. Perversely, Wilson grew morose just as things seemed to be looking up for him.

Admittedly, Wilson's situation was largely unchanged. But he complained that he had become the caricature of a struggling poet, afflicted by poverty, dressed in tattered clothing, and living alone in his garret with only "lank hunger and poetical misery" for company. A wiser man, Wilson felt, would give up the literary life and earn an honest laborer's living. As his anxieties over Martha and money mounted, Wilson lost weight, becoming shockingly emaciated. He fell ill, probably with pneumonia, and was bedridden at the tower in grave condition for months. His family was convinced he would die. But he didn't.

Wilson recovered and went back to work weaving. He also resumed writing, and, for the first time, politics figured in his verse. The ideas of God-granted liberty and individual rights, recently articulated and won during the revolution in the American colonies, were spreading across Europe. Weavers in Scotland were beginning to question their treatment by the owners of looming operations, and Wilson joined the attack, anonymously publishing a series of satirical poems describing certain recognizable Paisley mill owners as cheats. One of these poems resulted in a civil suit against Wilson, who defended himself by arguing that the poem was not about the plaintiff. Nothing ever came of the case. In the meantime, Wilson kept up a proper appearance. He placed second in a speech contest in Edinburgh—his was in verse—and then landed a job as an assistant editor on a fledgling literary magazine. Word spread that his book had been recommended to Robert Burns himself, and that the great poet had actually sent for a copy.

Wilson then did something inexplicably weird. One day in May 1792, he went to Glasgow, apparently to visit a printer. While he was away, a mill owner named William Sharp turned up at the sheriff's office in Paisley waving two documents. One was the manuscript of a long, inflammatory poem titled "The Shark." It was about a boozy mill owner who exploited his workers. Sharp believed he was the subject of the poem—a complaint the sheriff found reasonable, given that the second document was an extortion letter.

The letter informed Sharp that a copy of "The Shark" was with a printer and would be published at once unless Sharp returned a payment of five guineas within three hours, whereupon the poem would be destroyed. The note was signed "A.B." Nobody had any idea who A.B. was, but Sharp accused Alexander Wilson of being the author of the poem. Wilson was arrested later that day. He spent the next two years in and out of jail, regularly changing his story.

Wilson confounded everyone by admitting that he had written the letter. But he refused to identify the author of the poem, or to say whether he was part of a conspiracy. Eventually, he admitted to writing the poem as well. But he insisted, just as he had in the earlier case, that any similarity to an actual person in "The Shark" was purely coincidental. This was a crude defense—the blackmail attempt made it clear that the poem was aimed at Sharp—and Wilson was fined £60 ($270), about a year's salary, which he of course did not have. More ominously, a review of the offending poem was launched under the provisions of a new law prohibiting the publication of revolutionary materials. Wilson was threatened with a charge of treason.

Over the course of many months, Wilson was interrogated, fined, jailed, released on bond, and jailed again when he failed to appear in court. A judge awarded £50 ($225) in damages to Sharp. Wilson, unable to pay the damages or the fines, skipped more hearings. This led to contempt charges and still more fines. At one point Wilson was made to burn copies of "The Shark" in public, and endured the humiliation of having his bail paid anonymously by Martha McLean, who could no longer openly have anything to do with Wilson. The Paisley jail became a second home. It was a squalid, oppressive existence. The food provided to the inmates was so bad that prisoners often avoided starvation only if they could afford to buy meals from a commissary on the premises. Wilson borrowed from friends to stay alive and to get out when he could. Ironically, it was at this time that Wilson published his one truly popular poem—a first-rate comedy about an argument between a husband and wife titled "Watty and Meg." It sold unexpectedly well. But not well enough. Wilson was soon broke again and back among the "wretches." Jail, he said, was a daily horror show. He felt entombed by "the rumbling

of bolts, the hoarse exclamations of the jailor, the sighs and sallow coun-
tenances of the prisoners, and the general gloom of the place." During
one of his releases, in the spring of 1794, Wilson decided to go to America. Taking care not to tip off the authorities, Wilson hastily scraped together the fare. On May 23, he sailed for Philadelphia aboard the *Swift*,
accompanied by his sixteen-year-old nephew, William Duncan. "I must
get out of my mind," Wilson said to a friend just before leaving.

Crossing the Atlantic was then a common but still hair-raising experience. In addition to the risks of bad weather or other misfortune, the
ships were usually overcrowded and disease-ridden. Wilson waited until
he and Duncan had safely arrived in Philadelphia before writing to his
family about the trip.

They'd gone first to Belfast, Ireland, and had a look at the *Swift* that almost decided them against going. Surveying the throng of passengers, 350
in all, Wilson doubted half would survive the voyage in the dank, cramped
spaces below decks, where the berths were no wider than a coffin. The good
news, as they chose to see it, was that passage on deck was all that remained available. After they determined themselves to be among the fitter
specimens in the crowd, Wilson and Duncan gamely got aboard, never to
see Scotland again. They were seasick for a few days but soon felt better
in fair weather and gentle seas. Once away from land, one of the passengers, a physician, revealed that he recently had been tried as a seditionist
and condemned to death in Ireland. Rum was found and everyone drank
to the doctor's health and the cause of liberty the world over. In three
weeks of pleasant sailing "only" three passengers died, an old woman and
two children.

In the middle of the voyage, the *Swift* passed for two days through a
maze of "ice islands." Wilson was astounded at the size and number of the
icebergs. Some were more than twice as high as the ship's tallest mast. At
one time he counted thirty-four of them surrounding the vessel. A
steady breeze pushed the ship onward until they got through. But soon after they were hit by a terrific storm—the most violent Wilson had ever
seen. A day later, one of the sailors fell overboard. He swam strongly after the ship and came agonizingly close. But despite every effort, the man
could not be rescued.

After fifty days at sea, the *Swift* entered the calm waters of the Delaware

River and proceeded to the town of Newcastle, where Wilson and Duncan disembarked and set out on foot for Wilmington. They were "happy as mortals could be" as they walked through a flat, densely wooded country overflowing with unrecognizable vegetation and the calls of many remarkable birds. In Wilmington they asked about work for weavers, but none were needed and they decided to continue on to Philadelphia, another thirty miles upriver. They stopped at farmhouses along the way and were disappointed at finding the residents less welcoming than they had been led to expect. On reaching Philadelphia, they were impressed by the city's sprawl, which extended some three miles along the western riverbank. But Wilson was distressed to find no more than twenty looms running in a city of nearly fifty thousand inhabitants, where everything was very expensive and there was no demand for journeyman weavers.

Mulling what to do next, Wilson was meanwhile agape at the richness and natural beauty of the New World. Nothing about it was familiar— not the trees nor the bushes nor the animals. Even the air was different. The midsummer heat and humidity were tremendous—Wilson noticed that just sitting still in trousers and a waistcoat he sweated as he never had before. Like most Europeans, Wilson had believed that America's oppressive climate, where dense heat alternated with numbing cold, was hostile to wildlife. But walking in the forests around Philadelphia, he and Duncan found themselves in a veritable Garden of Eden. They were amazed at the number of squirrels scampering among the trees, and the size of the snakes sunning themselves by the footpath. They feasted on apples and peaches, delighted to find the local orchards without the high walls and fierce guard dogs encountered in Scotland. Nowhere on earth, Wilson imagined, could anyone find such an "agreeable spot" as Pennsylvania. Wilson could not identify a single one of the many birds they saw, but he was struck by the intensity and variety of their colorations. One day he shot several cardinals in order to make a closer inspection. Holding their warm, scarlet bodies lightly in his hands, Wilson wondered what they were.

3

A NAME FOR EVERY LIVING THING

Grus americana: The Whooping Crane
The members of a flock sometimes arrange themselves in the form of an acute-angled triangle; sometimes they move in a long line; again they mingle together without order, or form an extended front; but in whatever manner they advance, each bird sounds his loud note in succession, and on occasions of alarm these birds manifest the same habit.
—*Ornithological Biography*

Arriving in America nine years apart, Wilson and Audubon found themselves at the edge of a large, misunderstood continent. Like many of their fellow immigrants, each had come to the New World to get away from difficulties in the Old. Their ambitions, like their backgrounds, were vague. Neither of them could have been described as an artist or a naturalist; neither had aspirations as a scientist. Both would become all of these things. For the time being, they merely increased the population of interesting North American fauna by two.

Most of the country's 5 million immigrant citizens lived along the Eastern Seaboard. The frontier lay just beyond the Blue Ridge Mountains. Thomas Jefferson's purchase of the Louisiana Territory in 1803 had doubled the size of the young nation, pushing the border across the Mississippi River and all the way to the Rockies, but this tremendous area— some 900,000 square miles—had scarcely been visited in three hundred years of European exploration and conquest. Little was known about the interior topography of North America apart from a skeletal outline of the major waterways. Even less had been discovered about the plants and animals living in the western two-thirds of America. The same was true with respect to the uncounted tribes of American Indians living between the two oceans.

European naturalists, disinclined to let a shortage of facts get in the way of a good story, had been busily describing and cataloguing New World flora and fauna from afar for a long time. They'd made a mess of it, but then this was a confusing time for biology, especially the study of natural history. By the end of the eighteenth century, intellectuals on both sides of the Atlantic had been swept up in the Age of Reason. The movement was the product of Enlightenment philosophy, which held that traditional lines of authority—specifically the church and secular monarchies—were inferior to rational thought and the proposition of universal human liberty. These ideas had led more or less directly to the Declaration of Independence and the establishment of American democracy. Inevitably, the same principles resulted in a clash between European science and a group of American amateurs who challenged the views of the leading naturalists of the era—including one of the shining lights of the age, Carolus Linnaeus.

Linnaeus, the father of modern taxonomy, was the Swedish botanist and physician who in 1735 formalized a naming strategy for all living organisms. A man of wide interests, Linnaeus dabbled in politics and economics, and spent many years trying (unsuccessfully) to grow tropical food crops in Sweden. His lasting contribution to biology was *Systema Naturae*, a compendium of species names, which he expanded and revised many times. Over the course of several editions, Linnaeus devised the binomial identification system still in use today. In the Linnaean system, each plant and animal is given a two-word name, with the first a Latin term signifying the genus to which it belongs and the second a specific or "species" name. So, for example, the gyrfalcon (*Falco rusticolus*) and the peregrine falcon (*Falco peregrinus*) can be seen to be two distinct species of similar birds belonging to a single genus.

Giving names to plants and animals is, of course, as old as language itself. Sorting them into categories is likewise an ancient practice. A thousand years before Linnaeus, Aristotle wrote at length about the "history" of animals and also about their parts. He emphasized the importance of morphological characteristics in distinguishing one animal from another, as well as the fact that morphology itself could be subdivided. For example, skin is an irreducible or "uniform" part of an animal, whereas a foot is composed of skin and several other parts, like muscle and bone. A close observer of animal behavior and anatomy, Aristotle also recognized a parallel principle of organization, in which similar species could be grouped into assemblages called "genera." Aristotle's definition of a genus was broad. Birds and fishes are examples of Aristotelian genera, and Aristotle regarded all terrestrial quadrupeds as belonging to a single genus. But despite their many important shared characteristics there are also unmistakable differences between, say, a lion and a porcupine. This led Aristotle to insist on the supremacy of *species* as the fundamental unit of natural history. "[W]e must take animals species by species and discuss their peculiarities severally." And so it has ever been.

Linnaeus also emphasized the species as the fundamental unit of life. His binomial system was intended to make it easier to keep track of plant and animal taxa—whose numbers were expanding as European explorers pushed into new places across the globe. For several decades following the publication of *Systema Naturae*, students and colleagues sent Linnaeus specimens, mainly plants, from all over the world. He named them based on what he saw as their intrinsic qualities, like rocks whose origins could be explored with a hammer. Linnaeus believed the identity of a species was inherent in its appearance and that he didn't so much choose a name as diagnose one. "The thing is, that each Stone, Plant, Animal itself shall tell the ignorant its own name so that it will be understood by everyone who has learnt the language," Linnaeus said.

Linnaeus never imagined how truly extensive this language was. Late in life he realized that there were probably so many plants in the world that it would be hard to name them all. But he believed the number of species on earth was not incomprehensible. He estimated the total at 40,000. About half that number would be plants, with the next largest group being approximately 12,000 insects. Linnaeus thought there were maybe 2,000 species of birds and perhaps 200 mammals. He was low.

It's a testament to the diversity and abundance of life that although we know Linnaeus was off in his estimate of how many species there are, nobody today really knows *how far* off. There are something like 1.7 million named species. But that's only a small fraction of what's out there. New species are discovered continually, and we're not going to get a handle on the total anytime soon. Current guesses put the number at anywhere from 8 million to as many as 100 million, with 30 million being a generally accepted estimate. That includes a lot of bacteria, but also 4,300 mammals and nearly 10,000 birds. Linnaeus rightly suspected that there are many species of insects, though his estimate of 12,000 is amusing in retrospect. Beetles alone make up 300,000 known species. About one out of every three living things on the planet is a bug, and thousands of insect species thrive in anonymity in tropical forests.

Just as there were many more species than Linnaeus imagined, there was a need for more genera than he created to manage them all. As new species turned up in far-flung parts of the world like America, they were made to fit into a preexisting taxonomical scheme that seemed increasingly artificial. Linnaean taxonomy relied on morphology rather than behavioral traits or reproductive compatibility—features of natural history that required study in the field. This created confusion when unrelated species with a few coincidental similarities in appearance were crowded into the same genus. But this was only one of the shortcomings of the Linnaean system.

In Linnaeus's day, the idea that species were the "words" of the language of biology was widely shared. Naturalists thought of nature as a book. And since nature was the product of divine Creation, this book was a kind of scripture. The study of nature was thus a pious attempt to read God's book of life. But this raised a difficult issue. If the book of nature was a bible, then it was not meant to be edited. God was presumed to have created all living things at the same time and in a state of harmony that was immutable. Simply put, the plants and animals in the world were fixed. They were all of life that ever was or ever would be. The book of nature was written in indelible ink.

For most of his life Linnaeus believed this was so. "We count so many species as there were in the beginning," he wrote in *Systema Naturae*. But he gradually came to the conclusion that at least some species arose over time. Linnaeus was sure these processes were so slow that nature could be regarded as essentially stable. Like many of his contemporaries, Linnaeus was groping his way toward a concept—evolution—that would not be articulated for another century. He didn't get there because he didn't realize that, just as new species could develop, the reverse was also true, and even God's creations sometimes passed out of existence. Linnaeus had no concept of extinction.

To be fair, the evidence for extinction was still thin. Fossils—the gateway to former life forms—had long been seen as natural curiosities. But, as clues to the past, their meaning was murky. The presence of plant and animal shapes found in solid rock, and especially the appearance of fossilized marine life on mountaintops around the world, had puzzled people for centuries. There were imaginative explanations—though not to the point of guessing the truth—that whole worlds of living organisms had come and gone in the eons before us. It was believed by some that ocean life—possibly seeds or spawn—had been carried up to the mountains during the biblical deluge. Speculation during the Middle Ages centered on some kind of geological hoax perpetrated within the earth's mantle, where supposed "plastic forces" created rocky simulations of living things. Earlier, the Greeks had thought it possible that the sea had once covered the land where marine fossils turned up. Aristotle believed such fossils might be the residue of creatures trapped in crevices of formerly submerged rocks. Leonardo da Vinci thought the fossilized assemblages of corals and shells found in the mountains of Italy argued against a biblical interpretation. He noticed they were intact and arranged in the same way as in the ocean. Da Vinci concluded that it was impossible for such objects to have been transported to the mountains in a pristine condition— especially by way of a violent, forty-day flood. Linnaeus took a pragmatic view of fossils, naming them as if they were any other extant species.

All of this would have to be rethought, and soon, because people had begun finding large, unusual-looking bones on both sides of the Atlantic. The discoveries in America were particularly important because they pointed up the shortcomings of Linnaean taxonomy, and also because they sharpened the dispute between American naturalists and another European authority, the great French scientist and nature writer Georges-Louis Leclerc, comte de Buffon.

Count Buffon—or just Buffon, as he was usually called—was a contemporary of Linnaeus. Born in 1707 to a middle-class family in the small town of Montbard in Burgundy, Buffon was an unremarkable student. But he had a curious mind and was fascinated by mathematics and science—as well as money, power, fancy clothes, and beautiful women. Drawing on reserves of ego, ambition, and literary ability, Buffon launched an unlikely but meteoric career as a celebrity naturalist. In 1739, King Louis XV of France appointed Buffon keeper of the Royal Botanical Garden, a prestigious, essentially administrative position. The "garden" was much more than a royal arboretum. It was actually a well-organized academy that offered coursework in medicine and natural science, and which had a small faculty as well as many specimens of plants and animals from around the world. Buffon devoted himself to expanding and cataloguing the collection, called the King's Cabinet of Natural History. This work morphed into one of the most important and all-encompassing scientific publications of the eighteenth century, the *Histoire naturelle, générale et particulière, avec la description du Cabinet du roi*—*Buffon's Natural History*. The first three installments of this encyclopedic undertaking appeared in 1749. By the time of his death in 1788, Buffon had completed thirty-six volumes, including an edition illustrated with copper engravings of mammals from every corner of the world.

The subject of *Buffon's Natural History* was everything. Buffon endeavored to explain all that was known about the physical world, including its origins. He covered geology and anthropology, the formation of the planets, reproduction, astronomy, meteorology, mineralogy. He wrote about the oceans and air and continents. He covered physics and botany and zoology and, of course, taxonomy. Buffon liked naming things every bit as much as Linnaeus did, though the two profoundly disagreed on how to catalogue the taxa. Buffon thought the Linnaean system was flawed and far too generous in the way it defined species. Buffon, for example, thought all quadrupeds were variants on just thirty-eight mammalian species. Buffon didn't care for purely morphological analyses, and he poked fun at the way shared characteristics sometimes led Linnaeus into highly improbable groupings of animals that were obviously distant from one another. Buffon saw nature as more varied and more of a continuum. Nature, Buffon insisted, "works by insensible degrees." Taxonomic associations based on one or a few physical traits inevitably produced arbitrary divisions.

Buffon based his definition of a species on reproductive compatibility instead. A species, Buffon decided, comprises those closely related organisms that can interbreed and produce fertile offspring—a definition still widely accepted. Buffon offered a classic example: "The ass resembles the horse more than the water spaniel the hound, but nonetheless the water spaniel and the hound are only one species, since they together produce individuals that can themselves produce others, whereas the horse and the ass are certainly from different species, since they together produce only defective and barren individuals." In other words, the sterility of a mule, the hybrid that results from breeding an ass and a horse, is a dead end in nature. A species, Buffon said, was marked by the persistence of its generations through time—a "chain of successive existence."

Buffon's Natural History was massive, expensive, and despite Buffon's nebulous background in many areas of natural history, widely read. Prior to writing the *Natural History*, Buffon's interests had centered on physics and celestial mechanics. He worked on the "problem" of infinity, a trouble-some concept useful in mathematics but perplexing as an aspect of reality. He also conducted experiments in optics and rocketry, including attempts to calculate the size and configuration of the propellant required to send a rocket into space. Intrigued by the story of Archimedes setting the Roman fleet ablaze at Syracuse by means of reflected sunlight, Buffon had invented a "burning mirror" that could melt iron at close range or set fire to buildings two hundred feet away.

Buffon understood nature as a process—one involving a multitude of fluid interactions and changes taking place over time. He believed the earth was much older than the biblical claim of a few thousand years, and also that conditions on the planet had varied throughout its history. Life, he proposed, was a cosmic accident made possible by affinities between organic molecules that cohered into organisms. Anticipating Darwinian evolution, Buffon stated that all life forms were influenced by environmental conditions and were subject to incremental variations that ultimately gave rise to the plants and animals as they appeared in the present.

These brilliant (and probably heretical) insights led Buffon to speculate a little too freely on some of the taxa that were distributed around the world and now had come to the attention of naturalists in Europe.

Buffon never went to America. He studied accounts of North American wildlife and examined specimens submitted to the king's collection, measuring and comparing them closely with European species. Many of the ideas he formed about the New World were based on reports that were inaccurate, mean-spirited, or poorly translated. Buffon's focus on North American fauna was also a notable departure from the existing interest in the natural history of the New World, which had focused on plants. European horticulturists saw the botanical wealth of America as a potentially important resource given the depleted plant stocks in Europe.

Buffon detected several things about American animals. For one, it was clear that some species in the New World were unique. There were no turkeys or rattlesnakes or bald eagles in Europe. These belonged to the exotica of America. But it was equally apparent that America was home to many animals—deer, bears, beavers, porcupines, foxes, wolves—that also lived in Europe or Asia. Buffon supposed that America must have been colonized by animals that long ago proceeded across a former land bridge to North America, presumably to escape hunting and crowding in the Old World. Once there, some maintained their original forms, while others diverged and gave rise to novel species. What was most remarkable to Buffon concerned the animals common to both the Old and New Worlds: Animals from America were smaller than their counterparts in Europe.

Buffon proposed an unorthodox explanation for this discrepancy. The differences between Old World and New World animals belonging to the same species, Buffon determined, must be the result of environmental differences between Europe and America—most important, the harshness of the North American climate. In the New World, wrote Buffon, "nature is always rude and sometimes deformed." America, he said, was well suited to lower life forms like reptiles and bugs, but was otherwise a gloomy and disadvantaged environment for living things. "The air and the earth overloaded with humid and noxious vapors are unable either to purify themselves or to profit by the influence of the sun, who darts in vain his most enlivening rays upon this frigid mass."

Buffon described a kind of ecological withering that was the reverse of evolution, in which animals responded over time to an oppressive climate by becoming less fit. America was a land of stunted, less vigorous survivors. Buffon called this process "degeneration," and he claimed it as an example of the kind of morphological changes wrought by nature over long periods. "These changes are made only slowly, imperceptibly," Buffon wrote. "The great worker of Nature is Time; as it always moves with an equal, uniform, and regulated pace, it does everything; and these changes, at first imperceptible, become noticeable little by little, and finally leave results about which one cannot be mistaken."

The idea caught on. Europeans were already convinced of the inhospitable environment in America. From the time they first set foot in the New World, European explorers had reported its many unpleasantries. There were frightening snakes, tormenting insects, sour fens, and forbidding forests shrouded in fogs and poisonous airs. The land, unlike Europe, had not been improved through the industry of its native people. Although much of the continent was near the same latitudes as Europe, North America was much colder in the winter and endured awful heat and humidity in the summer.

Buffon argued that the degenerative effects of the North American climate could be seen even in livestock brought over from Europe—

which he insisted also grew smaller than their ancestors. He stopped short of claiming that the same thing happened to the human colonists, though some of Buffon's adherents said as much. What finally brought a response to Buffon from America was what he said about the New World's aboriginal people—judgments again made without any direct observation to back them up. Indians, he said, were no different from the animals of America. They were a degenerate species. Because Indians were about the same size as Europeans, Buffon defended his theory with a wildly racist assessment of their many other deficiencies:

> Although the savage of the new world is about the same height as man in our world, this does not suffice for him to constitute an exception to the general fact that all living nature has become smaller on that continent. The savage is feeble, and has small organs of generation; he has neither hair nor beard, and no ardor whatever for his female; although swifter than the European because he is better accustomed to running, he is, on the other hand, less strong in body; he is also less sensitive, and yet more timid and cowardly; he has no vivacity, no activity of mind; the activity of his body is less an exercise, a voluntary motion, than a necessary action caused by want; relieve him of hunger and thirst, and you deprive him of the active principle of all his movements; he will rest stupidly upon his legs or lying down entire days.

An answer to these brutal words—and to the whole theory of degeneration—would be offered, and when it came it would mark the beginning of American science.

In 1705, a farmer mucking about on the banks of the Hudson River near Albany, New York, found something odd. Spring floods had eroded the riverbank, exposing a foreign object. It was a gigantic tooth, about the size of a fist and weighing almost five pounds. Further excavation at the site unearthed the remains of a large animal that had presumably owned the tooth, including what appeared to be a thighbone approximately seventeen feet long. These additional parts were so badly decomposed that they crumbled instantly upon being dug up and could not be identified. The tooth, meanwhile, went on a journey.

It was sent to the Royal Society in London, in a box labeled "tooth of a Giant." The society was arguably the most respected scientific institution in the world. Its president at the time was Sir Isaac Newton. Everyone there agreed that it was a very big tooth indeed. Beyond that, things got hazy. For a while the prevailing feeling in both London and America was that the tooth might have belonged to a giant of the sort mentioned in the Book of Genesis. As more teeth and bones were discovered in America, this theory gained momentum. Cotton Mather, the influential Boston cleric, examined some of the relics and wrote a series of letters to the Royal Society affirming that they were indeed the remains of biblical giants drowned in Noah's flood. It was all perfectly obvious to Mather. God, disgusted with the wickedness of the world, had caused the children of normal-sized parents to become giants by putting something in their food. Although the giants proved highly troublesome, they were in the end insufficient punishment, so God drowned the earth, the giants included. Mather was an avid collector of sensational natural anomalies, and kept track of weird birth defects in animals and humans. He seemed to take a special pride in the apparent size of his supposed giants—who he calculated must have been about seventy feet tall. This, Mather noted, was bigger than other giants, mythical or biblical. It was also significant, he said, that they had been found in America, making them even more "curious and marvelous."

There were, of course, alternative theories about the tooth, which happened to look a lot like some other big teeth the Royal Society already had in its collection. Debate as to what they belonged to was lively. Perhaps they came from large sea creatures, maybe whales. Elephants, believed to have been brought to England by the Romans, were also considered. No one suggested they were from animals no longer living on the planet, as that would have been inconsistent with the biblical history of the world. Even Isaac Newton still believed the earth was no more than six thousand years old.

But things were changing. There was growing interest in comparative anatomy, and a number of English naturalists argued that the large teeth and oversized bones that suddenly seemed to be turning up everywhere were not, in fact, human. The discussion shifted to a mystery animal, one presumably still out in the world somewhere. In America it was dubbed the *incognitum*—the unknown. Then, in the early 1720s, reports began to circulate that Mongol tribesmen in Siberia sometimes scavenged ivory from enormous tusks found attached to the frozen carcasses of huge, ele-phantlike creatures that occasionally emerged when the tundra thawed in spring. It was frankly difficult to understand how elephants—tropical an-imals—had ended up on the icy steppe. The same difficulty existed in North America, which was decidedly not elephant country. One possible explanation was that the earth's orientation to the sun was different long ago, and that temperate regions had once been warmer. Meanwhile, a new term entered the discussion, thanks to the Mongols who called their mystery animal *mammuts*. The mammuts had teeth similar to the ones be-ing found in the West.

In 1739, a French military expedition traveled down the Ohio River by canoe, floating into a region of the country as yet unmapped by Euro-peans. They found the river broad and clear and more beautiful than any they had ever seen. Flanked by forests extending to the horizons, the river carried them deep into a shadowland of towering trees and thun-dering game. Great herds of bison and deer and elk rumbled through the woods, following thoroughfares created by their regular tramplings. These lanes, in places wider than two wagonways, formed a network connecting surface mineral deposits and marshes that were rich with salt. Animals gathered at these "salt licks" in large numbers, making them fa-vored hunting spots among the Indians. About six hundred miles west of Fort Pitt, on the eastern bank of the river in what would one day become Kentucky, the party made camp not far from a large marsh that stank of sulfur. Scouts were dispatched to explore the swamp, which was at the juncture of several major game trails. They soon returned laden with an assortment of astonishingly large bones and tusks. When the main party hurried down the trail to investigate, they discovered a natural grave-yard—a fetid, muddy wetland piled with enormous skeletons.

For the next several decades, the bones and teeth retrieved from "Big Bone Lick," as it came to be called, fueled the controversy over the *incog-nitum*. Benjamin Franklin, serving as a colonial emissary in London in the 1750s and 1760s, joined in the debate as to whether these remains were from some species of carnivore. Dissimilarities between the grinding teeth of the *incognitum* and the molars of elephants convinced some nat-uralists that the animal was indeed a meat-eater. Franklin thought so too at first, but in the end sided with those who argued it must have been an herbivore because its tremendous size would have made the *incognitum* too slow and awkward to pursue prey. Interest in the fossils remained so high that during the Revolutionary War George Washington took time to dig up ancient bones at several battlefield sites.

It was just before the end of the war that the governor of Virginia, Thomas Jefferson, along with the other governors of the new states, received a questionnaire from the French ambassador asking for a summary of natural resources and political institutions in America. Only Jefferson found time to respond, although it took him five years to do so. His response came in the form of a slim book, *Notes on the State of Virginia*, which had developed into a more elaborate reply than the ambassador probably expected. The book marked a transition in the approach to natural science in the New World and would eventually precipitate a revolution in American thought about the land it was overspreading.

In his book—it was the only one he wrote—Jefferson provided a detailed guide to Virginia's flora and fauna, including tables giving the sizes and weights of animals; to its geographical boundaries and internal topography; to its rivers, including their length, breadth, and navigability; to its mineral deposits, including discussions of mining operations and valuable ores and gemstones; to its population, military capabilities, laws, cities and towns, forms of government, and religion; to its agriculture and manufacturing; to its currency; to its buildings and roads. In his discussion of the people of Virginia—whites, slaves, and aboriginals—Jefferson vigorously defended American Indians against Buffon's scathing assessment. But in the same breath, he advanced a contradictory and confusing racial theory that seemed to argue for and against slavery all at once. Jefferson, who was serving as ambassador to France when the book first appeared in Paris in 1785, held off publication in the United States for two more years, anticipating that it would outrage people on both sides of the slavery issue.

Jefferson had reasons to make such a thorough inventory of Virginia. Emerging from revolution, America found itself mired in debt and an object of skepticism in Europe. The new republic appeared to be not only impoverished and materially pathetic, but also politically unstable. Europeans continued to wonder if there was anything of value in the wilderness of the New World beyond the narrow beachhead claimed by the former colonies. Jefferson saw it in reverse. America, he believed, was a land of unimagined natural wealth and diversity—a country that would someday exert itself as an economic force. As one of the architects of American independence, Jefferson felt obliged to correct the American image abroad—and to provide assurance to allies and creditors that the young nation's current straits were only temporary. The French, who sided with the Americans in the Revolution and whose trade policies were seen as more friendly than England's, were exactly the people Jefferson wanted to impress.

Jefferson was also instinctively drawn to the challenge of merging science and statesmanship—disciplines he did not regard as so separate and distinct as we do now. Like other adherents to the principles of the Enlightenment, Jefferson believed that all knowledge and all forms of social organization could be derived from the study of natural history. Jefferson saw a chance to show the rest of the world what America was made of, and, by extension, what America stood for. Here, too, was an opportunity to answer Buffon. When Jefferson turned his attention to the size and vigor of American animals in his *Notes*, he began with the big quadruped that was by then being called the mammoth.

Jefferson did not think the large skeletons found in America were the remains of elephants. Nor would he entertain any thought that they belonged to an animal that no longer existed. Jefferson did not believe in extinction. "Such is the economy of nature," he wrote, "that no instance can be produced of her having permitted any one race of her animals to become extinct; of her having formed any link in her great work so weak as to be broken." Instead, he declared that mammoths were one of God's proofs against Buffon's theory of degeneration in the New World. Mammoth remains hinted at an animal with "six times the cubic volume of the elephant," Jefferson wrote. The teeth of the mammoth and the elephant were different, and Jefferson noted that elephant remains had never been discovered in North America. Jefferson considered—and rejected— alternative theories in which elephants and mammoths could be one and the same. Could elephants be more adaptable to cold climates than was believed? No. Could an "internal fire" deep in the earth once have warmed the higher latitudes to a range comfortable for elephants? There was no evidence of such. Was it possible that the angle of the earth's axis relative to the sun had changed, and that northern regions were formerly warmer for that reason? Maybe. But Jefferson concluded that, given the maximum shift anyone could conceive, these northern elephants would

have had to have lived some 250,000 years ago! Here Jefferson declined
to invoke biblical time lines, noting instead that many mammoth bones
had been discovered lying in the open air and could not possibly have remained intact for so long given such exposure.

Jefferson thought there was only one reasonable explanation. Nature,
he said, had drawn a "belt of separation between these two tremendous
animals," and in so doing, "assigned to the elephant the regions South of
these confines, and those North to the mammoth, founding the constitution of the one in her extreme of heat, and that of the other in the extreme of cold." Given the efforts of the Creator to thus distinguish these
two animals by disposition and by geography, was it not then "perverse"
of man to believe they were the same beast?

But Jefferson was less interested in the precise identity of the mammoth than he was in what the beast suggested about the faunal environment of the New World. Jefferson was well versed in Indian legends
concerning the mammoth, which the Indians sometimes called the "big
buffalo," and had heard reports that Indian tribes in the north and west of
the continent claimed the animal still existed in remote areas. Jefferson's
presumption was that remnant populations of the mammoth represented
greatly reduced numbers as the animals retreated ahead of the settlers
advancing into North America. It was much the same thing as was happening to the Indians. Some years later, when Jefferson dispatched Meriwether Lewis and William Clark to explore the American West, he
would instruct the party to be on the lookout for mammoths. But even
without a live mammoth to point to, or certainty of what the animal was,
its existence refuted the concept of degeneration.

> But to whatever animal we ascribe these remains, it is certain such
> a one has existed in America, and that it has been the largest of all
> terrestrial beings. It should have sufficed to have rescued the earth
> it inhabited, and the atmosphere it breathed, from the imputation
> of impotence in the conception and nourishment of animal life on
> a large scale: to have stifled in its birth the opinion of a writer, the
> most learned too of all others in the science of animal history, that
> in the new world . . . nature is less active, less energetic on one
> side of the globe than she is on the other. As if both sides were not
> warmed by the same genial sun . . .

Jefferson backed up his velvety demolition of Buffon's theory with hard numbers. In table after table, Jefferson showed that animals common to both North America and Europe—from elk to flying squirrels—were in many cases bigger in the New World, and that there were so many species unique to America that no one could doubt the natural vitality of the continent.

During his time in Paris, Jefferson met with Buffon on several occasions and tried to talk him out of his ideas about degeneration. He found Buffon polite but indifferent until Buffon was presented with an ambitious argument. Jefferson prevailed on the governor of New Hampshire to send a moose to him in France. The governor dispatched a troop of soldiers who shot a sizable bull. The animal was dressed and skinned, and after the skeleton had been cleaned and dried, its hide was stitched together such that it could be draped over the bones in a semblance of its original shape. After some delay, the "moose" arrived in Paris and Jefferson showed it off to Buffon. Amazed at the animal's size—it was as big as a large draft horse—the aged naturalist agreed that he would have to amend his theory. Buffon had always maintained that an "error corrected" equals a truth told. But he died almost immediately after viewing Jefferson's "moose."

Jefferson had been less good-humored in responding to Buffon's claims that American Indians were impotent and cowardly. He denounced Buffon's characterization of the Indians as an "afflicting picture indeed which, for the honor of human nature, I am glad to believe has no original." Unlike Buffon, Jefferson had firsthand knowledge of Indians, whom he described at length as being brave and intelligent and passionate—and quite obviously members of the same species as Europeans. This argument, especially when coupled with Jefferson's racist discussion of American slaves—in which he weakly endorsed limited emancipation but described blacks as being in most respects inferior to whites—muddled the meaning of *Notes on the State of Virginia* for many American readers. But for the generation of naturalists who arrived in its wake, Jefferson's little book was a revelation. Jefferson had identified the limits of European understanding of New World natural history. In doing so, he had established two fundamental principles that would guide the future study of native fauna.

First, Jefferson proved the importance of direct observation. Buffon, relying on secondhand information and poorly preserved specimens collected on the opposite side of the world, had got many things wrong. North American fauna were not the shrimpy, defective creatures Buffon had pronounced them to be. Animals could not be correctly identified and described from afar, but only through actual contact with them in the field. Logically, only Americans could accurately classify American fauna. Second, Jefferson showed that America was a robust environment, home to many species not found elsewhere in the world—including some that were perhaps no longer walking around. The Linnaean system was woefully short of genera and severely underestimated species diversity. American naturalists had already discovered and described species previously unknown to science that demanded new nomenclature. And Jefferson had left open the door for the discovery of many more. Listing more than 120 species of North American birds, Jefferson anticipated this was only a beginning, as there were "doubtless many others which have not yet been described and classed." Within a few decades, naturalists who were curious about fauna that Jefferson scarcely considered—mollusks, insects, fishes—would fan out across the country and find new species at an astonishing pace.

Twenty years after *Notes on the State of Virginia* was published, Jefferson, recently reelected to the presidency, received a fan letter from a citizen just back from a visit to Niagara Falls. The letter was brief, consisting mostly of praise for the president, a man "so honourable to Science and so invaluable to the republican institutions of a great and rapidly increasing Empire." Somewhat apologetically, the writer also mentioned two birds he had shot on his trip, one of which seemed to be an unknown species of jay. Based on his observation of this and several more exotic species in the region, the writer wished to alert the president that "many subjects still remain to be added to our Nomenclature in the Ornithology." If it was not too much of an impertinence, the writer wished the President to accept a drawing, which accompanied the letter, of the two birds.

The letter was signed "Alexander Wilson."

4

LESSONS

Falco plumbeus: The Mississippi Kite
He glances toward the earth with his fiery eye; sweeps along, now with the gentle
breeze, now against it.   —*Ornithological Biography*

W ilson's letter to Thomas Jefferson was less about his respect
for the president—though that was real enough—than it
was about his recently formed determination to produce
an ornithology of American birds. Only months before, he had begun
practicing his drawing by making repeated likenesses of a stuffed owl.
Untrained as an artist, Wilson knew his initial efforts looked comical—a
crude owlish head sitting atop a body that more closely resembled a
lark's. But his technique improved rapidly, and the drawing he sent to Jefferson was a competent rendering of a handsome gray bird perched on a
branch, its tail angled sharply downward and its head cocked forward as
if it were studying something on the ground below. Wilson acknowledged that this unknown species of jay was similar to the Canadian jay,
which had already been described and classed by Linnaeus. But he
thought the plumage and shape of the bird's crest sufficiently different
that it must be considered a separate species. Wilson's claim of having
seen many other birds not yet formally described echoed Jefferson's pre-
diction two decades earlier in *Notes on the State of Virginia*.

The president was impressed, and wrote back to say he admired the
"elegant" drawing he'd received. He also asked Wilson for assistance in
identifying a bird he had spent twenty years wondering about. This bird,
Jefferson wrote, was found everywhere in America but was difficult to

observe. It was almost always perched on the highest branches of the tallest trees in the forest. Despite having chased them—on occasion through "miles" of woods—Jefferson had never gotten a good look at one. He'd also offered to reward anyone who could shoot him a specimen, but none of the young woodsmen he knew had managed it. The elusive bird appeared to be about the same size as a mockingbird and was generally brownish, with a lighter coloring on its breast. What was most notable, however, was its song, which Jefferson described as a glorious serenade, not unlike the nightingale's.

In retrospect, this exchange is an amusing demonstration of the primitive state of American natural science at the time. The jay Wilson "discovered" was in fact a Canadian jay and not a new species at all—as he was later pained to learn. As for the bird that so beguiled Jefferson, Wilson could only conclude that it was the ordinary wood thrush, a common bird also known as a "wood robin" that was not mysterious to anyone who spent time in the forest. Jefferson was, however, rightly smitten with the song of the wood thrush, which was so lovely that it taxed Wilson's descriptive powers a couple of years later when he completed an essay on the bird and its habits for *American Ornithology*:

> With the dawn of the succeeding morning, mounting to the top of some tall tree that rises from a low thick shaded part of the woods, he pipes his few, but clear musical notes, in a kind of ecstasy; the prelude, or symphony to which, strongly resembles the double-tonguing of a German flute, and sometimes the tinkling of a small bell; the whole song consists of five or six parts, the last note of each of which is in such a tone as to leave the conclusion evidently suspended; the finale is finely managed, and with such charming effect as to soothe and tranquilize the mind, and to seem sweeter and mellower at each successive repetition.

This lyrical, overwrought style, characteristic of the times and also of Wilson's poetic sensibility, contrasted with his drawing of the wood thrush—a frozen profile in which Wilson showed the bird's beak open, as if it were caught singing. Like all of his images, this one bore the caption "Drawn from Nature." But it was nature flattened, as though the bird had been pressed onto the paper like a flower preserved between the pages of a book. Nature was less vivid in Wilson's drawings than it was in his prose, and in this Wilson was a reflection of the moment in which he lived. America was then the epicenter of several worlds in collision—a country of revolution and radicalism premised on the triumph of reason, a civil nation thinly established on the shore of an immense land where the raw power of nature flooded the senses. Jefferson's *Notes on the State of Virginia* had in effect been a second declaration of American independence, this time from the tyranny of European science. In answering Jefferson's call to arms, Wilson was awed by what he saw in nature and by the responsibility of rendering it properly. But he wasn't ready, or talented enough, to throw away tradition. This limitation added a sorrowful tinge to the graceful but immovable images in *American Ornithology*, which was so much like its creator—ambitious yet bound by convention. Wilson allowed his writing to soar, but not his birds.

Wilson's interest in ornithology arrived late in his short life, after years of struggle and restlessness. In the summer of 1803 he wrote to a friend back in Scotland that he was determined to "make a collection of all our finest birds." He was just shy of his thirty-seventh birthday. He would be dead in ten years.

In the summer of 1794, Philadelphia, which had so impressed Wilson and his nephew when they first saw it sprawled on the opposite shore of the Delaware River, was in reality a devastated city just coming back to life. Still the provisional seat of government—Philadelphia was the federal capital under the Articles of Confederation—the city had been decimated by yellow fever the previous summer and fall. The fever was a terrifying, frequently fatal disease that produced rashes, lethargy, breathing difficulties, black vomit, and a ghastly yellowing of the skin. It turned up initially along the riverfront but spread quickly, sending panicked citizens fleeing to the countryside. Many who left did so on the advice of Dr. Benjamin Rush, the city's most prominent physician. Rush, who was also a political leader and a signer of the Declaration of Independence, was among the handful of doctors who first realized an epidemic was under way. He believed that the fever was caused by airborne poisons given off by putrefying garbage—especially the spoiled cargoes that were sometimes dumped on the wharves along the Delaware and left to rot.

Rush thought that a great load of ruined coffee, lying out under the August sun and fouling the air over the city immediately before the outbreak of fever, was particularly suspect.

As the city emptied, those who stayed behind saw the hellish effects of the fever. City officials commandeered deserted homes and stables to house the sick. In reeking hospitals the dying and the dead were confined together and then abandoned by their physicians, left to be tended only by ill-trained nurses, some of whom stole their patients' food and took no notice of the filth accumulating around them. The sky itself turned black, as buckets of tar were burned in the streets in hopes of sanitizing the air.

Rush no doubt saved many lives with his advice to get out of town—mainly because people who left were more likely to escape his own widely practiced treatment for the fever. Rush adhered to an old-fashioned, two-stage remedy that began with a massive dose of purgatives, which doubtless exhausted and dehydrated an already desperately ill patient. This was followed with a heavy bleeding of the victim. Rush, who greatly overestimated the amount of blood in a typical human body, advised the removal of several *quarts* from fever sufferers. In both phases of the treatment, Rush emphasized that it was important not to err on the side of caution, but to take the most aggressive measures possible. This approach, which by itself could be enough to kill a healthy person, contributed to the deaths of many fever patients.

Yellow fever was actually transmitted by mosquitoes. It probably arrived in Philadelphia with infected refugees who'd fled the recent uprising in Saint-Domingue—and who also seemed somewhat resistant to the disease. All of this was the subject of keen speculation, but nobody at the time really understood how the fever spread or what to do about it. A few doctors who were more familiar with tropical diseases prescribed fluids and cool baths, and their fortunate patients survived at higher rates. But the disease ran rampant. Racing through the city in a matter of months, it left five thousand dead—about one out of every ten Philadelphians. The following spring the city still appeared deserted. Weeds grew in the streets. Many businesses were boarded up; some had been looted or burned out.

But by midsummer, as Wilson and his nephew hiked along the Delaware toward the city, things were returning to normal and a general cleanup had restored a sense of well-being. Wilson, shocked as he was at the prices of almost everything and by the number of Caribbean refugees wandering the streets, still perceived the wealth and opportunity pulsing in the city. When he couldn't find work as a weaver right away, he accepted a position at an engraving shop—where he got a taste of the printmaking business in which he would one day make a name. Perhaps for the first time in his life, Wilson felt happy. In letter after letter home, he wrote about the wonder of America, and how grand a city Philadelphia was.

Philadelphia was then America's most successful seaport, prospering on a brisk export trade in agricultural produce—principally flour—and on the import of manufactured goods. Built on an orderly grid of tree-lined avenues fronted by sturdy, somewhat unimaginative brick buildings, the city was dominated by a burgeoning class of merchants and seamen. Market Street, which ran east–west from the Delaware waterfront, bisected the downtown area. It was twice as wide as the other streets, and the roofed stalls of meat and produce sellers occupied the center of the boulevard. Newcomers gaped at the abundance on display in the marketplace and at its tidiness. The butchers, especially, were immaculate. They dressed in sparkling white smocks and sawed the bones as they cut meat—an appetizing improvement over the European practice of breaking the bones. Every inn and hotel in the city served feastlike meals daily, though the rough table manners of the Americans offered a challenge to anyone too dainty to grab a portion.

By day the streets were clean and quiet, and it was generally agreed that no city in the world was better lit at night. Philadelphia looked rich, and it was—a city triumphant in the wake of a revolution launched from where it stood. Wilson said that coming to America was like being a tree that had been transplanted. After a period of adjustment to his new environment, he could feel himself blooming anew amid the bounty of the New World. Any of his old friends who dreamed of coming here should do so at once, he thought. No matter what a man's occupation was, there were "a thousand other offers" of employment to contemplate in America, and it was all but assured that you could "live ten times better" here than in Scotland. For Wilson, one recurring measure of the young country's greatness was how well Americans ate. "When I look round me here on the abundance which every one enjoys," Wilson wrote to a friend back in Paisley, "when I see them sit down to a table loaded with roasted, boiled, fruits of different kinds, and plenty of good cyder, and this only the common fare of the common people, I think on my poor countrymen, and cannot refrain feeling sorrowful at the contrast."

After a few months, Wilson and Duncan found work at a loom just outside the city and spent the winter weaving. The following spring Wilson headed for New Jersey, where he found eager buyers for the cloth he peddled. When he got back he decided to try something new—teaching school. Having little education himself, Wilson managed as best he could by becoming both an instructor and a student at once, furiously going through his next day's lessons until late in the evening, learning just fast enough to stay ahead of his pupils. He practiced his grammar and read history. Finding he had a special affinity for mathematics, Wilson was soon reading Newton's calculus. He taught himself surveying and earned a little extra income from it. He even managed to make a few of his own instruments.

Wilson settled in at a school in Milestown, Pennsylvania, about twenty miles northeast of Philadelphia, where most of his pupils were Pennsylvania Dutch. They spoke German, as did the family with whom Wilson boarded, and so he learned German even as he drilled the students every day in English. He found his neighbors pleasant and honest, and filled with aspirations for their children. But they were also strange—governed by superstition and odd religious dogma. They followed phases of the moon in timing activities such as the slaughter of livestock or cutting their hair. They treated physical ailments with charms and spells, and believed the countryside was haunted. But Wilson was gratified by their commitment to his school. He was well thought of in the community and could count on his salary in full as it came due.

America suited Wilson's taste for exploring the countryside, and also his deepening passion for wingshooting. Hunting in America, where wild places were never far away, was a thrilling elevation of the senses. The abundance of game and birds, especially waterfowl, was amazing. The latter passed along the East Coast for months every autumn in massive, noisy migrations. Ducks and geese of every kind funneled down the Delaware watershed en route to the marshes of the Chesapeake Bay and eventually on to their tropical overwintering destinations far beyond. From the end of summer through Christmas, the markets were hung with a seemingly limitless bounty: swans, geese, pigeons, woodcock, grouse, quail, and a kaleidoscopic assortment of ducks. Mallards, redheads, teal, and widgeon could be had for pennies, although a brace of prized canvasbacks sometimes commanded several dollars. For someone like Wilson, happy to do his own shooting, the arrival of September commenced an annual rite as these birds of passage poured through, each species arriving and departing on its own schedule.

It began with blue-winged teal, which Wilson learned was the first of the duck "tribe" to head south out of its breeding grounds. By early September, teal congregated in such numbers along the mudflats of the Delaware River that a hunter could often kill a large number of them with a single discharge of his shotgun. Although the birds were wary and fast-flying, a hunter could sneak up on them merely by hunkering down and pushing a small boat ahead of him though the shallows, taking care to remain concealed until the last minute. Teal were delicious, and they grew fat in their days along the Delaware until they fled south with the first frost.

Canada geese—which were shot in the spring as well as the fall— were more difficult to hunt, as their sharp eyesight and skittishness made them impossible to pursue in the open. Hunters had to conceal themselves near places regularly overflown by flocks of geese, and it was possible to decoy the birds within range by various means, some as crude as shooting a goose or two and impaling them on stakes that were then set out near the gunner. Many hunters tamed geese they had wounded and used them as live decoys, tethered and eager to call to other geese flying overhead.

But it was canvasback hunting that seemed to inspire the most imaginative and relentless techniques. Their ranks now immensely reduced, these large, tasty waterfowl, which got their name from the white plumage that wraps their midsections, once migrated across America in great numbers. The duck waters around Philadelphia produced crops of an aquatic plant known as "wild celery," which grew so thick in places that it was impossible to row a boat through a stand of its submerged stalks. Canvasbacks love the root of this plant, and when it comprises the bulk of their diet, the taste of canvasback flesh is unequaled. It was not uncommon for rafts of canvasbacks to form in open water near stands of wild celery, and to remain there in safety through the daytime before coming closer in at night to feed.

Temporary measures were sometimes adopted to regulate duck hunting, usually in times when waterfowl numbers appeared low. As early as

1727, the colony of Massachusetts had briefly outlawed nighttime hunting. But, for the most part, anything went. On moonlit nights, when the canvasbacks were thick on the Delaware, it was common practice to guide a boat silently under the shadow of the shoreline and then drift into a flock of feeding ducks—whereupon the stillness was broken by a blue flash and a booming report that echoed over the water as the hunter raked the ducks where they sat, killing many at a time. Another method, used late in the season, involved painting a boat white and setting chunks of ice or snow along the gunwales. The hunter—also dressed in white—approached a flock from upstream and reclined hidden in the boat, allowing it to float in among the ducks as it if were a chunk of drifting ice before he rose up and fired. The method that most intrigued Wilson was "tolling," in which a well-hidden hunter ordered his highly trained dog to scamper along the shoreline, usually with a brightly colored handkerchief tied about its midsection. The canvasbacks mistook the dog's actions for the movement of other ducks paddling close to shore and, curious, would swim in to investigate.

Wilson eagerly took up these sports, so different from his casual walking hunts over the moors near Paisley. It would have been hard to envision a more dramatic demonstration of nature's bounty than the annual flights of ducks and geese that passed over his head each autumn and again every spring. Their numbers, like the vision itself, are now so much diminished that it is all but impossible to conceive what it was like. The throngs of geese and ducks that Wilson saw were but a fraction of the waterfowl migrating along the Eastern Flyway, a number that was itself a fraction of the unimaginable masses overflying the continent.

Although there were other Scottish immigrants in the area, Wilson avoided people he thought might know about the circumstances under which he'd left his homeland. One exception was a man named Charles Orr, who lived in Philadelphia and occasionally visited Wilson out at Milestown. They wrote each other often, with Wilson sometimes corresponding in verse. Evidently, he enjoyed Orr as a compatriot and captive audience. The great thing about letter-writing, he once told Orr, was that it afforded you an opportunity to speak your mind without fear of interruption.

Time slipped away. William Duncan moved to upstate New York, to establish a farm. In 1798 Philadelphia was again gripped by a yellow fever outbreak that emptied the city. Through the summer and into the fall, people died by the thousands. Wilson could scarcely believe the deserted streets—no more than 8,000 of the city's 65,000 residents remained in town. It was possible, Wilson wrote to his family, to stand in any public square and hear no other human being "except for the drivers of the death carts." But the plague passed with the onset of winter and Philadelphia again recovered. Before he knew it, Wilson found that he'd been teaching for five years—and that he was on the verge of *something*, either an epiphany or a nervous breakdown. Or maybe both. He began to feel imprisoned by his responsibilities. He periodically complained of being ill. At one point he even resigned his post, only to be coaxed back to work with a promise of additional sick leave from the school's trustees. In the summer of 1800, Wilson's letters to Orr began to confide his innermost feelings—which were suddenly jumbled and anxious. In one letter, Wilson suggested they had much to reveal to each other as "lovers of truth," adding, oddly, that they were both "subject to the failings of Human Nature." Wilson couldn't quite seem to stay on one subject. He said he planned to begin an earnest campaign of frugality. Did Orr think that was a good idea? Could he speculate on the benefits of such a program? Wilson admitted he was writing in haste and urged Orr to write him back the same way. In a long, nearly inscrutable passage, Wilson hinted at something he wished to discuss that was so mysterious that even he couldn't tell for sure what it was:

> I, for my part, have many things to enquire of you, of which at different times I form very different opinions, and at other times can form no distinct decided opinion at all. Sometimes they appear dark and impenetrable; sometimes I think I see a little better into them. Now I see them as plain as broad day, and again they are as dark to me as midnight. In short, the moon puts on not more variety of appearance to the eye than many subjects do to my apprehension & yet in themselves they still remain the same.

Alarmingly, Wilson added that he had "many things of a more interesting and secret nature" to talk over with Orr. Perhaps Orr would find these "things" funny. A few days later, Wilson again wrote to Orr—who, not surprisingly, showed a growing reluctance to write back—and this time solicited Orr's opinion on marriage and family, a topic that Wilson said had been on his mind since a fateful walk in the woods the previous spring.

It was in the middle of May, Wilson wrote. The forest was in full bloom, and Wilson noticed many birds "in pairs" building nests in which to mate and raise their young. Continuing on his hike, Wilson saw a colt nuzzling its mother. Then he heard the bleating of lambs "from every farm," and after that he became aware of insects "in the thousands" at his feet and in the air around him, all "preparing to usher their multitudes into being." Suddenly, as if from a voice out of the heavens, the words "multiply and replenish the earth" formed in his mind. For a moment, Wilson said, he "stood like a blank in this interesting scene, like a note of discord in this universal harmony of love and self-propagation." He perceived himself in this flash of clarity for what he was: a wretch, living outside of normal society, a man with "no endearing female" who saw in him "her other self" and no child to call him father.

"I was," Wilson wrote, "like a dead tree in the midst of a green forest."

Hurrying home, Wilson found his landlords playing happily with their children. He was mortified. What good had he accomplished? What was the point of all his study and his books? Did it not strain the bounds of decency that a man such as he—learned now in science and in literature, and susceptible to "the finer feelings of the soul"—should not continue his line? There and then, Wilson vowed to fulfill the biological imperative. He would marry. He would raise a family. Bachelor to the core, he promised to do all this even though he could anticipate "ten thousand unseen distresses" that would befall him in the bargain. In any event, Wilson said, what he most wanted Orr's advice on was this: Was it not a crime to "persist in a state of celibacy"?

Of course, Wilson quickly admitted, he'd forgotten about all of this as soon as he was back in his room and immersed in his mathematics. Almost as an afterthought, Wilson said he had lately considered a modified version of his plan. It would not be necessary, strictly speaking, to get married in order to contribute "towards this grand work of generation" and to become "the father of at least *one* of my own species." Evidently there had been more than sap rising in the Pennsylvania woods that season. But Wilson said no more about it—certainly nothing about who might be his partner in such a furtherance of the species. He told Orr that, after thinking it over, he'd decided the whole idea seemed indecent and had abandoned any further thought of launching a little Wilson outside the bounds of holy matrimony. Exactly what additional thoughts he may have entertained he kept to himself.

And with that, he signed off.

Another year passed. In early 1801, Wilson was asked to speak at a patriots' rally in Milestown to mark the inauguration of Thomas Jefferson as president. Although he still felt he was something of an outsider—Wilson would not become a citizen of the United States for three more years—his speech was a resounding success. He chose to speak principally of liberty, which he called "the great strength and happiness of nations, and the universal and best friend of man." With a nod to the veterans of the Revolutionary War present in the crowd, Wilson exhorted his listeners to be protective of the freedoms gained by force of arms and to be mindful that the great American experiment was being closely watched around the world. Children should be taught to feel the highest regard for their country, and for the importance of preserving their rights, which were not granted to them by other men, but by God himself. Wilson so stirred his audience that the speech was transcribed and widely printed in pro-Jefferson newspapers. Wilson, carried away by the enthusiastic response to his rhetoric, basked in glory for weeks afterward.

But Wilson's moods were like the rising and falling flight of a bird that beats its wings only intermittently, traveling forward on an undulating line that is always in part a free fall to earth. In May, only months after his speech, Wilson sent Orr a panicky note asking him to come see him so that they might discuss an urgent matter. Wilson said he was quite distracted by something that had happened, and was in fact making plans to leave Milestown as soon as possible. Staying on was out of the question, and he could confide his reasons to nobody but Orr. Orr, he said, was the only friend he had now—apart from "one whose friendship" had brought ruin to them both, or soon enough would. Wilson said he would await Orr at the schoolhouse and to please come out that same day.

Apparently, Wilson had fallen in love with someone, possibly a married woman, and his reputation as well as hers was now at risk. Wilson must have told Orr the whole story, but if he ever revealed the details of this affair to anyone else, he did so in private conversation or in letters that do not survive. Orr found Wilson in a miserable state when he visited him that evening, and the next night, after Orr had gone back to Philadelphia, Wilson led his horse out onto the road in the night and stole away, leaving behind everything he owned. He never went back.

In the months following his disappearance, Wilson wrote Orr a string of increasingly pitiful letters—begging for information about rumors that might be circulating in Milestown and especially for any word of the "one" who'd broken his heart. He spent some time in New York City, a place he didn't care for, and briefly contemplated going home to Scotland. Eventually he found a teaching post near Newark, New Jersey. It paid poorly and Wilson remained deeply depressed. At one point he asked Orr to consider something they had often talked about—opening their own school together. But Orr became slower in writing back, and then he stopped entirely, devastating Wilson. In a tortured letter, Wilson told Orr he still loved him, even if the reverse was not true anymore. He repeated that he no longer had any friends, and as for what was being said about him back in Milestown, he was indifferent to expressions of either love or hate from anyone he'd known there. He just didn't care about anything now. A week later he wrote to Orr to apologize and take it all back. Orr should regard everything Wilson had told him as the rantings of a crazy person, but he should never doubt Wilson's undying friendship. He said he had never experienced such unhappiness and that it would be a long time before his mind recovered. "Past hopes, present difficulties, and a gloomy futurity," Wilson wrote, "have almost deranged my ideas and too deeply affected me." Without even a hint that he saw better days ahead, Wilson also mentioned that he had secured a new teaching position, this one at a school in Gray's Ferry, just across the Schuylkill River from Philadelphia. His predecessor there had been a boisterous and ineffective former sea captain, and the pupils appeared to be an unruly lot. He said he regarded the prospect of returning to yet another classroom with the same feeling as a condemned man walking to the gallows.

As it turned out, the move to the Union School of Kingsessing at Gray's Ferry was the most fortuitous of Wilson's life. The schoolhouse, a squat, one-room building with a steep roof and shuttered windows, stood in a glade near the main thoroughfare leading south out of the city. The road passed out of the city's busy streets and into the countryside, running by nurseries and the U.S. Arsenal before arriving at the river crossing about four miles from downtown. On the opposite shore, the highway entered a woodsy neighborhood made up of a number of taverns and a few blocks of wooden houses thrown together during the yellow fever exodus ten years earlier. It was also where an elderly man named William Bartram lived quietly on an estate known for its elaborate botanical gardens, which were said to include most of the known flora of North America.

Bartram, Philadelphia's most eminent naturalist, was a living legend. He was the son of John Bartram, formerly the "King's Botanist" before the Revolution. The elder Bartram had been revered in America and all over Europe both for his expertise in New World plants—Linnaeus considered him the world's most accomplished botanist—and for a series of expeditions he had made to collect plants and explore the continent. William, who from an early age showed an enthusiasm for drawing birds and trees, accompanied his father on several of these trips, most importantly in 1765 to northeastern Florida where he stayed on and established an indigo plantation near the banks of the St. John's River. The enterprise failed. But in 1773 William returned to Florida and again explored its northeastern palmetto jungles and savannas over the course of a four-year sojourn among the area's planters and the native Seminole Indians. In 1791, Bartram published a book, *Travels through North & South Carolina, Georgia, East & West Florida*, based on the field journals he kept during his expedition. It offered a vivid account of a wild place that seemed to Bartram a kind of Garden of Eden, and included detailed lists and descriptions of the many plants and animals he had encountered. Bartram's description of the Alachua savanna, an immense opening of sawgrass and wetlands just south of present-day Gainesville, evoked the intoxicating wildness of the place:

> The extensive Alachua savanna is a level, green plain, above fifteen miles over, fifty miles in circumference, and scarcely a tree or bush of any kind to be seen on it. It is encircled with high, sloping hills, covered with waving forests and fragrant Orange groves, rising from an exuberantly fertile soil. The towering Magnolia grandilora and transcendent Palm, stand conspicuous amongst them. At the same time are seen innumerable droves of cattle; the lordly bull, lowing cow and sleek capricious heifer. The hills and groves re-echo their cheerful, social voices. Herds of sprightly deer, squadrons of

the beautiful, fleet Siminole horse, flocks of turkeys, civilized communities of the sonorous, watchful crane, mix together, appearing happy and contented in the enjoyment of peace, 'till disturbed and affrighted by the warrior man. Behold yonder, coming upon them through the darkened groves, sneakingly and unawares, the naked red warrior, invading the Elysian fields and green plains of Alachua.

Travels was an instant sensation, though it was better received in Europe, where it quickly went through nine editions, than in the United States, where reviewers complained about Bartram's ornate style and his high regard for Florida's Indians. Bartram undeniably overcooked his prose, but in recounting his many adventures with the people and animals of the southeastern United States, he was often hugely entertaining. In one of his most talked-about escapades, Bartram described his killing of a large rattlesnake. In a momentary rage after nearly stepping on the angrily coiled specimen while hiking through a swamp near St. Augustine, Bartram whacked the animal with a stick and then cut off its head. He was instantly overcome with guilt—Bartram regarded the rattlesnake as a marvelous example of natural form and function—though he felt a different sensation after dragging it back to camp and being served a portion of its flesh when the local governor had it cooked up for dinner the same evening. Bartram admitted he could bring himself to taste the meat, but not swallow it.

This kind of adventure was riveting to casual readers, but Bartram earned even more respect for his enlargement of what was known of the country's natural history. Bartram drew sketches of and described snakes, frogs, turtles, and many sorts of mammals, bringing them to life with sometimes startling immediacy. He reported that Florida swamps in the springtime reverberated with the bellows of male alligators, and that when these reptiles issue their calls, "vapor rises from their nostrils like smoke." Bartram discovered a great many species not previously known to science, from the gopher turtle to the Florida panther. Among his most significant contributions were observations on bird migration. Bartram noted the transitory appearance in Florida each fall and spring of the many birds that bred in the North and overwintered in the South. And he assembled a new list of American birds—215 in all—that nearly doubled Jefferson's compilation. Bartram probably had even more bird data than he included in *Travels*, and his use of unconventional naming schemes in place of Linnaean binomials denied him full credit for many species he was certainly the first to formally describe. But later naturalists came to regard Bartram's *Travels* as the true starting point of American ornithological study. Three years after the book first appeared, Bartram was the only American named to an international list of "all living zoologists."

Bartram was sixty-three when Alexander Wilson came to Gray's Ferry, and was busy drafting illustrations for *Elements of Botany*, the first botany textbook published in America. Wilson's schoolhouse was less than a mile from Bartram's Garden, which he soon discovered. Long devoted to rambling before and after his teaching day, Wilson loved hiking among the unusual and stately trees and shrubs that abounded in the garden. He was more quickly acquainted with Bartram's cypresses and azaleas than he was with Bartram himself, as it apparently took the shy schoolteacher the better part of a year to become a regular visitor at the old stone house built by Bartram's father three-quarters of a century earlier.

But by the spring of 1803, Wilson was corresponding with Bartram and was spending time in the famous naturalist's library, where he was learning plant and animal classification. He had also begun taking drawing instruction from Bartram's niece. Wilson regretted not having more free time to pursue these new interests, and remarked how difficult it was to draft proper images when he was forced to work by candlelight. In March, he sent a note to Bartram thanking him for his letters of encouragement, which he said were like "Bank Notes to a Miser." Wilson worked on images of birds and flowers, and drew an interesting shrub Bartram had pointed out to him, sending the picture—which he deemed a "feeble imitation"—to Bartram with a request that he supply its Linnaean and common names.

One of the works Wilson studied in Bartram's library was an age-mellowed copy of *The Natural History of Carolina, Florida and the Bahama Islands* that the book's author, the English naturalist Mark Catesby, had presented to Bartram's father. It was, before Bartram's *Travels*, the most complete and the most beautiful zoology of North America. The two-volume book consists almost entirely of 220 etchings of plants and animals that Catesby had observed and drawn during two lengthy expeditions to the New World between 1712 and 1726. The pictures depict animals familiar now in North America, but also some that were completely unknown to Wilson. The schoolteacher's head, for years preoccupied with grammar lessons and the figures of the calculus, now filled with colorful images of fishes and reptiles and mammals and, especially, birds. The first volume was devoted to birds. Wilson saw birds that he knew and some that he didn't, many depicted in ways suggesting their personalities. In Catesby's most ambitious drawing, a bald eagle with wings outstretched and talons flaring dives high above a river to capture a fish that has just fallen from the grasp of an osprey seen hovering helplessly in the background. The complexity of this drawing—it is one of only two in which Catesby drew a landscape as a backdrop—is remarkable, and the fact that most of the rest are much simpler indicates how expensive and time-consuming engraving and coloring prints could be. Some of Catesby's animals are posed against neutral backgrounds; most are either perched on or standing by trees or shrubs that are carefully classed and named.

Catesby had a soft style—the original drawings were made in watercolor—but he used bold, saturating colors. There is an arresting degree of detail in the engravings, with the lines of even the softest feathers clearly delineated. His blue jay is typical. The bird stands on the limb of a smilax bush in a scolding posture, its tail cocked high and its head canted upward with its beak open to reveal a wagging tongue. The bird's signature crest is erect, and the fine feathers along its belly stand out excitedly.

Wilson found Catesby's book irresistible, and he seemed to begin thinking almost immediately about undertaking a project to expand on it. With only a hundred species of birds represented, the *Natural History* wasn't even close to a comprehensive catalogue of North American species. But Catesby had found the right approach in using the available printing techniques and figuring out how to market such a book.

There were several ways of reproducing drawings or paintings. All were labor-intensive and expensive. Images were typically traced and then cut into wood or engraved on stone or metal, usually copper. When these templates were inked and pressed onto paper, a black-and-white copy of the original image resulted. Depending on how rapidly the woodcut or engraving wore down, it could be reused many times to mass-produce copies.

If the finished image was to be in color, however, this added another demanding step—hand painting. Using the original as a guide, a colorist—or sometimes a team of colorists—painted over the black-and-white print, filling it in one color at a time, like a paint-by-numbers. When well executed, a hand-colored print was almost indistinguishable from the original and from its sibling prints—even though each reproduction was, in truth, a unique work of art.

Printmaking thus involved several skilled disciplines, with the engraving in particular requiring talent often equal to that of the original artist. This meant that the biggest obstacle facing any illustrated book was the cost of making it. Catesby did his own engraving, partly so he could control the quality of the prints but mainly because he couldn't afford to hire an engraver. Even then, the finished book figured to be so expensive— not to mention the normal risk of less-than-hoped-for sales—that Catesby had had to ensure in advance that the project would pay for itself. He did this by producing the *Natural History* in installments and selling subscriptions to buyers who agreed to pay for each batch of "birds, beasts, fish, serpents, insects, and plants" as it was received. He also decided to make the book available in black and white. One uncolored installment, or "Number" as it was called, cost one guinea—a pound and a shilling (about $4.80). Catesby then advertised a luxury version. "For the Satisfaction of the CURIOUS," he stated in a prospectus, "some Copies will be printed on the finest Imperial Paper, and the Figures put in their Natural Colours from the ORIGINAL PAINTINGS, at the Price of Two Guineas."

Catesby's *Natural History* made a terrific impact. It was widely reprinted and translated for many years, and found its way onto the shelves of several royal families. Virtually all of Europe's most influential naturalists regarded it as the definitive work on North American wildlife. Linnaeus himself based many of his taxonomic listings of New World plants and animals on Catesby's observations. Like William Bartram decades later, Catesby was struck by the coming and going of the birds through the South each fall and spring. At the time, there was still much uncertainty about migration, and many myths about where birds went in the winter persisted. It was thought that some spent the winter in the deep recesses of caves. Another surprisingly durable theory was that some species, such as swallows, dived to the bottoms of lakes and remained there until the return of warm weather.

Catesby was humbled by his success, and was at pains to apologize— quite unnecessarily—for his primitive style. He took more pride, it seemed, in having endured the rigors of his expeditions, which were considerable. Catesby made all of his drawings in the field, working whenever possible from live-caught specimens. He traveled in unsettled areas, hauling his kits of paints and papers and dissecting instruments, and often lived in the open. He was impressed by the many species he encountered—and by the violence they perpetrated on one another—as he advanced deeper into the tropics. In South Carolina, he lived through a powerful hurricane that left the carcasses of deer and bears hanging from tree limbs, and watched snakes feasting on animals fleeing ahead of the deluge. Inevitably, Catesby experienced the heart-stopping run-in with a rattlesnake that seemed obligatory among early American naturalists. After awaking at an inn in Georgia one morning, Catesby had just sat down to tea in the next room when he heard the maid who'd gone to make up his bed start to scream. She had discovered a rattler between the sheets that Catesby had vacated only minutes before. Catesby concluded that the snake had climbed into bed with him to warm up—it was February—but he couldn't guess how long they'd kept one another company. In any case, the snake did not care to be disturbed at this point, as Catesby noted when he investigated the scene and found the serpent "full of ire, biting at everything that approached him." Tellingly, Catesby's painting of the rattlesnake included a separate close-up of one of its fangs.

For the first time since the days when he had dreamed of being a poet, Wilson felt he'd found an objective—and a means of achieving it. He continued to work at his drawing, routinely submitting his renderings of birds and plants to Bartram for correction and advice. He got to know the Philadelphia engraver Alexander Lawson, a fellow Scot, who provided additional instruction. In the spring of 1804, Wilson sent Lawson a note explaining his frustration at not having more time away from his teaching duties to tend to his "itch for drawing," which he said he'd gotten from Lawson. He then told Lawson of his idea for an ornithological study of America, confessing that he was famous for having big ideas that came to nothing, but saying he would appreciate his friend's backing just the same. "I am most earnestly bent on pursuing my plan of making a collection of all the birds in this part of North America," Wilson wrote. "Now I don't want you to throw cold water, as Shakespeare says, on this notion, Quixotic as it may appear. I have been so long accustomed to the building of airy castles and brain windmills, that it has become one of my earthly comforts."

Wilson had taken lodgings near his school with a family named Jones, and in this, too, he was fortunate. The Jones house stood between two creeks that merged into a pool at the base of a low cliff in a thicket a short distance away. Wilson spent hours before and after school lazing atop this hill, reading poetry and studying the sunlight filtering through the beech trees overhead, or looking down at the water, which reflected the laurel branches hanging beside the pond. The grove was full of birds in the spring and summer—so many species that Wilson's observations there would become the basis for much of his ornithology. He kept track of the intermittent appearances of hawks and orioles, goldfinches and whippor-wills. Once, while walking in Bartram's woods not far away, he saw a species of woodpecker he was sure was new.

Wilson was sometimes joined in his poolside bower by Bartram's niece. Her name was Nancy, though Wilson called her by her nickname, Anna. Whether they were ever more than the closest of friends is unclear. A few lines in several of Wilson's poems hint at a greater affection. Wilson seemed, in any event, content and focused on his future—even when Lawson ignored his plea for support and instead tried to talk him out of attempting to publish an illustrated ornithology. Given the more than two hundred birds already known, plus the many more Wilson intended to add to the list, Lawson calculated that the cost of engraving, coloring, and printing such a work—in which Wilson also planned to include a scientific narrative giving the natural history of each species—would easily run to several thousand dollars a copy. No one would pay so dearly, Lawson said, and no publisher would risk investing in a book that might end up costing as much as a small farm.

Wilson never shared these reservations. He kept at his drawing undeterred. Within two years of his coming to Gray's Ferry he had assembled a fair collection of drawings of the larger birds in the area and was hard at work on the warblers and other small species. His students, amused by his interest in nature, constantly brought Wilson all sorts of plants and animals for his enjoyment. He received a whole basket of ornery crows from a boy in his class, and wondered if the child would next turn up with a load of live bullfrogs. One day a student caught a mouse in the schoolhouse and turned it over to Wilson, who considered how best to pose the animal for drawing. He finally decided to kill the mouse and mount it in the claws of his stuffed owl, but as he watched the animal struggling against a string with which he'd tied it up, Wilson's heart melted. When he accidentally spilled a few drops of water near it, the mouse quickly drank them up and then, to Wilson's mind at least, looked up at him with terror in its eyes. He let the mouse go.

Wilson's perpetually erratic mood stabilized during this time, or at least its extremes subsided in his new, invigorating surroundings. But he still had his moments. Bartram and his niece had promoted Wilson's interest in birds and drawing partly as a way of pulling him out of the tailspin he was in when he arrived. They understood that his long walks in the woods were not entirely about his devotion to nature, but were in fact Wilson's way of escaping his tormented thoughts. On one of these walks, he had accidentally dropped his gun—which shockingly went off. Stunned by the concussion of the blast and the whoosh he felt as the shot charge narrowly missed his chest, Wilson had gone home badly shaken. He confided to Bartram how ironic it would have been if his life, so amply punctuated by times when he almost wished he were dead, had ended in an accident that looked like a suicide. Bartram didn't know whether to be relieved or worried sick.

And while the birds seemed to lift Wilson's spirits, his work held his mood in check. Wilson was better paid at the Union School than he ever had been, but he knew now that teaching was not for him. He hated its confinement above all. Indeed, he was now convinced that the grinding repetitiveness of the classroom was killing him. "Close application to my profession, which I have followed since November 1795," he wrote to a friend, "has deeply injured my constitution, the more so, that my rambling disposition was the worst calculated of anyone's in the world for the austere regularity of a teacher's life."

5

A BEAUTIFUL PLANTATION

Troculus colubris: The Ruby-Throated Hummingbird
I ask of you, kind reader, who, on observing this glittering fragment of the rainbow, would not pause, admire, and instantly turn his mind with reverence toward the Almighty Creator, the wonders of whose hand we at every step discover?
—*Ornithological Biography*

While Wilson walked in the woods and practiced his drafts-manship, drawing and redrawing his owl, someone else was watching the birds thirty miles away. The eighteen-year-old who now called himself John James Audubon had arrived at his father's estate, Mill Grove, in late summer of 1803. The final leg of his journey from France had proved more difficult than the ocean crossing. Two weeks earlier, Audubon had left his ship the instant it docked in New York and walked all the way into Greenwich Village, where his father had arranged a line of credit with a bank. Audubon, excited by the city, per-haps failed to notice an uneasy quiet in the streets. Yellow fever had bro-ken out in New York that summer, and by the time Audubon made his way back to the docks he was feeling unwell. His condition deteriorated so quickly that the captain, a man named John Smith, hired a carriage and hurried him out of the city. He ended up at a boardinghouse run by two Quaker ladies who cared for him as his condition first turned grave and then, amazingly, improved just as rapidly.

Audubon's first weeks after finally reaching Mill Grove were awk-ward. His English was all but nonexistent, and his exact status at the es-tate was ambiguous. The elder Audubon was having trouble managing his property from France, and was at odds with both his American agent in Philadelphia (who, among other things, evidently was to handle John

James's modest allowance) and with François Dacosta, the man he'd sent over from Nantes to develop the lead mine on the property. Audubon's father and Dacosta had entered into an agreement for shared ownership of Mill Grove that was a continually evolving tangle of bonds, mortgages, and promises to split future proceeds from the mine. To the extent that anybody was actually running the place, it seemed to be the tenant farmer, a Quaker named William Thomas. Thomas tilled the land, tended the livestock, operated the lumber and grist mill, and took care of the large house. Audubon, apparently oblivious to these arrangements, assumed he was in charge of Mill Grove. But he showed little interest in accepting any daily responsibilities. Instead, he went hunting.

For a young man already in love with the outdoors and fascinated by wildlife, Mill Grove was a dream come true. It was near the confluence of Perkiomen Creek and the Schuylkill River, twenty miles northwest of Philadelphia. Audubon would recall the place later in his life as his "beautiful American plantation." The house, already forty years old, was impressive—a sprawling, three-story stone structure topped by a dormered shake roof and several tall brick chimneys. Inside, it was a warren of small rooms and low ceilings. The floors were wide-planked southern yellow pine worn to a warm patina. The house and a compound of outbuildings stood on a hillside, at the end of a long drive. A wide veranda ran the length of the house in the rear, overlooking an expanse of lawn and pastureland falling away to the south on a long slope above Perkiomen Creek. The Perkiomen, more truly a river than a creek, was eighty yards wide at the foot of the hill, where it ran over a low dam built to power the mill. Being close to the main crossing point of the creek, the house featured a small addition on its west end, with a tavern in the basement and rooms for travelers above. The famous lead mine was in the front yard, only twenty paces from the entrance to the house. Its shaft was twelve feet across and went straight down for some distance before angling off beneath the hillside.

Audubon spent little time in the house. Every day he was up at dawn and into the woods with his gun. The countryside, just then beginning to color with the onset of fall, was spectacular. High bluffs flanked the grounds, and the ravines were cathedrals of old-growth beech and oak and chestnut. Hemlocks stood on the ridgetops. The bottoms, especially along the creek, were shaded by immense, thick-bodied sycamores. Recent surveys at Mill Grove have found 176 species of birds in the forest.

In Audubon's day there were more, including flocks of passenger pigeons that appeared from time to time.

The intensity of Audubon's curiosity about the birds and animals in the forest was unflagging. In the evenings he practiced his violin and flute, but he also retreated to an upstairs room where he assembled a growing collection of specimens—nests, eggs, shed snakeskins, and now and then a freshly dispatched bird or small mammal that he practiced drawing. He was always reluctant to come home at the end of the day, and usually only returned after the dew had begun to settle and he had a full game bag hanging against his damp trousers. In a crevice in the rocks on one of the cliffs above Perkiomen Creek, Audubon discovered a grotto that became a favorite retreat. Phoebes nested there, and under his constant attentions the birds became so tame that Audubon could hold them in his hands. Curious as to whether they returned to the same nesting place every year, Audubon tied threads around their feet in hopes of identifying them in subsequent seasons. Audubon would later recall this as a time when he had not a care in the world, passing each day afoot in the woods, dressed in fancy coats and shirts with lace cuffs, or riding over the fields on one of his fine horses. The reality may have been more modest—it took him some months to save up for a new gun and a hunting dog—but Audubon's claim of having spent these days in a kind of nature-induced trance was true.

Shortly after he got to Mill Grove, Audubon learned that a new family was moving in at a big house only a half-mile down the road. Their name was Bakewell. They were originally from Derbyshire, in England, and more recently by way of New Haven, Connecticut. Evidently they were well off. Expensive stocks of fancy-bred sheep and cattle arrived shortly, and the Bakewells renamed their estate Fatland Ford after a local legend about the richness of its soil. Like Mill Grove, the house at Fatland Ford—far bigger and grander than Audubon's—commanded stunning vistas of the rolling countryside to the south and west. On a clear day, you could see from Fatland Ford all the way to Valley Forge.

Audubon was curious about the Bakewells. It was said that they had several handsome daughters, though he was more intrigued by the rumor that William Bakewell, the father, raised pointing dogs. But Audubon kept his distance. These people were, after all, English—countrymen of the enemies of his father. And although Audubon had slipped effortlessly into the role of young prince on his American plantation, he was painfully aware of his limited education and social experience, and that there were only a handful of English words that made sense to him. The Bakewells were sure to be much too sophisticated for his company.

But one day right after New Year's, Audubon came upon William Bakewell when they were both out grouse hunting along Perkiomen Creek. Bakewell was friendly and reassuring, and insisted the young man come to Fatland Ford for a visit and a formal introduction to the Bakewell family. Audubon said he would, and after some delay, he nervously went.

Audubon never forgot that day. He went down the lane to Fatland Ford in the morning. A servant answered the door and quietly led him into the parlor, where he found himself alone with a girl who was sewing by the fire. She seemed momentarily surprised by her visitor, but stood politely and offered Audubon a seat. Her father, she said, was out but would return shortly. They sat. Audubon could not take his eyes off the girl, who continued to sew and now chatted amiably with her guest. Her name was Lucy. She was the Bakewells' eldest daughter. In two days she would be eighteen.

Between stitches, Lucy studied the young man squirming in his chair and staring at her. She'd heard of her reclusive neighbor. The reality was unexpectedly pleasant. He was full of energy and most definitely handsome, although his hair, which hung to his shoulders, took some getting used to. But he was friendly, and his accent was cute. Lucy found his odd use of archaic expressions like "thee" and "thou" utterly charming. Despite the language problem, they managed to understand one another. Soon they were talking about England and France, and comparing impressions of their new homes in America. When Lucy spoke of the moors in Derbyshire, Audubon sensed that they shared certain feelings about wild places. He found himself hoping that her father would take his time getting back. She was pretty, he thought. Maybe not classically so, but she had lovely gray eyes and a sweetness that seemed to fill the room. Audubon was happy to see a pianoforte in the corner. When William Bakewell at last appeared, he saw that the two of them were getting on well and suggested that Lucy prepare lunch. Audubon would later recall that he and William Bakewell ate "over guns and dogs," lost in talk of hunting. But his most vivid memory was of Lucy's tiny waist as she went to the kitchen ahead of them.

"She now arose from her seat a second time," he later wrote, "and her form, to which I had previously paid but partial attention, showed both grace and beauty; and my heart followed every one of her steps."

Audubon's feelings for Lucy advanced quickly in the days that followed. He got to know all the Bakewells, which in addition to Lucy, William, and Mrs. Bakewell, included five more children: Thomas, who was seventeen; his eager little brother William, who was five; plus Eliza, who was fourteen and exceedingly pretty; and the two little girls, Sarah and Ann. After Audubon's visit to Fatland Ford, the Bakewells called at Mill Grove on several occasions. One cold evening, everyone went skating on Perkiomen Creek—where Audubon demonstrated impressive skill. He also had a fine time pushing Lucy around the ice on a sled. On another occasion, Audubon led the Bakewells up the cramped stairway to his specimen room, where they were impressed by his collection of stuffed birds and other animals. Shyly, he took out a few crayon drawings of some birds and a mink. He was an intense young man, though in his eagerness to impress he was prone to rash claims. He foolishly told the Bakewells that a portrait of George Washington hanging above the mantel had been presented to his father, "Admiral" Audubon, by Washington himself after the "Battle of Valley Forge." Audubon was ignorant of the fact that Washington had only camped his troops at Valley Forge, and that the general had visited not Mill Grove, but Fatland Ford. No doubt he got by with these lies because the Bakewells by then wanted to believe that Audubon was the aristocrat he seemed. If they doubted his boast of having studied painting with Jacques-Louis David, they apparently let that one pass as well.

There was no denying that Audubon had many talents. He danced well, played music, and was an accomplished horseman. He could fence and swim, and he was a superb shot. He seemed to know everything about birds and animals. His curiosity about nature never rested. Audubon was always in a good mood, always full of ideas about what to do or where to go to see something interesting. It gave William Bakewell pause to hear that young Audubon had led his daughter to some hidden place in the bluff above Perkiomen Creek—but he relaxed when he was reassured that they were only up there to look at phoebes. He was less forgiving when Audubon, on skates and armed with a shotgun, talked Tom Bakewell into tossing his cap in the air for a target.

One afternoon in late winter, Audubon led a hunting party after ducks. The season was not yet far enough advanced for a spring flight of waterfowl, but there must have been a few early arrivals and some ducks always stayed through the winter. The hunters moved up frozen Perkiomen Creek on skates, being careful to avoid the patches of open water they called "air holes." The group was still a long way from Mill Grove when darkness fell, leaving a fair distance of treacherous river ice between them and home. Undaunted, Audubon volunteered to lead the way. Tying a white handkerchief to a stick, Audubon held it aloft and told everyone to follow him. The others adjusted the still-warm ducks hanging from their belts, looking around doubtfully at the gloom. Then they were off, gliding down the creek beneath the bare branches of the overhanging trees, now and then passing by a gurgling air hole. The frigid night air stung their faces. At the head of the line, Audubon's white signal bobbed along like a beacon in the dark sky. Suddenly, it disappeared.

Audubon had fallen into an air hole. Instantly, the current swept him under, pushing him along beneath the ice and away from all sight and sound. His friends rushed to the place where he'd gone through. An eternity seemed to pass as they stared, horrified, into the swirling blackness. There was nothing to say, nothing they could do. The night was a clear, frozen envelope of silence surrounding them. They shifted on their skates. The ice groaned. Then they heard a cry many yards downstream. Audubon had somehow found his way up through another air hole. He was dragged coughing and shaking onto the ice, where someone stripped off a coat and wrapped it around him. As they got him to his feet, Audubon told his companions that in the shock of going under he'd lost consciousness. It was by pure chance that he'd popped up through another opening and regained his senses before being pulled down again.

Audubon worked hard at his drawing. His favorite subjects were birds, but they frustrated his efforts to translate nature onto paper. In France, as a boy, he'd collected birds with his father along the Loire River, but when he drew them in pencil and crayon the results were "miserable." The objects of these early sketches looked like what they were—dead birds. Audubon depicted them in "stiff, unnatural profiles," a manner he would later find all too common in conventional ornithology. The elder Audubon was unstinting in his encouragement, but warned his son that "nothing in the world possessing life and animation" is easy to imitate. At Mill Grove, Audubon tried to solve the problem by taking his crayons and pencils to the grotto above Perkiomen Creek, where he made countless attempts at drawing his beloved phoebes as they flitted about. Sometimes he made rough outlines of birds in the field, then shot them and returned to his room, where he laid them out as best he could in the same positions. This didn't work, as "they were dead to all intents and neither wing, leg, or tail could I place according to the intention of my wishes." He even tried tying threads to the head and wings of his specimens to support them in lifelike attitudes. But when he compared these clumsy models to the real, live thing, he said, "I felt my blood rise in my temples."

These efforts so demoralized Audubon that at one point he stopped drawing for a month. Instead, he walked every day through the woods, looking at birds and waiting for inspiration. Audubon later claimed that during this time he began to dream about drawing birds, and long before daylight one morning he sat up in bed with a start. As Audubon told it, he ordered his horse saddled—probably he had to do it himself—and rode off at a gallop to Norristown, about five miles away. There he bought wire in various gauges and, leaping back on his "steed," returned to Mill Grove. He passed up breakfast and instead grabbed his gun and bolted down the hill for Perkiomen Creek, where he shot a kingfisher. He gently carried the bird home by the bill and then went back down to the mill for a soft board. Filing points onto short lengths of wire, Audubon skewered the bird through the head, legs, and feet, and then, laying it on its side against the board, drove the wires into the wood to maintain the body in a fixed position. A final stiff wire was stuck under the tail to hold it up at a jaunty angle. Audubon was so excited he began to draw immediately, giving no further thought to time or hunger until he had finished. That kingfisher, he later said, marked the real beginning of his career. As he worked on his drawing, he reached over periodically and carefully opened the bird's eyelid, and every time he did this it was as if the kingfisher had sprung back to life.

Audubon eventually added an important refinement to what he called "my method of drawing." He marked off the surface of his mounting board with squares, and matched this grid with lightly penciled duplicate squares on his drafting papers. This allowed him to get the proportions and the foreshortenings of perspective just right. As for the scale, it was always a simple one-to-one. Audubon drew every bird as he saw it, exactly life-sized. It was a practice from which he never deviated.

Months streamed by in a delicious haze. Audubon was in love. Lucy was smart and bold, and she shared his enthusiasm for a day in the woods. He was thrilled at how well she kept up with him, and impressed by her riding skills. In England, Lucy had ridden with the hounds. She was at ease in the forest, and increasingly, she was attached to her companion at Mill Grove. They began to talk of marriage. When Audubon got sick just before the holidays in the fall of 1804, he went to Fatland Ford to be taken care of. His illness lasted weeks, and at one point it looked as if he might die. But once again he bounced back to life. Lucy read to him while he recovered. By early February he was well enough to go out for a ride.

Audubon did have one nagging concern—his father's overseer, François Dacosta, who seemed intent on gaining control of Mill Grove. Evidently the two argued over who was giving orders to whom, and the elder Audubon got wind of it back in France. In truth, Audubon's father had never completely explained to his son that Dacosta was an equal partner in Mill Grove. He wasn't satisfied with Dacosta's slow progress in opening the lead mine, but their arrangement had not changed. It meanwhile dawned on the younger Audubon that his say in the management of the estate didn't amount to much, and that it was all but impossible to convey to his father on the other side of the world how unsatisfactory this was to him. The elder Audubon, having also heard of his son's possible engagement, was already doing everything in his power to prevent a marriage between Audubon and Lucy. Audubon's father suspected Lucy might only be after a wealthy husband. He wrote to Dacosta, urging him to find a way to delay his son's plans, and, if need be, to let the Bakewells know that young Audubon, despite outward appearances, was not rich and could not expect anything in the way of support from his family in France if he were to marry "in his present condition." In a follow-up letter, Audubon's father warned Dacosta to stop complaining about his son, whose conduct must be the result of "bad advice and lack of experience." Young Audubon was, after all, not yet twenty. The elder Audubon felt certain that the Bakewells had "goaded" his son into bragging that Mill Grove was his.

The old sea captain's vision remained sharp. Even from across the ocean, his view of the situation was penetrating, and his response was a masterly demonstration of finesse and fatherly concern. He wrote to Dacosta, reassuring him that everyone in Philadelphia—except, apparently, young Audubon—understood perfectly that Dacosta's rights and interests in Mill Grove were the same as his own. He said he had written to his son advising him as much and admonishing him to be a more respectful member of the household. He told Dacosta that sending young Audubon home to France, as Dacosta now proposed, was out of the question. All of the elder Audubon's reasons for having his son in America were as before. Instead, he artfully suggested how Dacosta could act in his stead to bring the boy under control. Having repeated his command that his son not get married at such a young age, Audubon advised Dacosta to go easy:

> Only an instant is needed to make him change from bad to good; his extreme youth and his petulance are his only faults, and if you have the goodness to give him the indispensable, he will soon feel the necessity of making friends with you, and he can be of great service if you use him for your own benefit.

If Dacosta followed this advice, Audubon said, his son could be "reclaimed" and would be fit to assume the duties at Mill Grove that he had thus far ignored. If this could be accomplished, the elder Audubon said, he would be "under every obligation" to Dacosta, adding, "This is my only son, my heir, and I am old."

Unfortunately, both Dacosta and young Audubon ignored all this advice. In late February, Audubon announced he was going to visit his father to set things straight. He demanded funds for the trip, and Dacosta complied with a "letter of credit" Audubon was to use to book his passage in New York. The letter was bogus—Audubon was laughed out of the bank to which Dacosta had sent him—but he successfully prevailed on Lucy's father to arrange a loan of $150. On March 12, he boarded the *Hope*, bound for France.

Audubon stayed with his family at their big house near Nantes for just over a year. After recovering from the surprise of his son's unexpected return, the elder Audubon soon perceived that Dacosta thought he was in some way being swindled. He undertook to settle matters at Mill

Grove once and for all. While his son hunted and explored the country-side—taking care not to be recognized by anyone who might report him for conscription—the elder Audubon replaced certain papers of agreement that had apparently miscarried en route to Dacosta, and agreed to some much-needed repairs at Mill Grove. Short of funds, he also sold a portion of his share in Mill Grove to his neighbors in France, a family named Rozier.

The Roziers had a son, Ferdinand, who had once visited young Audubon at Mill Grove and wanted to go back to America. The elder Audubon, sensing the advantage to his son of being associated with Ferdinand—who was hardworking, serious, and eight years older than John James—encouraged a joint venture. In March 1806, John James Audubon and Ferdinand Rozier formed a legal partnership. In ten written "articles of association," they agreed to proceed to the New World and to enter into commercial ventures as equal proprietors. Much of the agreement centered on Mill Grove, where they would now jointly control half of the plantation. But it also stipulated that they would work together in whatever business seemed suitable and at whatever place they chose, "whether inland or maritime."

On April 12, 1806, Audubon and Rozier sailed aboard the *Polly*, an American ship bound for New York. Audubon's papers gave his home as Louisiana. Rozier's said he was from Holland. The crossing was eventful. A man was killed in a duel over a lady's bonnet, the ship was looted by a British privateer, and a storm drove them temporarily aground in Long Island Sound.

Audubon and Rozier spent most of the next year haggling with Dacosta while they tried their hands at business. Rozier found work with an importer in Philadelphia. Audubon, in a monumental mismatch of vocation and personality, took a job as an apprentice clerk in a countinghouse in New York. The business was owned by Lucy's uncle, Benjamin Bakewell. This friendly arrangement probably prolonged Audubon's employment in a position for which he was clearly unsuited. He visited Mill Grove and Lucy when he could, and continued to seek his father's approval for their marriage. Audubon corresponded now in his own peculiar English, blending odd formalisms with imaginative spellings, as in this letter to his father in the spring of 1807:

I am allways in Mr. Benjamin Bakewell's store where I work as much as I can and passes my days happy; about three weeks ago I went to Mill Grove . . . and had the pleasure of seeing there my Biloved Lucy who constantly loves me and makes me perfectly happy. I shall wait for thy Consent and the one of my good Mamma to Marry her. Could thou but see her and thou wouldst I am sure be pleased of the prudency of my choice . . . I wish thou would wrights to me ofnor and longuely. Think by thyself how pleasing it is to read a friend's letter.

Audubon and Rozier grew restless. Convinced they would never devise a workable partnership with Dacosta, they decided instead to sell him most of their share in Mill Grove for just under $4,000 and a promise of future payments when the mine came in. They mortgaged what was left for $10,000. Rozier, meanwhile, considered returning to France. Then they started to discuss something entirely different. Why not go west? Settlers were making their way into new territories west of the Alleghenies. Some took a southern route by way of the Wilderness Road. The road followed the old trace blazed by Daniel Boone in the 1770s along Indian trails and bison tracks from the Cumberland Gap in Virginia, across southeastern Kentucky, angling north all the way to the Ohio River. The trace was now becoming a busy turnpike. The other way west was to travel overland to Pittsburgh and then float down the Ohio and into whatever future was out there. The fast-growing town of Louisville sounded promising.

Rozier and Audubon agreed that there were likely to be commercial opportunities in Kentucky. Audubon encouraged this view, while thinking to himself how fine the hunting would be and how many birds must live in the wilds of America. He said goodbye to Lucy—who said she'd be waiting for him to return once he found them a home in the West. There are discrepancies in the record as to when they actually left Philadelphia, and whether they were much delayed on the way to Pittsburgh, but sometime between the end of August and the start of October 1807, Audubon and Rozier headed off. At first they made splendid time, reaching Lancaster, a distance of more than sixty miles from Philadelphia, in one day. The roads were good and lined with pleasant taverns. Crops of hemp grew in the fields. But the roads worsened. A team of six horses was needed to keep their coach moving over increasingly rough terrain. The jostling ride was exhausting. Sometimes, they got out and walked, finding a faster pace that was also easier on their aching backsides. In a place called Walnut Bottom, beyond Harrisburg, they had a wonderful meal in a clean tavern where they were served, Rozier happily noted, by "pretty girls." Rozier was likewise impressed by a species of tree he'd never seen before, called a hackberry. On the third day of November, bone-chilling rains commenced just as the stage entered the steepest section of mountains. The passengers all commented on the treacherousness of this stretch. Four days later, as the rain abated and the afternoon turned unusually hot for that time of year, they descended a final time—cautiously on foot now—and arrived in Pittsburgh.

Audubon and Rozier spent twelve days in Pittsburgh, staying at the Jefferson Hotel. Despite its captivating location, the town was a dismal place. It had been built in the shadow of British Fort Pitt in the 1760s, and was situated in a lovely valley where the Allegheny and Monongahela Rivers met and the surrounding hills formed a kind of natural amphitheater. The two rivers merged there to form the mighty Ohio, whose broad beginnings wandered north from the city before turning south and west and heading into the forever and ever of the frontier. But the town itself was a grimy black scar. Smoke and ash from coal fires powering the businesses and warming the homes occupied by four thousand residents rose in a towering pall. More smoke poured from several nearby coal mines that had caught fire years before and continued to smolder. Every surface exposed to the air was coated in soot. People choked and wheezed and went grimly about their business beneath a perpetual dark cloud hanging over the narrow streets and the low, ugly buildings.

But business *was* good. Pittsburgh was already becoming a manufacturing center and was sending a diversifying assortment of supplies down the Ohio on the heels of the settlers who would buy these goods at the other end. The trade included nails, cloth, glassware, wire, buttons, rope, iron implements, and lead. There were eight boat and barge builders in town, and so many keelboats, arks, and Kentucky flatboats now regularly descended the Ohio from Pittsburgh that nobody could keep count. With fair weather and high water, it was possible to reach Louisville in as little as ten days. The estimated value of all trade passing through Pittsburgh exceeded a million dollars a year, and with the promise of regular steamship travel arriving soon, there was talk of a coming boom. Audubon and Rozier were elated at all of this, and also at discovering several French-speaking merchants with whom they arranged to acquire inventories. Rozier considered these people honest and easy to deal with.

The two men bought passage on a flatboat for $15, which included the transport of a small amount of merchandise with which they planned to open a store. The boat moved swiftly down the smooth current, but it was crowded and uncomfortable. Rozier and Audubon slept in the open, with only their coats for blankets. Rozier found the monotony of river travel almost unbearable. Occasionally the boat careened to a sudden halt when it ran aground and the passengers were forced into the chilly November water to drag it off a sandbar. Rozier thought the boat's captain, a man named Morris, singularly unpleasant. He treated the passengers roughly, invented additional charges that he collected by threat of force, and used the foul language of "a low class."

Louisville waited for them just over seven hundred miles downstream. It stood on the slightly elevated south bank of the Ohio, immediately below the mouth of Bear Grass Creek, at a mile-wide bend in the river. Here the velocity of the current increased forcefully over a two-mile stretch. Boats lazing along at a gentle three miles an hour suddenly shot forward at ten to thirteen miles an hour, pitching violently through a section of almost invisible but dangerous rapids, as the water suddenly dropped twenty-two feet in elevation. The "Falls of the Ohio," as this place was called, were caused by immense submerged rock shelvings that lay in terraces across the river bottom. In periods of high water, a skilled pilot could run the rapids on almost any line. But when the river was low, the jagged ledges emerged and the channel divided into frothy chutes that funneled through openings in the rock, and only the most experienced and daring local rivermen could bring a boat through.

The town of Louisville had been laid out in the 1770s, when General George Rogers Clark first built a fort there during his campaign against British and Indian forces in the Revolutionary War. About twenty families of civilian pioneers had tagged along with Clark's small flotilla of boats when he descended the Ohio from Fort Pitt—somewhat to Clark's astonishment, as he gave them no encouragement in what seemed to him an incautious adventure into a wild country still being contested by several armed factions. By the time Audubon and Rozier landed at Louisville—probably sometime before Christmas—they found a civilized-looking town of about thirteen hundred citizens. There were at least two hundred sturdy brick homes, some three stories high. Many of these were on a busy-looking Main Street, which was also lined with shops and commercial operations.

Audubon and Rozier liked what they saw. Businessmen—many of them French settlers—were making fine livings in Louisville. Thanks to the Falls, which naturally slowed the passage downstream and necessitated overland transfer for anyone or anything going upstream, Louisville was the principal trading city between Pittsburgh and New Orleans. Some sixty thousand tons of goods now moved annually downriver to New Orleans. About one-tenth as much came back north—on keelboats that were sailed, rowed, poled, and sometimes dragged upstream. There was already talk of building a lock and canal on the south bank of the river that would have one terminus near the little waterfront community of Shippingport, which was home to fewer than a hundred people, though several were well-established French merchants and boat builders. Audubon and Rozier found store space for rent in town, and also got acquainted with the French in Shippingport. Audubon listened excitedly to their accounts of the local bird shooting, which featured great slaughters of migrating passenger pigeons and waterfowl.

In March the partners returned to Philadelphia for more goods, and so that Audubon and Lucy could be married. The wedding took place on April 5, 1808, at Fatland Ford, with a Presbyterian minister presiding. A few days later, Rozier, Audubon, and Lucy boarded a stagecoach for Pittsburgh. This time the trip seemed harder. With his new wife along, Audubon now took more notice of how horrible the roads were the farther they got from Philadelphia, especially in the mountain passages, where they were little more than ruts winding through the rock and mud. Lucy quietly endured the coarse language and drunken behavior they encountered at the taverns along the way. The inns—usually little more than saloons with a couple of sleeping rooms above—were crowded with unsavory travelers. Strangers shared their beds with one another and with the host of bedbugs that thrived between the infrequently washed sheets. A young woman who made the journey across Pennsylvania in 1810 said the physical hardships were only exceeded by the threat of unwanted attention from wagoners, who sometimes skulked about the sleeping quarters after long nights of drinking. Few settlers returned from the West, she speculated, not because the land there was so wonderful but because coming and going between civilization and the frontier was so arduous.

But Lucy made no complaint and seemed perfectly enchanted by her dashing new husband and the great adventure they were on. One day, as they climbed a steep, rocky section of road, with Audubon walking behind and Lucy riding inside to stay out of a cold rain, the coach overturned and was dragged on its side some distance before the team could be brought under control. Audubon pulled Lucy, bruised and shaken, from the coach, then helped set it upright. On they went, that day and the next and for many after that, over the mountains and then down the river to their new life.

6

THE FORESTER

Colymbus glacialis: **The Loon**
When it has acquired its perfect plumage, which is not altered in colour at any successive moult, it is really a beautiful creature; and the student of Nature who has opportunities of observing its habits, cannot fail to derive much pleasure from watching it as it pursues its avocations.   —*Ornithological Biography*

A spell of Indian summer came to Pennsylvania in October 1804. Alexander Wilson, desperate to escape the smother of his schoolhouse and now eager to see the country and all its birds, organized a small party of travelers. There were three, to be exact: himself, his nephew William Duncan, and a young man from Milestown—probably a former student—named Isaac Leech. On a warm morning, they met beside the Schuylkill River and set out. Their destination was Niagara Falls.

Duncan, hardened and countrywise from his years on the farm in upstate New York, served as unofficial guide. Wilson believed his nephew, carrying only a walking stick and a small knapsack, would find his way over field and swamp and mountain. In any terrain, Duncan seemed able to divine a path even where none was apparent, and he could read the signs of animals that might afford either a meal or a threat. Leech was an eager, rosy-cheeked boy, dressed in spanking new oilcloth and evidently sure of his safety so long as he was in the company of Alexander Wilson. Wilson himself was elated—even under an impressive load. He carried his trusty double-barreled gun, and a leather belt heavy with shot, flasks of powder, and a stout dagger. His knapsack contained clothes, some cakes and cordials, plus his drawing kit of crayons, pencils, and paper.

They walked that day through a gilded land. Leaves skittered across the path as they passed by orchards heavy with fruit and rattling fields of corn drying on the stalk. The sun shone sulfurously through the wood-smoke from farmhouse chimneys, and masses of blackbirds swept across the sky. They spent their first evening on the road in a snug tavern. At dinner the guests sat facing each other at a long table heaped with meats and bread and hunks of bacon. A pint of beer was passed around, everyone drinking in turn. They were off again before dawn, waking to Venus shining in the east and a canopy of stars hanging overhead like a shimmering veil. Wilson, sobered at the natural beauty around him, thought ruefully of his school and the endless drilling of the A-B-Cs that was surely a torture to student and teacher alike.

Wilson and his companions carried on. One day they came to what had been a towering forest, long since leveled by a storm. Many of the trees had burned from lightning strikes so that their remains lay in a charred and twisted mass. The deadfall was so thick that the path entered under the trunks of the downed trees, which made a tunnel only wide enough for the travelers to walk single file. In the midst of this hellish scene, the group paused to look around in amazement. Suddenly there was a commotion nearby and a bear rushed at them. The animal skidded to a halt as the men shouldered their guns, hearts racing. After a long moment the bear ran off as fast as it had appeared. For the rest of the day, they watched every stump and bush apprehensively. The forest grew ever gloomier, until they came at last to a house where they were put up for the night, comforted by a roaring fire and the pleasant faces of three plump children—though the owner's tales of hunting wolves and wild-cats in the area troubled their thoughts when they finally lay down to sleep. As they walked off down the road the next morning, a grouse flushed close by, going up on pounding wings, cackling as it rose into the chilly air. Wilson, snapping his gun up, brought the bird down in a roar and a puff of feathers that drifted slowly to the ground.

In a maple wood, near the banks of the Susquehanna River, the party came into a glen filled with spice and dogwood. Brilliant yellow leaves lay on the path. Wilson, stepping smartly along this shimmering carpet, was startled when the ground in front of him shifted oddly. In an instant he saw a shape at his feet twist into life as a rattlesnake, perfectly camouflaged on the trail, slithered away at an angle. It looked to be at least nine feet long. When Wilson jumped back and reflexively brought up his gun, the snake stopped short and threw itself into a threatening coil, tail buzzing ominously. Wilson squinted down the length of his barrels and thumbed one hammer. The rattling tail moved so quickly it was an almost invisible blur. Blood pulsed in Wilson's temples. But then he felt Duncan next to him. Don't shoot, Duncan pleaded. Rattlesnakes don't want trouble, he said, only to be left in peace. We're the ones who don't belong here, Duncan whispered, not him. Wilson took a deep breath and lowered his gun.

Days passed in a hypnotic rhythm of long marches and dazzling scenery. Sometimes the trio walked easily along smooth trails through agreeable woods; other days they scrambled up sheer mountains. They came to streams alive with trout, and upon finding a small boat on the shore of a marsh-fringed lake, whiled away a few hours shooting ducks. They spent a nervous night surrounded by howling wolves, and once thought they heard a panther creeping into their camp. They met with a few Indians and many farmers, and platonically eyed one or two of the farmers' daughters. They endured a wild ride on a small ship that bore them across Lake Ontario. At last they reached Niagara Falls, covering the final miles enveloped by a growing roar they could scarcely believe.

Wilson and his friends stood transfixed before the cataract. The falling waters rose back up from the river far below in a great billow of white, roiling vapors. The noise was deafening, and rainbows hovered in the mist. Bald eagles and ravens and vultures soared above the falls. They were feasting on fish in the river, and also on carrion from the many animals that must have tried to swim the river above the falls and were instead carried over the precipice. The three friends made a harrowing descent to the base of the falls by means of a slippery, chancy-looking ladder that was hung from a tree root at the edge of the chasm. Then Wilson and Duncan walked hand-in-hand along the glistening rocks until they entered into the dark, wondrous space behind the falls, between the trembling earth and the crushing waters—a place Wilson later described as the "porch of death," where they stood paralyzed amid whirling floods and terrible sounds, and where they could not see or hear or even breathe.

Wilson's return from Niagara was a remarkable trek. He and Leech parted company with Duncan at Aurora, New York, on the shore of Lake Cayuga, north of Ithaca. It was now mid-November. The travelers washed in an icy stream, then found a tavern where they could warm up by a fire. Wilson was annoyed at the drunken tradesmen carousing there until late at night. At five the next morning they were on their way again. Wilson set a brutal pace, taking Leech's gun from him when the boy fell behind. They held to this for several days, with Leech grunting and struggling to keep up. The road worsened, and it began to snow. Wilson sang to encourage his young friend onward, ignoring his own condition, which was not so good. Wilson's threadbare pantaloons had worn through and the soles of his boots were gone, leaving him all but barefoot in the icy slush. One evening they arrived on the east bank of the Mohawk River, where Wilson shot a medium-sized bird he could not recognize. He skinned it for a closer inspection after he got home. The next day the road became a muddy rut, and it was all Wilson could do to keep Leech moving. At noon he shot three more birds—these were like jays—including the one he later drew for Thomas Jefferson.

At Schenectady they caught a stagecoach for Albany, where they remained two days before boarding a sloop that took them down the Hudson to New York City. Wilson spent $12 on new trousers and boots, leaving him unable to afford coach fare the rest of the way. He said goodbye to Leech and set off for Philadelphia on foot, arriving at Gray's Ferry a week later with seventy-five cents in his pocket. On the last day, he walked forty-seven miles. In all, Wilson had traveled nearly thirteen hundred miles in two months, mostly on foot. He told Bartram he couldn't wait to make a longer trip:

> Though in this tour I have had every disadvantage of deep roads and rough weather; hurried marches, and many other inconveniences to encounter, yet so far am I from being satisfied with what I have seen, or discouraged by the fatigues which every traveler must submit to, I feel more eager than ever to commence some more extensive expedition, where scenes and subjects entirely new, and generally unknown, might reward my curiosity, and where perhaps my humble acquisitions might add something to the stores of knowledge.

Wilson said he planned to work hard to improve his drawing for this purpose. Over the winter, he practiced. It was a cold season. Both the Schuylkill and the Delaware froze solid, and Wilson hunched over his drawing table. He also wrote—this time an epic poem of more than two thousand lines titled *The Foresters*, which described the trip to Niagara. He told his nephew Duncan that he worked harder on this than on any poem he'd ever written and that if it wasn't any good he'd never write one that was.

Wilson gave the stuffed skin of his unknown species of bird to Charles Willson Peale for display to the public. Peale, part naturalist and part showman, had opened his famous Philadelphia Museum in 1786. It had become one of the wonders of the modern world, housing the first complete reconstruction of a mastodon skeleton, plus an enormous collection of living and stuffed animals, including many that had been brought back by the Lewis and Clark expedition. The museum was well known even in Europe, where it was said to be worth a trip across the Atlantic. Peale's collections were so extensive that many naturalists, including Wilson, used them to study specimens that were difficult to locate or draw in nature.

Wilson also sent drawings of twenty-eight birds to William Bartram, asking his honest opinion. These, Wilson said, represented birds that were found in Pennsylvania or that passed through the state. He also sent more drawings to Thomas Jefferson—as an apology for his earlier mistake with the Canada jay. Meanwhile, Wilson talked Alexander Lawson into giving him instruction in engraving and set about making several copper plates of his drawings. Wilson was convinced that, if he did the engraving himself as Catesby had, it would be possible to publish a ten-volume work incorporating hand-colored plates of all the American birds into a letterpress giving a written natural history for each species—and to make the venture profitable with as few as two hundred subscribers. Once the first volume was completed, he could use it to sell the rest. Concerned that his firsthand observations were still limited to Pennsylvania and upstate New York, Wilson also began thinking about an expedition to the frontier—the real frontier, beyond the settled territories just west of the mountains. Early in 1806, Wilson suggested to Bartram that they undertake a journey down the Ohio River, at least as far as St. Louis and possibly down the Mississippi to New Orleans.

Wilson had recently spoken with a local man who'd made this trip only a year before. He told Wilson that nothing could have been simpler or more pleasant. The Ohio was a gentle waterway, easily navigated in a small boat. The weather never got too cold nor the mosquitoes too fierce. One could sleep in the open without worries. The man, who had no interest in natural history, said he hadn't even bothered taking a gun or fishing tackle along. Wilson was excited. Perhaps, he suggested to Bartram, they could get President Jefferson to endorse the expedition in some official way—or at a minimum to provide advice and introductions to influential citizens they might call on during their travels.

By chance, just as Wilson was mulling this idea, news circulated that President Jefferson planned to send a team of explorers to the West the following summer, on a mission to investigate the length of the Mississippi and several of its major tributaries and surrounding regions. Wilson thought he and Bartram—who was acquainted with the president— should apply to join the expedition. Bartram, however, was not up to it. Wilson probably had a hard time not thinking of his friend as the adventurer, driven by curiosity about nature, who had explored the wilds of Florida. But that was decades ago. Bartram was now in his late sixties. His eyesight was failing and his appetite for the rigors of such a trip had faded.

In February 1806, Wilson wrote to Jefferson himself and asked to be named to the Mississippi expedition. He told the president he was presently composing a new illustrated ornithology of American birds— a work that would correct the deficiencies of Catesby and others. He said he had already completed more than one hundred drawings and two plates had thus far been engraved. But any comprehensive study of North American birds would necessarily have to include species found in the Western territories, as many of these were absent from the Eastern Seaboard. So the trip suited Wilson's purposes—and vice versa. Wilson pointed out that he was single, well accustomed to the hardships of travel in the wild, and able to leave on short notice. Finally, Wilson wrote, he wished to undertake this mission with the primary purpose of enhancing the reputation of the president, whom he awkwardly addressed as "Your Excellency."

Jefferson never answered.

As it turned out, Wilson got a better offer. In April he quit his job at the Union School in Gray's Ferry to accept a position as an assistant editor for a new edition of the twenty-two-volume *Ree's Cyclopedia*. The publisher was Samuel Bradford, a well-connected Philadelphia bookseller who, among other claims to fame, was married to the mayor's daughter. Wilson could scarcely believe his good fortune. He was freed at last from the tortures of teaching—and had been hired at the handsome salary of

$900 a year. But the best part was that Bradford was interested in Wilson's bird book.

Although Wilson thought his preliminary attempts at engraving his own drawings were passable, he realized that they would never be as good as Lawson's work—and also that doing his own engraving would eat away at the time he needed for fieldwork and drawing. When Bradford agreed to finance the first volume with engravings by Lawson, Wilson's course was finally set. Commingling his work on the encyclopedia with his ornithological studies, Wilson in the spring of 1807 drew up a prospectus for a work to be called *American Ornithology*. The prospectus offered a rationale for the book—Wilson went on at some length about the glories of American birds and the shortcomings of the European naturalists who had attempted to describe them—and gave a general idea of what the subscriber might expect. Wilson's plan was to issue installments, or "Numbers," every two months. Each Number would depict "at least" ten bird species on three ten-by-thirteen-inch hand-colored plates, plus written descriptions of each species. The Numbers would continue "until the whole be completed." The subscription price was $2 per number. Wilson added that it was not, at present, possible to ascertain just how big the finished work would be, but that it was likely to consist of at least one hundred plates bound in "two handsome volumes." This plan was modified in the months ahead. When the first volume of *American Ornithology* was completed in September 1808, it depicted thirty-eight species of birds on nine colored plates that were inserted at intervals in a 160-page letterpress of written descriptions. It cost $12. With a total of ten volumes now projected, a subscription to the complete work was priced at $120. Among the earliest subscribers was the president of the United States, Thomas Jefferson.

7

THE EXQUISITE RIVER

Turdus polyglottus: **The Mocking Bird**
See how he flies round his mate, with motions as light as those of the butterfly! His tail is widely expanded, he mounts in the air to a small distance, describes a circle, and, again alighting, approaches his beloved one, his eyes gleaming with delight, for she has already promised to be his and his only. His beautiful wings are gently raised, he bows to his love, and again bouncing upwards, opens his bill, and pours forth his melody, full of exultation at the conquest which he has made.   —*Ornithological Biography*

The newly married Audubons and friend Rozier had spent a couple of weeks in Pittsburgh, arranging passage downriver and acquiring more inventory for the store in Louisville. Lucy, like other visitors to the city, found its smoky streets oppressive. But she was impressed by the goods to be had and by the hum of activity along the riverfront, where she managed to ignore that portion of the action occurring in the saloons and brothels catering to the watermen. Having set out so soon after their wedding, the Audubons were happy to be in one place for a time. In the evenings, Audubon and Lucy had their honeymoon. Lucy, in a letter sent back to England, coyly informed a cousin of the "most excellent disposition" of her new husband, hinting at an unspecified but powerful attraction that "adds very much to the happiness of married life."

Now twenty-one years old, Lucy was wildly in love with Audubon— and also committed to the obligations of marriage. These she construed as meaning she was henceforth first and foremost a partner and companion to a husband whose expectations and demands were hers to fulfill. Lucy apparently never hesitated or offered the slightest protest over Audubon's abrupt decision to take her away from her family and the comforts of Pennsylvania to a remote, thinly populated frontier town. While she had found the trip at times difficult, especially in the mountains, she took care to emphasize the positive. Without even mentioning the overturned wagon that might have killed her, Lucy gamely told her cousin merely that "great stones beneath the wheels make the stage rock about most dreadfully." Putting a sunny spin on the journey to Pittsburgh, Lucy added that she was sure anyone would have enjoyed the many beautiful sights they took in along the way—if only it were somehow possible to do so without enduring the "fatigues" of the actual trip. In any event, if this was where her life now led, then this was where she would happily go in the performance of her "new duties."

"As yet they have been light," Lucy said of her marital responsibilities, "and be they what they may I hope I shall ever perform them cheerfully."

Eager to proceed from Pittsburgh, the three found space, finally, aboard a flatboat. These cumbersome but serviceable craft, which were also called "Kentucky boats," were the workhorses of the river. Half barge, half houseboat, they came in many sizes and could ship great loads of people, livestock, furniture, and the like. A typical boat large enough to accommodate a single family and their possessions was twelve to fifteen feet abeam and thirty or forty feet long. One could be purchased for under $50. Vessels twice that size were not uncommon, and a large flatboat could carry seventy tons or more. All were built on a simple configuration. The hull was essentially a rectangular wooden box, flat on the bottom, sometimes with a slightly angled bow and stern. Fully loaded, a flatboat had only a couple feet of freeboard. Extra caulk and a pump were essential gear. A low, shedlike house sat amidship. Though austere, these shelters could be fitted out with brick fireplaces for cooking and some heat.

Flatboats were not so much piloted as they were passively ridden. Travelers were advised to let the current do the work of finding the channel as it meandered among the Ohio's many islands and sandbars, though the boats could be steered a little with a long sweep on the stern and oars deployed toward the bow. The trip downriver was usually smooth and safe, but a flatboat could be swamped if unevenly loaded or carelessly handled. Overnight changes in the level of the river could put a corner of an improperly moored flatboat under—and the rest might follow in short order. Tangles of fallen trees that collected in "snags" at the heads of islands were a common hazard—it could take several days to free a boat caught in a snag. In fair weather and high water it was considered prudent to put ashore as infrequently as possible and to travel through the night, though there were so many boats on the river that groups of pioneers often tied up alongside one another for company after dark. Encounters with hostile Indians or pirates were possible, but such risks diminished with each passing year as the river valley filled with settlers. Travelers were more likely to be accosted by entrepreneurs and pimps who converted flatboats into floating taverns. By the time the Audubons set out for Louisville, people were already talking about how crowded with towns and farms the riverbanks had become. The frontier was moving west. And however far you went, that was where you stayed—flatboats were one-way propositions. At their final destination, the boats were knocked apart and their timbers sold or used to build a house.

The Audubons' departure in late April came at an auspicious time. Spring brought high water and easy navigation on the Ohio. The boat, Lucy reported, was reasonably comfortable, with a cabin ceiling "just high enough to admit a person walking upright." The ride was surprisingly smooth, Lucy said, though on one windy section of the river the boat began to pitch sufficiently that she felt momentary seasickness.

Ashore, the new season had replenished the woods along the river with game, and it was quick work for Audubon to disappear into the trees with his gun and return with a turkey or a brace of wood ducks. Lucy packed bread and ham, plus some beer, for the trip. They bought milk, eggs, and an occasional chicken en route. The suddenly lush forests lent an almost submarine quality to the journey. Lucy found the dense wall of trees and flowers flanking the river remarkable, though she was disappointed that the closeness of the overhung shorelines and high bluffs limited the vistas from midstream. Even so, it was the river itself that bedazzled.

The name *Ohio*, puzzlingly, seemed to have been derived from an Indian expression meaning "bloody river." The French, however, who were probably the first Europeans to descend the Ohio, called it *La Belle Rivière*—"the beautiful river"—and settlers who came later agreed. The Ohio, it was said, was "beyond all competition the most beautiful river in the universe." At its head in Pittsburgh, the more powerful and crystal-clear Allegheny pushed across the darker current of the Monongahela at a right angle, so that the waters of the two did not mix for several miles. Below Pittsburgh, the Ohio blended and broadened and took on the color of the sky. An abundance of navigable tributary streams, many beautiful in their own right, gave the Ohio communication with a vast region on its way west. In fact, as Lewis and Clark had discovered only a few years earlier, it was possible to descend the Ohio, proceed up the Mississippi and Missouri Rivers, cross the continental divide, and then continue down the Columbia all the way to the Pacific Ocean. This great network of rivers seemed to many people proof that the young country's destiny ultimately reached across North America. Zadok Cramer, a Pittsburgh bookseller and expert on Ohio River travel, saw a link between America's rivers and America's future that filled him with optimism: "No country perhaps in the world is better watered with limpid streams and navigable rivers than the United States of America," Cramer wrote, "and no people better deserve these advantages, or are better calculated to make a proper use of them than her industrious and adventurous citizens."

The Ohio River's uniform breadth was striking—it was generally between four hundred and six hundred yards across along its entire length, except near Louisville and at the river's end at the Mississippi, where it was wider. Much of the land on either side of the river was a steady procession of hills standing in ranks, changeless waves on an emerald sea. Seams of coal had been found between Pittsburgh and Wheeling, but where the land had not been cleared, a formidable forest remained. The uplands were thick with oak, walnut, hickory, chestnut, and ash. Willows, locusts, mulberry, beech, elm, aspen, and maples filled the bottoms. Tremendous stands of cedar and cypress grew in the swamps below Louisville.

But it was the sycamore that was thought of as "king of the forest." An immense species, sycamores grow to over a hundred feet in height. Their smooth, pale bark is unusual, like skin, but they're more notable for the great diameters of their trunks. Historical records indicate that the largest individuals may have reached fifteen feet across. In Audubon's time, when myths grew as large as trees, this was believed to be only an average-sized sycamore in the Ohio River valley. It was said some monster specimens more than twenty feet in diameter lurked in the forest. The summer following the Audubons' arrival in Louisville, a man named Miller in Scioto County, Ohio, claimed that a hollowed-out sycamore on his land was so large that thirteen men on horseback had ridden inside it—and had room left over. In many places, all the trees in the forest huddled under a knitting of grapevines that entwined the highest branches and dangled heavily in the air between the canopy and the earth.

Game was everywhere, but things had changed in even the short time of Kentucky's settlement. The first serious influx of people from the colonies had begun around 1775, following a string of settler victories in local wars with the Indians. Early arrivals came from Pennsylvania and

Virginia and North Carolina. In many cases, they were failed or deeply indebted farmers looking for greener pastures. For a time the early settlers were at odds with one another. On the lawless frontier, vigilantes calling themselves "Regulators" often enforced a crude justice. After the Civil War, the Regulators merged with the Ku Klux Klan, committing lynchings and other atrocities. But in Audubon's time they helped maintain a general order, administering floggings and banishing unsavory types from respectable communities. Audubon, like many people in Kentucky, admired the Regulators, and later claimed to have ridden with them and observed their stern adjudications. Kentuckians also had problems with a large commercial land venture called the Transylvania Company, which had illegally acquired vast land holdings from the Indians. The company subsequently offered Kentucky property to settlers at inflated prices completely out of line for such a wild region. The company's chief scout and road builder was the hunter Daniel Boone. Boone recalled that as late as the hard winter of 1780–1781, residents of Kentucky had survived almost exclusively on buffalo meat. Three decades later, as the Audubons drifted toward Louisville, buffalo were becoming rare in Kentucky. So were wolves, which of all the animals seemed the least tolerant of human encroachment.

But that still left an abundance of wild birds, fish, and other animals beyond belief. Herds of elk roamed the Kentucky woodlands, as did cougars—or *painters* as they were locally known. Bear and deer were so common that they were often seen swimming across the Ohio, and sporting flatboaters kept a rifle handy to restock their larders from such encounters. Catfish as big as a hundred pounds were readily caught in the river, which also supported enormous perch and pike. Ducks of every sort and many geese lived along the waterways and back in the adjoining wetlands. The woods teemed with turkey and other upland species.

Kentucky had become a state in 1792, and its population continued to soar. When the Audubons got to Louisville in May 1808 there were nearly 400,000 settlers in Kentucky. About 20 percent were black slaves. Nobody counted the Indians, whose numbers were much reduced—pushed out of the territory and decimated by European diseases. The Shawnee, who'd put up the strongest resistance to the white invasion, probably numbered only a few thousand and had relinquished most of their land.

The Audubons took lodging at a hotel called the Indian Queen, which stood on the corner of Fifth and Main Streets in Louisville. It would be the only home Lucy would know during the two years they remained in the city. The hotel was a two-story wood-frame building. It was a decided improvement over the flatboat, but must have seemed to her a tremendous compromise after years of comfort at Fatland Ford. The ground floor featured a bar, a "boot room," and a dining area. The Audubons evidently had their own quarters upstairs, but had to pass through a common dormitory to get there. They bathed at a cistern in the courtyard, attended by a black slave. Even so, Lucy declared that she and her new husband were "as private as we please."

Lucy was less happy with the creeping minutes and hours that measured out her new life. The days were long and hot and dull, and there was an almost unendurable lack of anything for her to do while Audubon was down at the store with Rozier or, more often, out in the woods getting acquainted with this new country. Audubon and Rozier employed a clerk, so she wasn't needed at the store. Lucy loved books, and she regretted having time on her hands and nothing to read. "I am very sorry there is no library here or bookstore of any kind," she wrote to her cousin.

From the start, business was slow for Audubon and Rozier. They found they could mark up their goods to what would seem a sure profit, only to lose money more or less continually because of small volume. Audubon took advantage of sluggish business conditions by devoting his spare time— which is to say most of his waking moments—to hunting and drawing. He made friends with Louisville's experienced woodsmen and learned his way in the forest. On those few occasions when new inventory was needed for the shop, Audubon eagerly made the trip east, by horse and foot and boat, shooting and observing birds as he went. During his more extended absences, whether for business or birds, Lucy often stayed with friends. She was meanwhile convinced they would soon have their own house.

If Lucy was often bored, Audubon was quite the opposite. These years, he said later, were spent in "the most agreeable manner," and they enjoyed "the best pleasures which this life can afford." Even allowing for Audubon's readiness to exaggerate, Louisville seems to have felt like some kind of paradise to him. Within months of their arrival his portfolio had swollen considerably. By the time he and Lucy left, Audubon had completed more than two hundred bird drawings. He had also become a father for the first time. Victor Gifford Audubon was born at the Indian Queen Hotel on June 12, 1809.

Audubon was not unaware that his neglect of the business earned him ridicule in Louisville. He later said that only his family understood him; his friends and acquaintances made remarks about his slack work ethic that "irritated me beyond endurance." Characteristically, he saw such criticism not as a just assessment of his shortcomings but instead as an obstacle that he had overcome by force of will. Over time, his forays into the wild kept him from his family for days, then weeks, then months at a time. This, Audubon maintained, showed only that he'd "broken through all bonds" in giving himself over entirely to the study of nature. His journeys were long and exhausting as he "ransacked" the woods and lakes and prairies. But he went, he said, only for the purity of the experience. Though it did not seem to reflect well on him as a provider for his family, Audubon insisted for the rest of his life that his curiosity about nature, and about birds in particular, was his sole motivation. Not until much later, he maintained, did the idea of making a living from these activities occur to him. In Kentucky, Audubon did nothing. And he did everything.

Audubon was drawn to every kind of bird—from the smallest, blandest warbler or wren to the great eagles. He seemed to care as much for a crow or grackle as he did for the rose-breasted grosbeak or the magnificent ivory-billed woodpecker. But he was especially fond of birds whose social behaviors became demonstrative with the turning of the seasons. And probably no bird fascinated him more—or figured more prominently in his art—than the turkey.

Audubon no doubt had seen a few turkeys in Pennsylvania. But they were already growing scarce in the East by the time he arrived in America. In Kentucky, though, turkeys were plentiful. It was a striking bird, with a heavy body topped by a short neck and a small head. Audubon thought its fine table quality, its tremendous size, and its ungainly yet beguiling appearance—plus the fact that a domesticated version had become popular on both sides of the Atlantic—made the turkey uncommonly appealing. And because turkeys do not winter in the tropics like most true migratory species, their seasonal movements across a region could be closely studied. To this end, Audubon devoted himself. When, twenty years later, he described the turkey, Audubon poured all that he knew of the animal and its nature into what he wrote.

Turkeys, Audubon discovered, are "irregularly migratory, as well as irregularly gregarious." He commenced his observations in the fall, when the Kentucky evenings cooled and the sky seemed bluer and the forest recolored itself in the transparent air. The movement and gathering of turkeys are governed, Audubon said, largely by variations in the density of food sources in the areas where they live. Turkeys subsist on various foods, but mainly on mast—an inclusive term for the nuts and fruits that fall from trees and litter the forest floor. Audubon determined that as turkeys forage they are sensitive to changes in the density of acorns and other mast items, and that they proceed in the direction of increasing abundance, as "flock follows after flock" until some districts are empty of turkeys, while in others great aggregations are formed.

Turkeys begin collecting themselves into flocks in October, Audubon said, in anticipation of the fresh mast that will soon appear on the ground. Females, usually attended by a brood of adolescent chicks, avoid groups of males—which tend toward obstreperous behavior at any time, and are apt to kill young turkeys by pecking them on the head. The birds proceed through the forest in this segregated fashion until they come to a river. There they halt for a day, or maybe two. While they wait at the river's edge, the turkeys' moods grow agitated. Males preen and gobble and fan their tails. Females and the young strut and purr. Finally, on a clear day, the birds ascend to the highest parts of the trees, and at the signal of a single "cluck" by an old leader, the whole flock launches for the opposite shore. Audubon observed that the flight across was made easily by the "old and fat" but that the younger birds sometimes struggled in the air and, if the river was wide, would often fall into the water partway over. But they did not perish. Instead, the birds would fold back their wings and swim powerfully across the current, continuing on to the far shore. If the bank proved too steep to climb, the birds would fall back into the water and drift in the current until they found a way out, although even then a waterlogged turkey extricating itself from a river was quite a sight. In keeping with one of his main obsessions—hunting—Audubon observed that turkeys that have just crossed a major river are for a time disoriented and unalert to their surroundings, making them easy targets. In fact, much of what Audubon learned about turkeys came via his persistent attempts to kill them. He said that turkey nests were well hidden in the forest, as the hens varied the routes of their comings and goings, and usually covered the nest with leaves when absent. If a human did manage to find and tamper with a nest, the turkey would still return to it. But if a snake or a skunk raided the nest it was immediately abandoned.

Audubon believed that turkeys instinctively knew how much interaction with humans was safe. When the mast was thick on the ground and the birds assembled into massive flocks of both genders, they seemed fearless and would enter farmyards to continue feeding. Audubon felt that, under certain circumstances, turkeys could read his intentions. If, for example, he walked briskly through the forest, whistling to himself, he could pass within a few feet of a hen on her nest without the bird making a move. But if he attempted to sneak up on a nest, his stealth seemed to alarm the hen and she would run or fly off before he could get close. Still, turkeys' habits sometimes betrayed them. Audubon said that when turkeys nested on islands in the river—which they did often—he had only to discharge his gun and all the birds would run to the nearest snag of timber, where they would cower but remain, even as he walked up to the pile. It was a simple matter to shoot them where they stood, blinking stupidly at his gun barrels.

Like many birds, turkeys reserve their most extravagant behaviors for the mating season. In Kentucky, Audubon found, this period could begin as early as February. A female typically initiates the lovemaking by separating herself from the males and then calling to them. Turkey cocks converge on the place from which the call originates and begin to strut, tails fanned, chests puffed out and necks curved backward over their shoulders. Should they fail to entice the hen at once, the males soon find one another and fall into combat. Sometimes a weaker or younger bird is killed. Audubon was surprised to see that when this happens, the victor completes the subjugation of his rival by standing atop its dead body and "caressing" it in the same manner in which he holds onto a female during copulation. Audubon told the story of a hunting trip during which he got near enough to a crowd of strutting cocks that a single shot from his gun killed three. Instead of flying off, the remainder strutted and danced around the fallen birds and only departed when Audubon emerged from his hiding place and waved them away.

Once mated, Audubon said, a female turkey remains with the cock through the breeding season. Males, on the other hand, are promiscuous and gather large harems of faithful hens. After they lay their eggs, the hens avoid contact with the males. Audubon believed this was to keep them away from the eggs, which he thought a cock would destroy "for the purpose of protracting his sexual enjoyments." Audubon was appreciative of the turkey hen's devotion to her young, which she attends to single-mindedly immediately before and after hatching. A hen on a nest of eggs ready to hatch will not move from it under any provocation, Audubon said. It was even possible to erect an enclosure around a hen thus engaged. Hens are especially cautious about the weather, and go to great lengths to keep their chicks dry, as a soaking of their down-covered bodies is usually fatal. After the mating period, Audubon said, turkeys enter into a summer molt, when they are flightless and become emaciated and are not worth shooting or eating.

In those days, according to Audubon, the turkey's chief predators, besides humans, were owls and the lynx, a cat now virtually extinct in America. Lynx were great ambushers. Once a lynx spotted a flock of turkeys moving through the forest, it would scout the flank of the group to determine its direction of travel, then bound noiselessly ahead to lie in wait, taking the first bird that wandered too close. Owls were stealth aerialists, descending on roosting turkeys with their great silent wings stiffening just before the lethal collision. Turkeys, Audubon was amazed to see, had an interesting defense against owls. A turkey spotting an owl soaring toward it tipped ahead slightly while bending itself backward and fanning its tail at a slightly elevated angle, so that its back formed a kind of curved ramp. An owl crashing down on a turkey in this posture often ricocheted off in confusion and then departed in search of a less wary bird.

Audubon was captivated by the richness of America's wild procession. Once, having set a cage trap for turkeys, he was thrilled when he went out to inspect it one morning and found a healthy black wolf lying inside. It was a different time. Turkeys were so easily gotten, he said, that in the Louisville market they could be purchased for pennies—less than the cost of an ordinary chicken. A really big, "first rate" turkey of thirty pounds fetched only a quarter.

Audubon felt—correctly—that these kinds of close observations from the field were the essence of ornithology, and were much superior to the study of specimens far removed from their natural habitats. What he lacked in formal training, Audubon compensated for with years of actual experience among the birds. Long after all this, when Audubon began to publish his bird drawings, it was the turkey that he had engraved first. One of his fans among the English gentry so admired his portrait of the great bird that she asked him for a miniature of it—which she then had copied onto a seal as a present for the brash American. For many years after, anyone receiving a letter from John James Audubon found it sealed with a large blob of red wax bearing the impression of a strutting turkey cock.

Audubon's zest for killing wild animals is jarring to modern sensibilities, especially to people who cannot reconcile hunting with the idea of con-servation—the latter a cause now closely associated with the name Audubon. Today, most hunters, of course, regard themselves as conser-vationists, and their sport has become an essential tool in the manage-ment of game and in raising money to preserve wildlife. But Audubon was a premodern man. He hunted, as everyone did then, to put meat on the table. He also hunted for sport. At one time or other, Audubon killed specimens of all but a handful of the more than four hundred species of birds he ultimately painted, plus most of the quadrupeds of North Amer-ica, from squirrels to alligators to moose. He recognized and often spec-ulated about the impact overhunting could have on wildlife populations. But he was never deterred. He sometimes said a day in which he killed fewer than a hundred birds was a day wasted.

Audubon's skill with a gun was considerable. Although birds were more numerous and perhaps more easily approached in those days, the weapons at Audubon's disposal were quite inferior to contemporary sporting guns. Audubon carried both a rifle and a shotgun, though pre-sumably not at the same time. Rifles, used mainly on deer, bears, and smaller mammals, were of little practical use in taking birds except for large species that presented a sizable and relatively stationary target. When loaded with a ball, shotguns could also be used in this way, though they were far less accurate than a rifle with its grooved barrel that was de-signed for the purpose. Audubon killed most of his specimens with a shotgun, which discharged a cloud of shot more likely to bring down fly-ing birds. He no doubt used the smallest size shot he could to minimize tissue damage. The technique works wonderfully: Brought down at a fair distance with fine shot, even a small bird will show little or no outward evidence of its wound.

Shotguns in Audubon's time were configured more or less like their modern counterparts. They typically had two barrels, mounted side by side, each about thirty-four inches in length and something under an inch in diameter. A modern shotgun in 12 or 16 gauge would be somewhat shorter but otherwise look much the same. There was a big difference, though. Audubon's guns were muzzle-loaders. Unlike modern shotguns—which fire a shell that contains fast-burning powder, plastic wadding, shot, and a primer all in one piece that is loaded into the breech—shotguns back then had a closed breech. They were loaded from the front end, first with a measured charge of black powder, then with shot wrapped in linen wadding that was rammed down the barrel with a rod. A flint-loaded "lock" at the back end of the barrel ignited the main charge when the trigger was pulled and the hammer fell and produced a spark.

Care had to be exercised in handling the muzzle-loader. Accidentally discharging the first barrel while loading the second could cost you a hand. A more life-threatening—and maybe more common—mistake was the inadvertent loading of two charges into the same barrel, which could turn a shotgun into a small bomb. It took time to load such a weapon, plus a healthy respect for the dangers involved. It also took time to shoot one.

When a modern gun is fired, the discharge is immediate—indistinguishable, really, from the act of pulling the trigger. But there was a time delay between squeezing the trigger on a flintlock and the gun actually going off. First the spark ignited a primer, which smoked and burned and then lit the main powder charge, which in turn burned much more slowly than modern gunpowders. When Audubon pulled the trigger on his gun, it clicked, sparked, smoked, issued a flash of light near the breech, and finally, after a brief eternity, fired. Around 1825, percussion firing caps came into general use, replacing the flintlock in providing the primary ignition. These shot a little faster, though the main advantage of the percussion cap was that it worked in the rain.

Wingshooting, that is, taking birds in the air, requires timing and a sense of speed, distance, and angle that can be acquired only through experience. To the uninitiated it seems a loud and cruel pastime. To the hunter, there is something ineffable yet almost physical in the pleasure of taking a bird from the air. The tang of fall on the wind, the swing of the gun, its powerful slam against the shoulder, the long, slanting parabola of the stricken bird falling to earth—all of it is an experience that, for some, begs repeating.

Using a gun that is slow to shoot changes the geometry of wingshooting. Nineteenth-century hunters presumably accommodated themselves to the individual proclivities of their guns. Still, some challenging species— fast-flushing upland birds like grouse, or certain puddle ducks that leap vertically into the air and are away in almost the same instant—must have presented Audubon with many a difficult shot. No doubt he was happy when he did not have to take a bird on the wing. Nowadays it's considered unsporting to shoot a bird perched in a tree, or one sitting on the ground. In Audubon's time it was merely the mark of an efficient woodsman.

Audubon's eagerness to shoot the very birds he loved is today some-times excused as an unfortunate necessity—a function of having no camera, no modern optical device with which to "capture" his subjects unharmed. It was, the argument goes, a different era, with a different, less enlightened ethos. This is wrong. Many things *were* different in Audubon's time, but field ornithology has in truth changed little since then. Modern ornithol-ogists still collect bird specimens all over the world. They still shoot them with shotguns. Many of these same scientists are both conserva-tionists and avid bird hunters.

On short forays into the woods, when he could return home the same day, Audubon would have needed little equipment other than his gun, powder, and shot. He usually had along a game bag to carry his birds in. For longer excursions, Audubon had to consider how best to achieve his main objective—making new drawings. There were two options. He could take his drawing equipment with him, or he could preserve the birds against spoilage and carry them back.

One of the telling facts that argues against Audubon's claim of having studied under the French master Jacques-Louis David is that David, who was principally a portraitist, worked in oils. Although Audubon spent many hours struggling with oil paints later in his career—especially after his reputation grew and he thought he could knock off duplicates of his birds for a profit—the medium always confounded him. In Kentucky, where his technique matured, Audubon stuck to the media he already knew: watercolors, pencil, and pastel chalks, which he called crayons. A traveling kit for this work would have been quite manageable. But

Audubon would have been limited to working on smaller species in the field because he always drew the birds full-sized. For the bigger birds, Audubon bought the largest paper available, a truly enormous size called "double elephant," which measured about twenty-seven inches by forty. These sheets would have been unwieldy for foot travel, or even on horse-back—though conceivably they could have been rolled into tubes. But there was the additional matter of the boards—one to which the bird could be wired for posing, and a second to hold the paper—and these would have been more cumbersome to carry. Audubon most likely never used an easel, as it is easier to work with watercolors on a flat or nearly flat surface.

Audubon traveled light. He didn't go in for fancy camps. He liked to sleep in the open, or, when forced to by inclement weather, in lean-tos he fashioned in the woods. It seems likely that Audubon would have hauled his full complement of drawing equipment with him on only his most ambitious trips—where he could set up a base camp at a friend's cabin, or when he could ship his gear ahead by trunk. Otherwise, he either hustled home with his birds or skinned them on the spot.

Bird skinning was a technique well-known to naturalists in Audubon's time, and one still in general use by ornithologists today. It's not as crude as it sounds. A bird "skin" is not a flattened pelt of feathers, but rather something that looks quite like the whole bird. It's a simple form of taxidermy, really, in which the bird's innards are removed and replaced with inert material. Audubon probably stuffed his with straw, or cotton when he could get it. A well-skinned bird is a vivid, three-dimensional version of the real thing that looks like—a dead bird. Several collections of Audubon's bird skins still exist, and many of his specimens look as if they might have been on the wing only yesterday.

Skinning equipment was an even smaller burden than drawing gear. All Audubon needed was a scalpel or sharp knife, perhaps a pointed scissors, and a needle and thread. Methods varied—everyone tended to skin the way whoever taught them did it—but the general procedure was simple enough. A freshly killed bird was slit open along its abdomen, sometimes on the back or under a wing, though Audubon seemed to prefer opening the stomach with a long incision beginning immediately below the breastbone and continuing down to the tail. Using his fingers, Audubon removed the viscera and then gently pried the skin away from the ribcage. He disjointed the leg and wing bones. Using the point of his knife or scissors, he patiently separated the flesh within the wings and legs from the bones. All bones but the very tips of the wings and those inside the feet were extricated in this way. Removing the esophagus, tongue, and eyes allowed the skull to be carefully emptied and left in place. As he worked, Audubon inverted the skin as it pulled away from the parts he was removing, so that when he finished, the bird was literally turned inside out, like a sock rolled off a foot.

Once the skin was removed, it was turned right side out, then cleaned and dried. An experienced skinner could do a small songbird in about twenty minutes. A big, thin-skinned species like a duck took several hours. Bird skins were remarkably durable and could even be washed and wrung out before the feathers were stroked back into place with one's fingertips. But they were vulnerable to insects, which were encountered everywhere on the frontier and could be counted on to infest and ruin a bird skin unless it was treated with a "preservative." Audubon used the standard treatment: arsenic. A potent insecticide, arsenic was also known to be poisonous if ingested, but no one then understood the neurotoxic effects of chronic, long-term exposure to it. Audubon, like other naturalists and taxidermists in that time, routinely handled arsenic through most of his adult life. It came packaged in different forms. Audubon probably bought it in cakes, like soap bars, that he smeared directly into the cavities of his birds before stuffing them and stitching them up, being careful to hide the thread beneath the feathers. Audubon's surviving bird skins even now faintly retain the sweet almond smell of arsenic.

Birds of all kinds were so easy to find in Kentucky then that Audubon may rarely have resorted to skinning specimens except on his most extended forays. Later in his career, though, Audubon came to rely on skins in his work and had them sent to him from all over America. He used skinned specimens to correct proofs of his drawings and also, in some instances, to depict birds he'd never seen in the wild.

As Audubon settled into married life and acquainted himself with the diversions of the frontier, the polar ends of his personality became more distinct. There was the playful Audubon who neglected his work and his family to tramp the woods at his leisure. This Audubon—seemingly immune to physical hardships and eager to partake of every amusement— was suited to life at the edge of civilization. He was a popular figure—a gentleman merchant who could shoot and ride and dance with the best among them. Comfortable now with his English, Audubon picked up a Kentuckian's knack for tall tales and practical jokes. Once, Audubon and a group of friends presented a local flower fancier with what they said was a rare type of geranium, the "rat-tailed Niger." In fact, it *was* a rat, buried headfirst in a pot, its spindly, semi-dried tail protruding up from the dirt and tied to a short stake as if it were a leafless stem. Water and tend it, Audubon advised, and it will soon green and bloom. The man followed Audubon's instructions for days—until the smell convinced him that he'd been duped.

There was also the other Audubon—this one an artist testing the limits of a prodigious talent, teaching himself to draw birds as he actually saw them. In the quiet hours he spent over his drawings, Audubon experimented with his pencil and his colors. Gradually, over the course of the next several years, Audubon found more uses for his outlining pencil, using graphite for shading and rubbing to create undertones that brought added texture to the images. He sometimes worked over his pastels and watercolors with pencil, adding the striations of individual feathers or highlighting details in the feet. It would be a few years, still, before he released his subjects from conventional poses and set them free to fly and cavort on the page. But even at this stage, Audubon's birds were advancing beyond anything as yet seen.

Audubon destroyed his earliest drawings. A few that exist—including some that were made in 1805 during his brief return to France, as well as some from his later formative years at Mill Grove and in Louisville—are the equal of Alexander Wilson's at the height of his career. A sign of what was to come was Audubon's drawing of a belted kingfisher he shot at the Falls of the Ohio in the summer of 1808, shortly after he and Lucy arrived there. Audubon drew the bird in simple profile—yet it appears utterly real, from the rich blue of its fat, compact body, to its wispy head crest and powerful, spiky beak. The eye, especially, looks *alive*. Audubon was an emotional man, and at Louisville his feelings for the first time entered his drawings in a way that imparted the most human of all traits to his subjects: consciousness.

Audubon's carelessness about his business and the industry with which he developed his art were, for the time being, the affordable luxuries of a young man having a great time with little thought of the future. Later, when Audubon recalled his years in Louisville, one of his most vivid memories was of a party. It was the Fourth of July. In a stand of beech trees near Beargrass Creek, the forest had been cleared, the low branches cut away, and a sprawling lawn opened to the sky. Everyone in town came, bringing with them venison and ham and turkey and fish, plus baskets of peaches, plums, and a variety of succulent melons. Fires were kindled. A "barbecue" commenced. Fifes and drums played, as patriotic speeches echoed through the forest and a small cannon went off at intervals. Carafes of wine were passed, and stouthearted men filled their glasses from barrels of "Old Monongahela." Shooting contests were staged and horses were raced across the glen. Stories were told and hoots of laughter filled the air. At the call to dinner, the women sat first while the men tended their partners with the preening enthusiasm of turkey cocks in full strut. The men ate next. And then came the dancing, the men in their leather hunting shirts twirling women in fringed skirts to the thumping music of violins, clarionets, and bugles. At dusk the fires were relit and another meal appeared beneath a spray of stars overhead. "Columbia's sons and daughters," Audubon later wrote, "seemed to have grown younger" that day.

What a time it was for Audubon and Lucy and little Victor. Even as Ferdinand Rozier wrung his hands at the bleak numbers in their ledger, the Audubons were intoxicated with their life together. In the spring of 1810, Lucy's father oversaw the sale of Audubon's remaining interest in Mill Grove and deposited nearly $8,000 in Audubon and Rozier's account in New York. This was, for all practical purposes, the last of their money. The decision also severed one of the few remaining ties between Audubon and his family back in France—where the elder Audubon apparently took little notice. Lucy's father, complaining about the difficulties of the transaction, wondered pointedly about the lead mine—which was apparently beginning to produce ore. But Audubon and Lucy were untroubled by the disposal of their only remaining asset. Were they not a golden couple in a golden land?

8

MR. WILSON'S DECADE

Anas sponsa: **The Wood Duck**
The flight of this species is remarkable for its speed, and the ease and elegance with which it is performed. The Wood Duck passes through the woods and even amongst the branches of trees, with as much facility as the Passenger Pigeon; and while removing from some secluded haunt to its breeding grounds, at the approach of night, it shoots over the trees like a meteor, scarcely emitting any sound from its wings.

—Ornithological Biography

The years from 1803, when he first conceived of the work that would become *American Ornithology*, until his sudden death in 1813 were the happiest and most productive of Alexander Wilson's life. This was in spite of—or possibly because of—the hardships and physical complaints that were the inevitable lot of any serious naturalist in those days. He lived in the city now, walking each day to Bradford's publishing house, except when he could get away for some shooting. Wilson told Bartram about a day he went out in search of a nuthatch, leaving before dawn in light shoes. Soon he was far afield, slogging through muddy wastes over his ankles. He reached the confluence of the Schuylkill and Delaware Rivers, on the southern outskirts of Philadelphia, where he was surprised to see much of the forest cut down and, with it, the normal habitat of the nuthatch. He got home late in the evening, soaked and sweating. Contrary to common wisdom, he said, this seemed to have done him good and he planned to "repeat the dose," minus the wet feet. He teasingly begged Bartram not to tell this to Lawson, who already feared for his sanity.

In 1807, Samuel Bradford's company won the contract to publish Meriwether Lewis's account of his expedition to the Pacific with William Clark. Lewis came to Philadelphia to oversee the project and before long had befriended Wilson. The Lewis and Clark expedition had returned from the West with a number of bird specimens, though many had been lost on the way back. Lewis handed these over to Wilson to include in his ornithology, and he also supplied many observations about the distribution of species that Wilson incorporated into his written descriptions. One of the species formerly unknown to science that Wilson was thus able to depict was a small, striking, black-yellow-and-scarlet bird he called the "Louisiana tanager," later renamed the western tanager.

Wilson continued his close study of Pennsylvania birds, and combined bird collecting with subscription sales on several long trips up and down the East Coast. The first volume of *American Ornithology* was generally admired, though many literate and prosperous people could not quite bring themselves to subscribe. Wilson called on businesses, colleges, governmental bodies, and wealthy patrons of art and science. In New York, where he met an aged and infirm Thomas Paine, Wilson said he pounded the streets so relentlessly that he became a well-known figure—on par with the town crier. His reception was not always warm. Wilson, in turn, didn't like many of the settled parts of America. He found New York and Boston cramped and dirty, and thought most of New England a desert of stony fields and unpleasant towns indistinguishable from one another, all of them swarming with greedy lawyers.

Wilson was no more fond of the South when he went there one winter. He thought the region poor and its roads execrable. He was surprised and offended by the presence of so many blacks, whom he described as usually dirty and half-naked. White women stayed out of sight and white men stayed drunk on a vile apple brandy that they began drinking the moment they got out of bed each morning. It was rare, he wrote to a friend, to meet a man whose lips were not "parched and chopped [sic] or blistered with drinking this poison." The country itself was often arresting in its wildness, though rarely beautiful. Yet even when he was appalled at his surroundings, Wilson was a lively reporter:

> The general features of North Carolina, where I crossed it, are immense, solitary, pine savannahs, through which the road winds among stagnant ponds, swarming with alligators; dark, sluggish creeks, the colour of brandy, over which are thrown high wooden bridges, without railings, and so crazy and rotten as not only to alarm the horse, but his rider, and to make it a matter of thanksgiving with both when they make it over, without going through

or being precipitated into the gulf below as food for the alligators. Enormous cypress swamps, which, to a stranger, have a striking, desolate, and ruinous appearance. Picture yourself a forest of prodigious trees, rising, as thick as they can grow, from a vast flat and impenetrable morass, covered for ten feet from the ground with reeds. The leafless limbs of the cypresses are clothed with an extraordinary kind of moss, from two to 10 feet long, in such quantities that 50 men might conceal themselves in one tree.

Wilson didn't care for the people he met in North Carolina, describing them as "ignorant, debased and indolent." All through the South he marveled at how lazy and slow the whites were, which he blamed on their dependence on slaves to do all the work. In South Carolina, the roads were long and sandy; he found Charleston to be a pretty town, clean and full of delightful gingerbread houses. But plantation owners were occasionally so hospitable that he was sometimes detained longer than he wanted to be, and once, when he needed to replace his horse, he had to accompany a country gentleman to the beach, where the deal was finally concluded "amidst the roar of the Atlantic." The new mount was a handful, cantering off along the surf's edge with him for fifteen miles.

Wilson saw and shot birds along the way, including many species that were familiar to him but that did not overwinter in Pennsylvania. Near Wilmington, North Carolina, he collected an exceptional specimen of the ivory-billed woodpecker, which he painted for *American Ornithology*. Now extinct, the bird was then still common in the South. It was a spectacular animal—similar to the pileated woodpecker but half again as big, with a heavy, black body, and a cartoonish red head and crest, and a pale beak the size of a railroad spike. Wilson's shot only wounded the bird and he managed to capture it alive, whereupon it began to scream and bawl with a "piteous note, exactly resembling the violent crying of a young child." This frightened Wilson's horse and unnerved him, too. But he managed to cover the bird and, placing it on the saddle in front of him, rode into Wilmington—where the townsfolk rushed to their windows at the sound of its wailing. Stopping at a hotel, Wilson inquired after accommodations "for myself and my baby," ridiculously amused by his joke before unhooding the woodpecker and explaining himself. He locked the bird in his room and went to tend to his horse, only to find the woodpecker furiously hammering its way through the plaster and lath of the wall when he returned. Recapturing it, Wilson next tied it to a table—the bird was screaming again—and went out once more, to see if he could find some bugs to feed it. As he climbed the stairs on returning a short while later, Wilson heard the bird furiously pecking away and this time discovered it had demolished the table. Wilson managed to subdue the animal long enough to paint it, suffering numerous puncture wounds in the process. The bird refused all Wilson's efforts to feed it and died after three days.

Wilson got as far as Savannah. After some time walking the "beds of burning sand" that were the streets of that city during an uncommonly warm spring, Wilson wrote to Bradford saying he would soon take a ship north and that all of his thoughts were now of home:

There is a charm, a melody, in this little word home, which only those know, who have forsaken it to wander among strangers, exposed to dangers, fatigues, insults and impositions, of a thousand nameless kinds. Perhaps I feel the force of this idea rather more at present than usual, being indisposed with a slight fever these three days, which a dose of sea-sickness will, I hope, rid me of.

The trip had been expensive. Wilson later calculated the cost at about five times the value of the subscriptions he obtained, though this must have been an exaggeration. He was victimized by innkeepers who were "like the vultures" that hovered over the cities, and he struggled to locate people of means whom he could call upon in hopes of a sale. Sometimes he was forced to advertise *American Ornithology* in the local papers. Despite the many difficulties and Wilson's dim view of this section of the country, however, he wrote to Bartram in Philadelphia to say that the subscription list was now approaching 250. It was March 1809.

The second volume of *American Ornithology* was published in January 1810. That same month, Wilson again left Philadelphia, heading this time for Pittsburgh and the frontier. He most likely rode past Mill Grove on his way out of town, about a year and a half after Audubon had gone by the same route.

Wilson paused occasionally on his way west, showing his books to potential subscribers, chatting up amateur naturalists who knew the birds and mammals of the Pennsylvania mountains, and gathering anecdotes for contributions he planned to make to a popular Philadelphia journal, *The Port Folio.* Near the town of Carlisle, he visited a local attraction, a cave that stood at the foot of a perpendicular limestone cliff. Its opening was about nine feet high and slightly wider than that at the base. Wilson entered, carrying a candle. The floor of the cave was level and smooth, but interrupted by ice stalagmites three and four feet high. He saw a lone wren. Wilson proceeded into the mountainside for something like three hundred yards, passing through chambers where the ceiling rose two stories overhead, stopping at last at a point where the cave divided down several paths. Here the walls were damp, and still pools of water were at his feet. Wilson—in one of his moods—blew out his candle and sat down to meditate, indulging, he later wrote in a letter to Lawson, "in a train of solemn and melancholy contemplations, that forc'd themselves on my mind in this gloomy & silent recess." Evidently his spirits were more festive after he relit his candle—on his way out of the cave, Wilson captured several hibernating bats. He wrapped them in his handkerchief and put them in a pocket. Later that evening, as Wilson relaxed in the barroom of the tavern where he was staying, the bats woke up and, disentangling themselves, commenced to fly around the room.

In Pittsburgh, Wilson was struck by the number of keelboats waiting to descend the Ohio, which was choked with ice, and also by the thriving industry of the place. Under its clouds of smoke, the city was busy, and far more prosperous than it first seemed. Wilson sold nineteen subscriptions while waiting for the river to open, a success beyond all expectation. He searched the surrounding woods for birds, but found nothing of note. Wilson bought a one-man skiff for his passage down the Ohio, painting the name *Ornithologist* on its low stern. He left near the end of February, under warming skies, maneuvering his boat through chunks of floating ice that dotted the otherwise mirrorlike surface of the Ohio. Within a day the ice disappeared. Wilson had some biscuits and cheese, plus his gun and trunk, in the bow. He used a small tin to bail the *Ornithologist*, occasionally dipping it over the side for a drink from the crisp waters carrying him along. When he rowed, Wilson estimated his speed at six miles an hour. He passed many arks, some as long as seventy feet, carrying families, livestock, and all manner of trading goods. A much lesser volume of traffic came upstream, barges that were backbreakingly poled ahead at a rate of twenty miles a day. The sight of so many people

moving to the frontier impressed Wilson. It was as if all these human beings were, he wrote, "migrating like birds of passage to the luxuriant regions of the south and west." He covered more than fifty miles his first
day out, spending the night at a "miserable cabin" where he slept on corn-
stalks. He was back on the river before sunup.

The nights were still bitterly cold. It was the breeding time for owls,
and Wilson often heard their "hideous hollowing" echoing through the
woods after dark. He explored as he went, stopping off to visit the Big
Bone Lick and inspecting many of the Ohio's tributaries. He shot and
skinned a number of ducks, bundling the skins in his coat. Wilson found
a mix of people as the river carried him on—amusing Kentucky story-
tellers, a colony of Swiss immigrants living in a tidy community where
they were bottling a decent wine, and many desperately poor squatters
who were "roving the frontiers advancing as the tide of civilized population approaches." The fields were full of horses and cattle that appeared
half-starved, while fat pigs roamed the forests, feasting on that year's unusually large acorn mast. Later, when he headed off across Kentucky,
Wilson noted that the horse stock much improved.

On the morning of the seventeenth of March, having come many
hundreds of miles, Wilson spotted several turkeys near the river on the
Indiana side. He put ashore and gave chase, but did not succeed in getting
one. A short time later he saw another flock, this time on the Kentucky
side, and tried again, but still he could not get close enough to the keen-
eyed birds for a shot. The turkey would end up being one of the major
species he had yet to draw when he died, but on this morning his
thoughts were equally divided between the bird and the town of
Louisville, which he was nearing. By the time he gave up on the turkeys,
he'd lost several hours. Hurrying along through the afternoon, Wilson
failed to reach Louisville before nightfall. He went on anyway, confident
that he would spot the lights of the city as he approached it, but around
eight o'clock he heard the falls up ahead and grew uneasy. Steering his
boat close to the shore, Wilson advanced slowly until he found the mouth
of Bear Grass Creek and tied up there.

Wilson found a room at the Indian Queen. He may or may not have
known that a young, newly married couple named Audubon was living there. Perhaps they saw each other. The dining room at the Indian
Queen was legendary for bringing its boarders together, as it was necessary
to rush in at mealtime to claim a seat. Polite travelers were sometimes

astonished to find the meal completed and the room empty before they'd finished their first cup of tea.

What did happen is this: A day or two after his arrival, Wilson was out making rounds in search of subscribers when he entered Audubon and Rozier's store. Audubon never forgot the "peculiar character" Wilson appeared to be that day—with his fine, long nose, hollow cheeks, and burning eyes. He was dressed too formally for this part of the world—in a short coat, an overcoat, and fitted trousers. He had two books with him. Audubon thought the man looked nervous as he placed the volumes on the counter and explained what they were.

Audubon, of course, was agog at *American Ornithology* and its beautiful color plates. Without hesitation, he got out his pen and was about to add his name to Wilson's subscriber list when Rozier, who'd been watching from the back of the shop, stopped him.

"My dear Audubon, what induces you to subscribe to this work?" Rozier said in French. "Your drawings are certainly far better, and again, you must know as much of the habits of American birds as this gentleman."

Audubon wasn't sure if the visitor understood Rozier, but Wilson seemed suddenly put off. At the same time, Rozier's flattery had the intended effect, and Audubon put down his pen. Wilson asked if Audubon had any drawings of birds. He would like to see them if that was possible. It was. Taking down his large portfolio, Audubon showed Wilson his collection of paintings, which was now thick. Wilson was floored. He said he had never dreamed anyone else was at work on an illustrated ornithology. When Audubon told him that he hadn't given any thought to publishing his drawings, Wilson seemed even more taken aback.

Wilson asked if he might borrow a few of Audubon's drawings while he was in town. Audubon happily agreed. In fact, he said, if Wilson wanted to publish any of them he would be fine with that, so long as his name was mentioned somewhere in the process. Wilson was particularly interested in a species of flycatcher he didn't recognize. Audubon said there were plenty of them in the woods outside Louisville and offered to take Wilson hunting the next day. They went and Wilson collected several specimens. Wilson also got his first look at a flock of whooping cranes in the wild. Audubon, who claimed Wilson had until then seen only stuffed versions of the bird, told Wilson that immature whooping cranes could be distinguished from the pure white adults by their gray plumage. Audubon later complained that Wilson had included this observation in the third volume of *American Ornithology* without crediting him as the source. In fact, Wilson stated—correctly—that young whooping cranes are brown. Whatever information Audubon shared with Wilson, it was insufficient to make him tarry in Louisville. A few days later, having sold the *Ornithologist* for half what he had paid for it, Wilson left town on horseback, heading overland to the south.

This chance meeting between Wilson and Audubon seems, in retrospect, an improbable coincidence. Actually, it would have been more surprising if they had not happened upon one another on the frontier. Everyone coming into the country passed the same way, stopped off at the same taverns and towns, moved in the same limited circles of a far-flung but still very small population. Yet there's doubt about the particulars, as the only record of their encounter is Audubon's after-the-fact account. It would not have been beyond Audubon to invent details of such an episode showing himself to advantage. Audubon said that when he compared his own drawings with Wilson's at the shop it was apparent that his collection was "already much greater." Audubon also maintained that he and Wilson met a second time, two years later, when Audubon was briefly in Philadelphia on business. According to Audubon, he called on Wilson, who was busy with a painting of the bald eagle—a bird the two ornithologists depicted in virtually identical poses. He said Wilson was noticeably cool, taking him to see the artist Rembrandt Peale but avoiding all discussion of ornithology. After an uncomfortable couple of hours, Audubon excused himself, never to see Wilson again.

Audubon told these stories many years after Wilson's death, and also after reading in *American Ornithology* Wilson's claim that he had visited Louisville in March 1810 and found it a wretched backwater. There was not a single subscriber to be had in the town, and not a single new bird could he find in the woods nearby. "Science and literature," Wilson concluded, "has not one friend in this place." In a journal Wilson kept of his travels that was later edited and then lost, he talked of hunting near Louisville with "no naturalist to keep me company." Wilson never mentioned Audubon in print, and perhaps he never even talked to anyone about him. There is evidence that Wilson had been alerted to the presence of a naturalist named Audubon in Louisville by Lucy Audubon's uncle, Benjamin Bakewell—the same man for whom Audubon had worked as a clerk in New York. Bakewell had since moved to Pittsburgh and was a successful glassmaker there when Wilson passed through. And a different version of the missing Wilson journal reportedly did refer to a meeting with Audubon, and included an account of their seeing many passenger pigeons and sandhill cranes while out hunting together one day near Louisville.

Nobody ever asked Rozier about the meeting.

Wilson rode to Lexington, Kentucky, and then down to Nashville, Tennessee, through Natchez, Mississippi, and finally all the way to New Orleans, where he arrived in June. Passing down the western edge of the civilized world, Wilson moved through an unfolding spring. Birds were everywhere—owls, whippoorwills, grouse, passenger pigeons. Wilson made drawings and took notes as he went, although many of the paintings were lost when he forwarded them to Lawson from Nashville and they miscarried en route. He was accompanied for a portion of his trip by a pet Carolina parakeet. Wilson had wounded the large green-and-yellow bird in Kentucky and nursed it back to health. It lived in his pocket and would climb out and perch on his shoulder to amuse people wherever he stopped.

Wilson's account of this trip brimmed with high adventure and frequent encounters with scoundrels and cutthroats. In the barrens region of southwestern Kentucky, Wilson spent five days hunting and making drawings. It was a strange place, almost devoid of trees and covered with wild strawberries. Rumors circulated that tavern keepers in this part of the country were a dangerous lot, given to murdering unwary travelers and secreting their bodies in caves. Wilson actually met a man suspected of such a crime—and boldly accompanied him on a visit to a cave. On seeing that Wilson carried a pistol, the man turned pleasant and professed innocence of any wrongdoing. In western Tennessee a short time later, Wilson spent a night in an Indian village, lying comfortably on a deerskin. The next day he rode through the tribe's territory. The Indians were fascinated by his parakeet. Wilson thought them primitive but pleasant. The women were naked above the waist, and because they never combed their hair, had the appearance of wearing a "large mop" atop their heads.

At the end of April, Wilson was stuck in Nashville. It had rained steadily for a week. He gave up on his plan of continuing from there to St. Louis. With the season so far advanced, he was dubious of finding any

new birds on that route, and was also skeptical of finding many subscribers in that remote town. He decided, instead, to ride to Natchez.
This would take him through an unsettled and only rarely traveled section of wilderness:

> I was advised by many not to attempt it alone; that the Indians
> were dangerous, the swamps and rivers almost impassable without
> assistance, and a thousand other hobgoblins were conjured up to
> dissuade me from going alone. But I weighed all these matters in
> my own mind; and attributing a great deal of this to vulgar fears
> and exaggerated reports, I equipped myself for the attempt. I rode
> an excellent horse, on which I could depend; I had a loaded pistol
> in each pocket, a loaded fowling-piece belted across my shoulder,
> a pound of gunpowder in my flask, and five pounds of shot in my
> belt. I bought some biscuit and dried beef, and on Friday morning,
> May 4th, I left Nashville.

For a man unworried about his safety, it must be said that Wilson
went into the wilds very well armed. Most of the difficulties he met with,
however, were topographical.

> Eleven miles from Nashville, I came to the Great Harpath, a
> stream of about fifty yards wide, which was running with great vi-
> olence. I could not discover the entrance of the ford, owing to the
> rains and inundations. There was no time to be lost, I plunged in,
> and almost immediately my horse was swimming. I set his head
> aslant the current, and being strong, he soon landed on the other
> side. As the weather was warm, I rode in my wet clothes without
> any inconvenience. The country to-day was a perpetual succession
> of steep hills and low bottoms; I crossed ten or twelve large
> creeks, one of which swam my horse, where he was near being en-
> tangled among some bad drift wood. Now and then a solitary farm
> opened from the woods, where the negro children were running
> naked about the yards.

Most of the people Wilson encountered were poor settlers and min-
ers, plus several parties of ragged boatmen who were making their way
back north overland after delivering cargoes to New Orleans. They

warned him of bad roads ahead and marveled that he should be traveling by himself, especially without any whiskey. About seventy miles from Nashville, Wilson stopped at a travelers' way station called Grinder's Inn, which had been the site of a bizarre suicide the previous fall. Wilson, the first reliable reporter on the scene, questioned Mrs. Grinder, the main witness to the event. He later gave a full account of the affair in an issue of *The Port Folio*.

It seemed that a guest who had come there in October spent the evening behaving oddly, pacing and talking to himself, asking for spirits but drinking little. He didn't eat much, and when it was time for bed, announced that he preferred to sleep on the floor on his own bearskin and buffalo robe. But he did not lie down. Instead, he paced his room for several hours, talking loudly to himself—"like a lawyer," according to Mrs. Grinder. Then there was a shot, followed by the sound of something heavy crashing to the floor. There was another shot. After a few minutes, the man staggered back to the kitchen and asked for water, pleading with Mrs. Grinder that she "heal his wounds," which were grim. Part of his forehead was blown away, exposing his brain, and there was a hole in his side. The man careened about the camp all through the night, searching for water while the terrified Mrs. Grinder hid in her room. He died in the morning, while begging someone to shoot him and end it.

The man was Meriwether Lewis. Wilson inspected his shallow grave, which was marked only by a few logs laid over it. He gave Mrs. Grinder some money to fence the gravesite so as to preserve it from hogs and wolves. Then he went on, now in a melancholy mood that was "not much allayed by the prospect of the gloomy and savage wilderness which I was just entering alone."

In the summer of 1811, Wilson was introduced to George Ord, a wealthy young Philadelphia businessman with a lively interest in natural history. Two years later, Ord got Wilson elected to membership in the fledgling Academy of Natural Sciences, and the two men became frequent partners on shooting expeditions outside the city and across the Delaware in the swamps and along the coast of New Jersey. *American Ornithology* became the model for illustrated books about North American fauna, solidifying the academy's prestige and inspiring its members—like the brilliant young entomologist Thomas Say. Say, a founder of the academy who was rumored to sleep in its museum under the skeleton of a horse, went on to describe much of the New World's insect fauna. He also discovered several species of birds in the West, and was the first to describe the coyote.

Publication of subsequent volumes of *American Ornithology* came in fits and starts. There were many delays. Wilson was never satisfied with the colorists hired to finish the plates, and they were expensive as well. In the end, he colored most of the plates himself. Volumes three and four came out in 1811. The original run of two hundred copies soared to five hundred, and Wilson had booked something like $60,000 in subscriptions—much of which would never be collected. Many of his early subscribers were tradesmen in Philadelphia who ultimately fell off the list. Others defaulted or reneged as the project crept forward. Volumes five and six were delivered in 1812, the latter showing a profit to Bradford of $12,000. Wilson had by then quit his job on the encyclopedia and moved to Bartram's Garden to work on the ornithology. The seventh volume was finished in the spring of 1813, and the eighth was near completion that summer when Wilson came down with an illness that began when he'd gotten chilled swimming after a bird. He had completed seventy-six plates, depicting more than 250 species. He was now owed by his subscribers $48,000, but his share was being devoured by the mounting production costs. His physical condition deteriorated, and on August 24, 1813, Wilson died. He was forty-seven years old. George Ord, who'd been away from the city, returned to find he'd been made co-executor of the will, which Wilson wrote eight days before his death. The estate consisted of three copies of *American Ornithology*. Wilson left two to his father back in Scotland and the remaining one to his nephew, William Duncan.

American Ornithology was a literary work as much as it was a scientific one. Wilson got some things wrong—his nomenclature required extensive revision later on and he sometimes mistook birds with immature or seasonal plumages for distinct species. But he got the story of America, and in his simple, elegant drawings, he got America's birds. As a natural history, *American Ornithology* was an original—one that would serve as a template for Audubon. It was mostly words—just 103 engraved plates were interspersed with the lively, personal descriptions of birds and their habits that Wilson gleaned from years of observation. He claimed to have written virtually all of it in the field. Wilson was as happy describing the searching flight of a hawk as he was telling how a boy had fallen from a tree after he reached into a woodpecker's nest for its babies and found instead the large black snake that had just eaten the little birds.

In the final days of his short, strange life, Wilson no doubt thought about the enormity of the New World and the portion of it he had seen. Certainly the delirium of his illness must have seemed familiar, must have reminded him of the malaria-like fever that had overtaken him on his trip through the West years before.

Wilson had crossed the Tennessee River and was angling across what would later be the northwest corner of the state of Mississippi. The way was difficult, as what passed for a road took him through a succession of miserable swamps that left him damp and caked with mud. In places, he could not tell whether his horse was walking or swimming. Wilson was abruptly overcome by a "constant burning thirst." He grew weak. He stopped every few minutes to drink from the fetid waters he rode through. At intervals, he soaked his hat for relief from the broiling sun. Soon he could barely ride. When he camped for the night, Wilson was so parched and feverish that he barely slept. The next morning he managed to buy some eggs along the road. He ate them raw and felt a little better for it. For the next week, eggs were all he ate. Wilson thought his fever had ebbed but he could not get over his all-consuming thirst. Now he was in cane swamps so awful that drinking from them was unthinkable. It got hotter. The sun was a constant torture. Exhausted and hallucinating, Wilson began to lose sense of where he was and what he was doing. He was desperate for water. There was none.

After ten days of this, as he rode barely clinging to his horse, Wilson noticed the wind begin to stir the trees around him. The sun disappeared, as if in answer to a prayer. He found a meadow and rode into the open. The wind continued to rise. The sky was an odd color. A massive wall of clouds formed above him, and it began to revolve, moving lower as it turned. The wind increased. Wilson dismounted, dropping the reins. His horse skittered sideways, eyes wide with terror. Wilson walked a few steps to stand alone. This was America. He was very far from home. The Seedhills and his poetry and his weaving seemed to belong to another world, another life. There were no birds here, no learned friends, no welcoming hearth, only this wild, terrible moment. Wilson steadied himself. On either side of the clearing, the trees bent in opposite directions. Lightning stabbed at the forest canopy. The air fizzed and the ground shook beneath long, shuddering waves of thunder. Now the wind shrieked. Wilson turned slowly, amazed, and watched as trees exploded and debris lifted and spun toward the sky all around him. The world was coming apart, rising to the heavens. He looked up. A great black cloud was coming right at him. And for an instant, Wilson, who was so rarely happy to be alive, was only that. He tipped his head back, opened his mouth, and raised his arms high.

It began to rain.

II

THE BIRDS OF AMERICA

9

AT THE RED BANKS

Scolopax minor: The American Woodcock
Now and then, the American Woodcock, after being pursued for a considerable time, throws itself into the centre of large, miry places, where it is very difficult for either man or dog to approach it; and indeed if you succeed, it will not rise unless you almost tread upon it.   —*Ornithological Biography*

Ferdinand Rozier wanted to move on. After two years by the Falls of the Ohio with Audubon it seemed that, even though Louisville kept growing, their business was a dead end. Settlers passed by on the way west, an endless thread of humanity pushing America ever farther into the continent. Surely, Rozier reasoned, opportunity lay in that direction. Audubon, who at best had only a vague concept of their stagnating fortunes, was not immediately enthusiastic about a move. He loved Louisville. He may even have convinced himself that Lucy and Victor loved their hotel room. But Rozier persisted, and eventually Audubon agreed to have a look at the place where Rozier thought they might have a better chance. It was a tiny town called Henderson, perched on a bluff on the south side of the Ohio, more than two hundred miles downriver.

Henderson's origins predated the Revolutionary War, when it had been conceived as a primary outpost in America's early westward push. It was named for Richard Henderson, a North Carolina judge and land speculator. In the years just before the colonies declared their independence from Britain, Henderson became interested in opening up land in Kentucky after listening to Daniel Boone's reports of the richness and beauty of this wild region west of the mountains. Boone was one of the self-styled "long hunters" who prowled the forests along the frontier for years at a time. In the summer of 1774, Henderson and a group of investors formed the Transylvania Company, intent on buying a large tract of land in Kentucky from the Indians who lived there. The following spring, a party including Henderson and Boone met with 1,200 Cherokee at Sycamore Shoals on the Watauga River in what is now the state of Tennessee. The meeting lasted twenty days, though the actual negotiations apparently occupied only a small part of that time, the rest being devoted to feasts and general merriment—with a promise of liquor all around once the deal was completed. In the end, Henderson cut the most one-sided bargain since the Dutch bought Manhattan for less than $30. The Transylvania Company acquired 20 million acres of central Kentucky for well under a penny an acre.

Daniel Boone and thirty men were dispatched to begin construction of a road into Kentucky. Within a month Boone had established a fort on the Kentucky River. Another month later, Henderson held a meeting at Boonesboro, as the settlement was called, at which time measures were adopted to bring order to the territory. These mainly dealt with courts and militia, but one fortuitous provision called for Kentuckians to engage in horse breeding. In September of 1775, Henderson's company petitioned the Continental Congress to make Transylvania the fourteenth colony. The request was rejected, however, and on New Year's Eve of 1776, Virginia nullified the Transylvania Company's claim in Kentucky and took control of its holdings. Two years later the Virginia House of Delegates returned 200,000 acres, and in 1783 the state of North Carolina added back another 200,000 acres. But Richard Henderson died just two years after that, at the age of forty-nine. His name was still inseparable from the Transylvania Company's interests when it looked to secure its new holdings along the Ohio River, just below the mouth of the Green River. Well to the south and west of Louisville, this was considered a dangerous stretch of the frontier, a place where the Indians were unfriendly and river pirates lurked. In the spring of 1797, agents from the Transylvania Company paddling pirogues arrived at a place called the Red Banks, where they surveyed and platted a new town to be called Henderson. A small settlement there had already been established, mostly occupied by German squatters who were offered free lots if they would stay.

It seemed a good location. There was a loop in the Ohio below its confluence with the Green River, and within the bend the land rose. The bluff on the Kentucky side stood more than seventy feet above the river and was reputed to be the one place along this section of the Ohio that had never flooded. The clay and rock in the riverbank itself had a reddish tinge that gave it the name Red Banks. As the river turned back on itself here, it widened. At Red Banks it was nearly a half-mile across before it straightened and flowed west again, disappearing over the horizon, a glittering ribbon of reflected light.

The town was well laid out by the Transylvania Company's agents. It sat parallel to the river, occupying about a half-mile of the bluff-top. There were 264 lots, each an acre large, divided by streets a hundred feet wide. The terms of sale called for residents to construct log houses at least sixteen feet on a side, with a "dirt, stone, or brick chimney, and plank floor." Twelve acres in the middle of town were reserved for a park. Pretty as it was, Henderson did not thrive. A general store operated for a while, selling mainly whiskey and, oddly, ladies' hats. When Henderson's first saloon was licensed in 1799, gambling was prohibited on the premises and the owner was liable for anyone who consumed more liquor than "necessary." Concern for law and order was considerable—the sun-whitened skull of an Ohio River pirate supposedly hung on a pole just outside town for years. Currency was hard to come by, and tobacco was often used instead. The people spread throughout the surrounding countryside were so scattered that public elections took place over a three-day period in order to make sure everyone could get to the polls. Boxing matches were popular, as was horse racing, which was conducted down the broad, mostly undeveloped avenues in the city proper. By the time Audubon and Rozier visited in 1810, there were 160 people living in Henderson. Even at that, Audubon, when he later wrote about his first years there, exaggerated how small Henderson was, claiming there were only "six or eight" houses in town—one of which was an empty, one-room log cabin that became the Audubons' first home of their own.

What Rozier saw in Henderson is impossible to say. What Audubon found appealing was no mystery at all. The country around Henderson was largely untouched forest. A patchwork of wetlands and sloughs attracted massive flocks of waterfowl and wading birds. One place in particular caught Audubon's attention—a narrow, oval-shaped marsh on the western edge of town called Long Pond. It sat in a broad opening of the woods and was connected to the Ohio by a narrow bayou. In the coming years, Audubon would spend many seasons on the shores of Long Pond.

The fabulous fall duck hunting there would, above all, make a lasting impression on him. Poor though the prospects for commerce appeared to be in Henderson, the pull of the wilderness was irresistible, and Audubon agreed to relocate at once.

Lucy could not have been happy with her first view of Henderson when Audubon brought her and Victor down the Ohio a short time later. If she ever doubted the wisdom and resourcefulness of her optimistic young husband, this would have been the time. Louisville, where she had felt bored and culturally deprived, now must have seemed cosmopolitan by comparison. Audubon, sidestepping the whole truth again, later said their only decent piece of furniture was Victor's cradle, and that aside from some flour and ham they'd brought along, they relied almost entirely on Audubon's gun and fishing equipment for sustenance. The garden they planted their first year, he said, withered in the "rank" soil and was swallowed by weeds. Actually, things were not so bleak as that. The Audubons were arguably among the town's more affluent residents from the day they climbed up the Red Banks. Lucy even had with her a set of china and silver. Audubon and Rozier, meanwhile, invested in four "downtown" lots and put up a log store. They'd brought what they could of their inventory from Louisville, and also their clerk, a young man named Pope. Pope was a dubious asset, as he was more inclined to be off in the woods with Audubon than behind the counter with Rozier.

Not long after they got to Henderson, the Audubons met a local doctor named Adam Rankin, who lived with his wife Elizabeth and their children on a farm called Meadow Brook three miles from town. Elizabeth came from a prominent family—the Speeds. Her father, Captain James Speed, had fought with distinction in the Revolutionary War. The Audubons had known some of the Speeds in Louisville. In the isolation of a small frontier community, it was not surprising that Lucy and Elizabeth were soon close friends. The Audubons became frequent houseguests at Meadow Brook. Though it was no grand estate, the Rankins' wood-frame house was roomy and comfortable and, to Lucy especially, a refuge. When Audubon told Lucy after only a few months in town that he was leaving on an extended business trip, they were thrilled when the Rankins insisted that Lucy and Victor stay with them during Audubon's absence. It was not an entirely charitable offer. Elizabeth, who was impressed with Lucy's English refinement, asked if she would become a tutor to the Rankin children. Lucy, eager for something constructive to do, agreed. It was her first taste of work. It was not to be her last.

Audubon's "business trips" until then had usually been pretexts for extended hunting excursions. This time was different. Audubon and Rozier had scarcely set up shop when Rozier decided that Henderson was a mistake. He wanted to move still farther west, this time, he told Audubon, to the town of St. Genevieve. A French settlement, St. Genevieve was located in Missouri, about halfway up the Mississippi River toward St. Louis from the mouth of the Ohio at Cairo. It was almost three hundred miles away. Rozier, who had never gotten comfortable with English, longed to live again in a place where French dominated the conversation. Audubon didn't feel a similar impulse, but he was eager to see more of the frontier, and no less a man than Daniel Boone was now living in Missouri.

Lucy thought the whole idea was terrible. She was not fond of the obtuse Rozier to begin with, and Henderson was quite bad enough. The prospect of moving even farther away from her family and civilization just to trade one backwater for another was almost unbearable. In early December of 1810, with snow falling and the winter already well advanced, Audubon and Rozier abandoned their shop and set off downriver. They went in a keelboat, two slaves manning the oars, and a cargo of dry goods that included gunpowder and several hundred barrels of "Old Monongahela" whiskey. Lucy saw them off with the hope that it was the trip and not the destination that interested her husband.

And so it was. The passage to St. Genevieve proved difficult. The travelers were repeatedly delayed by low water and ice in the river. Near the mouth of the Ohio, they were forced to make camp for six weeks, shivering behind walls of snow with more than a dozen other stranded travelers. Audubon conceded later that this was as "dismal and dreary" an experience as one could imagine. Rozier, out of sorts and half-frozen, became the butt of many jokes. Audubon, predictably, made use of his time in the wild, diverting himself with fishing, shooting game, and getting acquainted with the local Osage Indians, who were friendly. The Indians showed Audubon trails in the woods and marveled at his shooting proficiency. His bird drawings entertained them enormously, and when they looked at the portrait Audubon made of one Osage, they all fell to the ground laughing.

Audubon was fascinated by flocks of swans, which seemed as confused by the frigid conditions as his campmates. The huge white birds would land and flatten themselves on the ice, as if swimming. They were hungrily watched by packs of wolves that made periodic attacks. This, Audubon thought, was a remarkable spectacle. The wolves would patiently stalk the swans at a distance, unable to comprehend that the sharp-eyed birds sitting so temptingly motionless were watching their every move. At last the pack would charge forward in a headlong snarl, only to watch the birds run off ahead of them, their huge wings pounding the ice so loudly it sounded like thunder until they became airborne.

Audubon was gone five months. Not long after the ice broke up, so did the partnership of Audubon and Rozier that had been agreed to in France with such high hopes for success in the New World. Audubon accepted some cash and several IOUs from Rozier in exchange for his interest in the inventory and headed home, traveling the last 125 miles on foot. When he arrived back at Meadow Brook in early April, he told Lucy that he wouldn't dream of taking her and Victor to St. Genevieve, which he said was smaller and more hopeless than Henderson. This wasn't true. St. Genevieve had more than 1,200 residents. There were at least twenty shops and a large church in town. Adjacent to the main business district was a seven-thousand-acre field that was jointly farmed by the whole population—the largest communal farm in America. Ferdinand Rozier stayed there, got married, and launched one of Missouri's most successful merchant families.

Of the many accomplishments achieved by anyone traveling the frontier in Audubon's time, staying alive was the most important and, at times, the least certain. Audubon spent years in the wilds of America, on horseback, in small boats, in terrible weather. He crossed the Atlantic Ocean many times. Dangers, both natural and human, abounded. But he claimed that the only incident in which he feared that his life was at risk from another person happened on his way home from St. Genevieve.

The weather had improved after Audubon left Missouri. Spring was breaking out across the countryside. He was alone, taking his time. He wore moccasins and carried only his gun and a small knapsack. One of the hunting dogs he owned at different times trotted at his side. After a long day following an Indian trace across a prairie, as the sun set and nighthawks zoomed overhead, Audubon was searching for a grove that might give him shelter for the night. He heard wolves howling in the distance. To his surprise, he happened upon a small cabin.

The owner turned out to be a tall, "brawny" woman. Audubon found her manner abrupt and was appalled at her slovenly appearance. But she said yes when he asked if he might stay the night, and soon he was warming himself by the fire. As his eyes adjusted, Audubon saw that they were not alone. A handsome young Indian was sitting motionless on the floor, his head in his hands. Audubon spoke to him in French. When the young man looked up, Audubon was taken aback to see that half his face was covered in blood. The Indian said he'd been hunting raccoons that afternoon when one of his arrows split as he drew his bow and shot violently backward, blinding him in one eye.

Unsettled, Audubon checked the time. On seeing the fine watch Audubon pulled from his pocket, the old woman was immediately entranced. She asked to hold the watch and offered Audubon dinner. Audubon ate his fill, fed some venison to his dog, and began considering a pile of animal skins as a possible bed when the young Indian started nervously pacing the room, exchanging odd looks with Audubon. At one point he pinched Audubon roughly on the side. As Audubon stared, the Indian drew a large knife and fingered its edge, again looking strangely at Audubon. Finally, Audubon got the message. Now he studied the old woman, who was still holding his watch. He asked for it back, wound it, and excused himself to go outside and see what the weather was—taking his gun along. Out in the dark, Audubon loaded balls in each barrel and checked his flints. He went back inside, called his dog over, and lay down, cradling his gun.

Presently two strapping young men, the old woman's sons, arrived and commenced drinking whiskey. The mother joined them. Audubon, hoping the trio would drink themselves into a stupor, tapped his dog—who seemed alert to a threat in the stale air of the little cabin. To his horror, Audubon saw the woman at last get up and, looking like an "incarnate fiend," put a long carving knife to a grindstone. Audubon felt a sweat break out on his body. The woman leapt up from the wheel, turned to her drunken sons and, screaming an obscenity, commanded them to kill Audubon and get his watch. Audubon rolled over to face them, cocking both barrels as he did so. Now the "infernal hag" walked unsteadily toward him. The Indian, evidently trying to help, struggled with the sons. Audubon was on the verge of standing and firing when the door burst open and two more large men entered the cabin. They turned out to be fellow travelers. Once Audubon explained the situation, the woman and her sons were tied up. The Indian danced merrily around them while Audubon and his new friends spoke long into the night, swapping tales of similar close calls. In the morning, they led the three would-be assailants—now sober and pathetic—into the woods and flogged them. Then Audubon burned the cabin to the ground before going on his way.

This episode—which was to become one of the stories that would help to make Audubon's reputation as a fearless frontiersman—is hard to swallow. The gothic setting, the lurid details, the spine-tingling escalation of danger, and the last-minute rescue are almost certainly embellishments of some event that, while it may have given Audubon a scare, was probably a more pedestrian confrontation. The half-blind Indian—whose presence at the cabin isn't explained—feels like a detail Audubon imported from another yarn. Still, something almost like this may well have happened to him. Audubon did stop at cabins in the wilderness on his travels, and not everyone he encountered would have been an upright citizen. Most likely, he decided to relate some actual close shave in the way any proper Kentucky storyteller would—with a boost to make it more entertaining. But of course it's impossible to say for sure. It always was with Audubon.

After his return from Missouri in the spring of 1811, Audubon made plans to open his own store in Henderson. He located new space in town and made a trip to Louisville for inventory. After three years on the frontier, things had not worked out the way he had hoped. The woods and the birds were wonderful. Audubon was now as strong and resourceful and knowledgeable in the wilderness as anyone. But his family's financial security steadily eroded, and as a businessman, Audubon had lost a little of his swagger. There was also the beginning of a change in his relationship with Lucy. During his long trip to St. Genevieve, Lucy had become indispensable as a companion to Elizabeth Rankin and a tutor to the Rankin children. The Audubons were invited to stay on at Meadow Brook, at least until the new store established itself. In a literal sense, it was now Lucy keeping a roof over their heads.

During the balmy interlude of a Kentucky summer, the Audubons lived in comfort. They were part of the social life of Henderson, such as it was, and they also communed with the wilderness stretching in every direction beyond the town's limits. When Audubon was not out hunting or drawing, he and Lucy often took to the fields together. Lucy, who was now twenty-four, still kept up with her energetic husband. Sometimes they would swim across the Ohio to the Indiana side and back, a mile-long round-trip. They enjoyed riding and were both in love with a remarkable horse named Barro. Audubon bought the once-wild mustang for $50 after trying him and finding that the ungainly-looking animal was a good jumper, a strong swimmer, and would stand still when Audubon shot at game from the saddle. Audubon rode him to Philadelphia and back on business, making side trips along the way that extended the distance to something like two thousand miles—at the end of which Barro appeared as fit as on the day they'd left.

The record of Audubon's comings and goings between Henderson and Philadelphia at this time is fuzzy. Evidently there were several trips, one of which was at Lucy's request. She asked Audubon to take her east to visit her family and to introduce them to little Victor. Always eager to travel, Audubon said they could leave almost immediately—on horseback. Lucy gamely agreed. Audubon rigged a seat on the front of his saddle where Victor, who was two, would ride. And they were off. At Louisville, they stopped after getting word that Lucy's brother, Tom Bakewell, was coming downriver in hopes of going into business with Audubon. Worried they might pass him by on the river, the Audubons checked into their former home, the Indian Queen, and waited.

It was November of 1811 when Tom finally got to Louisville. He had an exciting plan. Tom had been working in a mercantile office in New York and was now determined to open his own operation in New Orleans as a consignment agent for a trading company in Liverpool, England. He thought Audubon's French connections would be an asset in New Orleans. Audubon and Lucy were ecstatic. The deal was done on the spot. The new firm was to be called Audubon & Bakewell. Tom headed south. Audubon, Lucy, and Victor climbed on their horses. The weather was turning cold and the road home to Pennsylvania was long and difficult. Three grueling weeks later, they rode up the drive at Fatland Ford. Lucy, a stoic traveler, admitted that the rocky climbs and steep descents through the mountains had been almost too much for her.

"I can scarcely believe that I have rode on horse back nearly eight hundred miles," Lucy wrote to her cousin in England. "The country from

Louisville to Pittsburgh is flat rich woodlands; there are some cultivated farms which diversify the scene a little, but the chief part of the road is through thick woods, where the sun scarcely ever penetrates. We crossed a number of rivers and creeks. The rivers are all navigable and have their banks lined with great variety of Trees and Shrubs."

Lucy, thinking her cousin might want to trace their journey on a map, listed the main towns and cities they passed through before arriving at Pittsburgh and beginning the hardest part of the journey, across the mountains and on toward Philadelphia. The boulder-strewn roads, Lucy said, were "dreadful at all seasons of the year" and only her eagerness to see her family had kept her going.

Audubon stayed just long enough to ask for a loan from Lucy's father that Tom wanted to help launch Audubon & Bakewell. Then he was away again on Barro—first to Kentucky, where he would arrange trading partnerships in Henderson, and then down to New Orleans to meet up with Tom. It was on this ride that Audubon met a man named Vincent Nolte at a river crossing in the Alleghenies east of Pittsburgh. As Audubon told it, Nolte was riding a fancy horse that caught his eye. But when he drew near and complimented Nolte on his mount, Nolte impolitely suggested it was unfortunate that Audubon's was so inferior. Nolte then offered to meet Audubon for dinner at a hotel down the road, implying that he would wait for him to arrive. Unfazed, Audubon agreed. Nolte cantered off. Audubon gave Barro a kick and sped past, arriving at the hotel fifteen minutes ahead of Nolte—long enough to stable Barro and place two orders for trout for dinner. Nolte remembered their introduction differently, writing that he met Audubon in a hotel over breakfast one morning and thought him a strange but intriguing man. They had ridden on together, Nolte said, and took themselves and their horses downriver on the same flatboat out of Pittsburgh. Whatever the truth, the meeting between Aubudon and Nolte later turned out to be far more important to Audubon than he could have imagined at the time.

Lucy, pleased that her husband's business was going to reconnect them with her family, amused herself back in Philadelphia by imagining how fine life in New Orleans would be after several years in lesser places. But when Audubon reached Henderson, he was met with news from Tom that their venture was on hold. A growing likelihood of war with England threatened to halt trade between the two countries. Rather than continue downriver, Audubon returned to Philadelphia to wait with

Lucy. For some reason he went by boat, reluctantly parting with Barro for $120. In April, the Audubons learned they were expecting another child. Soon after that, in June of 1812, war was declared, and Audubon & Bakewell abruptly existed only in the minds of its proprietors. The following month, Audubon rode into Philadelphia to become a naturalized citizen. In a moment of rare candor, he gave his place of birth as Les Cayes, Saint-Domingue.

10

KENTUCKY HOME

Plotus anhinga: The Anhinga, or Snake-Bird
It gives a decided preference to rivers, lakes, bayous, or lagoons in the interior, always, however in the lowest and most level parts of the country. The more retired and se-cluded the spot, the more willingly does the Snake-Bird remain about it.
—*Ornithological Biography*

ack down the Ohio went the Audubons. They started out on an ark, accompanied by Lucy's younger brother, William. Lucy, now well along in her pregnancy, rode serenely as Victor smiled and played at her feet, while Audubon watched the forest passing by. It was fall now. The river was low, so at Louisville Audubon bought a light but spacious skiff and hired two black oarsmen to speed them toward home.

The weather was still warm. Audubon later recalled that it was October, though possibly it was earlier. The woods were beautiful—long vines heavy with colorful fruits hung among the changing leaves. Sunlight reflecting from the river lit the trees from beneath more beautifully, Audubon said, than any description a poet might render. Sometimes, in places where the river widened and filled with islands, Audubon imagined himself motionless on a vast lake. In the daytime they passed by many slow-moving flatboats. The Ohio valley was teeming with settlers. Near the mouth of a tributary, where the river passed by a beech woods, there was a sudden clamor onshore. It sounded like an Indian war party. Quickly, and anxious not to make a sound, they put the boat ashore on the opposite bank and waited to see what would happen. After a while Audubon laughed. It was only a group of Methodists holding a camp meeting. The rowers pulled at the oars again and they moved on. Audubon went ashore periodically to shoot a turkey or a grouse. They ate well. At night they watched the moon rise and listened for owls ghosting by overhead. There were many deer swimming across the river, a sign, Audubon knew, that winter was coming. He could not have guessed the catastrophe awaiting them in Henderson when they arrived.

The Audubons again went to stay with the Rankins at Meadow Brook. After a couple of days, Audubon opened the trunk in which he had carefully packed away more than two hundred of his drawings almost a year before. A pair of Norway rats was living in the chest, having raised a family of little rats that were now nested in the chewed and urine-soaked shreds of his drawings. Although some other drawings survived—how many isn't known—there were more than one thousand individual birds depicted on the ruined sheets in the chest, the bulk of all the work he had completed. Audubon could not believe his eyes. He felt a rush of heat and pain in his head as he staggered away from the trunk. For a few days he could not sleep and wandered around dazed. Finally, calling on a reserve of what he called his "animal powers," Audubon picked up his gun and his pencils and walked toward the woods to start over. Quickening his pace over the brittle leaves, Audubon told himself he was lucky. He had lost a treasure beyond calculation. But fortune had invited him to remake his drawings. He would make them even better now.

The loss of his paintings marked a turning point in Audubon's life. And his response to the incident signaled that his drawing was more to him than an idle hobby. He was by nature an irrepressible personality, but Audubon's innate optimism had never before been tested so harshly. Yet within a matter of days, he bounced back and resumed drawing almost as if nothing had happened. Years later, after his work became celebrated across half the world, Audubon insisted that at this stage of his life he had still not considered the possibility of publishing his art. This can't have been true. There is evidence to the contrary, and on at least one occasion long before he attempted it, he admitted to an ambition to sell his work. Audubon knew how good he was and he knew, too, that there was a public appetite for the wild images of America that crowded his brain and filled his portfolio. What does seem believable is that Audubon did not then see drawing as his life's work. He still thought of himself primarily as a shopkeeper. Despite the setbacks he'd already experienced, Audubon had yet to suffer the abject failure at business that would force him to earn a living through his art. But it was coming.

In starting over, Audubon also crossed a creative divide. At Louisville, Audubon had still been consumed by technical considerations in his drawings—in mastering his pencil and chalk and watercolors—until he had at last made his birds look like the real thing. But at Henderson and during the months he'd spent in Philadelphia, Audubon's field of vision had widened. He'd begun to set his birds in motion. For the first time, he'd made successful drawings of birds in flight. And his compositions became more complex. There were now more elements—more tree branches and flowers in the background, and more birds interacting with one another. With the loss of his earlier drawings, Audubon now began the long task of assembling a portfolio entirely in his new style.

Audubon then did something no one would have dreamed him capable of at this critical juncture. Just when it seemed he would most want immersion in his drawing, Audubon showed an interest in his business. Tom Bakewell had arrived at Henderson about this time, having walked most of the way from New Orleans, where he had abandoned the Audubon & Bakewell trading company. But he still wanted a partnership with his brother-in-law, and together they set about reestablishing the store in Henderson. Surprisingly, business improved steadily. In November, Lucy gave birth to a boy. They named him John Woodhouse. Unlike his sturdy older brother, John Woodhouse was delicate and fussy. This was hard on Lucy and also added to their imposition on the Rankins, who were now putting up the four Audubons plus Lucy's two brothers. Audubon, determined at last to find Lucy a real home of her own and to be closer to his shop, bought a house in town recently owned by a doctor. It was a story-and-a-half log cabin with a big front porch. Audubon bought several adjacent lots that included a small orchard and a pasture where they could raise some livestock and also maintain the ever-changing menagerie of wild animals that he brought home from his travels.

Audubon continued to hunt and draw, and to make long trading trips that usually turned into quests for new birds. But he was no longer the neglectful or inept merchant he'd been in his first years in Kentucky. Although its population was still well below one thousand, Henderson was beginning to grow. The state of Kentucky named the town to its roster of tobacco inspection stations, and Henderson became one of the country's leading tobacco markets. Audubon found domestic goods and hardware increasingly in demand, locally and from settlers passing by on their way down the Ohio. Early in 1814, Audubon and Tom Bakewell opened a second store at Shawneetown, Illinois, about thirty miles downriver. They hired a manager to run it and immediately began earning back several thousand dollars a year. Audubon tried his hand at real estate speculation and did well, shrewdly subdividing lots in Henderson at a profit. In a six-year period, Audubon bought and sold property worth $50,000. Lucy found that her husband's frequent long absences were now more tolerable. They evidently acquired or at least had occasional ownership interests in several slaves who tended the Audubon compound. The Rankins built a house in town and became frequent guests of the Audubons, restoring Lucy's sense of social position. She sent for her pianoforte, which was shipped from Fatland Ford, and also began acquiring a library.

In this small place, the Audubons loomed large. John James was known as a well-to-do man who was also a clever woodsman quick to accept a physical challenge of any kind. Fencing wasn't a popular diversion on the frontier, but people in Henderson knew of Audubon's skill and were impressed when he once easily bested a traveler who had boasted of his prowess with the broadsword. Another time, the whole town turned out to see one of the new steamboats plying the Ohio and were alarmed and then thrilled when Audubon dived off the ship's bow, disappeared for a time, and finally surfaced astern after swimming the length of the keel underwater. Lucy, meanwhile, was one of Henderson's leading lights, an object of admiration and envy.

The Audubons kept an unusual house. Their rooms were filled with music and books and lively talk of commerce and nature. Outside their door, the grounds were overrun with a motley assortment of beasts. When Audubon found a very young turkey cock separated from its broodmates in the woods and brought it home, the bird became tame—and popular with people in the village after it developed a penchant for following anyone who spoke to it. The turkey grew large, refused to commune with Audubon's domestic turkeys, and could be seen silhouetted against the sky each evening on the ridgetop of the Audubon house, the only place it would roost. During one of the turkey's absences into the forest, Audubon happened upon it while out hunting. He would have shot it had not his dog recognized the bird, which sat unperturbed while the two of them walked up to it. Lucy tied a red ribbon around the bird's neck to alert local hunters that it was not a member of the wild flock. But it was eventually killed by a man who didn't see the ribbon until he picked up the bird. The man apologetically brought the turkey to Audubon, who probably ate it.

Prior to its demise, the turkey had for a time shared the Audubon compound with a trumpeter swan. Audubon was not fond of swan meat—only the cygnets were palatable, he said—but he hunted them enthusiastically. One day he wounded a large male, shooting off a wingtip. Unable to fly, the bird landed on a pond where, after some exertion, Audubon managed to capture it. Knowing the huge white bird would amuse Lucy and the boys, Audubon carried it home—though not without a struggle, as it was a two-mile hike and the swan, which was strong, did not go willingly. Audubon cut off the damaged wingtip and confined the swan in a fenced area. The family named it Trumpeter. After a while it got used to captivity, though it could never quite be described as "tame." The swan often escaped and would noisily chase after Audubon's other animals—as well as the children, the servants, and any of the townspeople who got in its way. On a rainy night after almost two years with the Audubons, Trumpeter walked out a gate that had been left open and was never seen again.

There were more birds in Audubon's time. How many can only be guessed at. It's natural to think of all wild animals as less numerous now than they were before waves of human settlement swept over the continent. But this is not true in all cases. White-tailed deer, for example, thrive in areas converted to agriculture and also in the suburbs. There are more of them now than at any time in history. Wolves and bears and bison are increasing in number again and expanding their ranges. Bird populations are especially fluid, both from one season to another and over long periods. In the past two centuries, the forest in the eastern half of North America has been logged off and regrown several times. In each phase, the number of birds and the composition of species have changed. When Audubon lived in Kentucky, birds that require large, uninterrupted expanses of forest to breed in—like warblers—were more numerous. But the brown-headed cowbird, one of a number of "edge" species now more common across North America, was probably less populous then because it prospers along the interface between forest and land that has been cleared. Some species of birds have been introduced to North America from Old World and Asian stocks since Audubon's time. There were no house sparrows or starlings in America when Audubon lived. Now they're everywhere. Audubon never saw a ring-necked pheasant, the spectacularly beautiful Eurasian import to the northern prairies in the late 1800s that has since become one of America's most sought-after game birds.

Waterfowl, which crowded the autumn skies over North America two hundred years ago, are today much reduced, their numbers a mere remnant of what they were before market hunting and widespread destruction of wetland breeding habitat took place. No one alive today can really imagine what the former immensity of birds in America must have been like to see. The best descriptions there are to go on are those of naturalists like Wilson and Audubon.

Audubon was captivated by all birds. But ducks seemed to affect him with unusual power. He spent countless fall days, in the cold and dark on either side of dawn and in the ochre of dusk, haunting the sloughs and oxbows along the Ohio River near Henderson, studying and shooting ducks that streamed into Kentucky as winter descended in the North. Sometimes he went with his brothers-in-law, Tom and William, renewing their shared passions from earlier exploits on Perkiomen Creek. Other times, Audubon was a solitary figure in the murk of a duck day. He was never happier than when he was lying in wait with his dog and gun on a reedy shoreline as ducks materialized out of the gloom and settled on the water. Ducks, with their powerful, steady flight and splashy landings and takeoffs, were a parade of aerial variation. Audubon was beguiled by their behavior and by their multitudes. Because hunting was central to his ornithology, Audubon never made much of a distinction between sport and science, and, when it came to ducks, his blood ran hot. Here's how he described hunting the green-winged teal, a small, speedy duck that arrived in the Kentucky wetlands early each autumn:

He sees advancing from afar, at a brisk rate, a small dark cloud, which he has some minutes ago marked and pronounced to be a flock of Green-winged Teals. Now he squats on his haunches; his dog lies close; and ere another minute has elapsed, right over his head, but too high to be shot at, pass the winged travellers. Some of them remember the place well, for there they have reposed and fed before. Now they wheel, dash irregularly through the air, sweep in a close body over the watery fields, and in their course pass near the fatal spot where the gunner anxiously awaits. Hark, two shots in rapid succession! The troop is in disorder and the dog dashes through the water. Here and there lies a Teal, with its legs quivering; there, one is whirling around in the agonies of death; some, which are only winged, quickly and in silence make their way toward a hiding-place, while one, with a single pellet in his head, rises perpendicularly with uncertain beats, and falls with a splash on the water. The gunner has charged his tubes, his faithful follower has brought up all the game, and the frightened Teals have dressed their ranks, and flying now high, now low, seem curious to see the place where their companions have been left. Again they fly over the dangerous spot, and again receive the double shower of shot.

Audubon wrote this many years after the fact, and in a country far from Kentucky. But the vividness of the scene was undiminished by time. This is the kind of story duck hunters like to tell over and over, so that the reliving becomes inseparable from the original experience. It was not surprising that Audubon could recall decades later the chill of the morning air on a Kentucky marsh, or the fact that it was not unusual in those days for a single hunter to kill more than seventy teal in an outing.

Many a hunt lingered forever in Audubon's thoughts. And while he adopted a sometimes heartless posture in writing about them, Audubon was always precise in his observations about a given species' behavior and appearance. Once, while watching mallards feeding on a pond, he saw two of them shot with a rifle through an odd chain of events. Some of the ducks were dabbling in the shallows, scooping up plants and small aquatic animals from the bottom muck. Their feet churned and their tails rode straight up in the air. Others ducks executed small leaps from the water to pull down seeds from the reedtops. Anyone who had hunted mallards was familiar with their ability to leap almost vertically into the air from the water, but Audubon must have been one of the first naturalists to have recorded this kind of jumping for food. While watching this unusual performance, Audubon also noted that a few of the "older" birds had waddled into the forest to help themselves to acorns and beechnuts littering the ground. Suddenly a shiver passed through the flock and their contented mewlings ceased in unison. Wary, necks stiffened and heads turning nervously, the ducks listened to the sound of footfalls in the woods. Just as they were about to take flight, the ducks saw that it was only a bear snuffling through the mast. For a moment, the birds were at ease again—until the bear without warning bolted and disappeared among the trees. Presently, another figure appeared, this one darting from tree to tree in an effort at concealment. It was an Indian, whom Audubon at once perceived had been trailing the bear. Now the Indian was left to consider the lesser quarry floating in a huddled mass some distance from shore. Audubon was sorry for the Indian's dilapidated gun and the ragged blanket that was his only clothing. But he admired the man's sure actions, which he sat and watched for some time. He wondered if the mosquitoes, still hungry at the last of their season, were tormenting the Indian as he slowly brought up his gun. He wondered if the ducks would flee at the last second. An instant later smoke flashed from the rifle and the report traveled across the pond as the flock sped into the air, leaving behind two birds dead and upside down on the water. The Indian waded cautiously into the pond to retrieve his dinner, testing the depth of the water and the firmness of the bottom as he went. A short while later, as Audubon still looked on, the Indian kindled his fire and plucked his ducks, setting aside a feather or two with which to clean his gun before finishing up his meal and melting back into the forest.

Audubon could not decide whether with some birds it was more amusing to shoot them or only watch them. He loved woodcock. The woodcock is a medium-sized, snipelike bird with a plump body, strong stubby wings, a long bill, and large eyes that sit high up on either side of its head. Woodcock feed on worms and are migratory—though, as Audubon observed, they fly not in flocks but in long lines of individuals that arrive at one place so rapidly—and often at night—that their sudden appearance en masse can make it seem as if a large number were traveling as one. Audubon liked to stand on the bank of the Ohio in the evening when the woodcock were coming through and listen to them whiz by one by one, their dark forms flying over the broad river like rockets. The birds' preference for boggy areas and their rapid, erratic flight made them difficult to hunt. The hunter inexperienced with woodcock, Audubon wrote, shoots too fast or not at all, in which case "the game is much better pleased than you are yourself."

As he had at Louisville, Audubon threw himself into the local pastimes. He was no snob. One of his favorite pursuits at Henderson was

trot-line fishing for catfish—a sport, if it could be called one, that required no skill at all. Audubon, usually with a friend or two, would run a
thick, cotton line some two hundred yards long out into the Ohio. The
end was weighted down with a large stone. A hundred shorter lines were
fastened to the main line at intervals, and each of these had a hook at its
tip. For bait they used live toads. In May, prime catfishing season, toads
were in such abundance around Henderson that it was easy to catch a basketful. This, even Audubon admitted, was quite a few damp, warty toads
in one place—enough to make a lady swoon, though he reported that this
was not a problem in Henderson, where there were no "tragedy queens"
or "sentimental spinsters."

The toads were hooked through the skin of their backs so that they
would wriggle enticingly once submerged, though catfish are fond
enough of dead flesh that it would seem a small matter whether the bait
was alive when it went in the water or how long it stayed that way. The
trot-line was left in place for hours at a time. Or days. The fish were periodically hauled in and the lines re-baited. In times of high water and difficult currents, Audubon sometimes baited a single line and cast it into
the river, tying his end to a springy tree branch and leaving it to do the
work. Audubon enjoyed all this, he said, because it required none of the
patience of other styles of fishing. He could bear fishing for trout with a
rod, Audubon wrote, only if he could count on catching at least "fifty or
more in a couple of hours."

But even in such humble activities, Audubon was a determined naturalist. The same account in which he described this lazy man's technique
included a meticulous morphology of the catfish they caught:

> The form in all the varieties inclines to the conical, the head being
> disproportionately large, while the body tapers away to the root of
> the tail. The eyes, which are small, are placed far apart, and situ-
> ated as it were on the top of the forehead, but laterally. Their
> mouth is wide and armed with numerous small and very sharp
> teeth, while it is defended by single-sided spines, which, when the
> fish is in the agonies of death, stand out at right angles, and are so
> firmly fixed as sometimes to break before you can loosen them.
> The catfish also has feelers of proportionate length, apparently in-
> tended to guide its motions over the bottom, whilst its eyes are
> watching the objects passing above.

Audubon was a close student of the Ohio River itself. The river had its own personality, and the mood of its waters varied with the season. Audubon was especially interested in spring flooding. Melting snows caused the river to rise every spring, of course, but Aububon noticed that in some years when the snow in the Allegheny Mountains was unusually deep and the weather turned suddenly warm, heavy spring rains were also more likely—and that this combination produced floods in which the river rose and overtopped its banks. Henderson, famously high, never went under. But great expanses of the lowlands in the river valley did, and these areas Audubon eagerly explored by canoe. Paddling over the sluggish, silt-laden waters of the floodplain, Audubon gaped at the animals trapped on ridges of land that now became islands or waiting out the deluge in the highest trees. He saw many deer, bear, cougar, and lynx. Poor backcountry hunters often took this occasion to shoot the stranded animals for their pelts, leaving the carcasses to rot. It was like being in a different country while the water covered the land. Someone told Audubon about a cow that had swum out the window of a house that was built more than sixty feet above the river, while the family that lived there remained in the upper story.

You could never tell when the river would deliver a surprise. One day as Audubon walked along the bank of the Ohio in Henderson, he noticed a strange-looking man climb out of a boat and proceed up the hill toward town. Audubon later remembered the man as being fat and dressed in a loose, heavily soiled overcoat of yellow nankeen. Buttoned to the throat beneath it was a waistcoat of the same material, with enormous pockets. The man's tight pantaloons, meanwhile were buttoned to his ankles. He carried what appeared to be a bundle of weeds on his back. He had a long beard, an unusually broad forehead, and a mass of dark hair that hung past his shoulders. On seeing Audubon staring at him, the man approached and asked for directions to the home of a Mr. Audubon. When Audubon explained who he was, the man produced a letter of introduction saying, among other things, that Audubon was being sent an "odd fish." Audubon asked to see the fish. After a moment of confusion, the man—who was, in fact, a prominent naturalist and academic named Constantine Rafinesque—explained that *he* was the odd fish. Audubon, only slightly embarrassed, took him home.

As Lucy prepared dinner, the Audubons' unexpected guest relaxed a little, removing his shoes and pulling his socks down to hide the holes

at the heels. He said he'd walked a very long way before taking a boat
the final miles to Henderson. Audubon offered a change of clothes,
which Rafinesque politely declined. Audubon suggested they wash
up. Rafinesque did so "with evident reluctance." But as they ate dinner,
Rafinesque warmed to his hosts. He explained that he was on a field expedition in search of new and undescribed plants and animals. He was
clearly a man of great intelligence. And he was like Audubon in some
ways. They were nearly the same age. Rafinesque had been born abroad—
in Turkey—but was raised in France. His lingering accent nearly
matched Audubon's. A precocious student of natural history, Rafinesque
had read more than a thousand books by the age of twelve. He had been
overwhelmed by the natural wealth of America when he first visited in
1802. After a decade of further work and study in Sicily, Rafinesque
came back to the New World determined to explore all its corners.

Rafinesque had been told that Audubon included flowers and shrubs
in his drawings and was curious to see if there were any that were unknown to him. Audubon thought the man seemed impatient and skeptical—as if he were wasting his time with Audubon and not the other way
around. After dinner Audubon opened his portfolio, which Rafinesque evidently found impressive. At one page, however, he stopped Audubon and
declared—rudely it seemed to Audubon—that the plant depicted on it
did not exist. Audubon assured him that it did and offered to find it for
him the next day. But as it was still light out, Rafinesque begged Audubon
to take him right then. After a short walk, Rafinesque was holding several
examples of the plant in his hands and dancing a jig. Not only was it a new
species, he said, it was a whole new genus!

They sat up late that night, looking over Audubon's drawings and talking of natural history. A beetle flew near the candle on the table and Audubon grabbed it out of the air. It was a strong insect, he told Rafinesque,
so strong it could carry a candlestick on its back. Rafinesque said it
couldn't—whereupon Audubon put the candle on the bug, which marched
away with it. Rafinesque was dumbfounded. Finally they went to bed.
Audubon, who was lying awake thinking, was sure the whole house was
asleep when he heard a commotion in the guest bedroom. He ran down
the hall and threw open the door on a memorable tableau. Rafinesque,
naked and wielding Audubon's favorite violin, was swatting at several
bats that had entered his room. Audubon stared, uncertain whether to
laugh or to try to save his fiddle, which already looked the worse for

wear. Rafinesque, racing about, shouted that he was certain this was a new species of bat and that he must have specimens. Audubon shrugged and picked up the bow from his violin and, with a few swift fencing strokes, killed several bats. Then he went back to bed, more awake than before.

Rafinesque ended up staying with the Audubons for three weeks. Audubon gradually realized that, although he was generally smart and skeptical, Rafinesque could also be something of a credulous fool. As Rafinesque attempted to learn more about local flora and fauna, Audubon indulged his penchant for telling tall tales, supplying his visitor with a mixture of fact and hokum. He invented some mythical fish species, and even sketched a few of them for Rafinesque—who later reported the "discovery" of several of these new fish. One of them, the "Devil-Jack Diamond Fish," was described as being between four and ten feet in length. Audubon found some rock shavings that he offered to Rafinesque as examples of the Devil-Jack's armorlike scales. In his account of the fish, Rafinesque declared that it was impervious to bullets and that its scales emitted sparks when struck against steel. Rafinesque added that he had actually seen the Devil-Jack Diamond Fish, though "only at a distance."

When Audubon came home caked in mud one afternoon, Rafinesque asked where he had been. Audubon explained that he'd been hunting in a canebrake. In those days there were stands of native bamboo, or cane as the locals called it, around Henderson. Canebrakes were nearly impenetrable areas where the stalks, each one or two inches in diameter, grew to thirty feet in height. The cane was so densely packed together that the only way through was by cutting a path or by turning around and thrusting your body backward, heedless of your direction or of what you might encounter along the way. Rafinesque, eyes goggling at this description, said he would very much like to visit a canebrake. Audubon smiled to himself and said that would be no problem at all. Later, he wrote about what Rafinesque was in for:

If you picture to yourself one of these cane-brakes growing beneath the gigantic trees that form our western forests, interspersed with vines of many species, and numberless plants of every description, you may conceive how difficult it is for one to make his way through it, especially after a heavy shower of rain or a fall of sleet, when the traveller, in forcing his way through, shakes down upon himself such quantities of water as soon reduce him to a state of the utmost discomfort.

Audubon led Rafinesque out after breakfast a day or two later, taking him across the Ohio and into the woods on the Indiana shore. They walked a few miles through gentle woodlands and then came to a substantial canebrake. At first the going was easy, and Audubon thoughtfully hacked down a stalk here and there to make the passage even less difficult. But the stand grew thicker and their pace slowed. They turned their backs and shoved on, with Rafinesque pausing occasionally to pick up a plant he didn't recognize. When they came to a downed tree, Audubon and Rafinesque stood considering how best to get either over or around its immense crown when a bear hiding in the tree emerged with a snarl and rushed at them. Rafinesque turned to run, but only toppled into the cane, becoming hopelessly wedged among the stalks. As the bear hurried off, Audubon laughed at his companion, who was by now screaming for assistance to his feet. Once Audubon got him upright, Rafinesque suggested they go back the way they'd come. Nonsense, said Audubon, the worst is over.

And then the going got harder still. Audubon, watching the sky as slivers of it appeared here and there through the canetops, noticed it getting darker. A thick cloud "portentous of a thunder gust" moved over them. Audubon had hoped for as much. Panting and sweating profusely, Rafinesque struggled to keep up, aware now that he would be hopelessly lost on his own. As the rain started and then became a downpour, Audubon trooped on. He told Rafinesque to buck up and be a man, that they were almost at the edge of the brake—which he in fact knew to be at least two miles ahead. Drenched and despairing, Rafinesque begged for a rest. Audubon obliged, and offered Rafinesque a drink of brandy to steel his resolve. Off they went again. Rafinesque threw away his plant specimens, laboring with each breath in the oppressive air. Being in the canebrake in the rain felt like drowning. Audubon, smiling, with leaves and mud plastered to his sodden leather hunting shirt, kept going, bending their course slightly but steadily, taking Rafinesque in a series of wide circles. Eventually—and in consideration of the possibility that he might actually get them lost—Audubon led Rafinesque back to the river, where he blew his horn to summon a ferry to take them back across.

Despite Rafinesque's gullibility—or maybe because of it—Audubon grew fond of him. It was disappointing a short time later when the awkward visitor abruptly disappeared without so much as a word of goodbye. After a while a letter from him arrived, informing Audubon that he was well and extending his thanks for everything.

Rafinesque continued downriver and in the end reported the discovery of more than two hundred species of animals—bats, snakes, lizards, rats, and a great many fishes among them. He also collected more than six hundred plant species and estimated that at least a tenth were previously unknown. Rafinesque eventually became a professor of natural history at Transylvania University in Lexington, Kentucky, where he was forever an object of amazement to his students, who found him a ridiculous genius.

11

LEGIONS OF THE AIR

Ardea herodias: **The Great Blue Heron**
Its sight is acute as that of any falcon, and it can hear at a considerable distance, so that it is enabled to mark with precision the different objects it sees, and to judge with accuracy of the sounds which it hears. —*Ornithological Biography*

Audubon's determination to survey the natural history of American birds—however vaguely formed at this stage of his life—was apparent in the attention he paid to every species he encountered. Each bird possessed a distinct personality that Audubon fixed in his mind.

The cedar bird—now called the cedar waxwing—was a glutton. Audubon found that the cedar bird was especially fond of sugary fruits, like the berries found on the red cedar or mountain ash. With an abundant supply of berries, cedar birds sometimes ate until they were rendered temporarily flightless and could actually be caught by hand. Once, Audubon wounded several cedar birds. Hoping to nurse them back to health, he put them in a cage and fed them apples—only to watch the birds gorge on the fruit until they suffocated. When he dissected the birds, they were packed with apples "to the mouth."

Audubon thought goldfinches and purple finches were among the smartest birds. They learned a trick for escaping from "bird lime," a sticky substance that was used to capture small birds. When a goldfinch landed on a twig Audubon had coated with bird lime, he saw that the bird recognized its predicament at once. But instead of struggling, the bird pressed its wings against its body and fell backward, so that it hung upside down. Gradually the glue began to give, stretching into a long strand—

like the filament of a spider's web—until the goldfinch perceived it was about to break, whereupon it gave a flap of its wings and flew off.

Everything about the great horned owl interested Audubon—from its sailing flight to its "ludicrous" mating ritual, a weird, hopping dance that the male initiates and the female then mimics as the birds snap their bills at one another. Audubon loved birds of prey, and in his drawings he often depicted them in full, fearsome attack mode—stooping on small birds or carrying off their bleeding victims in the grip of razor-sharp talons. The great horned owl affected him differently. Audubon recorded that the owl hunted several species of large birds—such as young turkeys, grouse, domestic poultry, and various ducks—as well as just about any kind of small mammal. But his portrait of this owl, easily the eeriest of all his images, shows a pair perched passively on a mossy limb. With their enormous, haunted eyes staring straight off the page, the birds look imperious, almost affronted—stony monuments to everything wild that stood before the onrush of humanity across America.

Audubon had probably seen something very much like the look he imparted to the great horned owl. He discovered that he could get quite close to the bird in broad daylight, but that on cloudy days the owl was quick to detect danger. If they were happened upon near the bank of a river, owls invariably flew to the opposite bank—a tactic Audubon felt certain the bird understood "renders its pursuit more difficult." Audubon once almost got himself killed hunting owls when he happened to shoot one in a boggy willow thicket. Rushing to pick up the bird, Audubon failed to notice the sponginess of the earth beneath his feet until he all at once sank up to his armpits in quicksand. Feeling himself settling further into the ooze with each breath, Audubon froze. Fortunately, he was not alone that day. He called out to his companions, who managed to extricate him just in time.

Audubon always noted the flight pattern of each bird, as well as its style of nest. These, after all, are the elemental aspects of life as a bird. He thought it ironic that the nighthawk actually spends most of its time aloft during the day and usually roosts early in the evening. Audubon also maintained that no other bird could rival the nighthawk for aerial stunts, especially those performed by the male during courtship—the time Audubon invariably referred to as the "love season." The signature maneuver of the male nighthawk is a death-defying plunge from a great height. With its wings flared back, the nighthawk dives toward the earth at a steep angle as the watching female glides through the air nearby. At the last instant, only a few feet above the ground, the nighthawk thrusts its wings sharply downward, reversing direction and creating a loud, concussive *pop*, which Audubon likened to the sound of a sail filling and snapping taut in the wind. For all its acrobatic grace in the air, though, the nighthawk was a disappointing nest maker. The female, Audubon observed, lays her eggs anywhere—on bare ground, a rock, a high spot in a plowed field—without so much as a twig or a scoop of dirt added. Because the nighthawk's legs are small and set far back on its body, the bird can't stand or even perch, Audubon said, without resting its breast on the ground or a branch—an awkwardness that necessitates its landing "sideways" in a tree. A nighthawk thus at rest was easily approached. As always, Audubon's researches on this bird had a pragmatic side. Nighthawks, he noted, are good to eat.

American white pelicans were numerous around Henderson in the fall. Audubon observed them in large flocks sitting on low islands or swimming in the river shallows, often so densely packed together that he killed several at a time with a single discharge of his gun. Although Audubon found all birds beautiful, he considered the white pelican unusually handsome. This was due in part, he thought, to the bird's careful grooming of its plumage, which was frequently passed feather by feather through its long bill when the bird was at rest. Audubon was impressed at how different the bird was from its cousin, the brown pelican, in the way it fished. White pelicans, he said, never dive upon their prey from the air but instead swim after fish and sweep them up by extending their necks and thrusting their heads underwater. Sometimes a flock hunted together in a militaristically choreographed group deployment. One Indian summer afternoon, as the sun lowered and the day cooled, Audubon watched a flock of white pelicans lazing on a sandbar. The forest was changing its colors and the red of the sunset touched only the tops of the trees. A commotion started in a small bay a little way off from the flock, which was instantly alert. The birds waddled into the water, where their ungainly land movements disappeared and they began to glide forward across the current in a surging mass toward the place where a school of small fish had begun thrashing the surface. The fish, Audubon said, seemed at play. They made the water sparkle. As the pelicans approached, the splashing continued. The birds swam closer together and, nearing the shoal, spread out their wings so that they formed a solid wall pushing forward. Now the pelicans propelled themselves faster still, sending the fish fleeing ahead, into ever shallower water, herding the school toward its demise. When the fish were at last trapped against the shore, the pelicans moved in, heads lowering, and devoured them by the thousands.

Audubon made notes and kept journals of his field observations. Years later, when he was writing about America's birds, he consulted these records for the traits and the descriptions of each species, sometimes in conjunction with an examination of more recently killed specimens. But he relied, too, on his memory. However far he traveled from the lush forests of Kentucky, his days there went with him. Wherever he was, Audubon seemed always able to see the woods and the birds as he'd seen them as a young man. He could remember how white a pelican looked in the afternoon sun and how cool it was in the shade of a towering sycamore as he leaned against its smooth trunk. He took with him the feel of his gun pounding into his shoulder and rubbing against his cheek where it was pressed to the stock. He remembered what it was like when the stillness of a pallid dawn was split by the whistle of wings cutting through the air, sometimes like a gentle breeze and other times in a pro-longed *aaahhhh*, like the sound of silk tearing. Audubon could forever hear the calls and songs that rang through the trees, as well as the sounds of rivers and storms and horses. He could feel the pull of a swamp against his shins and recall the torment of mosquitoes and withering heat spells and terrible winters when life on the earth seemed to stop and the rivers ceased to flow. Much of what Audubon saw and remembered now exists only in remnants, and some of it is gone entirely. For everything that Audubon took from America—and he took a lot—he left behind a spir-ited portrait of a country that is no more.

The Carolina parakeet—or parrot as it was also known—was already in decline when Audubon began observing it in Kentucky, though its numbers had been so great that the bird was still seen in immense flocks across much of the eastern portion of North America. Like the passen-ger pigeon, the Carolina parakeet was disappearing in defiance of the usual precondition for extinction, which is rarity. Animals that go extinct typically shrink to very small numbers over a long period of time before they reach the vanishing point. Populations become isolated and contract to a handful of individuals, which are wiped out one by one. Usually this is a natural process. Species average about a million years on earth, and many more animals have gone extinct than exist today. But in the cases of both the Carolina parakeet and the passenger pigeon, the birds persisted in huge numbers right up to the time when they went very suddenly extinct. It's now believed that both species were adapted to survive and breed only in massive flocks of millions upon millions of individuals, so that even when many remained there were not enough. The last time anyone saw a Carolina parakeet in the wild was in 1905. The passenger pigeon had disappeared five years earlier. The very last individuals of both species died in zoos not long after.

The Carolina parakeet was one of the few species of bird that Audubon worried about. The only parrot native to North America, it was a large, noisy resident of the forest, as common at it was beautiful:

Bill white. Iris hazel. Bare orbital space whitish. Feet pale flesh-colour, claws dusky. Fore part of the head and cheeks bright scarlet, that colour extending over and behind the eye, the rest of the head and neck pure bright yellow; the edge of the wing bright yellow, spotted with orange. The general colour of the other parts is emerald-green, with light blue reflections, lighter beneath. Primary coverts deep bluish-green; secondary coverts greenish-yellow. Quills bluish-green on the outer web, brownish-red on the inner, the primaries bright yellow at the base of the outer web. Two middle tail-feathers deep green, the rest of the same colour externally, their inner webs brownish-red. Tibial feathers yellow, the lowest deep orange.

But loss of habitat and a great continuing slaughter—by market hunters after the bird's extravagant feathers and by farmers trying to save their crops from marauding flocks—devastated a species that many then regarded as a pest. Audubon, whose published drawing of the Carolina parakeet was from specimens he eventually shot in Louisiana, observed the bird in decline while he was still at Henderson. Carolina parakeets, he wrote, were fond of cockle-burs, the small, spiny fruit that is found, as Audubon noted, "much too plentifully" across the eastern and southern parts of America. Cockle-burs were—and still are—a great nuisance, sticking to clothing and livestock. The parrot ate cockle-burs with abandon, plucking them from the stem and then manipulating the bur while holding it with one foot until its "joint" was aimed at the bird's mouth—whereupon it would squeeze out the inner flesh and then drop the barbed husk to the ground. Anyone with cockle-burs on their property should have been glad to have Carolina parakeets alight and dig in, thought Audubon, though he was careful to add that while there was as yet no known use for the cockle-bur, it could not be assumed that it would not in the future prove useful in "medicine or chemistry," as had other plants thought to be of no value.

The problem for the Carolina parakeet, Audubon said, was that it loved every kind of fruit and grain "indiscriminately," corn being about the only farm crop it wouldn't eat. A flock of Carolina parakeets—think of a roiling, deep green ocean falling out of the sky—could lay waste to a large area of cropland. Farmers hated the birds and killed as many as they could. When feeding, the Carolina parakeet was oblivious to its surroundings and easily approached. Even after being shot at, the birds remained easy targets. Younger parakeets, Audubon reported, were "tolerable" table fare. But mainly the birds were shot just to be rid of them. Audubon described how farmers walked up to Carolina parakeets feeding on stacks of grain and shot them until the farmers got tired of it. At the sound of gunfire, the round of killings began:

All the survivors rise, shriek, fly round for a few minutes, and again alight on the very place of most imminent danger. The gun is kept at work; eight or ten, or even twenty, are killed at every discharge. The living birds, as if conscious of the death of their companions, sweep over their bodies, screaming as loud as ever, but still return to the stack to be shot at, until so few remain alive, that the farmer does not consider it worth his while to spend more of his ammunition. I have seen several hundred destroyed in this manner in the course of a few hours, and have procured a basketful of these birds at a few shots.

Carolina parakeets issued a sharp, screeching call—a "scream" to Audubon's ears—that was hard to endure at close range. Although they could be tamed by being repeatedly dunked in water, a lamentable practice with which Audubon was evidently familiar, Carolina parakeets could not mimic human speech and never gave up their own call, which made the birds "so disagreeable as to render them at best very indifferent companions." The bird was wild and wanted to stay that way.

In the fall of 1813, while on his way by horseback from Henderson to Louisville, Audubon saw a low smudge in the sky, at first like a dark cloud, pulsing and growing larger. Presently he heard a rumble, and in the same moment the smudge became a surging mass of dark points. It was a flock of passenger pigeons, flying directly at him. There seemed to him to be a great many birds, even by passenger pigeon standards. Passenger pigeons were almost certainly one of the most abundant bird species to have ever lived. A darkly beautiful, medium-sized bird, the passenger pigeon looked like a slightly larger version of the rock dove—the bird we know as the common city pigeon—only more richly colored. Its sleek, rounded head was slate-blue, as were its shoulders and back. This coloration blended into a deep reddish-brown on the chest. Seen at a glance, the passenger pigeon looked purple. From the moment European settlers arrived in North America, they were awestruck by the incredible numbers of "wild pigeons" that traveled in immense groups, ceaselessly traversing the continent in search of food. So huge were these flocks that they were more like storm systems than assemblages of birds, and they moved with the speed and power of hurricanes. Alexander Wilson reported seeing a flock that he estimated at more than 2 billion individuals.

As the line of birds approached Audubon, he climbed down from his horse and made an attempt to count what at first seemed to be successions of discrete flocks. But he soon lost track, as the "flocks" merged into an endless, indistinguishable black column proceeding across the sky, lengthening, and stretching out toward the opposite horizon. Mounting his horse and moving on, Audubon found the pigeon numbers increasing as he went. Although it was midday, the sky darkened. Audubon said it reminded him of an eclipse. Pigeon droppings fell like snow, and Audubon felt himself lulled into something like a trance as he listened to the rush of wings overhead.

Audubon rode on, surprised that not a single bird landed or even strayed near the earth. There was no acorn mast in the area, and Audubon concluded that the pigeons were in transit, flying fast and high. Once, he tried a rifle shot on the flock, which was far out of range of his fowling gun. He was amazed to find that, despite their numbers, he could not hit a pigeon or even startle the flock with the report from his gun. By the end of the day, Audubon reached Louisville. The pigeons were still flying, their ranks undiminished. Near the river the pigeons descended— not alighting but merely flying low over the broad Ohio. Audubon found the riverbanks at Louisville "crowded with men and boys incessantly shooting." The whole population was "all in arms," Audubon said, destroying pigeons by the "multitudes." When he went to bed that night, the pigeons were still flying, the roaring columns of the great flock spanning the sky. The next morning, they were still passing overhead. So it went for three consecutive days, with no pause as the birds streamed past. Nobody in Louisville could talk of anything else. Everyone ate pigeon meat all day. The air smelled of pigeons.

The passenger pigeon was a force of nature that even the imaginative Audubon was unable to exaggerate. Fast and sharp-sighted, the pigeons flew with great purpose, sweeping past areas devoid of food. When traveling like this, pigeons ascended to great heights and spread out their ranks to maximize the area they surveyed below. When they encountered an area with food, the flock descended in waves, like a succession of breakers rolling onto a beach, with the rear guard flying ahead and landing, and then the next group coming up and over them, and so on, spilling across the countryside until they covered it.

Some years after seeing the big flock in Kentucky, Audubon made a series of ingenious observations about passenger pigeons that are probably as good a description of the species as we will ever have. Audubon, who sometimes dissected his birds and sketched their internal organs, determined that passenger pigeons completely digested their food in about twelve hours. He also learned that pigeons killed in New York were sometimes found to be full of rice. Since rice grew only as far north as the Carolinas, Audubon was able to make a rough calculation of the birds' sustained speed. To arrive in New York with rice still in their crops, the pigeons would have to travel around a mile a minute, Audubon figured. Sixty miles an hour is a speed we now know is typical of some larger ducks, like mallards and canvasbacks.

Audubon reasoned that, if you knew how fast passenger pigeons flew, you could estimate how many birds might be in a "typical" flock. As with many of his scientific observations—which eventually involved several expert collaborators—he may have had help translating his own impressions from the field into a more rigorous form. But there's no doubt he sensed the enormity of pigeon numbers in the size and speed of their hurtling masses. Imagine, Audubon wrote, a column of passenger pigeons one mile wide. This, he said, was a modest premise. Now assume that this mile-wide flock passes overhead in three hours. This, too, would be conservative. If the birds are flying at sixty miles an hour, then the whole flock could be visualized as occupying a rectangular area one mile wide and 180 miles long—or 180 square miles. Now, assume a density of two birds per square yard—with a body length of about sixteen inches and a twenty-five-inch wingspan, this seemed plausible to Audubon—and you can figure the total number of birds in this 180-square-mile "layer" of pigeons at just over 1.1 billion. If Audubon were even close in his estimates, then the big flock he saw pass by over the course of three days in Kentucky might have contained more than 25 billion birds.

When a flock of passenger pigeons dropped out of the sky to feed, a great devastation ensued. The birds denuded and destroyed large sections of forest, and when a flock's presence was discovered, people would travel from far away to harvest the birds by the thousands. Once, near the Green River in Kentucky, Audubon happened upon such a killing field. It was in a stand of old forest, with little understory, where a flock of pigeons had come to roost each night after foraging in the area by day. Audubon arrived on the scene about two weeks after the birds' first appearance. He found a section of forest three miles wide and nearly forty miles long, littered with broken branches and limbs that had sheared off beneath the weight of the birds. Smaller trees as big as two feet in diameter were broken off just above ground level. Dispersed across this blasted landscape was a band of hunters and farmers armed with guns and long poles. Wagons parked in lines waited to carry away the spoils of the hunt, and some of the farmers had brought their hogs to feast on the fresh kill. As the afternoon went by, piles of debris were readied, forming tall pyres to be set afire after dark, and these were augmented with smudge-pots filled with sulfur and torches made from tarry pine knots.

The sun set and the sky went black. At last Audubon heard a cry. "Here they come!" And with a roar of wings that was deafening, a torrent of pigeons poured into the forest, searching for places to alight. Soon what remained of the trees filled with birds that seemed to land on top of one another, their dark forms congealing into throbbing masses that rocked precariously above the earth until the limbs beneath them splintered and gave way and came crashing down, sweeping away everything below and carpeting the forest floor with a tangle of fallen and crushed birds. The fires and torches were lit. An evil light filled the woods. The air was acrid and thick with smoke and pigeons flying in all directions, passing and repassing through their own shadows. People flayed at the birds with poles, knocking down hundreds. As men began firing into the flock, Audubon found the chaos so overwhelming that he could not even hear the reports of their guns.

The mayhem lasted through the night. Pigeons continued to arrive at the roost, though Audubon noticed that fewer came after midnight. In the gray light of morning, wolves howled along the edge of the forest as mounds of dead pigeons were shoveled into the wagons and hogs rooted through the corpses, the surviving birds flying off to another part of the world. Audubon, appalled yet transfixed by this scene, reminded himself that passenger pigeon populations could quadruple in a single breeding season.

In fact, Audubon thought it inconceivable that hunting—even the kind of slaughter he'd witnessed at the Green River—could diminish passenger pigeon numbers. Audubon believed that only the continued clearing of the North American forest threatened this remarkable bird, which seemed to him a mobile but permanent part of the American landscape. Passenger pigeons in flight, high and untouchable, flowed through the sky like a single organic body. Audubon recognized that, despite their swarming numbers, passenger pigeons actually flew in a replicating formation—that is, each bird followed the one in front of it exactly. Anyone who has seen pelicans gliding in an undulating line along a beachfront has seen this graceful behavior, but in a flock consisting of hundreds of millions of pigeons rocketing through the air, the effect could be spectacular. When a hawk approached a passing flock of pigeons, Audubon said, the birds rushed together—like the current in a river being forced into a narrow gorge. The noise of their wings as the birds merged in the air was incredible. Folding into a column that appeared to be a "single mass," the flock veered through a series of wild maneuvers, diving toward the earth before leveling at the last instant and thundering along close to the ground, then rising in a vertical ascent almost out of sight, then twisting, falling, and diving again. The pigeons careening through the air at the point of attack thus initiated an elaborate pattern that was sustained as all the birds following behind repeated the identical twists and turns when they arrived

at the same point—even long after the hawk had departed. This left a living sculpture arcing across the sky. As thousands and then millions of pigeons retraced the pattern, a sinuous line of birds writhed overhead like
"the coils of a gigantic serpent."

Audubon was always on the lookout for new species—or, as he called
them, "non-descripts." It was a confusing business. As the country was
explored and settled, people encountered birds not yet known to Western science, although this in itself was not always easy to ascertain. Ornithologists on both sides of the Atlantic had often mistaken immature
specimens or birds with plumage variations for distinct species. Scientific
names competed with one another, as did a myriad of common names by
which birds were known in different locales. Audubon's enthusiasm for
discovering new birds was another indication that he was at this stage in
his life interested in more than just making handsome pictures. Although
his training in natural science was virtually nonexistent, Audubon was
generally familiar with published bird descriptions and, much more important to him, was by now on the most intimate terms with American
birds in the wild. On a chilly winter day in 1814, while returning up the
Mississippi River from a business trip, Audubon made an incredible
discovery.

    As Audubon huddled amid the cargo on deck to stay out of a cold
wind, he was entranced by flocks of ducks and swans passing high over
the river. The boat's skipper, a Canadian, noticed Audubon's attention
to the birds and offered to watch the skies with him. Presently, a large
bird sailed toward them, passed directly over, and continued on. The
Canadian was excited. It was, he said, the Great Eagle, a rare species
sometimes seen diving for fish on northern lakes—in the manner of an
osprey, or "fish hawk" as they were then commonly known. The bird also
occasionally followed hunting parties through the woods to feed on the
remains of freshly butchered animals. The Canadian told Audubon that
this eagle nested on rocky cliffsides. Electrified, Audubon listened closely
to the captain while he followed the bird with his eyes until it shrank to a
dark spot in the distance and vanished. Audubon was quite sure it was unlike any eagle he'd ever seen before and different from any that had been
formally described. He did not see the bird again for several years.

It happened again near the Green River, where Audubon had gone with friends to catch crayfish and quite unexpectedly stumbled upon a mated pair of the mysterious eagle. The birds were tending a nest on a precipice near the river's confluence with the Ohio. Audubon first noticed a splotch of droppings at the base of the cliff and assumed he was standing below an owl nest. But one of his companions more familiar with the area assured him that this was the home of a pair of "brown eagles." The birds were away from the nest. Audubon and his friends hunkered down to await their return.

Eagles, which undergo plumage changes as they mature and which are often seen only at a distance, can be difficult to identify. Audubon rarely had the use of binoculars or a telescope, and such equipment did not figure significantly in his fieldwork. It took long experience and good eyes to recognize the differences between eagles and several other large raptor species. Golden eagles and bald eagles were well-known as the prevalent eagle species in America. The term *brown eagle* was the common name for an immature bald eagle that did not yet possess its signature white head and tail. Alexander Wilson had complicated things by describing a species he called the "sea eagle," though he indicated a strong suspicion that it was in fact a juvenile bald eagle. This was based, in part, on Wilson's observation of a captive brown eagle that in its fourth year acquired a white head and tail.

But Audubon's friend at the Green River said this particular pair of birds, which was feeding a brood of chicks in their nest, didn't seem to conform to any description of an eagle. For one thing, they appeared to be much larger than any known eagle. He said he had also observed them diving for fish on the river—something he had never seen the bald eagle do. Bald eagles, as everyone knew, only got fish by stealing them from fish hawks. Audubon assured his friend that bald eagles did not nest on cliffs either. (Neither of these assertions was true, as Audubon himself would eventually learn.) Barely able to control his excitement, Audubon looked to the heavens. Two hours crawled by. Suddenly a noise issued from the nest—the whining of the chicks at the approach of a parent. Audubon, heart thumping, craned around in search of the great bird he was already daring to hope was the same one he'd seen on the Mississippi. At last he saw it, a huge eagle gliding toward the nest with a large fish gripped in its talons. As it delivered the fish to its young, the bird hung precariously from the edge of the rock almost in the manner of a swallow, with its tail spread and wings cupped against the cliff. Audubon was ecstatic. Presently, the second bird returned. It was even larger than the first—a sure indication, Audubon believed, that it was the female. She, too, carried a fish. But as she came near the nest, the eagle spotted Audubon and his companions and, with a shriek, dropped the fish and flew away with her alarmed mate. Audubon ran to retrieve the fish. It was a five-pound perch. Audubon made up his mind to come back the next day and shoot the eagles and their whole brood. But it was raining the following morning, and when he went back the day after that, the birds and their young were gone.

Two years went by. Audubon searched for the eagle in vain. Then, while walking from Henderson one day to visit Dr. Rankin at Meadow Brook, Audubon saw a large bird flush from a hog pen. The bird landed in a tree overhanging the road ahead. Audubon, his hands shaking, charged his gun and walked slowly forward. The eagle casually studied him, even as Audubon raised his gun and sighted down its barrels. Audubon fired and the eagle fell dead on the road. Thrilled, Audubon grabbed the bird and ran back to show it to Rankin—who confirmed that he had never seen an eagle like it.

Audubon saw this eagle only a handful of times afterward—twice near Louisville a few months later, where he tried unsuccessfully to shoot another specimen, and again at the confluence of the Ohio and Mississippi Rivers in the fall of 1821, where he watched transfixed as a pair flew majestically past his boat, heading downstream. He never saw the eagle again in the wild, though he did eventually examine a similar bird in a museum in Philadelphia. Audubon's drawing of the bird he shot at Henderson was a heroic profile showing the eagle perched on a promontory overlooking a sailboat serenely cruising by far below. Claiming his right as the first formal describer of the bird, Audubon thought the species deserved a grand name. Calling it the "noblest bird of its genus that has yet been discovered in the United States," Audubon proposed a name wreathed in glory—a name he said was synonymous with courage and the freedom that had blossomed in the New World. Audubon named it the Bird of Washington.

By the time Audubon published his description of the Bird of Washington, more than fifteen years after he had first seen the bird, it had morphed into an epic creature. Its flight, said Audubon, was quite different from the bald eagle's, and in fact it was so unlike a juvenile bald eagle that Audubon dismissed the possibility out of hand—though he took satisfaction in pointing out Wilson's misidentification of that bird as a so-called sea eagle. Instead, Audubon compared the Bird of Washington to the white-tailed or "cinerous" eagle, which he called the "true sea eagle." Apparently he was referring to one of the two Eurasian eagles that occasionally find their way into parts of North America. As if determined to complicate matters further, Audubon suggested that the white-tailed eagle in its juvenile phase was sometimes mistaken for an osprey. Even more perplexingly, he also gave "sea eagle" as an alternative name for the Bird of Washington.

Against this muddled backdrop of intermingled taxonomy, Audubon offered many characteristic differences in plumage, bill structure, and so forth between the Bird of Washington and the white-tailed eagle. One claim above all seemed to set the Bird of Washington apart from other eagles, however. Audubon gave a weight for the Bird of Washington of over fourteen pounds, a length of forty-three inches, and a wingspan of ten feet, two inches. That's about 50 percent larger than the biggest bald eagle. Not even the California condor, the largest North American raptor at well over twenty pounds, has that great a wingspan. Audubon thought it obvious that no other New World bird approached the magnificence of the Bird of Washington. "All circumstances duly considered, the Bird of Washington stands forth as the champion of America . . . henceforth not to be confounded with any of its rivals or relatives," Audubon wrote. "If ornithologists are proud of describing new species, I may be allowed to express some degree of pleasure in giving to the world the knowledge of so majestic a bird."

Audubon appears to have been wrong. There are only two American eagles, the golden eagle and the bald eagle. On closer examination—much of it by Audubon's critics—the Bird of Washington was widely dismissed as merely a juvenile bald eagle and not the undiscovered lord of the skies. However, this conclusion is also questionable, as nobody could ever explain the extraordinary size of Audubon's specimen. A printing error in Audubon's published account is doubtful—it's a stretch to think there would have been matching mistakes in the weight and the wingspan, the latter being given twice. The same would hold for Audubon's measurements in the field. It is all but inconceivable that Audubon would have recorded a wingspan of over ten feet if it were really closer to the six or seven feet typical of eagles. Nor does it seem plausible that he could have mismeasured *both* the wingspan and weight—or that in doing so he would have been off by exactly the same factor.

What is the truth? Perhaps Audubon, eager to claim the discovery of a major new bird, exaggerated the bird's dimensions. Maybe he had no field notes and simply made up the bird's size and weight long after the fact. Maybe the bird he shot just happened to be unusually large. Some species of birds vary considerably in size, especially from one region to the next. Canada geese, for example, range in size from small ones scarcely larger than a duck to giants that are nearly double the size of common specimens.

What about the chance that Audubon was right—that the bird he shot and drew actually was a separate species, possibly a rare individual from a remnant population that was in the process of going extinct? Could there have been a Bird of Washington? Almost nobody, from the time of Audubon's published account of the bird until now, has seriously considered that this might have been the case. But there are reasons, apparently overlooked, to think twice. And the evidence is all right there in Audubon's own account.

First, there was Audubon's observation of a mated pair with their young near the Green River. Though they could have been golden eagles—assuming Audubon was mistaken about their great size—these could not have been immature birds. Bald eagles tending a brood would have had the characteristic white heads. But more important is Audubon's drawing of the Bird of Washington. Like all of his bird drawings, it was done to life size—the image a precise copy of the bird placed against a measured grid. It was the same with his drawings of the bald eagle and the juvenile bald eagle, which he also eventually published. A comparison of the three images, using actual measurements of Audubon's original prints is revealing.

Although each of the three eagles is posed differently, it's obvious, even without measuring, that the Bird of Washington dwarfs the bald eagle. Looking at the three prints side by side, it's not even close. The Bird of Washington is positively massive, filling the double elephant paper to the edges. The adult and immature bald eagles, though large, impressive birds, occupy dramatically less space.

The measurements tell the same story. In Audubon's drawing, the adult bald eagle is 30¾ inches long. The juvenile bald eagle—which typically has a longer tail than the adult—is slightly under 34 inches long.

The Bird of Washington is 40 inches in length. The longest toe on the adult bald eagle is 3 inches long. On the juvenile, it's 2¾ inches. The longest toe on the Bird of Washington is 4 inches long. Most telling of all, the visible section of folded wing—that is, the outer portion of a single wing that you would see with the wing held against the body—measures 24 inches on the adult bald eagle, and 23⅝ inches on the juvenile. The same wing section on the Bird of Washington measures 29½ inches long. Assuming the inner wing sections and shoulders are proportionally larger, the wingspan of the Bird of Washington would thus exceed that of the bald eagle by about two feet—making Audubon's claim of a ten-foot wingspan plausible.

None of this is conclusive. If the Bird of Washington really was only a juvenile bald eagle, Audubon may be forgiven the error. Like other naturalists of his time, he made this kind of mistake over and over again. But nobody ever managed to do it quite so extravagantly—or to leave behind so many unanswerable questions—as Audubon did with the Bird of Washington.

By 1815, the Audubons' life on the frontier had settled into a comfortable rhythm. The stores at Henderson and Shawneetown did steady business, meeting the modest local demands for whiskey and dry goods including everything from fencewire to ammunition. Audubon hunted and fished and painted as he pleased, while Lucy managed a crowded, slightly chaotic household that often included friends and relatives who came out from Pennsylvania to sample life in the West. It was mildly astonishing to the Audubons, who could not have been happier, when most of these visitors retreated East, complaining of Henderson's discomforts and backward social life. Meanwhile, Audubon and Tom Bakewell, eager to expand their commercial interests, hit on the idea of building a steam-powered millworks that would grind grain and saw lumber. This was, to say the least, a highly speculative venture. The demand for such an expensive and technologically advanced mill was far from obvious. But with boatloads of settlers still coming downriver, the two men—especially the entrepreneurial Tom—assumed the need was imminent. They hired a mechanic, drew up plans, and began looking for property along the riverfront. Audubon, always easily excited by the hint of a golden opportunity conceived by somebody else, saw his horizons expanding in seemingly every direction: Lucy was pregnant again.

When the Audubons' first daughter was born that year, they named her Lucy. The baby's arrival coincided with what seemed the beginning of a new, even more luxuriant chapter in their charmed lives. It did not work out that way. Little Lucy was sick. Sick at first, as infants sometimes are, and then gravely sick. Nothing could be done for her, and in agony the Audubons watched their baby girl slipping away at the very time they also saw their own fortunes suddenly collapse in the construction and immediate failure of the mill. By the time little Lucy died in the winter of 1817, at the age of two, the heartbroken Audubons were facing financial ruin. They buried their daughter in a temporary grave in the garden until they could move her to a cemetery in the spring. They could not have imagined a crueler time. But it was coming.

12

EVER SINCE A BOY

Falco borealis: The Red-Tailed Hawk
It sails across the whole of a large plantation, on a level with the tops of the forest-trees which surround it, without a single flap of its wings, and is then seen moving its head sidewise to inspect the objects below.   —*Ornithological Biography*

The happy, prosperous life the Audubons had made for themselves on the frontier had been an early version of what later generations would call the American Dream. But this dream dies fast sometimes, and for the Audubons it did just that.

The mill was only part of the problem, though it was a big part. Almost from the time construction began on it in the spring of 1816, the mill devoured capital, grinding up Audubon's savings faster than it would ever go through wheat or wood. Audubon and Tom Bakewell took on investors as the project swelled. When it was done, the mill was gargantuan—standing some six stories high on the waterfront side, with clapboard siding and rows of double-hung windows looking out over the Ohio River. Crumbling remains of its stone footings still lie, like the partially excavated skeleton of a huge beast, on the mill site today, in what is now a tree-lined city park.

In his lifetime—and ever since—Audubon's failure in business was blamed on his frequent absences on hunting expeditions and his dislike of business routine. Whether he was lazy or merely at times careless about his responsibilities depends on how much value you attach to the paintings and the wildlife observations he was making when he was off in the woods—work that it is now all but impossible to put a value on.

Audubon himself guiltily alluded to his birding as time he had subtracted from business duties that did not hold his interest.

But the truth was more complicated. Audubon's business failure was in many respects caused by factors he could neither have foreseen nor controlled. A more charitable view is that Audubon's main fault was a misjudgment of how much and how fast he should expand in good times—a failing that is often the flip side of the American Dream.

The years following the successful conclusion of the War of 1812—some called it the second war of independence—brought an economic boom to the country. The war's interruption of trade with Europe had created a renewed overseas hunger for American goods—mainly livestock and agricultural produce, ranging from primary crops like cotton to specialty items such as ginseng and bourbon whiskey. England, meanwhile, suffered several crop failures in a row. Prices spiked and then settled back to a comfortable, seemingly stable level.

But the banking system in Kentucky was primitive and the currency fluid and unreliable. The Kentucky Insurance Company, formed in 1802 to insure river traffic, operated briefly as a regional bank. It was joined by the Bank of Kentucky and then by the federal banking authority, the Second Bank of the United States. In 1818, the Kentucky Insurance Company failed and the state chartered forty-six new banks to serve the region. They were soon derided as the "Forty Thieves." Speculative ventures in real estate, manufacturing, and milling multiplied. Barter was still a common way of doing business, and shopkeepers and farmers typically traded on credit between harvests. Credit had never been easier to come by. Soon the whole economy of the state was overextended—mired in debt and bloated with heavily leveraged enterprises that had little or no prospects for the future. Some aspects of the Kentucky economy were simply unsustainable, notably the increasingly unpopular slave trade in which free blacks were hunted down to be resold and black families were split apart and shipped south to work on plantations.

The collapse came in 1819, with the onset of a nationwide economic depression. In the Panic of 1819, prices fell sharply and businesspeople who owed money to creditors and investors could not pay. When the banks and then the state of Kentucky itself were asked for help, none was forthcoming. In fact, few people at that time construed intervention in economic matters as a responsibility of government. As for the banks, they went broke right along with the businesses they served. The Bank of

Kentucky began issuing its own paper currency. Its value fell almost as fast as it could be printed.

Against this background of economic malaise, Audubon had his own special problems. The mill, when it wasn't idle, produced far less revenue than expected. Then, in 1818, his father died in Nantes. After protracted litigation, Audubon and Rose, his half-sister from Saint-Domingue, ended up inheriting nothing from the elder Audubon. At the same time, Tom Bakewell, now married and with two children of his own, wanted to reduce his investment in the business partnership with Audubon—and was asking for the return of several thousand dollars he'd borrowed from his father. In a convoluted exchange of credits and countercredits that had become all too common in the depressed Henderson economy, Bakewell gave Audubon a note—supposedly worth more than $4,000—that he had accepted as payment for the *Henderson*, a steamboat Bakewell and the mill engineer had built in yet another get-rich-quick scheme. Weirdly, both Bakewell and Audubon also owed money to the boat's purchaser, a Mr. Samuel Bowen. In handing over the note to Audubon, Bakewell created an absurd closed circle of demands in which everyone owed everyone else money and nobody had either the wherewithal or the inclination to pay. It was up to Audubon to straighten out this mess by either getting cash for the note or seizing the boat. Meanwhile, the only viable collateral involved—the vessel—chugged off downriver with Bowen at the helm.

Audubon, rashly it would seem, gave chase. His pursuit of Bowen and the *Henderson*, which took him all the way to New Orleans and back, eventually culminated in the confrontation in which he stabbed Bowen. Their fight in the middle of the street near the mill, in turn, led to both criminal and civil proceedings against Audubon—in which he prevailed but from which he never recovered. The details of this episode—mostly long since lost or confused—do not add up to a coherent explanation for any of it.

Bowen evidently took off in the spring of 1819. Audubon, hastily equipping his skiff and bringing along a crew of two slaves to man the oars, followed. But why? Did he actually expect that a small boat rowed by two men could overtake a steamboat making a fast getaway? Besides, did Audubon know where Bowen was going? Once he reached the confluence with the Mississippi, Bowen could have turned north for St. Louis or south for New Orleans. Or he could have put in at any place in between.

More to the point, what was Audubon's purpose? Even if he managed to catch up with Bowen and get either the money or the boat, the change in his fortunes would have been negligible. It's possible—in fact it seems likely—that Audubon was looking for an excuse to get out of town. Harried by his creditors, still distraught about little Lucy's death, and generally miserable over his sorry state, Audubon probably welcomed a chance to disappear into the wilderness. And the longer the better.

Whatever his thinking, Audubon remained several steps behind Bowen all the way—both going and coming home. By the time he reached New Orleans and got himself before a judge to bring suit against Bowen—an action that for some reason required Audubon to post more than $16,000 in bonds—the *Henderson* had already been surrendered to other creditors. Audubon may well have wondered then if there was *anyone* in the whole wide world who was not owed money that one way or another had to come out of his pocket.

Audubon caught a steamboat back north—again just behind Bowen. Because of either a lack of funds or bad weather, Audubon decided to walk the more than two hundred miles home from the confluence of the Ohio and the Mississippi. He must have gotten to like this walk, since he made it two other times in his life—once a few years earlier after parting ways with Ferdinand Rozier, and then five years after this, when he headed north with Victor on his way to Philadelphia.

It was shortly after his return to Henderson—and to the fresh horror of still-mounting debts—that Audubon injured his right arm and then nearly killed Bowen one-handed when they fought in the street. A local judge, in dismissing an assault charge against Audubon, admonished him that he had committed a very serious offense in "not killing the damned rascal." Even so, it was apparent that Audubon had few friends left in town. By summer, Bowen was back on his feet and suing Audubon for $10,000. Audubon, sensing that the community would back his enemy, asked for a change of venue—which he got. After Bowen twice failed to appear in court to press his case, it, too, was dismissed.

But by then Audubon had lost everything. An old friend in Shippingport bought Audubon's house, a few pitiful real estate holdings, and what was left of his interest in the mill for just over $20,000. But with a depression on and the currency deflated, $20,000 wasn't what it used to be. And it was still only a fraction of what he owed. Adding to this crushing burden was the mixed news that Lucy was pregnant again. Audubon, feeling himself at the edge of the abyss, gave every penny he had to his creditors. Feeling compelled now to leave town for good, he asked Lucy to wait while he went to Louisville and figured out what to do next. Audubon left Henderson, alone and "poor and miserable of thoughts," as he later wrote. As he walked along the road leading east, Audubon scowled at the birds he saw. They looked, he said later, "like enemies."

Audubon seemed to have no clear concept of where he was going. He had a vague idea that he wanted to visit his mother and half-sister in France. In Louisville he was arrested and jailed over unpaid loans. A judge helped him file for bankruptcy—a move that in those days got you out of jail but not out of debt. Broke and distraught, Audubon made his way to Shippingport, where he was put up by friends. Lucy joined him there soon after. When he asked his hosts to recommend him for a job on a riverboat, they politely declined. Audubon had a look in his eye that seemed to warn everyone he was on the verge of disappearing forever.

This was Audubon's lowest moment. For the first time since he'd arrived in America, he had nothing. No money. No property. No job. No home. His father was dead and he was disinherited. His adopted mother was on the other side of the world. Audubon had nothing to look forward to but another mouth to feed.

And so he started drawing. Looking at a pair of chalk portraits he'd made for his hosts years earlier when he lived in Louisville, Audubon thought he might now try to earn a few dollars doing portraiture, possibly even taking on students in drawing. He was startled when a number of people responded to an advertisement for his services. Soon Audubon had a fair business going, painting and teaching. One of his specialties was portraying the dead. People liked to have deathbed portraits of their loved ones, and word spread that Audubon was good at them. He later even claimed that a Louisville clergyman had his recently deceased young daughter disinterred so that she could be drawn by Audubon. How this kind of work affected Audubon's already depressed mood can only be imagined.

After a few weeks of painting, Audubon had enough money to rent an apartment in Louisville. Fall was on the way. But before they could move,

Lucy gave birth—this time to another daughter. They named her Rose. While Audubon waited for Lucy to get back on her feet, it seemed to him that the world looked a little brighter. He was earning a living again. His family would shortly be in its own home once more. Watching his new daughter nursing at Lucy's breast, he told himself she was the most beautiful little girl he had ever seen. She lived for seven months.

By the time Rose died, Audubon had also run out of portraits to paint. Shippingport and even nearby Louisville needed only so many chalk likenesses of their citizens, and people didn't die fast enough for Audubon to make a living off that end of the business. A friend told Audubon about a temporary opening for a taxidermist at the new Western Museum of Cincinnati College. The job paid $125 a month. Audubon applied and was hired. For a few months the grieving Audubons lived something approximating a normal life in Cincinnati. Audubon liked his work stuffing fish and birds. More significantly, his portfolio of bird drawings—now virtually his only possession—was much admired by people at the college. Audubon was assured that it was a thing of great value, something that would one day bring him fame and fortune. Unfortunately, praise for his work was all Audubon received for his tenure at the museum. After repeatedly promising him his pay, the curator instead let him go in April of 1820. Lucy, who'd anticipated this, had already opened what amounted to a small private school where she taught a handful of students. Audubon's attempt to become a teacher at a local girls' school didn't work out, so he, too, advertised for his own students. A number enrolled, but the one whose talent caught Audubon's eye right away was a boy named Joseph Mason. Audubon thought he was "about 18 years of age." In fact, Mason was only thirteen years old. But he had a prodigious knowledge of botany and was a brilliant flower painter. Audubon admired Mason's work so much that he experimented with it, adding birds to the flowers and shrubs the boy willingly drew for that purpose.

Spring moved into summer. Audubon's thoughts—for the first time in a long time—turned to the future. His course seemed at last inevitable, or at least unavoidable. He began planning a trip through the country, one not unlike the expedition Alexander Wilson had been on when he had paused in Louisville a decade earlier. Audubon was determined now to complete his drawings and observations of American birds. He expected this would take him down the Mississippi, through

Arkansas, into Louisiana, eventually over to the Florida Keys, and then up
the East Coast. The precocious Joseph Mason was to go along, as company and as a collaborator. Lucy, whose suffering must have been all but
unendurable with two dead children and a bankrupt husband in the space
of only a few years, grimly agreed to stay on in Cincinnati, where she
would continue teaching and try to collect some of the salary Audubon
still had coming. With no money to pay his fare, Audubon spent months
looking for a boat captain who would give him passage in exchange for
his services as a hunter and scout. At last one said yes. His name was Ja-
cob Aumack. Aumack, a plainspoken man much accustomed to the hardships of frontier travel, was a prudent skipper known for the care he took
on passages downriver. He was in command of a large flatboat bound for
New Orleans with cargo and a slightly motley crew of four, as well as a
handful of passengers. Late in the afternoon of October 12, 1820,
Audubon and Mason stepped aboard and the boat was pushed out into
the current. Audubon, writing in his still groping English, confided to his
journal that the outcome of this enterprise was far from certain—though
he would do his best:

If God will grant us a safe return to our families our Wishes will
be most Likely congenial to our present feelings Leaving Home
with a Determined Mind to fulfill our Object=

Without any Money My Talents are to be My Support and My enthusiasm my Guide in My Dificulties, the whole of which I am
ready to exert to meet keep, and to surmount.

One more time, Audubon set off down the Ohio River in the hope that
something was out there for him in the vastness of the American frontier.
Only now he traveled chastened and without pretense, dressed in buckskin and homespun, carrying with him only his gun, his drawing kit, and
his precious portfolio, plus several letters of introduction. These he and
Lucy had managed to obtain from prominent Kentuckians whose names
and reputations might open doors far away. Such letters were then a common way of establishing contacts in new, sometimes remote places. One
of Audubon's letters was from Henry Clay, the future secretary of state

in the administration of John Quincy Adams. Clay, who had been elected to the House of Representatives from Kentucky, had also helped negotiate the Treaty of Ghent, which ended the War of 1812. He would eventually run (three times) for the presidency, but at the moment was better known as one of the brokers of a deal in the Congress to give equal representation to free and slave states—an arrangement dubbed the Missouri Compromise. Clay was one of the most famous men in America.

In his short letter, Clay stuck to the most general sort of endorsement, "recommending" Audubon to government officials and private citizens, while rather pointedly mentioning neither birds nor painting. He stated that he was personally acquainted with Audubon, and had also the assurances of many who had known him longer and better, that he was a man of outstanding character. Audubon, Clay wrote, was now embarked on an expedition to what was then the American southwest in pursuit of "a laudable object connected with Natural History." Audubon was well qualified in this undertaking, Clay said.

The river was low as they set out—Captain Aumack managed only fourteen miles in their first day. The next morning, Audubon and Mason led a hunting party ashore and returned after a short foray having killed a woodcock, twenty-seven squirrels, a barn owl, a turkey buzzard, and thirty partridges. Audubon also knocked down what he thought was a yellow-rumped warbler still in its juvenile plumage, a bird he was "perfectly convinced" had been misidentified by Alexander Wilson as the "autumnal warbler." (Actually, Wilson was correct, as Audubon later conceded.) As the hunters relaxed on deck cleaning their guns, flocks of ducks and meadowlarks streamed by overhead on their way south. Signs of the season were afoot. A couple days later, the passengers awoke to find the woods heavy with frost and saw deer swimming in the river.

Audubon fell into a routine, hunting at first light, then dissecting birds, making drawings, and writing in his journal during the day as the boat coasted on. It was unseasonably cold. Audubon felt ill the first week out, and working in the cramped cabin to stay out of the icy wind gave him headaches. In early November they put ashore near Evansville, Indiana. Audubon persuaded Mason and one of the passengers to take the skiff across the river to Henderson and retrieve his hunting dog, Dash, who'd been left behind in the Audubons' hurried departure many months before. Despite a fierce wind that made the trip far chancier than it should have been, they were successful. Audubon, delighted to have his dog back, was in a bleak mood all the same. He made a morose sketch of the place and reflected that it was almost inconceivable that he had lived there for eight years and thought himself happy. When they shoved off the next morning and the current swept them past the blank walls of the mill, he hoped he would never see it again.

The weather was slightly better that morning, a scarlet sunrise hinting that an interlude of Indian summer might be on the way. But the effect was partly due to thick smoke that filled the air and had Audubon blinking back tears. It was said in Kentucky that smoke sometimes drifted in from prairie fires set by Indian hunting parties to the west. Puzzlingly, Audubon observed that the wind had been from the east—always a portentous direction—for days. It grew chilly again. This cold spell lingered, and a string of rainy days made everyone cranky. Audubon was uncharacteristically annoyed by a fellow passenger named Shaw, who owned a fair portion of the cargo. Audubon thought him weak and self-centered, and said he reminded him of "some Jews" who live well at the expense of others. Audubon's feelings about the man were undoubtedly inseparable from his bruised ego, as Shaw's conspicuous wealth must have offered an unhappy contrast with his own circumstances.

Audubon consoled himself with his daily hunts and with many new observations of birds, which he carefully recorded. One evening, just before sunset, he watched a barred owl that had been chased from its roost by a flock of crows. The owl rose rapidly into the sky "in the manner of a Hawk" until it disappeared from sight. When the owl came back into view, it was flying erratically, "as if Lost." It then flew in circles and crazy zigzags until darkness came and Audubon could not tell what became of the bird. This was, he said, highly unusual and fascinating behavior that he had never seen before.

Summer seemed to have turned almost overnight into winter. The cold continued, and the leaves were all gone from the trees. Rain and sluggish currents slowed the travelers' progress. One day, they floated only seven miles. They ran aground from time to time, forcing the crew over the side and into the frigid river to free the boat. As nerves frayed, Audubon came to doubt the wisdom of the trip altogether. Out of the blue in mid-November, Captain Aumack grew testy and apparently had a falling-out with Audubon. Without giving any of the details of what had happened, Audubon hinted in his journal that he had been grievously mistreated by the captain, who, among other complaints, had developed misgivings about the arrangement for Audubon and Mason's free passage. Evidently their disagreement raged through the better part of the night. Audubon wrote a note to his sons—in the unlikely event they ever happened to read his "trifling remarks"—advising them that they should never permit themselves to take on obligations to men who are "not Aware of the Value or the Meaness of their *Conduct*." They should also, he warned, be wary of understandings with "owners" and "clerks," and they should avoid ever accepting anything they couldn't pay for.

The next day at dawn, Audubon, exhausted and in an agitated state, went ahead by himself in the skiff to the confluence with the Mississippi. Studying the eddies where the clear water of the Ohio was subsumed by the muddy surge of the Mississippi, Audubon was overcome by emotion. He tried to think casually about his previous visits to this place, but the roiling waters held his gaze, and anxious thoughts came unbidden. Despite his awkwardness with language and his frequently rough manner, Audubon was sometimes capable of expressions of surprising sensitivity. Audubon thought he perceived that the pretty, transparent Ohio tried to resist as it disappeared into the Mississippi's southbound murk. And then it occurred to him that he was staring into a watery metaphor for his own life:

The meeting of the Two Streams reminds me a little of the Young, Gentle, man Youth who Comes in the World, spotles he presents himself, he is gradually drawn in to thousands of Dificulties that Makes him wish to keep to himself apart, but at Last he is over done and mixed, and lost in the Vortex—

Later that day, as the flatboat came into the Mississippi and they turned toward New Orleans, Audubon again felt a foreboding, noting in his journal that he had become the victim of an "involuntary fear" he could not shake as "every moment" carried him farther away from his family.

One morning when it was too rainy to hunt, Audubon sat down and composed a long journal entry seemingly addressed to Victor, though he obviously meant it for both his sons. It amounted to a brief autobiography, offering a carefully edited version of his birth at Saint-Domingue, his removal to France, and his eventual arrival in America. In a confessional tone that revealed his uneven state of mind, Audubon admitted to contradictory feelings about his time in Henderson. It was, on one hand, the place that saw his best and happiest days. John Woodhouse had been born there—a great blessing. Business had been good too, and for years he and Lucy had felt close and certain of themselves and their future. But it was also the place where disaster had befallen him. Audubon wrote of having too many partners and taking on too much debt, and of confronting too many unforeseen events that "reduced" and "divided" everything the family had achieved. Now he was embarked on a new chapter in his life, one forced upon him by bad luck but also by a disposition that he believed made it necessary for him to pursue his only abiding passion. His confession was sharply at odds with his later claims about when the idea of publishing his work first formed:

> Ever since a Boy I have had an astonishing desire to see Much of the World & particularly to Acquire a true Knowledge of the Birds of North America, consequently, I hunted when Ever I had an Opportunity, and Drew every New Specimen as I could, or dared *steel time* from my Business and having a tolerably Large Number of Drawings that have been generally admired, I Concluded that perhaps I Could Not do better than to Travel, and finish My Collection or so nearly so that it would be a Valuable Acquisition—My Wife Hoped it might do Well, and I Left her Once More . . .

Audubon found the passage south painfully tedious, largely because the weather forced the travelers to remain in the cabin so much of the time. Yet scarcely a day passed that he did not record observations of birds—as well as the occasional geological feature or some aspect of the lives and characters of the settlers and Indians the party encountered. Audubon began seeing bird species with which he was unfamiliar. Some of these he drew and later included in his published works; others, like the "fin-tailed duck" and the "imber diver," disappeared among many future corrections of his taxonomy. Sometimes the stormy weather so retarded the boat's progress that Audubon had time to hike the woods. One day, after a bone-chilling and sleepless night during which everyone aboard had gone repeatedly over the side to keep the wind from pushing the boat hopelessly aground, Audubon discovered a small, quiet lake where he shot several geese and ducks and found the largest mussels he had ever seen, recording them as "muscles" in his journal. Later that afternoon he caught a catfish that weighed over sixty pounds. Audubon reported happily that such a large fish was easily dispatched by "stabbing it about the Center of its head."

But a day later, having caught another, smaller catfish, Audubon wrote that this one survived for over an hour during the same stabbing treatment. Apparently in a brutal mood, Audubon tied a line around the foot of a bald eagle Captain Aumack had wounded, lashed the other end to a large pole, and pitched both the bird and the pole overboard to see what would happen. Surprisingly, the eagle swam off rapidly, flailing the water with its huge wings and dragging the pole along with it. As he amused himself watching a frightened Mason attempt to recapture the eagle with the skiff, Audubon noted the bird's mate circling overhead and crying out with "true sorrow." An hour later the eagle accepted a fish from Audubon, but the next day it hissed at him whenever he came near.

As they passed through the Arkansas territory, the flora and fauna began to change. Audubon wrote to the territorial governor imploring him for assistance in exploring the region, but heard nothing back. Spanish moss now hung in the trees. Audubon was on the alert for alligators and was eager to see them—though the chilly weather did not cooperate. Ivory-billed woodpeckers became a common sight, and their calls reverberated through the forest. Dash, it turned out, was pregnant. Audubon referred to her in his journal as "my slut Dash." After she finally gave birth to a litter of pups, Audubon and Mason decided to perform a gruesome experiment. It was said that the flesh of the Carolina parakeet—or "parrokeet" as Audubon wrote in his journal—was toxic to a dog's heart. Audubon and Mason shot ten parakeets, boiled them, and fed them to Dash—who showed not the slightest ill effect.

For many weeks, Audubon had been seeing numbers of large, long-necked black birds he took to be a species of pelican unfamiliar to him. Above Natchez, Mississippi, at the mouth of the Yazoo River—a beautiful, clear stream flanked by willows and cottonwoods—Audubon spotted a whole flock of the strange birds roosted near the water. Audubon and Mason took the skiff and floated past the birds, then went ashore and crawled back toward them. When they were finally in range, about forty-five yards away, Audubon carefully picked out a group of three perched on a dead branch and stood and fired at them. All three birds fell.

But when he and Mason rushed forward to retrieve the birds, they discovered them swimming off with the larger flock. All the birds dove at the approach of the two men, and on resurfacing took to the air after running over the surface of the water for a good fifty yards. Audubon was fascinated—and then noticed that one bird, obviously wounded, could not fly. He and Joseph raced back to the skiff and went after the bird, which swam ahead up the river, diving repeatedly. After a mile of inching closer to the bird, Audubon sensed it was tiring, as each dive lasted a shorter time than the last. Finally Mason readied his gun as Audubon pulled on the oars. The bird came up again, close by now, its head and neck like a snake. Mason fired, killing it. Audubon, nervous and exhausted from the chase, was flummoxed once he brought it over the side. The bird looked something like an albatross, but Audubon could not even guess at the genus to which it belonged. And while Audubon surely determined the bird's identity later, exactly what it was remains uncertain, since he never mentioned this incident again.

Most likely it was an anhinga—a bird Audubon eventually encountered all across the southern United States. The anhinga turned out to have several other names, including "black-bellied darter" and "snake-bird," all of which Audubon somewhat confusingly used in his later description of the species. It is, beyond question, a magnificent bird, with its long neck, sharp beak, and broad, fanlike tail. Although this design suggests a bird made for long, soaring flight, Audubon learned that it is actually the most powerful of all freshwater diving birds. It is also among the most averse to capture. Audubon said that an anhinga even slightly wounded falls immediately into the water—whereupon it swims off rapidly underwater, surfaces, and goes down again and again in a desperate effort to escape. When seriously injured, the anhinga, like certain other waterfowl, sometimes dives to the bottom and, taking hold of some vegetation, stays there until it drowns—a heartrending form of suicide familiar to duck hunters. Audubon's drawing of the anhinga, showing a male and a female perched atop dead tree trunks overlooking a swamp, their heads and necks serpentined to the side in sinuous curves, is one of the most elegant he ever painted.

On Christmas Day, 1820, Audubon got a present. Captain Aumack shot a great-footed hawk, a bird Alexander Wilson had heard of but, Audubon gleefully noted, had not been able to observe and describe. Audubon's sudden attentiveness to Wilson's inventory of species seemed to indicate that he now viewed Wilson as a rival. Audubon himself claimed to have seen this particular hawk many times, but admitted he had never managed to shoot one. They flew very fast, and as they passed through the air issued a loud, whistling roar that Audubon likened to the swooshing near miss of a cannonball. This hawk was unusually active, rarely soaring passively on the air but always flying furiously and falling on its prey—smaller birds that it seized on the wing—in spectacular dives. Quite a few seemed to be at this place, and Audubon speculated that the abundance of overwintering ducks was the chief attraction for them. The specimen Aumack collected that day turned out to be an old female. Audubon went to work on a drawing of it, and later dissected the bird, finding in its stomach the remains of a teal. Audubon was right to be impressed with this bird—which we now call the peregrine falcon. The sleekest and most deadly of aerial killers, the peregrine falcon is the fastest living thing on earth, achieving speeds of nearly two hundred miles per hour when stooping on its prey—which usually dies upon impact in midair.

The next morning the flatboat at last came beneath the bluffs at Natchez. It was the first contact with a civilized settlement in two months and nine hundred miles of travel. Audubon thought the city pretty and romantic. Goats grazed on the hillsides, and the town was well laid out with tree-lined streets—though the buildings and houses were a mostly ramshackle collection of small, woodframe structures. The two thousand or so residents overlooked a busy waterfront, where all manner of arks and flatboats were tied up. Aububon was impressed by the bustling traffic of horsecarts and pedestrians, and also by the number of sawmills along the river and several immense rafts of logs, some bound for New Orleans. Audubon realized he was seeing a small fraction of the removal of the forest from the vast interior of America. One raft operator boasted to Audubon that his last delivery to New Orleans of logs he'd "stolen" off government land had brought him $6,000.

There was a decent hotel—built in the Spanish style—and several crowded taverns that Audubon, penniless, could only stare into as he ambled past. On the boat, floating through the backcountry and living off the game he shot, Audubon had known he was poor without really feeling it. The men had helped themselves equally to the food they had, sharing the cooking duties and supplementing Audubon's game feasts with hunks of bacon they chewed cold after cutting them from the slab kept hung by the fireplace. Audubon said that no one ever ate a freshly plucked and fire-roasted duck with more gusto than he did on that trip. But, in a town, one needed money to eat. Audubon managed to find two people willing to pay him $5 each for their portraits—which he speedily produced. The recipients were so delighted with the results that one of them actually paid. Audubon treated himself to dinner at the hotel that evening, where he was repeatedly embarrassed when he picked up his food with his fingers, a habit acquired on the boat. Audubon thought bitterly to himself that less hardened men—especially eastern "dandys"— would do themselves good to live as he had, by day hunting through tangled, treacherous woods and at night going to sleep in soaked, mud-caked clothes on a buffalo skin nailed to a board. This would teach them what it was to sweat and to be hungry and so occupied with staying alive that their imaginations would be kept "free from worldly thoughts." Those who dared, he added, should leave their "high heeled boots" at home but not their "corsets," which would come in handy for cinching down their shrinking bellies when food was in short supply.

Audubon stayed in Natchez less than a week. On the last day of 1820, he and Mason spent the morning on the flatboat packing their gear. Audubon had run into a friend from Shippingport, who offered to take Audubon and Mason on to New Orleans in his keelboat. Audubon jumped at the chance to ride in greater comfort and felt a rush of gratitude when his friend sent a man to the flatboat to help with their belongings. Feeling as if things were looking up a little, Audubon went to town and had breakfast before going aboard the keelboat and putting off once more into the wide, brown river. They tied up to the stern of a steamboat heading south and were soon making good time. That afternoon, when he got out his drawing kit, Audubon realized something terrible had happened. One of his portfolios—a small one—had been among the things he had entrusted to the porter. It was now nowhere to be found. The portfolio contained about fifteen drawings, including at least three "non-descripts," plus a portrait of Lucy and some "silver papers" used as protective liners between his drawings. Audubon, imagining the portfolio ripped open and cast aside on the Natchez waterfront, pictured his drawings tacked up in the cabins of various flatboats or decorating the walls of houses owned by "low characters" who would have no concept of their worth. He felt sick.

The next morning, New Year's Day, Audubon stared glumly at the passing country, which had become flat. It seemed scarcely possible, but exactly twenty-one years before, he had been a cadet training at the naval school in Rochefort in France. It all felt far away and long ago. He believed an account of his life and travels since that time could fill a big book. But his experience had been "dearly purchased," and this morning he thought the only thing to be said of him could be recorded in a single sentence. "I am," he wrote in his journal, "on Board a Keel Boat going down to New Orleans the poorest Man on it."

Audubon and Mason arrived in New Orleans a week later—where Audubon's intention of continuing across the Gulf of Mexico to Florida met with reality. He had no money with which to go on. He had no money with which to go back. After nearly three months away from his family, Audubon felt the constant weight of his loneliness for Lucy and the boys. On his first night in the city, Audubon dined with friends of the keelboat's owner and found himself disgusted by their boisterous behavior. Audubon thought these people talked too loudly and laughed too hard at "dry" jokes that left him at a loss. At one point the party was entertained by a pet monkey that was permitted to caper around the dining room. Audubon, unhappy and feeling out of place, refilled his wine glass many times. He finally excused himself after dinner—everyone else was headed to the theater, a diversion he could not afford—and returned to the boat with a headache. The next day, hungover and depressed, Audubon went to a parade commemorating the sixth anniversary of the Battle of New Orleans—where a pickpocket lifted the letters of introduction he'd taken along in hopes of meeting the governor. Back on the boat, Audubon was lampooned as a "green horn."

Audubon had reached the end of all the rivers he had been on since he and Lucy had set out for the frontier on their honeymoon. Now it seemed he could go no farther. Seeing and drawing the birds of America remained his goal, but he no longer had any clear idea of how he would achieve it. Desperate for money, Audubon looked for work as a portrait painter and found a little. In one ten-day stretch during his first month in town, Audubon managed to earn $220. He resolved to stop blaming his circumstances on poor luck and to instead become a "wiser" man. But it would be a long time before he was a happy one again. For the next several years, even after being reunited with his family, Audubon would bide his time in Louisiana, painting and teaching, working and waiting for something good to happen.

Audubon didn't care much for New Orleans, though it was the cultural capital of the southwest and home to many painters and musicians. New Orleans was the fifth-largest city in the country and second only to New York in shipping tonnage. The city was also a principal immigration point and on the way to becoming the country's leading slave trading center. The population of 27,000 featured a mélange of skin tones and dialects that Audubon found disagreeable, as well as odd social arrangements between the races, many seemingly contradictory and difficult to sort out. There were, of course, many slaves in Louisiana. But there were also a fair number of free people of color. Almost incomprehensibly, a few of these free blacks actually owned African slaves. Everywhere there was evidence of the mixing of races and peoples. Audubon was fascinated by the weird speech of the Cajuns, who spoke what seemed a backcountry blend of French, Spanish, and English, but he was not impressed by their knowledge of the country. Early in his stay, Audubon reported seeing on the streets some pretty "white ladies," though he also admitted to being curious about a "quatroon ball," as he called it, which he would have attended but for the $1 admission. Quadroon balls were popular events at which women of mixed race mingled with white men. In fact, relationships between white men and mulatto women— as long as they stayed short of marriage—were widely accepted and often arranged by the young women's mothers. Women of color were especially popular as mistresses to prominent white men, who provided for their paramours in accordance with the implicit social code. All of this was not unlike the laissez-faire attitude back on Saint-Domingue, and it may be that New Orleans reminded Audubon uncomfortably of his own heritage. In any case, Audubon said he much preferred "rosy Yankee or English cheeks" to the many "citron" faces he encountered in the city.

But the countryside around New Orleans more favorably impressed Audubon. The land here was flat in a way that sometimes reminded him of France, and the typically warm weather made the vegetation lush.

More important, southern Louisiana teemed with birds, both locals and migrants that overwintered there. Birds of every description could be seen in the New Orleans market, though it was in Audubon's estimation the "dirtiest place" in any city in America. The market's filthy stalls sometimes made him wish he'd remained in Natchez, but Audubon could not stay away from the daily display of so many members of the "feathered tribes." Ducks and geese and herons could usually be had, plus an ever-changing assortment of songbirds. Audubon was dismayed at some of the prices—$1.25 for a brace of ducks seemed outrageous—but amazed at how cheaply other species could be bought. One day he found a freshly cleaned barred owl for only twenty-five cents.

The Mississippi River between New Orleans and Natchez was flanked by plantations that grew mainly sugar and cotton. Both were labor-intensive crops. As more and more African slaves arrived, the plantations grew in size and prospered. When word of his skill as a portrait painter spread, Audubon started getting work at some of these country estates and from the businessmen who traded with them. Usually the job began as an assignment to paint the woman of the house. Some of the wealthy and bored plantation wives found Audubon's presence pleasant enough to ask him to stay on and paint other family members or offer drawing instruction to their children. Audubon leapt at these opportunities, but soon learned that these temporary positions required more patience and diplomacy than he had to give. The women were sometimes fickle and could be cruel when they grew tired of him or thought him insufficiently attentive. Some of the children were ill-behaved or without talent. In a few instances, his clients grew uncomfortably close to the poor but still dashing Audubon. Women talked among themselves about how handsome and clever he was. One bit of gossip hinted that Audubon was a philanderer and no longer cared for his wife, whom he supposedly said had begun to show her age "like a beautiful tobacco plant cut at the stem, and hung to wither."

But Audubon had little choice about what to do with himself. The jobs sometimes included room and board—which was important, as on several occasions he was unable to collect the agreed-upon salary. These engagements also left Audubon time to explore the fields and swamps and continue his own work. By mid-February, Audubon had completed twenty new drawings—including four of birds "not described by Wilson"—which he sent north to Lucy.

In this dashing self-portrait made shortly after his arrival in England, Audubon looked the conquering hero. His nervous caption was closer to the mark. (John James Audubon, *Self-Portrait*, 1826, pencil on paper. University of Liverpool Art Gallery and Collections)

Mill Grove. Audubon's first American home, where he invented his technique for drawing birds to scale—and where the girl next door was a pretty young Englishwoman named Lucy Bakewell. (Used by permission of the Mill Grove Audubon Center's Archives)

This unpublished painting of the belted kingfisher, made by Audubon at Louisville in 1808, hints at the enormity of his talent, although this simple profile is not characteristic of his mature style. (Used by permission of the Houghton Library, Harvard University)

William Bartram, the eminent Philadelphia botanist and mentor to Alexander Wilson. Bartram's accounts of his expeditions to Florida before Audubon was born were among the first and most important natural history studies undertaken by an American. (Portrait by Charles Willson Peale, 1808. Used by permission of Independence National Historical Park)

The house at Bartram's Garden, where Alexander Wilson taught himself ornithology. (Used by permission of the American Philosophical Society)

Alexander Wilson. Complicated, morose, brilliant, he created *American Ornithology* as the first attempt at a comprehensive description of the birds of the New World. (Portrait by Rembrandt Peale. Used by permission of the American Philosophical Society)

Wilson taught himself to draw birds by practicing studies of a stuffed owl such as this one. The flat, immobile pose was the accepted method for ornithological depictions—until Audubon changed everything. (Used by permission of the Ernst Mayr Library of the Museum of Comparative Zoology, Harvard University)

The elegance of Wilson's raptors showed how far he had come as an artist. This is the Mississippi kite that was copied by either Audubon or his engraver and appropriated for *The Birds of America*. (Thomas Cooper Library, University of South Carolina)

Napoleon's nephew, Charles-Lucien Bonaparte. One of the leading naturalists of his day, Bonaparte "discovered" Audubon, but their long-running relationship was rocky. (*Charles-Lucien Bonaparte as a Young Man* by Charles de Châtillon. Pencil drawing. Used by permission of the Museo Napoleonico, Rome)

George Ord, whose campaign against Audubon in Philadelphia grew into an obsessive hatred of the ornithologist. (*Portrait of George Ord* by J. Henry Smith, after John Neagle's portrait of 1829. Used by permission of the American Philosophical Society)

Audubon was forty-eight and at the halfway point of his "great work" when Henry Inman painted this portrait in 1833, seven years after *The Birds of America* had begun publication. (Private collection)

The artist Frederick Cruikshank apparently saw a younger Lucy Audubon than the one who posed for this melancholy portrait, circa 1831. Two years earlier she had written to Audubon that she was old and gray and that the last of her teeth were gone. (Collection of the New-York Historical Society)

Audubon's adventures on the American frontier—so unimpressive to the scientific establishment in Philadelphia—made him an object of fascination in Britain. He sketched himself in buckskins in this 1826 self-portrait while he was in Liverpool.

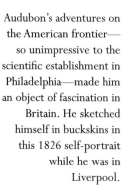

Otter Caught in a Trap. Audubon loved this grisly tableau so much that he painted it over and over again. Not everyone was equally fond of it. (John James Audubon, 1826, oil on canvas. University of Liverpool Art Gallery and Collections)

The shop of Robert Havell Jr. on Oxford Street in London, where most of the engravings for *The Birds of America* were made. (Courtesy of the Kentucky Department of Parks, John James Audubon Museum)

Scratched and blurred but still magnificent, 250 uncolored prints of Audubon's snipe were struck from one of Havell's original copper plates by the Audubon Museum at Henderson, Kentucky, in 2002—more than a century and a half after it was engraved. Finished prints for *The Birds of America* were completed by teams of painters who hand-colored such black-and-white images. (Photograph of copper plate #308 © C. Wesley Allen. Used by permission of C. W. Allen and John James Audubon Museum, Henderson, Ky.)

John James Audubon, in a rare daguerreotype from 1850, the year before he died.

Difficult as it was to scratch out a living, Audubon managed to send a few dollars to Lucy from time to time. Young Mason, who might have become another worrisome obligation, had meanwhile turned out to be very much the opposite. He seemed a steadying and cheerful influence on Audubon, who wrote to Lucy that Mason now drew flowers "better than any man, probably, in America." Audubon believed the boy's skill would serve as an advertisement—proof that Audubon was a superb instructor and mentor to budding artists. He added that the cost of having Mason with him was next to nothing and that the boy's company was "quite indispensable." As one month followed another in Louisiana, Audubon suffered through one of the unhappiest—and yet one of the most productive—periods of his life. He missed Lucy and the boys. He struggled to earn enough money to get by. New Orleans seemed perpetually unkind to him. Audubon's mood was volatile. He worked hard, especially on a drawing of the brown pelican, a bird of which he was particularly fond. But sour feelings were never far from his mind. "I rose early," he wrote in his journal in mid-January, "tormented by many disagreeable thoughts, nearly again without a cent, in a Busling City where no one cares a fig for a Man in my situation." Still eager to join a government-sponsored expedition to the Pacific, he could get no answer to his requests for a position on one as a naturalist and artist. Audubon called on local painters and art instructors, who were mostly dismissive of his talent and who also said he charged too much for his work. An exception was the painter John Vanderlyn, who thought Audubon's birds remarkable. But such bright moments were few. Audubon complained about everything. On the streets he saw people who avoided him and vice versa. Even the weather at times seemed intolerable. The almost perpetual warmth that attracted so many birds was sometimes swept away by a sudden wintry blast, and on a couple of occasions it snowed. Audubon and Mason, confined to cramped, dingy apartments much of the time, lived in a state of perpetual anxiety. Again and again, Audubon confessed bleak thoughts in his journal entries. As he and Mason moved around, they hired a woman to cook and clean for them when they could afford it. More often, they were broke, sometimes living back aboard the keelboat.

One day as he walked down a back alley to avoid being seen with his bulky portfolio, Audubon was stopped by a woman wearing a veil. She seemed young, perhaps only in her teens. She asked Audubon about his

work, and what he charged for portraits. She then wrote down her ad-
dress and asked him to call on her in half an hour. When he arrived and
went inside, the young lady pulled back her veil. Audubon thought she
was the most beautiful woman he had ever seen. She asked if he could
draw her likeness. He assured her that he could. Then she asked if he
could draw her naked. Audubon, later confiding his reaction in his journal, was speechless. "Had I been shot with a 48 pounder through the
heart," he wrote, "my articulating powers could not have been more suddenly stopped."

After a walk around the block to steady his nerves, Audubon went
back and began to prepare his drawing equipment. The woman disappeared behind a curtain, undressed, and arranged herself on a couch.
When Audubon pulled the curtain back, he dropped his pencil. She
smiled at him and he started drawing. Audubon worked for an hour.
When he stopped, the woman dressed and then talked with him at
length, offering suggestions for improving the uncompleted drawing.

Every day for the next week and a half, Audubon returned to work on
the drawing. When the subject of payment came up, Audubon—who
would have happily worked for nothing—said she could pay him whatever
she liked. The woman answered that she would buy him a new gun and
have it inscribed. On the last day they met, the woman wrote her name
at the bottom corner of the picture, as though she were the artist and not
the subject, and together they framed it. When Audubon received his
gun, the barrels bore an engraving in French that, translated, read: "Do
not refuse this gift of a friend who is grateful to you—may it equal yourself in goodness." Though he called at her apartment several times after
that, the woman was never in and Audubon did not see her again.

Did this all really happen—or was it one of Audubon's extravagant
lies? There's no proof that it isn't the truth, and there are a handful of
reasons to believe that some episode at least similar to this did, in fact,
take place. Audubon gave the woman's last name as "Andre." His journal
entry dated February 21, 1821, mentions his drawing a likeness of a "fair
Lady" named Andre—and includes a hint that he may have more to say
about this picture at a later date. Then, on March 11, 1821, Audubon reported a shooting excursion with Mason on which he tried his new "Sou-
venir Gun." He later gave his old gun to Mason, so he must have gotten a
replacement for it. Perhaps more important is the fact that Audubon did

not compose his written account of his sessions with Andre for publication, and never spoke of them as a way of advancing his career or burnishing his ego.

Instead, it seems to have been written for an audience of one—his wife. Audubon often juggled letters and diary entries, sometimes copying sections of his journal into his correspondence. In a long letter to Lucy that he composed over a period of days toward the end of May 1831, Audubon included a section from his journal that he called "The Fair Incognito," which told the story of the Andre drawing. Audubon scrawled a note to Lucy at right angles across the letter, saying he was providing this account for "my only friend." He admonished her against "participating" in the story—whatever that meant—and asked that she share it with no one, except her brother William if he would promise not to repeat it.

During this long period of separation—and others they endured—the Audubons were sometimes impatient and cranky with one another in their correspondence. But neither was ever intentionally cruel. Audubon, though he was on occasion insensitive in relaying events that could have aroused Lucy's jealousy, surely would have seen that this incident could have been especially hurtful. For him to have invented the story—or to have added salacious overtones to a more benign episode—for the purpose of wounding Lucy's feelings would have been quite out of character. What seems more probable is that this was actually a kind of preemptive confession—Audubon's effort to erase any tinge of guilt he may have felt about what happened.

Lucy, many miles and two rivers away, tried hard to look on the bright side of their lengthening separation. It could not have been easy. Victor and John Woodhouse, whom she was now teaching, consumed all of Lucy's time. Weary and losing weight, Lucy said she was often too tired even to play the piano. Her father had recently died, and in her grief Lucy had begun to dwell on "happier times" when she was growing up in Derbyshire. She said she could still picture her favorite places there "as if no time had elapsed." Of course, much time and many events were now between Lucy and her childhood. During a springtime visit to relatives in Louisville, she wrote to her cousin in England, going over recent events with an economy of emotion that didn't quite match the circumstances of "the various losses and misfortunes of my husband's affairs," as she put it.

"[F]or the last year he has supported us by his talent in drawing and painting which he learnt from David as a recreation in better times," Lucy wrote, stretching the truth with every syllable. Whether Lucy actually believed that Audubon once studied with David or she was merely an accomplice in perpetuating this myth, Lucy clearly intended to place her husband in the best possible light. Left on her own with two children to raise however she could, Lucy managed to make it sound as if Audubon were taking care of everything.

"This last year I have spent in Cincinnati where Mr. Audubon combined a drawing school with a situation at the Museum, and taking portraits of various sizes and kinds," Lucy continued. "[A]t the same time he is prosecuting a large work on Ornithology which when compleat he means to take to Europe to be published. The birds are all drawn from nature the natural size and embellished with plants, trees, or views as best suits the purpose. It is his intention to go first to England and I hope it will be in my power to accompany him . . . Mr. Audubon is now out on a tour of research for the birds he has not. At present he is in New Orleans and it will be a year before he returns." In what was perhaps an attempt to ensure that she and Audubon were in agreement about all of this, Lucy mailed the letter by way of Audubon, who got it ten days later and added a postscript, sending his best wishes to England.

Here, of course, was still more proof that Audubon's plans for publishing his drawings had developed long before his trip to Philadelphia and his meeting with Charles-Lucien Bonaparte. But Lucy's letter to her cousin was more telling for what she left out. That same spring, Lucy was writing to Audubon that she was running out of patience with his vague plans to travel to England and his ineffectual attempts to land a position with an expedition to the West. Her letters, he wrote in his journal, "ruffled" his spirits. Lucy begged Audubon not to return to Kentucky a failure, and demanded that he at least give some thought to how they could put together enough money for Victor to go to college. Audubon, who was living hand-to-mouth as it was, sent back an exasperated reply. He told Lucy she was much too timid. If he had to go to England without a penny in his pocket he would do it, he said, confident that he would always find a way to get by. What really annoyed him were Lucy's endless demands for money. Where she seemed now to see him solely for his ability—or inability—to provide for his family, Audubon said he thought of Lucy only as the object of his undying love.

"Wert thou not to give me hints about money I should be sorry," he wrote acidly, "as I know it is as necessary for the support of *thy life* as thy affection is to the comfort of *mine*."

In June of 1821, a family named Pirrie invited Audubon and Mason to spend the summer and fall at their home near Bayou Sara, about 125 miles upriver from New Orleans, near the town of St. Francisville. Oakley Plantation, as it was called, was a revelation. On the day he and Mason arrived, Audubon saw that the land was different from the level country around New Orleans. There were hills and long ridgetops dense with hardwoods. Beautiful flowers grew on immense magnolia trees, and Audubon reveled in walking over the hard, red-clay ground beneath soaring beech trees. He grew dizzy at being "surrounded" by thousands of warblers and thrushes, and—too entranced to think of unpacking his gun—admired a fine Mississippi kite that glided by high overhead. A few weeks after their arrival, on the Fourth of July, Audubon composed a long, detailed inventory of the birds he was studying at Oakley—more than sixty species. All of these were of interest, though Audubon seemed quite partial to mockingbirds, which readily imitated every kind of sound and bird call—sometimes confusing him. Mockingbirds were also unusually bold, willing to chase every other species of bird except for the larger raptors.

Early one Sunday morning in August, Audubon and Mason hiked to a lake about five miles distant from Oakley and on their way discovered a landscape unlike any Audubon had ever seen—a world of water and gnarled forest that would become an important backdrop of his work. At first they passed among the crowded trunks of a vast magnolia woods. Audubon shot two wood ducks on a small pond and watched as a pair of red-shouldered hawks descended and made off with them. A little later, he and Mason stopped to watch a large, brilliantly colored spider spinning a web coffin around a fly it had just caught. Audubon surmised that this was how the spider preserved its food when it was not hungry.

They came finally to a place where the land fell off, and beneath them in the dawn light spread a fantastic swampland of red and white cypress trees, their kneelike roots rising up from the mist-shrouded water by the thousands. In the distance was the lake. Audubon and Mason trudged through the mud and ooze of the swamp. At the lakeshore, they saw a number of big alligators lying in the shallows, obviously unconcerned at their approach but perhaps not unawares. Audubon studied a beautiful ibis perched on a log some way out from shore, but thought better of shooting it, as he had no boat with which to retrieve it and was afraid the alligators might come to life if he sent his dog in.

The woods near the lake were filled with birds, including a blinding variety of fat, vividly hued warblers. Audubon shot several species, including a stunning male specimen of the yellow-throated warbler. Later in the day, Audubon heard what he thought was surely a wood pewee, but he was unable to find the bird. When he went back a few days later, he heard it again. It turned out to be a young Mississippi kite. Audubon shot it, but the baby bird did not fall and instead remained high in its tree. Suddenly its mother returned, carrying a large grasshopper—which the wounded bird refused. The mother then carried her offspring away to another tree. Audubon followed and killed both with a single shot.

Audubon went back again and again to the cypress swamp, awed at its richness. Perhaps it was about this time that he began to think how pleasant it would have been to have grown up on a sprawling plantation in such a place—a fantasy he eventually decided to claim was the truth.

In late August, Audubon worked on a drawing that would later be incorporated into one of his most famous images—and the focal point of a raging controversy. The finished drawing, which was probably completed several years later, depicts a group of mockingbirds seemingly under attack by a rattlesnake coiled among the branches of a yellow jessamine tree. It's a startling, imaginative picture. Audubon, eager to display the reptile in a posture that would "render it most interesting" to other naturalists, showed the snake—mouth gaping and fangs bared—striking at one of the birds. The mockingbirds, meanwhile, are shown in varying attitudes to illustrate different aspects of male and female plumage— Audubon's trademark technique. The bird closest to the snake recoils into the air, a look of terror in its eyes.

In the swelter of late summer in Louisiana, Audubon painted only the snake—a 5½-footer he killed for the purpose—laboring sixteen hours straight, until the stink of the corpse's rapid decay forced him to stop.

Eliza Pirrie, at fifteen the youngest member of the Pirrie family, worked eagerly by his side making her own drawing of the snake. Eliza had become Audubon's prize pupil and sole excuse for staying on at Oakley. She had six brothers and sisters, all but one of whom—a married sister not living at Oakley—had died. Audubon was teaching her drawing, and also music, dancing, and arithmetic. Audubon enjoyed this work. Eliza had a sweet disposition, and although she was not pretty, the thirty-six-year-old Audubon took note—perhaps not appropriately—of the "good form" of her mature body.

In the fall, Eliza fell ill. Relapses kept her bed-ridden for an extended period, and the Pirrie family physician finally ordered her to cease her lessons. Audubon observed a special affection between doctor and patient, and surmised that this was the real reason Eliza was no longer permitted to study with Audubon. The doctor meanwhile said she could eat as much as she pleased—a treatment, Audubon dryly noted, to which Eliza eagerly applied herself. In October, Audubon and Mason were fired. The Pirries allowed them to stay on for a bit as guests, but everyone seemed cool toward their continued presence in the house. Audubon busied himself with ornithological studies, particularly in going over the mistakes he had found in Wilson's *American Ornithology*—which, knowing Wilson was highly regarded in Louisiana, he prudently kept to himself. When it finally came time for Audubon and Mason to leave, Mrs. Pirrie objected to the $204 bill Audubon presented for his services. She accused him of trying to cheat her. Audubon listened patiently and then wrote up an invoice for her husband. Mr. Pirrie, a good man who tended to drink too much, was apologetic about his family's behavior and assured Audubon he would be paid in full. He never was.

Audubon and Mason went back downriver to New Orleans, where Audubon cut his hair and bought more fashionable clothes in an attempt to make himself presentable in the city. Shocked at how altered his appearance was, Audubon wrote in his journal that he now resembled a handsome bird "robbed of all its feathering." He said he would not miss Oakley Plantation, which he crabbed was an "abode of unfortunate Opulence." But he was sorry to be parted from the woods around Bayou Sara, and wrote in his journal that he wished his lungs could somehow remain filled with their sweet air forever. Only two months after his leaving Oakley, Eliza Pirrie had passed by on the street in New Orleans without deigning to acknowledge him. Audubon could console himself with the knowledge that he'd come away from the Pirries with a large cache of his best work yet.

Audubon continued to draw new species—including the black-bellied darter—and he added to his morphological notes on the brown pelican. Audubon had to think about how best to fit a full-sized swan onto his paper, finally solving the problem by turning the bird's neck to the rear as it glided on the water, as if it were about to eat something it had just swum past. A moth was later added to the background to fill that role.

Audubon could not decide which was worse—waiting anxiously for Lucy's next letter or receiving one filled with her annoyance, which left him even more depressed. Finally they agreed that Lucy and the boys would come south and join him. After weeks of meeting one boat, then another, each vessel the one that he was sure they would be aboard, Audubon was at last reunited with his family when the steamboat *Rocket* arrived and they stepped ashore in New Orleans a week before Christmas in 1821. Together for the first time in more than a year, the Audubons walked to a little house he'd managed to rent for $17 a month.

Lucy had brought all of Audubon's earlier drawings with her, and as he compared them with his more recent ones, he realized how greatly his work had improved despite his gloomy frame of mind. Determined to start the new year on a better note, Audubon hired a local hunter to bring him new specimens—ninety-nine different birds in as many days—promising himself that he would paint them as fast as they arrived. With his schedule already crowded with drawing lessons, Audubon felt the weight of financial worries lift a little.

But a few months later, Audubon lost one of his most valued students. He decided to try his hand at commercial art in Natchez, where fewer artists vied for work. For the better part of the next two years, the Audubons bounced from place to place and job to job, up and down the lower Mississippi River with their boys and young Mason in tow. Lucy got work as a governess in New Orleans, and once again the couple parted for a time. Audubon struggled to find work at Natchez, eventually landing the first of several jobs teaching drawing at local academies. He tried to learn to paint in oil. Mostly he hunted. Lucy and the boys joined him at Natchez and Lucy found another job as a governess. Audubon tried painting landscapes. Then he taught fencing. In the summer of 1822, Joseph Mason, homesick and weary of their hand-to-mouth existence, reluctantly went back north. Everyone was sorry to see him go. Audubon gave Mason some paper and chalks and the gun he'd owned since 1805, thinking to himself that most of the birds he had killed from Philadelphia to New Orleans had fallen in front of it.

Then Lucy was offered a position by a wealthy widow in West Feliciana, at Bayou Sara, in the heart of the Louisiana country Audubon loved so much. The woman, Jane Percy, lived on a plantation called Beech Woods, and ran a neighborhood school attended by her daughters and their friends. Lucy was to earn $1,000 a year and have the use of a cottage adjoining the schoolhouse. Audubon, who was still smitten with Bayou Sara, joined his wife there for a time. But rumors of his strained departure from nearby Oakley Plantation haunted him, and he soon had a run-in with Mrs. Percy—who didn't care for his portraits of her daughters when he attempted them in oils. Lucy, who had long since determined that Audubon needed to find a publisher for his birds, told her husband to get on with it. In October 1823, she handed over what little money she'd managed to save, and Audubon and Victor departed for Philadelphia.

In better days, when business was good at Henderson, Audubon had bought the first six volumes of Wilson's *American Ornithology*. After leaving them behind when he went to New Orleans, Audubon found it difficult to consult Wilson's work. It was hard to find anyone who owned *American Ornithology*, much less anyone willing to loan it to him. Audubon attributed this unwillingness to the high cost of the book, which he believed was due to its rarity.

Actually, Wilson's work had become much more than a collection of pricey color drawings. Audubon probably did not comprehend how much American science had advanced in recent years—nor did he imagine the exalted place *American Ornithology* occupied in that world. When George Ord was elected to the Academy of Natural Sciences of Philadelphia in 1815, two years after Wilson's untimely death, his self-appointed mission to complete Wilson's work became inextricably linked with the academy's emerging reputation as the country's leading scientific institu-tion. *American Ornithology* conveyed a prestige and an authority to the academy that had been considerably augmented over the intervening years. As academy members traveled from one side of the continent to the other on government expeditions, and scientific papers began ap-pearing in the academy's *Journal* in 1817, American science took on a rigor that had its center of gravity in Philadelphia.

Even as Audubon was preparing to depart on his journey to Philadel-phia, the young French naturalist Charles-Lucien Bonaparte was hard at work on corrections to Wilson's taxonomy. Many of the corrections turned out to be wrong, but the point was being made that American natural history studies were now subject to peer review. And in a rever-sal of the long-standing practice of European scientists determining New World taxonomy from afar, Bonaparte had come to Philadelphia and was working on American birds in collaboration with Ord. Audubon, having never heard of George Ord and probably unaware that *American Ornithol-ogy* was still a work in progress, set off for Philadelphia believing it would be self-evident once he got there that his superior drawings made his or-nithology preferable to Wilson's. He was wrong. Against Ord's energetic opposition to him throughout the city and the orchestrated campaign to prevent his election to the academy, Audubon never had a chance.

Audubon's humiliating defeat in Philadelphia, coming at the end of five years of financial and psychological torment, could well have de-stroyed his ambition once and for all. It did not. Audubon had struggled with the erosion of his wealth and status as both unwound over several years, but he remained amazingly resilient in a more acute crisis. Audubon departed from Philadelphia, forcing himself to look on the bright side, as he did throughout his life when sudden misfortune befell him. In New York, to which he'd fled, Audubon amused himself for a day or two sitting as a model for his painter friend John Vanderlyn, who was now in New York and at work on a heroic full-length portrait of Andrew Jackson. Jackson, a busy man who would become president in a few years, had only time to sit for Vanderlyn's work on his face. The still trim and muscular Audubon, Vanderlyn realized, was a nearly perfect body double for Jackson. As a favor in return for his friend's help, Vanderlyn put Audubon's face on a soldier standing in the background of the paint-ing. During the long hours he posed, Audubon had time to sort things out. He felt himself "strange to all but the birds of America," and was eager to get back to the woods and the comforting solitude of the wilderness. And he was thinking, too, of the next step after that. When Audubon reflected on what had happened in Philadelphia, it seemed that Ord had actually done him a favor. Audubon now understood that he would be better served taking his birds abroad, to Europe, where prospects for their publication and sale would be better. In London or Paris, he had been told, there were many talented engravers who could do justice to his drawings—and many wealthy people who might be able to afford such a lavish and costly work.

After a slow bird-watching detour across upstate New York and a brief visit to Shippingport—where he begged a few dollars from friends despite his wild appearance—Audubon made his way back downriver aboard a steamship. He arrived at Bayou Sara in a sorry state. Carrying a portfolio of drawings that would one day be among the most treasured of American artworks, Audubon was broke, dirty, and dressed in rags. A skiff delivered him ashore at midnight in a driving rain. He'd been gone more than a year. It was now late November. St. Francisville was mostly deserted, owing to a recent outbreak of yellow fever, but Audubon managed to borrow a horse so he could ride to Lucy at Beech Woods. The night was warm, but in the rain and dark Audubon got lost. When he finally rode up to Lucy's cottage, it was morning. Audubon walked in, dripping and exhausted. Lucy, who was already busy giving a lesson to her pupils, stood and rushed to his arms.

Audubon was astonished to learn that Lucy was now earning almost $3,000 a year and had already put away $1,000 in savings. As the year 1825 began, Audubon could start making plans to travel to Europe. To stay out of the way at Beech Woods, where he was still at odds with the Percys, Audubon occupied himself by teaching dance. One evening, he instructed a class of sixty young men and women. They were all but hopeless—Audubon could scarcely coax a graceful step from the lot. After lumbering around the floor to Audubon's fiddling for a while, the class demanded that he show them how it was done. Clearing a space for himself, Audubon began to dance alone, playing his violin and singing lustily. The class burst into wild applause. After the students were dismissed, the young men remained behind in hopes of a fencing lesson from their dance master. Audubon obliged. He went home that night exhausted.

Audubon and Lucy settled down to work and save toward his trip to

England. It was a pleasant time. On hot afternoons, the Audubons would ride together to a small lake, where Lucy swam naked while Audubon lolled on the beach admiring her. Audubon continued his teaching, but he was also busy hunting and drawing and staying in touch with several of his newfound friends in Philadelphia—notably Charles-Lucien Bonaparte, with whom Audubon was eager to remain on good terms. This turned out to be hard at times. Some field notes that Audubon had mailed the prince miscarried, causing Bonaparte to think briefly that Audubon had ignored his promise to send them. Audubon corrected the situation, but blundered badly in criticizing the first volume of Bonaparte's American bird studies. Although he was delighted to see that it included his drawing of the great crow blackbird—now known as the boat-tailed grackle— Audubon was not impressed with the book and particularly regretted sharing his intimate knowledge of the wild turkey with Bonaparte. Thinking he was speaking confidentially, Audubon wrote to Reuben Haines, one of the academy members who had nominated him for membership, saying Bonaparte's book was riddled with mistakes and that Bonaparte had appropriated some of Audubon's observations without attribution. Audubon said he felt misled and betrayed. Haines—rather stupidly, the prince said—forwarded this letter to Bonaparte, who was livid about it.

But the storm passed. Audubon did his best to please a number of people back East who had asked to be sent various plant and animal specimens. One request was for an alligator heart. Audubon thought he could do better. Visiting a nearby pond he knew to be crawling with alligators, Audubon shot one small enough to be put in a barrel for shipping. His ball struck the animal atop its skull, seemingly killing it. Audubon and a few men from the plantation hauled it back to Beech Woods, where it attracted the attention of Lucy's students. When they asked Audubon to prop open its mouth and he started to oblige, the alligator, which was not dead but only stunned, suddenly became alert and began thrashing violently. Audubon coolly grabbed a rope tied around the animal's neck, threw it over a tree branch, and hauled the alligator into the air, where it continued to struggle and gasp, scratching at the rope with its forefeet. The next morning the alligator was still slightly alive. Audubon lowered it into a barrel filled with whiskey and hammered on the top as the alligator swished around dazedly in the spirits.

Audubon had an equally dicey experience with a live rattlesnake that escaped several times from a tub in Lucy's kitchen before Audubon succeeded in quieting it in a bath of spirits. He had an easier time collecting insects—young John Woodhouse helped—to be sent to the entomologist Thomas Say.

In the spring of 1826, Audubon was at last ready to go. He packed up more than four hundred drawings, put $1,600 of his and Lucy's savings into his pocketbook, and headed off to New Orleans to find a ship to England. Lucy, supportive but perhaps irked at the prospect of yet another long separation, earmarked part of the money for a new piano Audubon was to send home. He bought passage on the *Delos*. Having some time before the ship was ready to depart, Audubon screwed up his courage and made several calls to ask for references. He got in to see the governor, who wrote up a general letter of introduction, exaggerating the length of Audubon's residence in Louisiana while offering a slight understatement of Audubon's life's work, which the governor characterized as "procuring drawings and preparing manuscripts in relation to the birds of America."

More valuable still was a letter of introduction Audubon received from a rich merchant named Vincent Nolte—the very same Vincent Nolte who had chuckled at his horse Barro when the two men met in the wilds of Pennsylvania more than a decade earlier. Audubon had seen Nolte on the street when he first got to New Orleans with Joseph Mason, but had avoided him out of embarrassment. Nolte was wealthy and powerful and busy, and Audubon had been ashamed to be none of those things. Then one day, as the two men passed each other and Audubon tried to hide his face, Nolte had stopped and seized Audubon by the hands. Nolte told him to stop being ridiculous—he was more than glad to see him. Nolte insisted Audubon bring his portfolio around, and when he did, Nolte heaped praise on the drawings and, delighted to see Audubon after several years, said he was eager to be of service. He now gave Audubon two letters of introduction. By far the more valuable of the two was addressed to a Mr. Richard Rathbone, a prominent cotton importer in Liverpool.

On May 17, 1826, at seven o'clock in the evening, a steam-driven tender pulled alongside the *Delos*, put a line on her, and for the next ten

hours towed her down through the Mississippi Delta and out into the
Gulf of Mexico. Once clear of land, the ship began to roll and Audubon
was immediately seasick. While he stayed up on deck to settle his stomach, Audubon diverted himself by drawing an almost perfect replica of
the state seal of Louisiana on his letter from the governor.

13

EDINBURGH

Sylvia aestiva: The Yellow-Poll Warbler
Its sojourn is of short duration in Louisiana, for it moves gradually eastward as the season advances, leaving nothing but the recollection of its passage through the land.
—*Ornithological Biography*

It was raining when Audubon stepped onto the wharf in Liverpool on July 21, 1826, after sixty-six brutal days at sea. New Orleans had been scarcely out of sight when Audubon regretted his decision to come that way rather than via New York. The Gulf of Mexico was dull and airless in the summer, or raked by eastern trade winds that checked the ship's progress. The heat was tremendous and most of the passengers chose to sleep on deck beneath a large awning. Repeatedly becalmed, the *Delos* needed almost three weeks to reach Cuba. The crew catered to Audubon's curiosity about every kind of creature, however. When he wasn't shooting and drawing seabirds, Audubon dissected and sketched the fish the crew brought over the side. There was a big shark and many dolphin fish. One day a crewman harpooned a "porpoise," using a five-pronged spear called a grains. The animal—actually a bottle-nosed dolphin, a mammal—was hauled aboard by its tail. Audubon noted the large quantity of black-looking blood that issued from the wound and took a step back when the animal gave out a loud groan and died. Audubon killed time sketching the crew and his fellow passengers. The officers of the ship, a capable lot, wore tall top hats.

The North Atlantic proved much the same as the Gulf—only cold instead of hot. The *Delos* moved imperceptibly to the east, spending long days rolling on a glassy ocean with no wind. Audubon suffered when they were becalmed and equally when they were under way. Anytime the wind picked up and the ship gathered speed, he became seasick. The *Delos* moved beneath his feet in ways he could never anticipate, so that Audubon felt constantly buffeted and off-balance. Eating was often hard. When Audubon cut into a large cheese and maggots poured out of it, his stomach revolted.

As the days wore on, Audubon thought about his life, replaying his triumphs and mistakes over and over, preoccupied by "curious fits of thoughts." When his meditations turned to Lucy, a "confusedness of ideas" rushed through his mind and he wrote in his journal that it made him feel as if he were traveling through a "dismal, heavy snowstorm." Audubon did not record—at least not coherently—his feelings about his purpose in going to England, though this must have been much on his mind as well. On its face, it was a preposterous undertaking. Audubon had no clear plan. He thought he might find a way to sell his drawings, or possibly copy them for sale. Or he would be happy to find a position as an artist and naturalist in residence at one of England's fine, musty museums. Of course, Audubon dared dream that he might publish his drawings with an engraver—as Catesby and Wilson had done. But this was an idea so presumptuous it must have struck him as absurd even to think about it. Audubon had more than four times as many drawings as Wilson—and they were huge! Engraving and printing them would require the most ambitious, time-consuming, and labor-intensive publishing enterprise in history. And one that would be by far the most expensive. How could Audubon, a humble backwoodsman with no reputation and no money, dare hope he could land in a new country and pull it off?

A more dismaying realization may have been that he seemed to have little choice but to try. When, after his retreat from Philadelphia, Audubon feared he might die "unknown," it was the first time he ever admitted to himself the importance of gaining acclaim for his bird drawings. For most of his life until then, Audubon had told himself he was a businessman with a hobby. And while he often imagined one day completing his study of American birds, he had never formed a concrete objective beyond that. Now he shuddered at the prospect of continuing as a teacher, toiling for a pittance to instruct the distracted children of rich Southern farmers—though he had no qualms about relieving his wife of the money she had earned doing exactly that. For a long time Audubon had been able to tell himself that if all else failed, someday, somewhere, he could make a living painting birds. But when he went aboard the *Delos*, he was taking the final step. If he failed now, he failed at everything.

Early one evening on the ship, Audubon and another passenger drank a bottle of porter. Audubon, retiring to the cabin to write in his journal, apparently found another bottle to keep his glass full. In a long entry marked by increasingly unsteady handwriting, Audubon free-associated about his trip. He had long dreaded the voyage itself, he wrote, and now that he was at sea being "swung about, rolled, heaved, bruised and shifted around probably around half a million times," it was even worse than he had anticipated. His thoughts lurched wildly. Audubon reported sighting near the ship a bird never before described by anyone and wondered where George Ord, an "academician" of all things, came off questioning his veracity as a naturalist. The world was full of things nobody knew anything about. If Audubon said a turkey could swim—because he'd seen it with his own eyes—then who was Ord to laugh at him? But then who was he to be going off to Europe? Audubon wondered "where the devil" he was running to. England? The home of Milton and Shakespeare? The country that cried for Byron? The room whirled. Audubon seemed suddenly intimidated. "Oh England," he wrote shakily, "renowned isle! How shall I enter thee? Good God, what have I pronounced—am I fit to enter her dominions at all? My heart swells."

As it got dark in the cabin, Audubon started to write about his feelings for Lucy. But he thought better of it and instead fell drunkenly into bed.

Even though it was the middle of summer, the streets of Liverpool were choked with coal smoke. Audubon—always sensitive to smoke—rubbed his eyes and wheezed. But looking around, he saw a world that was totally new to him. He found an inn and had breakfast, happy to take a meal on solid ground. Although he felt lonely, Audubon was impressed by the polite way people offered him directions. Several times as he walked through town, Audubon stopped short, startled by the sudden clatter of approaching hooves. But on turning to look for a horse bearing down on him, Audubon saw only plump Englishwomen walking along, their stiff heels clacking noisily against the cobblestones. They were quite pretty, he thought, with fresh, rosy complexions and lovely figures. There was some confusion at the customs house about his drawings—nobody had

ever seen such a portfolio before. In the end Audubon was charged a duty
of two pennies on each of the paintings.

Audubon checked into a hotel called the Commercial Inn. Three days
later, he surprised himself by sleeping in until ten o'clock. It was the beginning of a momentous day. He joked to himself that something in the
air he was breathing or the food he was eating must have undermined his
normal discipline of rising with the birds at dawn. Perhaps this was a reverse example of the "degeneration" the great Comte de Buffon had believed took place in America. Audubon wished he could have met
Buffon, whom he deemed a true original, a man who had cast both "light"
and "shade" over the study of natural history.

When he went later that day to call on Richard Rathbone, the man to
whom Vincent Nolte had recommended him, Audubon did not imagine
the sudden change in his fortunes that was about to take place. After
tracking him down and being invited for lunch, Audubon went to Rathbone's house and waited anxiously in the dining room for his host to appear. Staring out the window, Audubon broke into a sweat and for an
instant felt he was about to lose his nerve altogether. Presently, Rathbone
appeared and greeted him like a long-absent relative. They were joined at
lunch by Rathbone's wife and children. Audubon, unable to eat a bite,
simply looked and listened, amazed at the handsomeness and refinement
of this family. That evening, the Rathbones took Audubon to an art exhibition. The next day Audubon packed one of his several portfolios and
went back. He ended up joining the family on an excursion to their country estate, Green Bank, a short distance from the city. Audubon thought
the countryside lovely beyond description. At Green Bank, he was introduced to Rathbone's mother, his brother William, and several young
Rathbone women. Noticing the well-executed bird drawings on the walls
of the house when he started to untie his own portfolio, Audubon told
himself not to rush. As he fumbled with the string, he felt his heart
pounding "like a pheasant's." But his fear soon disappeared. Turning the
huge pages, each one a window onto his life in America, Audubon was
elated as the Rathbones told him again and again how wonderful his
drawings were. The Rathbones fairly glowed in his mind. They were like
"celestial beings" to him. On his return to the city that evening, Audubon
could barely contain his emotions when Rathbone said good night and
ordered the carriage to take Audubon on to his hotel.

The Rathbones, both Richard and William, turned out to be fabulously well connected. Their family had gotten rich in the cotton business and their father had also been a prominent abolitionist. The sons knew all of the city's richest and most influential people, and William would one day be elected mayor of Liverpool. Audubon, clueless and overwhelmed, could not have invented better or more influential patrons for himself. Over the course of several weeks, the Rathbones arranged for Audubon to meet a succession of Liverpool's leading lights, all of whom quickly converted to ardent admirers. One of these was William Roscoe, a neighbor of the Rathbones who was a writer, historian, naturalist, and art fancier. Shortly after Richard Rathbone and Roscoe hosted a dinner for Audubon, at which he was introduced to still more local celebrities, the Liverpool Royal Institution invited Audubon to exhibit his drawings in their hall for three days, beginning the last day of July. Audubon visited the hall over the weekend—to judge the light, he said—and also went to church.

Despite the sudden, vertiginous embrace of Liverpool's upper crust, Audubon worried about a few things. He'd had no word from Lucy yet. And he was unsure how to make his presence known to Lucy's sister Ann, whom he had not seen in many years but who was living in Liverpool after marrying a Scottish man named Gordon. In fact, upon his arrival, Audubon had briefly met Gordon and sensed that he might not be entirely welcome to call on his sister-in-law. Eventually he went to see her. It was awkward at first—Audubon kissed her and she did not kiss him back, apparently not convinced as to who he was. But as they spoke, Ann warmed to him. Soon they were talking about old times. Once she'd recovered from her surprise, Ann told Audubon he ought to cut his hair, a suggestion he didn't act on. Later, Audubon—writing in his journal as if he were speaking directly to Lucy—went on at some length about a friend of Ann's who was also present, a Miss Donathan, whose hair he found singularly beautiful. This kind of insensitive description of the attractiveness of other women would gradually become habitual in Audubon's correspondence to his wife.

On Monday, July 31, Audubon got to the Royal Institution three hours early to set up his drawings in its gallery. He selected nearly half of what he had, mounting them on purple plush. It must have seemed almost unreal that he had arrived in Liverpool a stranger only ten days before. At five minutes to noon, when the exhibition was to commence, he began watching the seconds tick by on his watch. When the doors opened, a great crowd, including many ladies, rushed in and at once began to sigh at the magnificence of Audubon's birds. More than four hundred people turned out in the space of two hours. It was the same the next day and the day after. The exhibition was held over. Audubon increased the number of drawings on display and was ecstatic when Ann, Mr. Gordon, and Miss Donathan attended the exhibition. Audubon was introduced to so many people he complained of fatigue from bowing. In the dining room at his hotel, everyone suddenly seemed to know who he was. Audubon now stepped lightly through the streets of Liverpool, memorizing their names and learning to navigate the city after dark. He liked England very much. The weather in August reminded him of early spring in America. Liverpool was lit by gas streetlights at night, and the shops lining the walks were warm and inviting. Audubon had expected the city to be crowded, but instead he found the streets pleasantly uncongested. The staff of the Royal Institution, stunned at the enthusiastic turnout for the free display of Audubon's drawings, suggested that he not only continue the exhibit but also start charging admission. Audubon was tempted. But he was concerned that showing his drawings for money would somehow cheapen them—and also discredit him as a naturalist and a man of science. The Rathbones and Roscoe offered conflicting advice, and in the end Audubon decided to keep the exhibition free. Head spinning, Audubon packed up his portfolio one morning in early August and was taken by carriage to the home of a man named Adam Hodgson. Hodgson, the recipient of Vincent Nolte's second letter of introduction, was a business partner of the Rathbones. He had arranged for Audubon to meet Lord Stanley.

Edward Stanley—Lord Stanley—was in a few years to become the thirteenth Earl of Derby. He was a member of Parliament and a naturalist of great stature in his own right. He had a keen interest in British birds. As a young man he had studied Buffon's work, and had since amassed a notable collection of bird drawings and specimens. Audubon was beside himself at the prospect of meeting Stanley, and quizzed Hodgson at length about how he should act. When Stanley was introduced and led into the room, Audubon's hair—according to his hilarious confession in his journal—literally stood on end. He felt he must have surely looked like a porcupine. Lord Stanley, exhibiting the ease and impeccable manners that Audubon had come to expect of Englishmen—though not necessarily from one of such elevated stature—greeted him warmly. Stanley was ten years older than Audubon. He was, Audubon noted, a fine-looking man, with lively eyes, a high forehead, and luxuriant sideburns that framed his face. As Audubon gaped, Stanley politely inquired about his drawings.

Flustered, Audubon produced his portfolio and nearly fainted when Lord Stanley spread the contents on the floor and then got down on his hands and knees to examine them. They were excellent, Lord Stanley said, utterly beautiful. Noticing one drawing in need of a minor correction, Stanley pointed out the error to Audubon, furthering Audubon's already high estimation of Stanley's ornithological sophistication. Stanley spent a full five hours going over the collection. Afterward, as they dined and Audubon allowed himself to relax ever so slightly, Stanley told him his work deserved recognition by the Crown. On taking his leave, Stanley invited Audubon to call at his home in London whenever his travels took him there.

In less than a month's time, Audubon had accomplished more in Liverpool than he had dreamed possible. It was as if he had been reborn after the long, watery journey that had brought him from America. Everyone urged him to exhibit his drawings across the three kingdoms of Britain. Each day seemed to bring a fresh extravagance. Private carriages waited on him for every engagement. He visited grand homes and lingered over sumptuous banquets long into the evening. He consumed wine and ale in quantities to which he was unaccustomed. Occasionally he took a little snuff with the men after dinner. Handsome, smitten wives and daughters drew near the long-haired woodsman and asked for stories of the American frontier. When asked how he had escaped death by the attack of some fearsome beast of the forest, Audubon assured his hosts that nothing more notable than a tick or a mosquito had ever bothered him in the wild. He imitated bird calls upon request and one evening drew the Rathbones a sketch of himself, bearded and dressed head-to-toe in buckskins, with a hatchet in his belt, a gun in one hand, and a brace of freshly killed geese slung over his shoulder. The further his experiences diverged from those of the tidy, citified people he entertained, the more fascinated by him they seemed to be. Liverpool was the perfect inverse of Philadelphia. Projecting the very same persona—half artist, half man of action—that had earned him scorn from America's scientific elite made him a hero in England. More important, the drawings that had been called inaccurate and outlandish by the followers of Alexander Wilson were now viewed with awe by men of far greater wealth and knowledge.

For Audubon, the overnight success was exhilarating—and also disorienting. Within days of his first exhibition, Audubon's nerves were frayed. His mood grew erratic. Late at night, he sat in his room at the Commercial and confided to his journal that he was tormented by inexplicable fits of despair. Aududon's daily entries were increasingly dominated by episodes of loneliness and a free-floating anxiety that repeatedly overpowered him, often in the dead of night. Once, while visiting the Hodgsons, he was awakened at three in the morning by the call of a blackbird. Unable to go back to sleep, Audubon dressed and tiptoed from the house, wandering the fields all the way to the seaside before returning for breakfast and a hasty return to his own quarters.

Just as in the journal Audubon kept six years earlier on his way to Louisiana, his daily diary took the form of an extended letter to his family—but this time he spoke exclusively to Lucy. He missed her terribly and still had not received any word from home. Every ship that arrived from America without a letter from Lucy was a crushing disappointment. The thought that he was on the verge of accomplishing what he'd set out to do only intensified his unhappiness at their separation. Although he was gratified by the attention and admiration of his influential new friends, he could not get over his shyness and discomfort in their presence. Sometimes, as he walked to the Rathbones' or the Hodgsons', his knees would weaken and Audubon would feel as if he wanted to run back to his hotel. He spent occasional restorative overnights at Green Bank. Though it was only three miles outside the city, Green Bank was a relief from the bustle of Liverpool—which had at first been so welcome but had just as quickly begun to wear on Audubon. Now the streets of the city seemed jarring and frightening. Discordant winds howled outside his rooms at night, keeping him awake and jittery. Audubon was distressed by the beggars and prostitutes who wandered the city. Looking out from his room at the Commercial, he could not believe the same moonlight illuminating the city outside the window also fell on the quiet countryside at Green Bank. And even out there, he was dismayed by the many areas posted against trespassers. Audubon was used to going wherever he pleased. Here people guarded their property with notices and dogs and sometimes guns booby-trapped to fire at anyone who, unawares, came too close. The more time he spent in Liverpool, the more claustrophobic it felt. Audubon visualized great throngs of people moving through the city, jostling and "encroaching" on one another, coming together in a whirling mix, like crosscurrents in a powerful flood.

Audubon also could not get used to the pace of his new life. The late dinners and rich fare of the people who entertained him disrupted his routine. He began taking breakfast at eight in the morning, a full two hours later than he was accustomed. Sometimes he slept too late for the walk he usually took at dawn. Audubon tried to draw, but found himself distracted and unable to get down on paper anything he thought was any good. Sorting through his emotions one morning when he managed to get out for an early stroll, Audubon stumbled into a confrontation that unnerved him even further.

As he walked along the banks of the Mersey River toward the ocean, Audubon saw a small boat haul up on shore. A stooped, disheveled man climbed out carrying a sack. Certain at once that the man was a smuggler, Audubon drew the sword concealed in his walking stick and yelled at the man to stop where he was. The man instead dropped the sack and took off at a run. But he was no match for Audubon, and an instant later was cowering before the wild-haired American. Audubon, only slightly out of breath, ordered the man to go back and pick up the sack, noticing as the pathetic figure trudged ahead of him that he seemed poorer and more beaten down than even the slaves Audubon had encountered in America. While the man retrieved the bag, Audubon watched in disgust as the accomplices pulled on their oars and fled the scene. The sack turned out to be filled with about fifty pounds of American tobacco. Audubon berated the man, telling him a smuggler was an enemy to his own country. Scared, eyes bulging, the man begged for mercy and offered Audubon the tobacco if only he would let him go. Audubon, who never smoked in his life, instead eyed a pair of pistols he hadn't noticed before in the man's belt. Seeing this, the man assured Audubon that his guns were not loaded. Audubon didn't believe him. But the man was so pitiful that Audubon began to feel less righteous by the moment. Reaching into his pockets, Audubon held out a handful of pennies to the man and commanded him to look him squarely in the face. With a warning to never do anything like this again, Audubon told him to get lost. The man croaked out a thank-you and ran off toward a hedge, where he vanished. Back at his hotel, as he was cleaning the mud from his boots, Audubon suffered a delayed reaction. What if the man had shot him?

As it was, Audubon was well supplied with his own demons without going looking for trouble. One evening about this same time, he returned to his room and began to record the day's events in his journal. Suddenly Audubon put down his pen and stared into space. At first he thought vaguely of America, and then in a frightening rush, as if he were being propelled through space, Aububon felt his whole consciousness transported by a mysterious force to the other side of the ocean. The sensation was not pleasant. A nameless dread flashed into his mind and Lucy appeared before him in a terrifying vision, cloaked in hideous garments. Frozen in place, Audubon could not move for an hour. At last he stumbled to his bed and fell onto his pillow sobbing.

By day, Audubon somehow held himself together for the business at hand. After first resisting the idea, Audubon had been persuaded to renew his exhibition at the Royal Institution with an admission charge of one shilling (about twenty cents). An advertisement was prepared for the papers. But Audubon continued to worry that this was a mistake, that his drawings would now fall under the unforgiving eyes of "the critics." He needn't have been concerned. People still came and the papers reviewed the exhibition favorably. Audubon was still the talk of the town. Even more important to him by now was the continuing affection shown him by the Rathbones, who in late August convinced him to give up his room at the Commercial and move in temporarily at Green Bank. Audubon had felt the Rathbones' hospitality was something he could trust ever since his first visit to Green Bank, when he overheard Richard Rathbone telling another guest that Audubon was a "simple intelligent," a description that flattered Audubon. The women of the Rathbone clan, including Richard and William's mother—the "Queen Bee," as Audubon called her—as well as their wives and daughters, were also taken with him. One daughter in particular, the lovely Miss Hannah, beguiled Audubon and evidently encouraged his attentions whenever they were together. Audubon, with a surprising lack of husbandly empathy, wrote to Lucy in his journal that she would surely like Hannah if only she could see the young girl's beautiful eyes, her smile, or the way she blushed when Audubon stared at her. Late one evening under a full moon, the Rathbone ladies invited Audubon on a walk that lasted until sunrise. Rambling across dewy meadows, they spoke of metaphysics, of the timeless imponderables of the universe, and of human volition and whence it comes. Back at Green Bank, Audubon slept only four hours afterward.

The Rathbones had encouraged Audubon to stay with them in the hope that he would find Green Bank more conducive to his drawing and painting. He did. Audubon worked on a magnificent drawing of the turkey cock—the one Mrs. Richard Rathbone had him reduce so she could have a seal bearing the image made for him. She was much less taken with a painting he did especially for her.

It was his bloody picture of an otter, which Audubon now boldly attempted in oils. As was the case with many of his drawings, which he copied and recopied many times over, this was a new version of a painting he'd first done in watercolor years before. In fact, it was the same picture he'd been in the middle of back in Henderson on the day the eccentric Constantine Rafinesque had shown up looking for him. Like many of his drawings, this one was meant to convey the ferocity of nature. It is arguably one of his most startling and gruesome images. Audubon depicted the otter in profile. One of its forelegs is caught in a leghold trap. The animal's head is turned toward the viewer, its mouth agape in a snarling grimace of pain. Audubon, whose head was filled with such violent images, was at least sensitive enough to consider the possibility that Mrs. Rathbone would find the picture disquieting. He wrote her a pleading note, hoping she would not be offended and would not feel obliged to accept the painting merely out of courtesy. Still, he was disappointed when the Rathbones offered only perfunctory thanks for the picture—which was promptly donated to the Royal Institution.

By the start of September, Audubon was preparing to take his drawings to Manchester, a milling and manufacturing center in the English midlands about forty miles east of Liverpool. He now carried many letters of introduction that would see him across Britain, and had also been assured of finding exhibition space at Royal Institution galleries in several cities. Audubon still had not received a letter from Lucy. He felt "desolate and alone," he wrote in his journal. It was almost as if his beloved wife had never existed. He wrote to Victor, who was still in Louisville, imploring him to let Lucy know he was desperate for news from her. In the month he'd been in Liverpool, at least eight ships had arrived from New Orleans. Audubon could not understand her silence. In a letter to Lucy,

Audubon said his latest exhibition had done well—how well he didn't go into—but that his concern about her was making it increasingly hard for him to write to her. Audubon said he wished their boys could someday see England, as he was most impressed by the education and manners of the young men he had met. He asked Lucy to make sure that John Woodhouse, now almost fourteen, tended to his lessons and that he practiced drawing from nature in the way Audubon had instructed him.

Manchester was much more crowded than Liverpool. Audubon didn't like it. The economy was depressed, the streets narrow and dirty. People were less friendly, it seemed, and having got used to the company of proper English ladies, Audubon was now sorry to be without it. In fact, respectable women in Manchester appeared to be outnumbered by the poor streetwalkers he encountered everywhere. Audubon rented exhibition space and even hired a boy to collect admission. But attendance was modest and his reception indifferent. Audubon caught a cold. Time passed slowly.

Then, on September 16, Audubon got two letters from Lucy—one from late May and the other from early June. He admitted in his journal that every time he'd thought of their last farewell, it had occurred to him that he might never see her again. Now he was much relieved, feeling the stirrings of optimism for the first time in many weeks. One of the letters included a small treasure, a drawing by John Woodhouse. Audubon promptly sent it to Hannah Rathbone, asking that she put it in her scrapbook. Lucy's letters cheered Audubon tremendously. "Thanks," he rhapsodized in his journal, "thanks to thee, my dear wife, for thy kindness!!" The only thing that would have made him happier at that moment, Audubon said, would have been to be in America and exhibiting his drawings there.

The actual plan, which had taken some time to coalesce, was for Audubon to carry on with a slow tour of England and Scotland until March. He intended to exhibit his work as long as there was an acceptable profit in it—meaning an income approximately four times greater than expenses, he said. At the end of the tour, if "accident or circumstances" did not alter his purpose, he would finish with a bigger, longer exhibition in London. While touring, he could continue to work on his paintings. At the conclusion of all this, he meant to find a publisher for his work, either in London or Paris. Recognizing that this last undertaking implied a stay of considerable length, Audubon wrote to Lucy urging

her to finish up her current term at Beech Woods and then move to Shippingport—or better still, New York City, where communication between them would be easier. Most preferable would be for her to join
him in England, and to bring John Woodhouse with her. Audubon regretted not having had them come over with him in the first place and
was now eager to put things right. If, for some reason, she could not
come, then he believed he would now be able to send her enough money
to live anywhere in the United States that suited her.

Attendance at his Manchester exhibition continued to be poor. Some
days only twenty or so people came to see it. But people routinely called
on Audubon in his rented rooms to inspect his drawings, and some extended invitations to dinner. In late September, Audubon was invited to
hunt partridge with a local nobleman, a Lord Stamford. Stamford's
gamekeeper provided them with two dogs and guns "no longer than my
arms," Audubon said. It was not yet pheasant season, though the concept
of open or closed hunting seasons was completely foreign to Audubon.
When a pheasant got up, he reflexively dropped it with a quick shot,
oblivious of the fact that they were supposed to be after a different
species. Then another pheasant flushed, with the same result. Audubon
continued to shoot at every bird he saw—until the gamekeeper inter-
vened and declared a halt to the slaughter. The hunt was most pleasant,
Audubon said, and from the rolling hilltops he'd seen Derbyshire, where
Lucy's family had once lived. Some days later, Audubon was asked to dinner at the home of Thomas Lloyd, one of the wealthiest men in England.
Audubon estimated his assets at £400,000, about $1.8 million then.
Audubon was agog at the number of servants who attended their table
that evening. He also remarked on how much trouble he was given by the
English habit of toasting one another with wine. It was hard to get
through such an evening without being in your cups by the conclusion.

Toward the end of September, Audubon moved his exhibition to
Manchester's Royal Institution, which offered him free space. Leaving
some two hundred of his drawings on display, Audubon returned to Liverpool to visit the Rathbones. Riding atop the carriage so that someone
else could have his seat inside, Audubon got soaked in a cold rain. At
Green Bank, he was pleased when Miss Hannah asked for his assistance in
framing a sketch of himself he'd made for her.

It was on this visit that Audubon received an important introduction.
Friends arranged for him to meet with a man named Bohn, a bookseller

from London who was staying in Liverpool. Bohn, who struck Audubon as unusually honest and knowledgeable on such matters, advised him about publishing his work—which Audubon had lately begun to refer to as *The Birds of America*. Bohn told Audubon he should go to London and meet with prominent naturalists there to find out which engravers and lithographers in the city might be up to the job of making colored reproductions of his drawings. He should also visit Paris and do the same, Bohn said, before deciding where best to undertake such a monumental project. Then, rather than wasting months exhibiting his drawings, Audubon should immediately publish a selection of his work and issue a prospectus for the rest. Implicit in this concept was the idea that Audubon would compose some sort of text to accompany his illustrations. The idea of becoming an "author" filled Audubon, a man more at ease in forests and swamps than among words, with trepidation. But this approach, Bohn assured him, would put his work before the largest possible audience in the shortest time. Audubon was all ears, eagerly nodding at everything Bohn said and agreeing that this was a plan he should adopt at once.

But while Audubon did not say so at the time, one of Bohn's suggestions was out of the question. Bohn told Audubon there was a large potential audience for his work among people with taste and the wherewithal to buy an expensive book. These people liked to entertain, Bohn went on, and would likely buy Audubon's book as much for its value as a conversation piece as for its artistic or scientific merits. But Audubon's drawings were far too large for this purpose. A book made from his life-sized paintings would dwarf everything else its owner possessed—it would be more like a piece of furniture than a functional part of a library or an adornment for a sitting-room table. People would have no place to put it and no inclination to look at it. The result would be sales to only a few public institutions and a handful of blue-blooded dilettantes. Bohn urged Audubon to publish at a drastically reduced scale.

Audubon's resistance on this point was insurmountable. He seems never to have given the idea any serious consideration at all. This was not an insignificant matter, and Audubon's determination to do it his way was in the end one of the hallmarks of his genius as an artist. Audubon saw the world through a lens all his own. And at a time when he was poor and in a precarious state of mind, Audubon's real strength was his allegiance to his personal vision. He could no more produce an image of a bird at a fraction of its size than he could paint one plaid. Drawing his birds life-sized was not simply a matter of accuracy; Audubon understood that scale was a big part of the impact the images made on the viewer. No one looking at one of Audubon's larger birds—a turkey or an eagle, for example—could fail to be impressed with its magnificence when it was shown as big as life. Whatever this would mean for the eventual sales of his work, Audubon could not know. Sure enough, just a few weeks later as Bohn again looked at the drawings he changed his mind. They should be published full-sized, Bohn agreed. He told Audubon that if he failed to find a publisher willing to do the job, then he himself would find one.

The minute Audubon arrived back in Manchester, he hurried to the gallery to inspect his drawings. He found the doorman drunk. Audubon fired him and then had a look at his birds. In the cool darkness of an empty room far, far from home, they looked "fresh and gay," as lifelike as he remembered them from the forests of America.

Audubon spent his next days touring the countryside where Lucy and her family were from. He was joined for much of the time by assorted Rathbones, including the seemingly ever-present Miss Hannah. Lucy, who would have been excited to hear of her husband's visit to Bakewell, the town bearing her family name, would undoubtedly have been less thrilled to know that he went with Miss Hannah leaning on his arm, the two of them lost in confused feelings that were neither "very happy nor very sad."

By the third week of October, Audubon had decided that his stay in Manchester was unprofitable and it was time to move on. But he changed his mind about going directly to London and instead made plans to head north, into Scotland and on to Edinburgh. It was a two-day carriage ride. The driver complained about Audubon's trunk and his oversized portfolio, but the trip was pleasant enough. Four passengers rode inside the carriage and another ten, including Audubon, on top. Audubon was surprised at how rapidly the countryside changed as they passed through it—flat one minute, hilly the next. Dense, inviting forests alternated with open vistas that Audubon found dull. There were black-faced sheep everywhere. Audubon saw some pheasants and thought to himself how much John Woodhouse would enjoy shooting in this place. After a time, the road passed alongside the North Sea, which he found picturesque. At a stopover, Audubon ate fish and took his first taste of Scotch whiskey. The locals drank it like water, he said, but he found it far too strong for his "weak head." The stage arrived in Edinburgh an hour before midnight on the second day. Audubon, glancing at the clean, gaslit streets lined with lovely stone buildings, checked into an inn called the Star, thinking that what little he had been able to make out of the city late at night looked wonderful.

Edinburgh, Audubon declared, was the most beautiful city he had ever seen—a gem perched between the Pentland Hills and the point of the Firth of Forth on the North Sea. The city was arranged on two parallel hilltops, which ran east–west on either side of a narrow declivity. On one side was the "Old Town," overlooked on one end by the imposing Edinburgh Castle, a centuries-old keep whose foundation incorporated the solid volcanic rocks found atop the highest point in the city. From this commanding height, High Street descended along the spine of the hill, flanked on either side by shops and churches and residences, all built of cut stone mellowed by time to a soothing shade of gray. At the far end of High Street was Holyrood Palace, the twelfth-century abbey that had once been home to Mary Queen of Scots.

On the opposite hilltop—reached by either of two main bridges—was the "New Town," an orderly grid of stone rowhouses, shops, and pubs of more recent vintage, largely built between 1750 and 1800. Princes Street, a broad commercial thoroughfare, ran right along the edge of the New Town where it faced the old, and rising beyond it was a neat latticework of streets and avenues, strategically interrupted by quiet public squares. On a plain to the south of the city, a wedge-shaped escarpment—a long-extinct volcano—rose sharply to over eight hundred feet. This was "Arthur's Seat," named for the Scottish legend who supposedly passed some meditative hours there.

The New Town was symbolic of Edinburgh's emergence in the eighteenth century as one of Europe's intellectual capitals. Home to artists and architects, Edinburgh had also been in the middle of the philosophical movement emphasizing human reason and the fundamental rights of man that had inspired America's founders. The origins of the modern age still hung in the clear air of Edinburgh. Audubon, well aware that the city was a great seat of learning, hoped to meet its current resident genius, the novelist Walter Scott.

On his first day in the city, Audubon slept late. He had breakfast at ten, and then found rooms for rent on George Street, a broad boulevard off St. Andrew Square in the New Town. A bedroom and a comfortable, well-furnished sitting room, from which he could see steamships plying the Firth, was to cost him one guinea—less than five dollars—per week. Later, as Audubon explored the city, he marveled at the castles and parks and could scarcely believe how clean and neat everything was. The cobblestone pavements and broad sidewalks were as smooth and uniform as the buildings that stood in regular formation everywhere.

After a long day hiking through the city, Audubon returned to his rooms thinking he'd like to take a look at his drawings, always a cheering prospect. While Audubon's mental state had improved since he'd gotten Lucy's letters, his moods still fluctuated. As he looked over his birds, Audubon was suddenly seized by a fear that they would never be published. He felt bereft and alone. Later, over dinner, Audubon still could not shake these anxious thoughts. He worried that Lucy was sick, possibly dead. He was unable to eat. As his food sat in front of him getting cold, Audubon felt tears coming on. He rushed from the restaurant to escape this "painful gloom" with a long walk. Back at his rooms later, he calmed down a little. There was a pair of stuffed pheasants in his sitting room. He admired them for a bit and then looked closely at himself in the mirror. Audubon was startled by what he saw—his own father looking back at him. He'd forgotten how much they resembled each other. Before he went to bed, Audubon wrote in his journal that these bouts of despair frightened him badly. He hinted darkly that he now and then worried he would someday overreact to one.

Audubon set out right away to call on people to whom he had letters of introduction. Nobody seemed to be home. He finally tracked down Robert Jameson at the University of Edinburgh. Jameson was one of the university's most eminent professors, an instructor in geology and natural history. Jameson was also president of the Wernerian Natural History Society, which he had founded in 1808. Named for Jameson's mentor, a somewhat obscure German mineralogist named Abraham Gottlob Werner, the Wernerian Society was the Scottish equivalent of the Academy of Natural Sciences in Philadelphia. The society met on Saturday afternoons when the college was in session, and papers read before the membership were often published by the *Edinburgh New Philosophical Journal*—which was edited by Professor Jameson.

Audubon got a brusque reception from the professor, who seemed busy and distracted. He told Audubon it might be several days before he had time to look at Audubon's drawings. When Audubon mentioned that he also hoped to show them to Walter Scott, Jameson seemed huffy. Scott, he said, was hard at work on a new novel and a biography of Napoleon—he was unlikely to make room in his schedule for the likes of Audubon.

Audubon told himself not to take offense at being so lightly dismissed. After all, he thought, wasn't he just as absorbed in his own work? The next day he took a long walk. Some of the "lower class" women he saw carried loaded baskets on their heads and walked in a pigeon-toed way that reminded him of Indian squaws. He went out to Leith, Edinburgh's port village. It was a beautiful day. A sharp wind rocked the boats in the harbor and waves broke along the shore. On his way back, Audubon was stopped by a woman who was nicely dressed and seemed well-spoken. But she told him she was poor and would do anything for him for some cash. Audubon held out his hands and said he was also poor, and a stranger. Hustling away from the woman, Audubon was shocked when she swore at him. Audubon realized that, even in so civilized a city as Edinburgh, he was an easy mark. He promised himself he'd be more careful. That night he relaxed at the theater, taking in the play *Rob Roy*. When he came home with a cough, the landlady at George Street offered him a glass of grog.

Audubon learned that one of the things keeping Professor Jameson busy was a collaboration with the naturalist Prideaux John Selby and a "Sir Somebody" on an illustrated book of British birds. The "Sir" was William Jardine, an Edinburgh naturalist of international standing who in just a few years would begin publication of his forty-volume *Naturalist's Library*, an account of the entire known vertebrate kingdom. All that Audubon knew was that these gentlemen seemed to have better things to do than look over his poor drawings. Still, he was feeling emboldened. He no longer suffered embarrassment about his appearance and didn't get flustered whenever someone asked him to open the big portfolio. He wrote to Victor at Louisville, telling him how fine Edinburgh was, but that he would soon be on his way to Glasgow and then Inverness before returning south, to London and eventually to Paris.

After four days in town, Audubon had met only a handful of the people recommended to him. The few who visited his rooms to look at the portfolio assured him that the drawings were splendid. But one person, a businessman named Patrick Neill, seemed to take a special interest. When Audubon called on Neill one rainy afternoon and told him he was ready to give up on Jameson and move on, Neill urged him not to go. Audubon admitted he'd become impatient, convinced nobody else in Edinburgh had the slightest interest in his work. But Neill was insistent and said he had an idea. Dropping what he was doing, Neill took Audubon to St. James Square and introduced him to a man named Lizars.

William Home Lizars was three years younger than Audubon. An artist at heart, Lizars had shown early promise with his richly textured depictions of ordinary events in Scottish life. He'd even had two of his paintings exhibited at the Royal Academy in 1811. But his father's death a year later had forced Lizars to take over the family printing and engraving concern. He was currently engraving illustrations for at least two major works—Selby's birds and a volume on human anatomy. Lizars had a thriving business and was highly thought of, though some of his clients worried that he paid his colorists too little to ensure their best efforts.

Lizars studied Audubon while listening to Neill go on about the drawings, in the end agreeing to accompany Audubon back to his rooms for a look at his portfolio. It was still raining as Audubon and Lizars walked toward George Street under a shared umbrella. Lizars talked all the way about what a brilliant illustrator Selby was. Once inside, Audubon offered the soggy Lizars a chair. He opened the portfolio and without saying anything began showing Lizars his drawings, one by one. A look of wonder came over Lizars's face. After a minute he could not contain himself. "My God," Lizars said. "I never saw anything like this before!" The next morning, before Audubon had a chance to go anywhere, Lizars was back—this time accompanied by Robert Jameson.

Professor Jameson suddenly had all the time in the world for Audubon. He quite agreed with Lizars that the drawings were extraordinary. After a while Jameson's praise became so effusive that Audubon grew wary. But he accepted Jameson's invitation to breakfast at his home the next morning. Later that day, he walked through Edinburgh feeling deliriously happy. In the evening, he stopped in at Lizars's shop, where he was impressed by Lizars's skill as both an engraver and a painter. Audubon was also happy to meet Mrs. Lizars, a beautiful woman and the first of such with whom he'd had a chance to spend any time since his arrival in Edinburgh. Audubon, in a rare moment of discretion, kept his appreciation of Mrs. Lizars's loveliness to himself. He bit his tongue again when Lizars got out some original drawings by Selby and Jardine. They were good, Audubon thought—about as good as what John Woodhouse could do. Was it possible that after all these years his work really was better than anyone else's? As he walked home through the silent streets just before eleven o'clock, Audubon marveled at what seemed to be happening to him.

And it continued the next day. Over a fine breakfast at Jameson's comfortable house, Audubon decided he had totally misjudged the professor. The truth was, of course, just the reverse—it was Jameson who had unwisely dismissed Audubon on their first meeting. Now all was forgiven. Audubon thought Jameson's friendliness all the more remarkable for how supremely intelligent the man seemed to be. Audubon found him fascinating, and was amused by their shared penchant for unfashionable hairstyles. The professor's, Audubon noted, was done up in multiple parts, so that it went in three directions—right, left, and straight up. Jameson assured Audubon he would do everything in his power—which was considerable—to introduce Audubon and his work to the world of science. Audubon departed, ecstatic, and had barely taken off his coat back at his rooms when Jameson showed up with a crowd of friends to look at Audubon's drawings. A steady parade continued throughout the afternoon. That night Audubon fell asleep thinking of Beech Woods, imagining himself in bed with Lucy.

Now things happened in a blur. Lizars was positively smitten by the action in Audubon's drawings—especially one showing a rattlesnake with a group of mockingbirds. When Audubon realized he had not yet shown Lizars some of his larger pieces, he insisted on doing so. Looking at Audubon's drawings of the wild turkey—one a great striding cock, and another a hen with her brood of chicks—Lizars was moved. He draped his arm around Audubon's shoulders as they looked at more. Lizars loved Audubon's drawing of a covey of partridges being attacked from the air by a hawk, and he was delighted by the painting of a whooping crane bending its great neck toward the earth to devour a baby alligator. When Audubon turned up his drawing of the great-footed hawk—the peregrine falcon—Lizars's arm dropped and he stood stock still. For a long moment he said nothing as he studied the picture, which shows a pair of hawks feeding on two freshly killed ducks. A solitary feather floats in the air above the birds, whose eyes seem filled with a savage lust. Blood empties from a gaping wound on one of the ducks, and falls in hot droplets from a hawk's beak. For a moment, Lizars was speechless. At last he turned to Audubon. "I will engrave and publish this," he said.

The room was still crowded with other visitors, so Audubon and Lizars did not strike a deal then and there. But later that day Audubon went to see Lizars—who poured him a glass of wine, followed by three glasses of Scotch. Lizars reiterated his desire to engrave some of Audubon's drawings. Lizars was impressed with the letters of introduction Audubon showed him. He told Audubon that they'd soon be unnecessary, as it would not be long before everyone knew who he was. That night, Audubon wrote in his journal that he felt at last "fame and fortune" were at hand, and that he could now see to the well-being of his wife and the education of his children. Money, Audubon said, didn't really matter to him. But it was necessary to have it, and so have it he would, on their behalf. As for himself, all he wanted was a plum for breakfast.

As it was now early November and there were no plums to be had, Audubon settled for boiled eggs the next morning. Soon his room was again crowded. Audubon showed his drawings while Lizars served as a kind of master of ceremonies, ushering the guests in and out at a dizzying pace. One of the people who called that day was the artist John Syme, a young but highly regarded portraitist. Syme and a few others remained with Audubon and Lizars for dinner. It was a lively evening, full of toasting. Everyone present agreed that Audubon should sit for Syme. Lizars immediately offered to engrave such a likeness.

Every day for the next couple of weeks, Audubon received a steady stream of visitors eager to view his work. Everyone who was anyone in Edinburgh was interested—from Sir William Jardine himself to the actress starring in the production of *Rob Roy* Audubon had attended only days before. Audubon made time to sit for John Syme now and again. What little private time was left to him Audubon used to work on a large oil painting of a hen turkey. When that was done, he amused himself by making a new sketch of his "Otter in a Trap." Audubon was also in demand as a dinner companion. The "constant round of parties, suppers and dinners," as he described it, was exhausting. It seemed all he did was eat and drink and show off his drawings. Meanwhile, the local Royal Institution offered him exhibition space. By mid-November, he was earning more than £5 (about $22) a day from admissions.

Audubon and Lizars continued to work out the details of publication even as the engraving commenced. They decided that *The Birds of America* would be published in installments, or "Numbers." Each Number would comprise five hand-colored plates from Lizars's engravings. Audubon knew a separate text would have to accompany the illustrations, but put off thinking about the letterpress for the time being. There was again discussion as to how big the plates should be—Audubon had once more been advised that his drawings were too cumbersome—but he would not be budged. Each Number, in keeping with the concept that had first occurred to Audubon on his long trip back to Bayou Sara from Philadelphia, would consist of a mix of different-sized birds, all full-scale, all printed on the same oversized "double elephant" papers. The initial plate would always be one of his largest drawings. It would be followed by a medium-sized drawing and then three of the smaller ones. Audubon, showing some marketing sense, anticipated that buyers would be so bowled over by the huge opening image in each Number that they would fall in love with the rest as well. But when he saw the smaller birds finally being engraved and colored, he realized how exquisite they were in their own right. Set in the middle of the enormous sheets of heavy paper, the smaller drawings seemed to Audubon to possess an "air of richness and wealth." A prospectus was drafted to announce the publication. It emphasized Audubon's long experience on the frontier, promising incomparable illustrations of American birds in their full, life size. *The Birds of America*, it stated, would be the most colorful and accurate work of its kind, showing both the male and female of those species where the two differed in appearance, and depicting the birds in natural settings, often in pursuit of prey amid lush foliage that was also meticulously represented.

Audubon agreed to pay for production of the first Number, which he would then take on the road throughout England in hopes of securing subscribers for the rest. Each Number was to be priced at two guineas—about $9.45. With upwards of four hundred drawings, a complete set of *The Birds of America* figured to ultimately cost about $822. Audubon calculated that if he could secure three hundred subscribers he would make a reasonable profit. This all happened so fast that Audubon had no time to worry about the abandonment of his plan to go to London or Paris for a publisher. Lizars's engravings were, in any case, dazzling. He felt certain that this was the right thing to do, and that he would pursue this course no matter what. Audubon had no illusions as to how easy this would be or how long it would take. It occurred to him that he might never set foot in America again.

Toward the end of the month it snowed, causing Audubon to recall wistfully his last warm November at Bayou Sara. Work on the first Number was going so well that several colored plates would soon be ready to exhibit at the Royal Institution. On the last day of the month, John Syme showed Audubon his finished portrait. It depicted a dashing Audubon in a heroic pose beneath a rose-tinted sky. He was dressed in a fur hunting coat, with leather bandoliers strapped over his chest and a shotgun cradled in his arms, one thumb resting on the hammers. The way his luxurious hair was pulled back from a high forehead and allowed to fall gently past his shoulders emphasized his long nose and large, sensitive eyes— delicate, romantic features that dominated an otherwise atavistic image. Audubon coyly said he wasn't sure if it was a good likeness, but that it certainly was a fine picture. The next day it was put up alongside his drawings at the public exhibit. Audubon said it felt good to have people staring at his portrait instead of at him for a change.

How could all this happen? How was it that the same man who had been blackballed in Philadelphia was now being lionized in England and Scotland? What explained Lizars's eagerness to engrave *The Birds of America* when Lizars's countryman Alexander Lawson had declared Audubon incompetent and thrown him out of his engraving studio in Philadelphia?

If Audubon was puzzled, he didn't admit to it. But he must have sensed that his long years of anonymity in the wilds of America, which had contributed to his being discredited in Philadelphia, were seen here in a more favorable light. Audubon knew that the British were enamored of roguish explorer types. One who was then popular was a wealthy and eccentric naturalist named Charles Waterton, who'd made four expeditions to South America, the most recent only two years before. Waterton had written colorful accounts of these travels, and was famous for his claim of having ridden on the backs of caimans. Audubon wondered if he should claim to have done the same with alligators. In any event, Audubon's lack of training in a scientific discipline did not seem to stand in his way in Edinburgh, as it had in America. Besides, if Audubon could not yet be called a man of science, Professor Jameson had it in mind to make him one.

Jameson urged Audubon to attend meetings of the Wernerian Society, and to present papers there on American zoological subjects. Audubon was understandably intimidated by this prospect. In addition to his shyness, which would surely translate into paralyzing stage fright before a learned assemblage, Audubon worried that he still did not write nearly well enough in English for such a purpose. In fact, Audubon's English was good. Years of obsessive journal-keeping and letter-writing had given him considerable practice. He still mangled an occasional word, but generally wrote quite acceptably in the stiff, slightly ornate style of the day. Plus, one of Jameson's colleagues at the university offered to edit Audubon's papers and straighten them out grammatically. Audubon still hesitated. He asked Jameson repeatedly if this was necessary. Jameson insisted that it was, and that delivering papers to the Wernerians would be the fastest way to become known by the educated and prominent persons on whom he would soon be calling for subscriptions. Audubon also understood that in appearing at the society he would be elected an honorary member—and that this would in turn lead to his election to learned institutions across Britain.

Audubon at first thought he would deliver a paper on the wild turkey, a bird he had observed perhaps more closely than any other, and whose habits he thought the Wernerians would find unusually interesting. But he changed his mind. Instead, he wrote about the turkey buzzard—the bird now called the turkey vulture—taking into consideration some experiments he'd performed on its sense of smell back at Bayou Sara the year before. The paper was adapted from an account he had planned to send to someone else, recast as a letter to Professor Jameson. Audubon completed it in a day, working until midnight. Just over a week later, on the afternoon of December 16, he took a deep breath and headed for the Old Town.

The university, which was on South Bridge Street, was an imposing structure. It faced the street, looking like a great, gray city unto itself. The entrance was a soaring walkway that passed beneath a cupola and opened onto an immense stone courtyard surrounded by tall, colonnaded buildings with high, arched windows and vertiginous balconies. As Audubon walked into the courtyard clutching his paper, plus a portfolio and drawing kit, the sound of his boots echoing over the stones mixed in his ears with the pounding of his heart.

The Wernerians met in a long room with a fireplace at one end. They sat in heavy, high-backed chairs on either side of two large tables. When Audubon walked in, a stuffed swordfish—an object of the day's discussions—lay on one of the tables. Audubon may have felt a little like the fish. Everyone was eager to meet and listen to the American woodsman. Audubon, who had at the last minute demurred on presenting the paper himself, listened as the society's secretary read it aloud to the members in his stead. It was substantial, occupying thirteen typeset pages when Jameson later published it in the *Edinburgh New Philosophical Journal*. Audubon gave a thorough account of the turkey buzzard's life history and behavior. But he focused on the bird's sense of smell, which Audubon believed made little or no contribution to its finding carrion on which to feed. Audubon wrote that he had learned when he was very young that turkey buzzards were attracted to carrion by the odor of its putrefaction. But when he began studying the birds in the wild, he became less sure. They seemed quite unable to detect his presence, even when very nearby, unless they saw him. Audubon stated that nature is parsimonious—that creatures may, for example, rely on keen eyesight or a sensitive ability to smell, but not both. To test which sense the turkey buzzard relied on, he had conducted a number of experiments.

In one, Audubon stuffed a well-cured deer hide with grass and placed it in a field so as to make it look like a dead animal. A turkey buzzard alighted on it almost at once, and made numerous attempts to tear into the "corpse." In a second test, Audubon hid a dead and rotting hog in a ravine, covering it with brush so as to make it invisible from the air. Although the hog soon stank to high heaven under the hot Louisiana sun, buzzard after buzzard soared right over it for days without one bothering to investigate. Audubon then took a young pig down into the same ravine and slashed its throat, allowing the blood-soaked ground to remain in plain sight while he hid the pig's body close by. Buzzards immediately spotted the blood and, convening on the spot, followed the blood trail to the pig and ate it.

Audubon's compelling report was well wide of the truth. He may or may not have done such experiments, but he was quite wrong about the turkey buzzard. While it is the case that most bird species have a very poorly developed sense of smell—bird brains tend to have extremely small olfactory receptors—the turkey buzzard is a notable exception. It possesses an acute sense of smell that is especially attuned to a compound released by rotting meat.

But of course none of the Wernerians were in a position to question Audubon. The minutes from the meeting instead praised him for "exploding the opinion generally entertained of the [turkey buzzard's] extraordinary powers of smelling." Audubon, gratified by the reception, relaxed a little. He opened his portfolio and showed the members his drawing of the turkey buzzard. They all thought it breathtaking. Audubon then got out his drawing equipment and demonstrated his methods, explaining how he wired birds to a gridded board and then copied them exactly onto paper on which he had lightly drawn matching squares. At the conclusion of the session, Professor Jameson—seconded by Sir William Jardine—nominated Audubon as a Foreign Member of the Wernerians.

Just before Christmas of 1826, Audubon wrote to Lucy. He was in high spirits, despite what had become a grinding routine of dinners and parties that often broke up in the wee hours of the morning, leaving him run-down and headachy. At one point, he went two weeks without dining once in his own rooms. His days, filled with drawing and writing, were exhausting. Still, he seemed to be realizing all his ambitions in one headlong rush. And, after another long silence from Lucy, during which he'd again feared the worst, two letters from her had finally arrived. The news that she and the boys were well made him happy and homesick. Even so, he said, his situation in Edinburgh bordered on the "miraculous." He expected Lizars would complete the first Number of *The Birds of America* by the middle of January—a mere six months after he had landed at Liverpool. Audubon thought the engravings were splendid. This was critical, he told Lucy. Even though his original drawings inspired the most effusive praise, if the reproductions were inferior, no one would want them. In the meantime, while Lizars was occupied with the engraving, Audubon's reception in Edinburgh had become a string of fantastic successes. He told Lucy he would soon be elected to the Wernerian Society. In fact, two of its most esteemed members—the great naturalists

Selby and Jardine—had recently called on him two days running to receive instruction in his drawing technique.

Audubon was throughout his life generous—careless almost—in sharing his artistic methods. He did so, certainly, to ingratiate himself with powerful patrons. But he apparently also did it believing that his technique was only as good as the painter who tried it. Five months in England and Scotland had finally convinced him that his own talents were unmatched. Every day seemed to bring fresh rewards. On a recent Saturday he'd earned the astonishing sum of £15, about $67, from his exhibit. He told Lucy he would take *The Birds of America* in search of subscribers throughout Scotland, England, and Wales, then over to the continent of Europe. He said that while he could not yet be positive of success, it now seemed probable.

And he said a lot more. Because he retained the habit of referring to Lucy as "thee" or "thou," as he had when he first met her as a teenager and knew little English, Audubon's letters to his wife sometimes had a whiff of formality, a remoteness he probably didn't intend. Now he told Lucy that more than ever he realized how important it was for a family to be together. Audubon thought the boys would benefit tremendously from a move to Europe. Victor, with his smart head for business, could work with him in keeping track of subscriptions and receipts. John Woodhouse, who seemed to have inherited his father's talent for drawing, could continue his education. Audubon even suggested that, if he were to die, "Johnny" could take over and complete his work.

But with Lucy, Audubon was strangely noncommittal. He said he wanted her to join him as soon as possible, that he missed her every second of every day. But he did not tell her to come. Instead, he asked her to tell him what she had in mind. Audubon said Lucy should follow her heart in determining her intentions—and then inform him what they were. Back in America, this must have seemed a tepid invitation. All the while that Audubon complained of Lucy not writing, she was feeling at a loss too. In late November she'd written her cousin, saying that "Mr. Audubon" was in England, though she didn't know where. But she said if things worked out and he went ahead with the publication of his bird drawings over there, she expected to join him the following autumn.

Audubon continued to attend meetings of the Wernerian Society as the new year began. The discussions at these sessions were lately much concerned with the growing evidence that multitudes of animals had once existed and gone extinct. Members often examined fossil bones and devised exciting descriptions of monstrous beasts—pterodactyls, mammoths, and assorted ancient quadrupeds. On January 13, "John James Audubon Esquire of Louisiana" was elected to membership. At the same meeting, Audubon delivered another paper—one that he read himself. It was a lively and entertaining account of the alligator. Audubon spoke at length about his own experience at close quarters with the fearsome reptile, sensing, no doubt, how much this impressed the Wernerians. His insistence that alligators never attack anyone who approaches them head-on was equal parts imagination and bravado. The group found the paper packed with "new information." Audubon promised that he would next deliver a talk on the animal that had long excited the most interest in the New World—the rattlesnake.

But two weeks later, at the meeting where the rattlesnake talk was scheduled, Audubon asked for an extension. Two more weeks after that, Audubon again showed up without the paper and requested another delay. To make up for it, he brought along two plates from *The Birds of America* that were fresh from Lizars's shop. Everyone thought they were wonderful.

Finally, on February 24, Audubon was ready. He brought to the meeting his drawing of the rattlesnake and mockingbirds, and with that as a backdrop, began reading a long, riveting account. He started off by suggesting that a close study of the rattlesnake's natural habits would disabuse anyone who believed that the snake mesmerized its prey. This so-called power of "fascination" was a widely rumored attribute of the rattlesnake. But Audubon assured his audience that the snake's hunting abilities had more to do with its speed, its eyesight, its ability to swim, and its powers of "extension," which, among other things, accounted for the rattlesnake's breathtaking climbing ability.

Audubon focused on an incident he said he had observed in the woods of Louisiana in 1821. He said he was lying on the forest floor watching a bird when he heard a commotion in the brush nearby. Presently, a gray squirrel sprinted into view, bounding along in leaps of several feet at a time. It was closely pursued by a rattlesnake. The snake, Audubon said, was stretched out to its full length and moving so fast that the squirrel could not gain any ground on it. The squirrel ascended a tree, running up its trunk and then scampering out into the highest branches. The snake followed. In fact, Audubon said, even though the snake climbed much more slowly than the squirrel, it still moved fast enough that the squirrel seemed almost paralyzed on the spot. Eventually, it leapt to another branch. Amazingly, the snake still followed—this time by stretching out almost two-thirds of its total length to span the gap and move over to the next branch. This maneuver was repeated several times, as the squirrel jumped from branch to branch. Finally, trembling with exhaustion and fear, the squirrel leapt to the ground, its feet spread wide to absorb the impact. In a flash, the snake tumbled after it, landing heavily near the squirrel. Before the squirrel could climb another tree, the snake at last overtook it, seizing it by the neck. The snake then wrapped itself around the squirrel and squeezed it to death—whereupon it let go and proceeded to swallow the squirrel tail-first. Audubon added that similar observations were confirmed by "one of our most eminent naturalists." He neglected to say who.

Audubon continued with general descriptions of rattlesnake behavior and hunting style. He said rattlesnakes were possessed of sharp eyesight, and that he had himself seen them hide after spying a bird of prey high overhead. He also had seen rattlesnakes cruising through the forest, their heads moving from side to side as they looked up into the trees in search of birds' nests. The snakes, Audubon said, cleverly avoided nests that were guarded by adult birds.

Audubon recounted a "well authenticated" story that illustrated the extreme toxicity of rattlesnake venom. Some years before, in Pennsylvania, a farmer was bitten by a rattlesnake. The fangs broke off in his boot and, having felt only a prick he attributed to a thorn, the farmer was unaware of what had happened. But after returning home he fell sick, and died in a few hours. Months later, the farmer's son pulled on his late father's boots—and promptly died as well. A brother of the son now inherited the same boots, put them on, and he died too. Finally a doctor was summoned to investigate the deaths, which mystified everyone. The physician found a fang imbedded in one of the boots and tested it by scratching a dog on the nose with it. The dog died.

Audubon concluded on a lurid note, describing the rattlesnake's "disgusting" mating ritual. In the spring, Audubon said, large numbers of male and female snakes join together, so that a single, writhing mass is

formed of thirty or more individuals. As copulation within this dense assemblage takes place, the snakes turn their mouths outward, open them
wide, and hiss furiously while their tails buzz with abandon. Approaching
such a ball of mating rattlers is quite dangerous, Audubon said, as the
snakes are quick to disengage and give chase to any intruder on the scene.

The substance of Audubon's talk suggests why it took him so long to
compose it. The creative process can be slow. Almost everything in
Audubon's account of the rattlesnake was pure fiction.

Rattlesnakes can climb trees and bushes, and all species of rattlers do
on occasion. But their arboreal abilities are limited. Unlike slender-
bodied snakes that are good climbers, rattlesnakes are heavy and have relatively stout bodies ill-suited to climbing. Nor are rattlesnakes fast, as
snakes go. They typically ambush their prey from a stationary hiding spot.
A gray squirrel can easily outrun a rattler on the ground and would have
no trouble at all escaping one that attempted to pursue it into a tree. Rattlesnakes do not kill by constriction. Nor do rattlesnakes have remarkable
eyesight. In fact, they see well only at close range—say under twenty
feet. The idea that rattlesnakes move through the forest scanning trees for
nests to attack was fantasy. Rattlesnakes sometimes bunch together near
their dens, but they do not mate in massed groups. They copulate in
pairs, one male and one female. As for Audubon's story about the farmer
and his sons, it was nothing more than a tall tale that had made the rounds
in America for years. The Wernerians were oblivious to all this, but
when Audubon's paper was reprinted later in America, it eventually had
to be retracted.

The debate that enveloped this paper—as well as Audubon's drawing
of the rattlesnake and the mockingbirds—simmered for years, though he
scarcely ever addressed it. What, exactly, had Audubon seen in the
Louisiana forest that caused such a blunder? It was suggested then, and
has been ever since, that Audubon must have confused his field notes with
others involving not a rattlesnake but a black snake—an accomplished arboreal performer that might well have chased a squirrel up a tree. But
this theory seems almost as far-fetched as the story in question.

For one thing, Audubon also reported that, after the snake had eaten
the squirrel, he approached it—tapping it with a stick to make it rattle.
He then killed the snake and dissected out the squirrel. Audubon had
plenty of experience with rattlesnakes, and such a close inspection would
have left no doubt as to whether he was looking at one. The chance of a

mix-up in his field notes seems equally remote. Audubon kept fairly detailed inventories of birds he observed, and he recorded these and events from the field in his journals. He also maintained that every bird he ever painted had been carefully measured "in all of its parts." Whether he kept separate, more detailed field notes from this time isn't known, but it seems doubtful. In the coming years, as work on *The Birds of America* progressed, Audubon had to acquire hundreds of specimens to complete his descriptions of birds he had in many cases painted years before.

What seems most likely, then, is that Audubon—feeling the pressure of a missed deadline and knowing that a credulous audience would be hanging on his every word—simply invented the whole account. And for the time being, it did nothing to undermine his growing fame.

Audubon had gotten word that Charles-Lucien Bonaparte was in Liverpool. In late December, he'd finally received a letter from Bonaparte— who was by then in London—asking what had become of some bird skins Audubon had supposedly sent him from New Orleans. Audubon, always concerned that he remain on good terms with the prince, wrote to Lucy asking her to look into how the skins had miscarried. Audubon had been worried about this for a while. He'd written to Bonaparte as soon as he'd gotten to England to ask about the skins—and also to urge Bonaparte to keep writing to him as he "traveled the great World." Audubon wrote again in early December, still worried he'd offended Bonaparte. He reiterated that he had sent Bonaparte a case of bird skins and also gave him the happy news that *The Birds of America* was in production in Edinburgh.

In the meantime, Audubon's sphere of admirers around Edinburgh kept expanding. Once again he collected letters of introduction for his next stop, which he now decided should be London. One of these letters came from the great Sir Walter Scott, Scotland's literary lion. Apparently Scott wasn't much impressed with Audubon's drawings, but thought Audubon himself interesting and authentic. Audubon had also been invited to dine and then spend the night at Dalmahoy, the country estate of a Lord and Lady Morton, eight miles distant from Edinburgh. The ride out over the Glasgow Road in the Mortons' ultra-plush carriage lulled Audubon into a near stupor. When the coach halted in front of Dalmahoy—a gothic, turreted mansion guarded by stone lions—Audubon expected to be met by a man of towering proportions. But Lord Morton was old and shrunken and frail. He spent much of the afternoon seated trembling in a chair on wheels in which he was pushed around the vast rooms of the house. The Mortons had asked that Audubon be sure to bring his portfolio along. Audubon, for his part, had hopes of securing an especially impressive reference from the Mortons. When it turned out that Lord Morton's poor health wouldn't allow even that much, Lady Morton obliged Audubon by asking for help from yet another nobleman, Lord Meadowbank, a barrister who was the chief advocate of Scotland. Meadowbank drafted a letter of introduction for Audubon to hand to the secretary for the king of England. Audubon, in a fit of gratitude, took Lady Morton's suggestion that he get a haircut. Recording this event in his journal—outlined in black—Audubon said that now he knew what it felt like to go to the guillotine.

In Edinburgh, Audubon also met a young landscape artist named Joseph Bartholomew Kidd. Audubon, much impressed by Kidd's talent, arranged to take lessons in oil painting from him. In early 1827, their friendship expanded into an ambitious partnership. Audubon, who'd begun thinking of a large exhibition of his drawings, offered Kidd one pound (about $4.50) per drawing to copy each of his watercolors in oils. Kidd agreed and commenced the work. As spring approached, Audubon found himself the head of a sprawling enterprise. Kidd was at work and Lizars had completed the first Number. The prospectus was now in circulation. Audubon had earned nearly $800 from his exhibitions and had added to his résumé election to several learned societies. How easy it all seemed now. In March, he had sent Lucy the first Number and the prospectus for *The Birds of America*. By May he had signed up nineteen subscribers to *The Birds of America*. Among them were the Mortons and also a woman named Harriet Douglas. Douglas, a rich woman from New York, was visiting Edinburgh when she met Audubon at a party at Professor Jameson's and decided to subscribe. Half a world away from home, Audubon had at last found an American patron.

14

DEAREST FRIEND

Colymbus glacialis: **The Great Northern Diver or Loon**
When travelling, or even when only raised from its nest, it moves through the air with
all the swiftness of the other species of its tribe, generally passing directly from one
point to another, however distant it may be.   —*Ornithological Biography*

L ondon, one of the great cities of the world, seemed to
Audubon almost deserted when he got there early in the
summer of 1827. In fact, most of its almost 2 million residents were present. But many of the naturalists and noblemen to whom
he had letters of introduction had gone to the country until the fall.
Audubon called at one empty house after another over the course of
three days. Frustrated, he put the letters in the mail—a decision he later
regretted when fewer than half the recipients bothered to respond. After
the quaint intimacy of Edinburgh, London's sprawling tangle of streets
was daunting. Audubon stayed briefly at an inn called the Bull and Mouth,
then found rooms for rent on Great Russell Street, in a quiet section of
the city near the British Museum and the apartment-lined avenues and
leafy public squares of Bloomsbury. It was the end of May. He had been
gone from home a year.

Audubon had been reluctant to leave Edinburgh, a town that suited
him. But he was eager now to sign up new subscribers. These he expected
would be found across England and Wales, and eventually in the capitals
of Europe. Audubon seemed to give little thought to selling *The Birds of
America* in America. He'd asked Lucy to show her copy of the first Number
and the prospectus to the libraries in New Orleans. But the suggestion

was a halfhearted one, since he at the same time reminded her that he had
no interest in subscribers whose ability to pay seemed suspect.

Audubon had spent April 5, his last day in Edinburgh, packing. It was
his wedding anniversary and three years to the day since his fateful arrival
in Philadelphia. Everything that America had denied him now seemed to
be his for the asking. Audubon the naturalist had been embraced by Scotland's scientific community, and England's would soon follow. Audubon
the artist was even more successful. People packed exhibitions of his
work. Others were quick to snap up the sketches and oils he was now
producing on the side. Departing Edinburgh, Audubon had traveled to
London by way of Newcastle, York, Leeds, Manchester, and Liverpool—
adding subscribers at every stop as people paraded through his rooms to
meet the artist and see his work. Three subscribers had even signed up
during his stopover at Prideaux John Selby's estate, Twizel House in
Northumberland.

Everyone was dazzled by the first Number. It opened with Audubon's
regal portrait of the turkey cock strutting through a canebrake. The second plate showed a pair of yellow-billed cuckoos cavorting in a pawpaw
tree. This was followed by plates of the prothonotary warbler, the purple
finch, and the Canada warbler. Each plate typified the Audubon style,
from the imposing heft of the turkey to the delicate twistings and turn-
ings of the small birds posed in their shrubs against a gleaming sea of
white. Audubon told subscribers that these five prints—spectacular on
their own—were a mere beginning. Lizars had commenced the second
Number already, and Audubon anticipated that it would be done by the
end of June. After that the Numbers would continue, one by one, until
all the birds of the New World were represented. When Charles-Lucien
Bonaparte stopped in to see him in London, it felt like they had come full
circle. Bonaparte was enthusiastic about the engravings. He even offered
to provide proper taxonomic descriptions for some of the birds. But he
never did.

Altogether, Audubon had landed forty-nine additional subscribers before reaching London—which, added to the Edinburgh list, brought the
total to almost one hundred. This was important, Audubon explained to
Lucy in a letter detailing his business strategy. The first one hundred
copies of a Number earned back the cost of engraving his drawings. After those were sold, the cost of additional copies was relatively small—
mainly paper and coloring. Audubon, like every author getting a first

taste of success, fantasized about the income he might expect in the future. If he could secure two hundred subscribers, Audubon told Lucy, his clear profit would be nearly $4,000 a year—more than enough to support them both in England "in a style of Elegance and Comfort." This was based on the supposition that Lizars could produce five Numbers—that is, twenty-five plates—every year. Audubon realized what that meant. It would likely take more than sixteen years to complete *The Birds of America*. Audubon, who had been only thirty-five when he'd gone off to Louisiana to complete his study of American birds after the collapse of his business in Henderson, now contemplated the sobering prospect that he would be approaching sixty when he finished. And this time—doubtless the best years of his life—would not be spent tramping the woods and shooting game beneath the wild skies of the country he loved. Instead, he now looked forward to a life of writing and drawing and selling subscriptions to his work. Still, if his health held up and the number of subscribers were to reach five hundred, he would earn almost $11,000 a year—an all but inconceivable fortune. Who knew what would happen? The copper plates wore down as the prints were struck, but Lizars assured Audubon that each would be good for 1,500 copies if needed. Perhaps all of this was on Audubon's mind when he told Lucy she should give his gun to John Woodhouse.

While he was at Leeds, Audubon received several letters Lucy had sent back in winter. The difficulty of communicating with one another across the ocean was magnified the longer they were apart. Letters were often delayed, or miscarried entirely. Audubon was frustrated that an expensive watch he'd bought and sent to Lucy when he first arrived in England had not gotten to her. Reports of storms and shipwrecks tortured him with the thought that letters from Lucy might have been lost. Most vexing of all was the impossibility of timely responses from either side of the Atlantic when letters routinely crossed paths during their long transits.

Lucy had written to say that she remained in Bayou Sara, but had left Beech Woods. Mrs. Percy's long-standing animosity toward Audubon had mutated into a disagreement over Lucy's pay. Her new position was at a smaller but friendlier plantation called Beech Grove, where she was again a schoolmistress to a group of local children. Lucy also asked Audubon about her hair. Was it all right, or should she change it? Audubon wrote back saying she should wear her hair however she pleased—and that he'd send her a fine English bonnet to keep it in place. But he didn't have an easy answer to something else she said. Lucy told him that if she could collect the tuition still owed her by Mrs. Percy, she would join him in England that very summer.

Audubon employed a variety of salutations when he wrote to Lucy. Sometimes she was "My Beloved Wife" or "My Dearest Lucy" or even "My Beloved Friend." Often she was "My Dearest Friend." Judging by the context of his letters, it seems unlikely that he attached any significance to which of these greetings he chose, even though the word *friend* seems wanting between husband and wife. In March, addressing her as his "beloved friend," Audubon had suggested that he would write for her to join him once he had reached London and secured sufficient subscribers there. After months of describing his torment at being apart from her, Audubon began to equivocate on when she should join him. The suggestion that Lucy's coming to England in some way depended on his financial success there—something they probably both understood without having explored the details—became the focus of their correspondence.

Now he wrote to his "dearest friend," picking his words more carefully than ever. Audubon told Lucy she must wait until at least the end of the year to come across. By then, he said, proceeds from *The Birds of America* would provide for them. If by some misfortune he failed, then he would come back to America and to her. But in the meantime, it was best to be prudent. Besides, he wrote, "Thou art quite comfortable in Louisiana, therefore wait with a little patience."

Audubon's letter, however, revealed contradictory thoughts. He had undergone a transformation of sorts in Edinburgh. While he still wrote to Lucy of his hoped-for success—and now presented it as a requirement for them to be reunited in England—he privately imagined that he had, in fact, already succeeded. This message, too, drifted through the lines he sent to Lucy. Perhaps she could see how his confidence ebbed and flowed. In low moods his thoughts invariably turned to other ideas for earning his living. Most of the time Audubon's head seemed more in the clouds than in tune with his wife. Lucy, scraping by as a teacher and piano instructor, must have felt the pangs of envy and desertion as she received Audubon's continuing reports of the social whirl that enveloped him—dinners and parties, nights out at the theater or off to some nobleman's grand estate. He had already decided against sending Lucy a copy of his journal, with its candid accounts of his frazzled nerves—and sent it instead to the lovely Miss Hannah Rathbone. Now, in the same message in which he insisted Lucy stay put until he was ready for her, Audubon referred to *The Birds of America* as "this Great work of mine."

Though he complained of being lonely, Audubon never concealed from Lucy the busy social life he led in London. One of the first persons he'd met on his arrival in the city was a man named John Children. Children had been an officer of the Royal Society, one of the oldest scientific institutions in the world, and doubtless the most influential. Children now worked in the antiquities department of the British Museum. He invited Audubon to show his drawings at a meeting of the Royal Society and escorted him to one. A proper gentleman, Children never quite got used to seeing Audubon carrying his large portfolio himself. But Audubon, forever recalling the loss of his drawings at Natchez, insisted on it. On May 24, Audubon and Children made their way to Somerset House, a vast complex of majestic buildings standing alongside the Thames River. The doorway to the society was just inside and to the left of the entryway off the Strand. Beyond was a courtyard so large that it looked as if all of Edinburgh University might have occupied but one small corner of it. Somerset House was the headquarters of the British Royal Navy. From these buildings, the power of Europe's mightiest military force was projected across the world.

The Royal Society, organized informally by a group of London scholars in the 1640s, had been granted its official charter by King Charles II in 1662. Christopher Wren, Edmond Halley, Isaac Newton, and Joseph Banks had all served as presidents of the society. In the 1700s, much of the debate over the strange, immense bones unearthed in America had taken place here. The society took an interest in all of the sciences, though as part of its charge as an advisory to the Navy it devoted special attention to practical studies of things like navigation and food preservation. The society had nearly seven hundred members, some of whom had started to grumble that election to the society had become entirely too easy. Even so, Audubon—who just a few months earlier had made his first nervous visit to the Wernerians—now found himself an honored visitor at the epicenter of the learned world. As the meeting progressed, Audubon listened politely to two numbingly technical presentations. One concerned the use of "chloride of lime" in abating the noxious or explosive gases that sometimes collected in the holds of ships. The second was a study of the relative cooking speeds of black versus shiny cook-ware. At the close of business, Audubon had a chance to mingle and show off his portfolio. He may have relaxed a little when someone mentioned that his friend Charles-Lucien Bonaparte had visited the society only five months before.

While Audubon was still wondering whether his command that Lucy remain in Louisiana would reach her before she showed up on his Bloomsbury doorstep, he got distressing news from Edinburgh. In mid-June, Lizars informed him that his colorists—the team of mostly young women art students who hand-painted the prints, one color at a time—were on strike. And they seemed determined to remain so. Lizars con-fided that all this was partly because of a competing project—Selby's book on English birds. The colorists, it turned out, were much better paid by Selby. This may have surprised Audubon after his recent happy stay with Selby at Twizel House. Now it seemed the second Number of *The Birds of America* could be engraved but would have to wait indefinitely to be colored. Lizars pleaded with Audubon to see if he might find col-orists in London who could do the work.

Audubon, full of swagger only weeks earlier, betrayed his frustration when he again wrote to Lucy. In one letter, Audubon said he had no doubt that their friends and relatives in America thought he was living extravagantly in England while his poor wife slaved to stay alive in Louisiana. But he insisted that it was he who should be envious of her. Lucy, he said, was fortunate to be where she was, to have steady employ-ment, and to be close to John Woodhouse. In another letter, he seemed vexed by his loss of control over his own family. Here in such a "Civilized Country," he wrote, it was really a terrible thing to have one's talents ap-preciated but to enjoy none of the comforts of domestic life. He lamented that although he was married, he now had no wife—and that everyone could see it. Audubon could only add that nobody in America really knew what was happening to him. He wasn't sure himself.

Audubon asked Lizars to send down some finished as well as some un-colored prints from the second Number, hoping he could find someone to complete the work or possibly take it over altogether. In Edinburgh, the colorists stayed out on strike as the summer wore on. One day Audubon called at a printing and engraving shop on Newman Street, just a few blocks from his apartment. Audubon may have been intrigued by the natural artifacts, including bird skins, that were also for sale in a zoological gallery connected to the shop. A questionable version of what happened next arose after the fact. What is certain is that of all the steps on Audubon's uneven road to immortality, none was more important than the one he took through the doorway of the shop owned by Robert Havell.

Havell belonged to a well-known family of painters and engravers. For years he'd worked in partnership with his father, Daniel Havell, on a series of much-admired illustrated books depicting local scenes. Robert Havell's work was distinguished by his skill with a relatively new engraving technique called *aquatinting*, which produced prints with remarkable gradients of shading and texture—similar, in a way, to the halftones later used in reproducing photographs. First introduced in Britain in the 1770s, aquatinting was a demanding process that only a few engravers attempted and even fewer mastered. William Lizars, good as he was, did not use aquatint.

Aquatinting was a refinement of the engraving process—which typically involved very little actual engraving. Strictly speaking, "engraving" means cutting the lines into a metal plate with a pointed tool. In Audubon's time, though, engraving had become a generic term for a printing technique called *intaglio*, in which an image is cut or etched into the surface of a metal or stone. Copper engravers like Lizars and Havell used engraving tools sparingly in their work—usually for captions or an occasional hard, deep line in the image. Most of the image was instead etched into the copper. Etching involved coating the copper plate with a layer of wax called a "ground." The image was traced onto the ground, and this tracing was then gone over with a sharp tool that cut through the ground to the copper—but not into the metal. When the plate was then immersed in a bath of acid, the acid would "bite" into the copper where it was exposed through the ground, etching the lines of the image onto the metal. When the ground was removed, the etched plate was inked, wiped, and run through a press where the black-and-white outline was transferred onto paper. Colorists then painted the image to match the original.

In the aquatinting process, the ground was manipulated to enhance the image. The plate was coated with a clear rosin dust that was then heated from beneath. As the rosin warmed, it coagulated and hardened, forming small dimples across the surface of the plate and exposing a fine, honeycombed pattern through to the copper. The engraver next applied varnish to "stop out" the areas he did not want etched. The plate was then put into a bath of nitric acid—or aqua fortis, as it was called; hence the term *aquatint*. After the initial etching, additional areas could be stopped out and the process repeated to achieve a deeper acid bite in the portions still exposed. When this was done multiple times, an almost seamless range of shading was achieved, in which the image transitioned from black through gray to white. When an aquatint was colored, it exhibited a depth and shape unmatched in other forms of engraving.

Looking over samples of Havell's aquatint prints, Audubon was no doubt impressed. And the feeling was mutual, as Havell at once recognized how extraordinary Audubon's drawings were. But when Audubon explained that there were more than four hundred to be engraved, Havell's face darkened. He was fifty-eight, he said, too old to take on a project that would take many years to complete.

Here the story blurs. Supposedly, Havell suggested that they visit a competitor who might have a young engraver up to the task. When the competitor showed them a finely aquatinted plate just completed by one of his engravers, they eagerly asked to meet him. To Havell's consternation, the engraver turned out to be his estranged son, Robert Havell Jr. The younger Havell, who was thirty-four, had lately been living away from London in order to pursue his artistic interests—contrary to his father's desire that he take up one of the professions. But in this moment, so the myth goes, Audubon brought father and son back together. Audubon asked them to try a sample plate, the prothonotary warbler. Two weeks later it was done, and Audubon, thinking it much better than Lizars's version, begged them to take over production of *The Birds of America*. The Havells agreed. Havell Senior would lead the coloring team, while Havell Junior and his assistants would do the engraving. Audubon danced a jig as the Havells congratulated each other on the launch of their new firm, Robert Havell & Son.

There's reason to doubt a lot of this. The firm of Robert Havell & Son was listed in the London business directory as early as 1823. If father and son had been apart, it seems they might have reconciled before Audubon came on the scene. Similarly, there's no evidence that a copper engraving of the prothonotary warbler was produced by the Havells, since the only one ever used in making any of the prints was the one engraved by Lizars. It is improbable that Audubon would not have insisted on using the better of the two engravings if such a thing existed.

However this meeting between the Havells and Audubon unfolded, Audubon soon enough decided to abandon Lizars. Had the only issue been the colorists in Edinburgh, Audubon might have stayed with Lizars, to whom he owed almost all of his recent good fortune. But the Havells offered additional advantages. Because Havell Junior would have help with the aquatints, he could complete the engravings faster than Lizars, perhaps saving Audubon several years in production. The Havells also had more ready access to paper and coppers, which Lizars had to order from London. Amazingly, the Havells sweetened the deal by undercutting Lizars's price by about 25 percent. Audubon could not pass on the opportunity. The Havells could produce *The Birds of America* faster, better, and cheaper. In early August he wrote to Lucy, telling her he had retrieved the copper plates from Lizars. The Havells had commenced the completion of the second Number and would soon begin the third. Not satisfied with the condition of all the plates from Edinburgh, the Havells eventually added aquatint retouches to several of Lizars's plates.

Audubon now told Lucy he imagined he would have to remain in England "as long as I will have Drawings to keep my work going on." He estimated five more years, at least. This was yet another wrinkle in his thinking, which to Lucy seemed to change from one letter to the next. Was Audubon saying that he anticipated returning to America at some point to paint more birds? One thing he was saying quite clearly was that the time when Lucy could join him continued to move further into the future. Now he told her—pretty unconvincingly—that if he were "substantially settled" by January he would then send for her. But he added that London was very expensive.

Audubon was also increasingly concerned about the supervision of his sons. Victor, still working as a clerk in Shippingport, didn't bother to answer his father's letters. Or maybe he didn't even get them. Who could be sure? Audubon continued to envision his elder son—Victor was now eighteen—as a partner in the business end of *The Birds of America*. Meanwhile, he repeatedly insisted that Lucy make sure John Woodhouse, who was not yet fifteen, practiced his drawing and his violin. Audubon was awed by the educated manners and social graces he saw all around him in England, and he dreamed of his boys' talents flourishing there someday. Early that fall, Audubon wrote to Victor and said that once Lucy and John Woodhouse had come to England and were comfortably settled there he would send for him, too—just as soon as he had another one hundred subscribers. Audubon said he thought he could help Victor find a position in a countinghouse in Liverpool. In a fatherly gesture, he sent along a little five-hole flute.

In late September, Audubon again wrote to Lucy, this time from Manchester, where he was embarked on a tour of several cities to collect subscriptions as they came due. He told Lucy that she might expect further delay in joining him. "Dearest Friend," he said, "Thou must not think me too tardy." Audubon tried to reassure Lucy that the only reason he still hesitated was to make absolutely certain that their finances were in order. He told her he would send her money for passage to England, but that until he did so she and John Woodhouse should stay put. He admitted this must sound "cooler than usual," but he insisted it really wasn't like that. On a happier note, Audubon informed Lucy that the king of England had become a subscriber. The third Number of *The Birds of America*—the first one done entirely by the Havells—was complete. It seemed to him much superior to the first two.

By the middle of November, Audubon was back in Edinburgh, well along on a tour that was taking him some eight hundred miles through Britain. He'd sold a subscription to the university in Glasgow, but was disappointed that many of his original subscribers in Scotland were balking at paying or had canceled entirely. He said the Scottish people's reputation for being tight with their money was deserved. Even so, he said he still hoped he would be able to send for Lucy after the first of the year. The Havells, in a burst of productivity that pleased Audubon greatly, had finished two more Numbers—meaning that despite his change of engravers, he had completed five Numbers in less than a year. Best of all, the engravings were his, free and clear. He had paid £173 (about $780) to Lizars and more than £350 (about $1,575) to the Havells. Lizars, desperate to regain Audubon's business, told Audubon he would match the price the Havells were charging if only he could have some of the work. Audubon diplomatically put him off, thinking he now had an insurance policy in Lizars in case anything went wrong in London.

From Edinburgh, Audubon went back to Liverpool—pausing at Twizel House for a couple of days to shoot pheasants with Selby and Jardine. Perhaps less certain of himself after the long and only partially successful collecting trip, Audubon was thinking again about other ways to make money. One idea he had was to limit the number of subscribers to *The Birds of America* to 150, keeping those proceeds for himself. Additional copies would then be printed and bound for booksellers in London, Paris, and other large markets, with Audubon collecting some sort of royalty on sales. He thought this could work because it was now clear from the reactions of everyone who saw *The Birds of America* that it was unique. There'd never been anything like it and probably never would be again. In the meantime, Audubon could always earn a little extra by doing small paintings of birds. These sold quickly, he said, now that he knew "the tricks of the trade." A few weeks later, Audubon changed his mind again, returning to his old idea of finding a permanent position as a resident artist—either with a public institution or a wealthy nobleman. He thought such a job might pay as much as £500 (about $2,250) a year, leaving all the money from *The Birds of America* as profit. That way, when the last engraving was done he and Lucy could go back to America to live out the rest of their lives at leisure. To Lucy, Audubon's talk about their joint "return" to America was premature, to say the least.

Audubon reported that his health was fine, and that he walked a good deal and still got up at dawn whenever he could, convinced that keeping to his habits from the woods was beneficial. But now Audubon, who was so often described as "simple" or "authentic," and who had kept his composure through so many reversals, made a surprising confession to his wife. He admitted that he was a hopeless perfectionist. After trying to paint in oils for years, he said he at last despaired of ever becoming competent in the medium. The only people who bought his oil paintings were friends, acting, he suspected, out of charity. This was so humiliating, he said, that he planned to give up oils for good. He knew he would regret this decision forever, he said, because "*Man* and *Particularly thy husband*, cannot easily bear to be outdone." Audubon said he wished he had "another life to spend."

Lucy could not have been entirely pleased with the way he was spending the one he had. Audubon signed off saying he was due at Green Banks to see Mrs. Rathbone and Miss Hannah. He told Lucy that he wished very much that she would write to both women. They were kind and gentle ladies, he said, and ought to be "thought of often." As if that weren't enough to make Lucy want to throttle him, Audubon added a warning so preposterous that Lucy must have wondered what he had been telling

people. Audubon said that Lucy should never intimate to the Rathbones—
or to anyone else—that the Audubons were poor. It seemed that everyone
in England was under the impression that Audubon was well off.

Audubon did not send for Lucy in January. Back in London and again co-
zily established on Great Russell Street, Audubon instead bought her a
piano, which he had shipped to New Orleans. He said he hoped she
would give it to Victor when he at last sent for her to come to England.
But now he told Lucy he "dare not yet invite Thee," even though he continued to make progress with new subscribers and the sixth Number was
under way.

Audubon did not send for Lucy in February, or in March. He did mention that he was thinking of going to Paris for a while. He reported selling several subscriptions to The Birds of America on a trip he'd made to
Cambridge. Audubon was happy to learn that Victor had visited Lucy.
His son had even taken a moment to add a few words to him in one of her
letters. Evidently Lucy worried that Victor was too skinny. Audubon assured her that he was only tall, and would soon enough put on weight. In
another letter a few days later—addressed once more to "My Dearest
Friend"—Audubon said he was still "imperfect in my thoughts" as to
Lucy joining him in England. He didn't send for her in April, either, nor
in May, nor all summer long. He had now been gone for more than two
years. In August he wrote to say that the Havells were starting on the
tenth Number. But although everyone continued to speak glowingly of
The Birds of America, Audubon found that he had to spend more and more
time replacing subscribers who canceled their orders. Once again, he
told his "dearest friend" that he was miserable without her. "My anxiety
to have thee with me as thou may well expect is greater every day," he
said. "We are growing older and have been parted so long that I feel as if
abandoned to myself."

About this time, Audubon again mentioned that he needed more
drawings to complete his ornithology. But instead of contemplating a return to America for this purpose, he once more implored Lucy to make
John Woodhouse practice his drawing. Audubon said he would gladly
send money for drawing supplies. He didn't explain whether he thought
Johnny's drawings could go directly into The Birds of America or serve only
as references for his own depictions. He also asked that, in whatever

spare time remained to him, John Woodhouse shoot and skin as many
birds as he could—and ship them to England as soon as possible.
Audubon said he was in need of turkeys and cranes and hawks, plus some
other species. But he said Johnny was not to worry about what was gotten and was instead to shoot and carefully skin every bird he could, no
matter what it was.

Audubon now began to talk about what a help Lucy would be to him
in London, especially when he had to be away on subscription calls.
Wearingly, he said he was still worried about money and wasn't ready yet
to send for her.

Lucy was understandably mystified. In June she'd written to Victor to
confess that she no longer knew what to make of Audubon's apparent in-
difference to a separation that seemed more permanent by the day. She
said she could not decipher the many conflicting messages that floated
among the disjointed lines he wrote to her. Audubon had warned her, she
told Victor, that it would be a very long time before *The Birds of America*
was finished and that he would most certainly want her and John Woodhouse to join him in England just as soon as it was possible. At the same
time, he told Lucy that England was "not what it was" and that she might
not care for it at all. If she decided *not* to come he would understand.

"What he really means I cannot tell," Lucy wrote to Victor. "Those are
his words and we must interpret them as we can."

Lucy chose to interpret them thus: She wrote to Audubon and told
him any thought she had of coming to England was now indefinitely on
hold. Audubon wrote back and told her, his "dearest friend," to please
"make up thy mind."

But he did not ask her to come.

Audubon's mood was up and down. He heard that he was being made fun
of back in Philadelphia, where everyone was shocked at his success overseas. In London, there were likewise people who thought his work over-
rated. Subscriptions ebbed and flowed, cancellations and new orders
staying in a precarious balance. Feeling especially low one day, Audubon
got out his painting of the white-headed eagle and altered it on the spot,
replacing the goose the eagle was shown feeding on with a lowly catfish.

Audubon had a friend named William Swainson. They'd met after
Audubon was approached by a man named John Loudon, who was

launching a magazine about natural history, to be called *Loudon's*. Loudon wanted Audubon to write something for the magazine. Of more interest to Audubon was Loudon's suggestion that Swainson, a zoologist who lived north of London in the country near St. Albans, write a review of *The Birds of America* for the inaugural issue in May. Audubon and Swainson had become close, thanks in part to the questionable arrangement Swainson proposed with respect to this review. Swainson bluntly told Audubon that he would compose a highly favorable notice if Audubon would provide him "at cost" with a full set of *The Birds of America* as so far completed. Audubon, who was more than happy to strike a deal, had a laugh. Despite the hopeful calculations he'd been relaying to Lucy, the truth was that subscriber numbers had not yet reached the breakeven point, and *The Birds of America* was still being produced at a loss. He sent Swainson a note promising him a copy of *The Birds of America* at a fair price that he would figure out. "I assure you my dear sir," he told Swainson, "that was I to take you at your word it would be a low bargain for you as the amount would be very nearly double that for which it is sold to my subscribers." A couple of weeks later, Swainson invited Audubon to dinner at his home in London. Audubon, who still suffered occasional bouts of paralyzing shyness, sent a note saying he would come at six that evening if it was convenient, nervously adding, "I am an extremely plain man, and always anxious not to be an Intruder."

After the flattering review appeared, Audubon let his guard down with Swainson—although he was briefly shocked to learn that Swainson had been corresponding for a number of years with an American colleague by the name of George Ord. Audubon, dying to unburden himself to a willing ear, confided to Swainson that his marriage had become an extended transatlantic misunderstanding. He told Swainson time passed "heavily" for him in London. He hoped someday that he and Lucy would call on Swainson at home in the country, but added that it would depend on "if I ever see my wife again."

At the beginning of July, Audubon sent a note thanking Swainson for having supplied him with a small white lamb that had been delivered "alive in a basket." The lamb now existed only on canvas in the "effigy" Audubon had painted of it being attacked by a golden eagle. Audubon said he'd also been hard at work on new versions of the turkey and the white-headed eagle, painting feverishly day and night. Apparently, Swainson didn't care much for the lamb-and-eagle painting, as he never said anything about it after visiting Audubon at his new apartment. Audubon had taken rooms on Newman Street, directly above the Havells' shop. It was handy, Audubon said, though he missed the open spaces of Bloomsbury.

By August of 1828, Lucy's growing impatience sent Audubon into a new tailspin. She informed him that she had borrowed some money from her brother William and had sent John Woodhouse to attend a school in Louisville. Lucy said she planned to follow him there and, unless she heard otherwise from Audubon, to make her own way in the world going forward. Audubon's already "despondent spirits" sank lower still. He told Swainson that thoughts of suicide had swept over him. Then, out of the blue, he asked Swainson if he would accompany him on a trip to Paris. He told Swainson he had put away his brushes, unable to even think about working. He said they could go to France whenever Swainson was free, and stay there as long as he cared to. Audubon spent the next few weeks researching travel options.

Audubon, accompanied by William Swainson and Swainson's wife, spent two months in Paris. Fourteen new subscribers signed up for The Birds of America. The trip was otherwise forgettable. Audubon had worried almost constantly that the story of his birth and adoption would be discovered. Returning to London in November, he was excited to find two letters from Victor waiting for him. He wrote back to say that he was happy to know that both Victor and now John Woodhouse were well situated in Kentucky. But he told Victor that it was unlikely he would visit them there anytime soon. Unless "some accident" befell his drawings, he had quite enough to carry on for the foreseeable future. He said he had 144 subscribers and was free of debt. He had begun to think about a "perpetual" exhibition of the oil copies of his birds now under way with Joseph Kidd in Edinburgh. Audubon thought he might send the collection to Russia for a while before establishing it permanently in London. In spite of it all, Audubon said, Lucy was resistant to the idea of joining him in England before he had acquired a "great fortune."

Victor was caught between his feuding parents, both of whom now vented their unhappiness to him. Audubon had learned that Lucy was disappointed in the piano he'd sent her, and this seemed to confirm his unreasonable conviction that he could never satisfy her material needs. In fact, the rooms above the Havells' shop on Newman Street—a narrow, quiet lane in the West End—were spacious and Audubon had even hired a young woman to clean and cook and mend his clothes. Without Lucy for company, Audubon was left to roam his apartment and stew. He continually pored over a growing clutter of pictures, drawing equipment, and books. Looking at his own drawings, Audubon said, transported him back to America. Every bird reminded him of where he'd been and what the woods were like where he'd shot it. It's doubtful these memories improved his general outlook. Audubon had now been gone for two and a half years. In truth, his mental state had been fragile for nearly ten, ever since the collapse of his businesses at Henderson. A decade of erratic mood swings, headaches, insomnia, nightmares, financial uncertainty, and the occasional hallucination now filtered into his strained communications with Lucy. He wanted her to come but would not send for her. He told her to stay in America and then despaired when she said she would. Just before Christmas, Audubon sent Swainson a note saying he had "the blues completely."

Christmas came and went, the holiday a hollow, haunted misery. Audubon had to decline the Swainsons' suggestion that he spend some time in the country with them, having accepted an earlier, less appealing invitation. And he was angry enough when Havell Senior took an unannounced vacation that he transferred the whole job of engraving and coloring *The Birds of America* to Havell Junior. Sometime after the first of the year, something snapped—on both sides of the ocean. Audubon decided to go home and, if she would agree, bring Lucy to England. Lucy, devastated by Audubon's recent letters, made up her mind to go to England in hopes of saving their marriage. If she'd had enough money to leave right then, the two might well have passed each other on the Atlantic.

In mid-January of 1829, Lucy wrote to Victor, telling him that he had in effect become the man of the family—he was old enough now to be her friend and confidant. She said a recent letter she'd gotten from Audubon was his most bitter yet, "severe" and "painful" and a sorry reward indeed for all she had done for him. Had she not, after all, supported everyone in the family for the better part of the past ten years? Somehow, she said, Audubon had gotten it in his head that she would never join him in England unless he could afford a "Princely domain." Spitefully, he'd told Lucy to let him know once and for all whether she would come over—otherwise a formal separation would be in order.

Truly, Lucy said, Audubon was "blind" to the real state of their affairs. Accordingly, Lucy said she would now act as her own agent, and would decide what was best for her and her sons. Her plan was to remain at the school at Beech Woods for another year. Then, in the spring of 1830, she would come for John Woodhouse in Louisville and take him to Europe to continue his education. Avoiding any direct mention of reconciling with Audubon, Lucy added that she felt this course of action was her "duty." Lucy, who had a lifelong fear of ocean voyaging, told Victor that the dangers of the Atlantic crossing would be nothing next to the pain she would feel at leaving him behind in America. But they would have to "trust to providence" for their happiness. If for some reason she could never return, she hoped Victor would go over to Europe and bring John Woodhouse home someday. She begged Victor not to say a word of any of this to anyone—especially because "circumstances may change." This included not so much as a whisper to Audubon. "Do not write to your Papa anything about it my Dear Son," Lucy said. "Leave it to me to settle with him."

At virtually the same moment, Audubon was writing to Lucy from London. No longer able to stand the uncertainty of her coming to England, he had decided to come to America for her. He said he expected to leave around the beginning of April. Although he had known he would someday have to go to America to continue his work, this was much sooner than he had hoped. But—evidently unaware of how odd this sounded in view of his repeated insistence that Lucy delay coming to him—he told her now that this was the only way he could "persuade" her to come over.

It's impossible, after more than a century and a half, to fathom exactly what was happening between Audubon and Lucy. The long, uncertain lines of communication between them surely made it hard for them to understand one another. But there was also an obtuseness on both sides of the ocean, two complicated halves of a relationship that were entrenched in positions fortified against one another—a husband and wife at loggerheads and perversely determined to remain so. Audubon's letters, brimming with erratic assessments of his finances and grim hints of his anxious mental condition, careen between professions of endless love for Lucy and an unfeeling effort to keep her away. Many contained worrisome references to Miss Hannah Rathbone. It seems obvious that Hannah and Audubon were smitten with one another, though how far the attraction progressed can't be known. Audubon thought about Hannah a lot, but he did not see her often after his first months in Britain. If there was a liaison between the two, it was short-lived.

But the Audubons' transoceanic spat went on and on. Lucy's letters, many of them from this time long lost, betray her stubbornness, her fear of ocean travel, and her concern for what was to become of Victor and John Woodhouse. Lucy still thought in terms of the family, whereas Audubon focused on himself. What she seemed to want—and most need—was a clear signal from Audubon in place of his vague and oft-delayed plan for her to join him. She never got one.

Audubon was also seriously worried about the effect his leaving London might have on the progress of *The Birds of America*. He had every confidence in young Havell to keep the job going, but doubted that everyone else would be so sanguine. John Children had agreed to oversee the project in his absence—a comfort, but only a partial one. Audubon feared that if word circulated among his subscribers that he wasn't personally supervising the engraving, many would back out. He was concerned enough that he initially planned to travel under an assumed name—after putting out a cover story that he was going to the European continent to sell subscriptions. But he eventually dropped the idea of going incognito, and instead considered notifying the papers in America of his arrival, since he would be traveling with copies of *The Birds of America* in the hope of landing some American subscribers.

For some time after Audubon announced his intention of coming to America, Lucy was quite unaware of it. The mail was so slow that in February she was still receiving letters he'd written the previous summer. Unsure if he was getting her letters on the other end, Lucy repeated her wish to join him in England—*if* that was what he wanted. But she could not tell. His letters were angry, she thought, not to mention ambiguous. Though she tried to dismiss his moodiness as a continuing "fit of the blues," this was not always easy. Transatlantic communications seemed to produce more misunderstanding than affection. Did he think she cared not for the piano he'd sent? It wasn't true, Lucy insisted. The piano was fine, she said, once she had it repaired. More important, Lucy still loved Audubon, but could not be sure that he loved her. She explained again and again that she could not leave for England immediately—that she had to see to the boys by finishing out her current contract so she could leave them enough money to get by. Being both father and mother to them,

Lucy admitted, was a trying occupation. Otherwise, she felt in quite good health. Lucy was forty, she reminded her absent husband. Actually, she was forty-two.

Audubon imagined that Lucy would be much surprised at his coming home. But he told her it was really the only way now. "I want and must talk to thee," he wrote to her. "Letters are scarcely of use at this great distance when 5 months are needed to have an answer." He would have much work to do in America, Audubon cautioned. Lucy should anticipate that he would spend all of his time drawing. Also, she would have to meet him halfway, as he did not wish to come any farther south than Louisville. This, he said, would be his only trip to America until the day came when he returned for good, ready to retire from "public life." Of course, he said, there could be no question but that she would go back to England with him. That would be settled, he said, when at last "our lips will meet" again. Sounding genuinely happy for the first time in a very long time, Audubon said that now that it was decided, he felt in "great spirits."

Sitting alone in his room, Audubon looked over the letter. Smiling, he signed it "God Bless thee Dearest Friend—thy Husband for Life, John James Audubon." Folding the letter carefully, Audubon closed it with a daub of red sealing wax, pressing it with the seal bearing the image of a turkey cock.

15

MY GREAT WORK

Turdus mustelinus: The Wood Thrush
[H]ow fervently . . . have I blessed the Being who formed the Wood Thrush, and placed it in those solitary forests, as if to console me amidst my privations, to cheer my depressed mind, and to make me feel, as I did, that never ought man to despair, whatever may be his situation, as he can never be certain that aid and deliverance are not at hand.
—Ornithological Biography

Audubon, now in his mid-forties, believed he had grown an inch taller during his lonely sojourn in Britain. Perhaps he was only feeling larger than life. On April 25, 1830, the sailing ship *Pacific* entered the Mersey River after a rough passage of twenty-five days from New York. Audubon and Lucy stood on the deck as Liverpool came into view and the pungent spring air of England drifted through the rigging.

Audubon had spent nearly a year in America, having reached New York in early May of 1829. Of the twin purposes he had in going home—to collect more birds and to reconcile with Lucy—the birds had taken a decided priority. Rather than rush to Bayou Sara, Audubon instead stopped in New York, then Philadelphia, sending letters west and south to Victor and Lucy. Apparently still convinced that Lucy needed a full accounting of his situation before she would join him, Audubon wrote to say that his net worth was now more than £1,500—nearly $7,000. A close reading of this total revealed that only about $1,500 of this was cash. The rest was mainly in subscription fees due him, plus the value of the coppers and prints thus far completed. Audubon mentioned that he also owned a watch he said was worth $450, a gun worth $90, plus "plenty of clothes." In an odd, quasi-legal plea, he told Lucy that he now pledged to her "myself with my stock, wares and chattels and all the devotedness of heart attached to such an enthusiastic being as I am."

Lucy was not to regard this as an attempt at persuasion, Audubon insisted. Rather, she was to "consult with thy ownself." He said he needed a yes or a no, and soon. Audubon asked now that Lucy come to Philadelphia, or at least as far as Louisville, as he had already suggested. He could not risk going to Louisiana for fear of missing important communications from Havell or Children. Much as he would love to see the magnolias and the mockingbirds, Audubon said he doubted he ever would do so again.

Audubon again turned to Victor for help. He wrote to his elder son that while Lucy seemed to want him to come to Bayou Sara as a proof of his affections, he needed to work on drawings of birds that were plentiful near Philadelphia. Victor's mother could not or would not understand how important it was for him to remain "east of the mountains." If she had to meet him by ascending the Mississippi and Ohio, she insisted it could not be for months yet. This caused Audubon anxiety, as he had hoped to sail back to England in the fall. Audubon also told Victor that he doubted he could visit him in Kentucky. Much as he wanted to see his sons, Audubon said he no longer had friends in Kentucky and had his hands full enough with critics and skeptics as it was. Word from England was that production of *The Birds of America* was progressing nicely, but that more and more subscribers lagged in their payments or had stopped paying entirely. Apparently there had been something like a revolt among the subscribers in Manchester. Every day away from England, Audubon felt, increased his financial risk, though he by now thought that he could always find new subscribers or coax back some who had deserted. When Havell wrote a troubled letter about the decline in subscriptions, Audubon quickly wrote back telling him not to worry. Havell was particularly concerned about a less-than-full payment he'd received from agents representing Charles-Lucien Bonaparte. Havell had given them the latest Numbers anyway. Audubon assured him this had been the right thing to do. Bonaparte was certainly good for the money, and when he got back to England Audubon would restore order among the other subscribers.

He was less confident about prospects in America. Audubon's friend Dr. Richard Harlan arranged for *The Birds of America* to be exhibited at the Academy of Natural Sciences in Philadelphia, but the academy itself declined to subscribe. Still, Audubon's spirits perked up considerably as he once more spent his time in the woods of America, shooting and drawing birds. He passed most of the month of August and some of September in Pennsylvania's Great Pine Swamp, finding it more forest than swamp and alive with birds. By October, though he'd found not a single new subscriber in America, Audubon had completed more than forty new drawings, including large, medium, and small species. He'd also found a new partner, a Swiss painter named George Lehman whom he'd met in Pittsburgh on his way back to Louisiana from Philadelphia five years before. Lehman was contributing backgrounds and botanical elements for the drawings. The work had gone well enough that Audubon was now willing to come as far as Louisville to meet Lucy. He planned to travel by way of Baltimore and Washington, where he hoped he might get in to see President Andrew Jackson. Audubon said he would be at Louisville by the beginning of December.

The more imminent their reunion became, the more nervous Lucy was about it. Once Audubon was back in America, the pace of their correspondence quickened and the issues between them came into sharper focus. And it turned out that much of the trouble really *was* about money—a subject Audubon had belabored seemingly out of all proportion. But Lucy now took her turn. Although she had begun packing and said she looked forward to joining him in England, she told Audubon that she wondered if he could truly afford an "idle wife." Lucy said that if she remained in her current teaching position at Beech Grove, she expected to earn $1,800 in the coming year. What, she wondered, did he think of that? Having been on the receiving end of Audubon's convoluted pleadings—for every time he'd begged her to join him there was a matching instance when he'd told her not to—Lucy now offered him an equally ambiguous proposition. She was packing, Lucy said, but was prepared to stay on at Bayou Sara if necessary. She hinted that the financial security of doing so was worth considering. Obstinately, she refused to say whether staying was or was not her preference. Instead, she insisted that Audubon decide, and that once he had made a careful "deliberation," she would follow his wishes. "You *must choose* what I shall do," Lucy said. "In the meantime I am getting all in readiness till I hear from you again." Lucy added that her savings would amount to between $700 and $800 once her "accounts" were settled at the end of the current term, though she could not be absolutely sure of this. "I am not famous for my economy," she wrote.

Lucy's wariness about Audubon's prospects was understandable. The failure of his businesses in Henderson had plunged the family into poverty for nearly a decade, a period during which Audubon was mostly absent and making little more than token contributions to their support. Then, with a glimmer of success before him in England, Audubon had turned ambivalent. "I thought that I would feel sufficiently settled, after balancing my accounts, to write to thee to come directly to England," Audubon had written her more than a year ago, "and I hoped so the more, as I am really and truly in want not only of a *wife*, but of a kind and true friend, to consult and to help me by dividing with me a portion of my hard labours—yet thy entire comfort is the only principle that moves me, and fearing that thou might expect more than I can yet afford, I refrained."

"I leave thee," Audubon had concluded, "from my heart perfectly at liberty to do whatever may be most agreeable to thee."

Lucy now demanded absolute clarity. If she joined Audubon in England, she expected that her days of providing for the family were over.

"I do not look to anything like labour after I give up these toils," Lucy said. "Do not think me harsh . . . but it is absolutely necessary for our happiness to be *sincere*."

Lucy's anxiety was not limited to financial worries. She hated the idea of traveling anywhere alone. Lucy still hoped Audubon might come all the way to Louisiana for her, but if not he could send one of the boys down from Louisville to accompany her back upriver. More tellingly, Lucy also wrote to Audubon wondering how much they'd each changed. When Audubon told her he'd cut his hair recently, Lucy answered that she was glad to hear it. It was, of course, quite handsome when long, she said, adding mysteriously that she didn't like to think of it long, as that brought "associations to mind which I wish ever to *bury*." Whether Lucy was talking about some former intimacy between the two of them, or a painful recollection of someone else's fascination with her husband, Audubon presumably knew what she meant. As for herself, Lucy thought Audubon would find her not much like the sweet, shapely, dark-haired young woman he'd left more than three years ago. In fact, she'd grown older in just the last few months and thought she might be entering menopause, though she could not yet be sure. Lucy said she felt she was likely to live many more years, but that was something she never took for granted. "I live, and regulate all concerns relative to me as if I was to be called to the other world at any moment," she said.

Independent of the outward changes going on with her, Lucy assured

Audubon that she still loved him and always would. "I am gray quite," she said. "No teeth and thinner than ever I was and of course older. But my heart [and] my head [are] the same and yours 'for better and worse' as the saying is."

Lucy, however, was unsure that Audubon could say the same. She wondered if Audubon's anxiousness about money was covering up something else. Did he, she now wanted to know, still love her?

"You say you must not speak as a 'man in love,'" she wrote to him. "I do not see why, if you do love, which there seemed some doubt of . . . I beg of you my husband to be plain and clear in your reply. If any circumstance has occurred to change your affection for me as you rather insinuate be explicit and let me remain where I am."

Audubon changed his mind about going to Washington. Instead he collected his gun and dog and got on a coach for Pittsburgh in late October. At Pittsburgh he transferred to a steamboat headed down the Ohio River, the once-adventurous passage now a regularly scheduled boat ride. At Louisville a few days later, Audubon rushed to the countinghouse run by Lucy's younger brother William, where Victor was working. Victor was so much taller and more mature-looking than he remembered that Audubon at first did not recognize him. Now he began to feel a pull he hadn't anticipated. After a few days visiting with Victor and Johnny, Audubon caught another steamboat, this one bound for Louisiana. Late one night in the middle of November, Audubon arrived at Bayou Sara, and once again made his way through the dark to Lucy's apartment. At dawn he walked in on her, tears streaming down his cheeks.

With Lucy at his side again, Audubon was now focused completely on the work ahead of him in England. One of the subscriptions he'd managed to sell in America was to the United States Congress, which he and Lucy had visited on their way to New York. They'd also had a brief audience with Andrew Jackson that must have reminded Audubon of how far he'd come since he'd posed as the president's body double years earlier.

Before leaving Victor and Johnny in Louisville, Audubon had drafted his will, virtually all of which concerned the continuation or disposal of *The Birds of America* in the event that he died before it was finished. Thoughts of death often came to Audubon just before an ocean crossing. He would leave it up to the boys, and to Lucy if she survived him, whether to press on with Havell or to abandon the project and sell off all of his original drawings. Audubon was meanwhile preoccupied with worry about the engravings. Children had written to say that Havell was working hard in his absence, but that Audubon should not stay in America a day longer than necessary. Children, fretfully monitoring the quality of the colored prints, had lately enlisted a friend from the British Museum to assist him. But only Audubon could really do the job.

Audubon wrote to Havell that he and Lucy expected to sail for Liverpool in early April, after a brief rest in Louisville. Mrs. Audubon, he said, was in good health but her "frame is delicate." Meanwhile, Audubon assured his engraver that he was taking full advantage of his time in America, having traveled some four thousand miles in the past two months. Audubon said he'd made a number of new drawings, shot and skinned lots of birds, shipped tree and shrub samples to England, and had managed to capture fourteen opossums and a "beautiful male turkey," which he had already sent to friends in Liverpool.

After they got to England, Lucy briefly went to stay with relatives in Liverpool while Audubon devoted himself to collecting moneys due and attempting to woo back lapsed subscribers—managing pretty well on both counts. When the Audubons finally got to London they got the unexpected good news that Audubon had been elected to membership in the Royal Society just months before. He went to a meeting and paid his dues of $225, taking a seat in the society's long meeting room and feeling quite out of place among the institution's past and present luminaries. He was well aware of the shock wave news of his election would generate back in America, especially in Philadelphia. George Ord, who had been conveniently abroad during much of the time Audubon was in Philadelphia the previous spring, had stopped in London and visited the Royal Society. The thought of Ord picturing Audubon rubbing shoulders with the society's august membership was delicious for Audubon. He immediately directed Havell to place the initials F.R.S.—Fellow of the Royal Society—first among the growing list of honorifics that followed his name on each plate of *The Birds of America*. A short while later, Dr. Harlan back in Philadelphia wrote to say that Audubon's election to the Royal Society had "confounded your traducers" and produced some "cadavourous stares" at the Academy of Natural Sciences, but that many people there had been happy for him.

Havell was by now at work on the seventeenth Number, bringing the total count of drawings engraved to eighty-five. Havell sent Audubon a note updating him on plates currently being colored. Page by page, Audubon's birds were multiplying—flying and attacking and perching daintily on the great white planes of Havell's double-elephant-sized paper. The paper itself—heavy linen stock from the J. Whatman Company— was thick and textured and amazingly durable. Audubon's original prints remain sturdy and supple today, after almost two hundred years. Each Number was shipped in a flat tin case. Eventually, most subscribers chose to have the prints bound in enormous leather volumes, each consisting of around one hundred plates.

Audubon learned after arriving back in England that many of the lapsed subscriptions were due to disappointment with the quality of the printing work, which he discovered had eroded in his absence. While Lucy visited her relatives in Liverpool, Audubon toured several English cities and got an earful. Mostly, people were unhappy with the finishing of the plates, especially the hand-coloring, which had become careless and in some cases unnatural-looking. Worst of all was a scathing letter from Charles-Lucien Bonaparte, echoing these complaints and also adding that some of the legends to the plates contained errors in the common and scientific names of the birds depicted. Audubon remained desperate for Bonaparte's approval, even though the prince had moved to Rome for good and was, at least in theory, a competitor because of his continued work on the expansion of Wilson's *American Ornithology*. Enraged, Audubon wrote to Havell insisting that he fire his letter engraver, and demanding an "overhaul" of all the coppers to correct engraving errors, plus a much closer supervision of the coloring. Chagrined at not having caught the mistakes himself, Audubon said he'd hung all of the Numbers up on a wall and was horrified at their unevenness. He warned Havell that if his firm could not fix the plates and improve the prints, he was prepared to abandon *The Birds of America* and "return to my Own Woods until I leave this World for a better one."

Stung, Havell fired back. He was "extremely hurt" by the tone of Audubon's letter. He granted that perhaps a few subscribers might have reason to complain, but he was not aware of any dissatisfaction among the London subscribers. And he insisted he could not believe the small corrections that were needed would impede future sales.

There may have been another reason for the growing uneasiness some subscribers felt about Audubon's work. During his visit to England in the spring of 1829, George Ord had renewed his attack on Audubon to anyone who would listen, and apparently some people did. Swainson sent Audubon a sarcastic note complaining about several people—including Charles-Lucien Bonaparte—in which he said he was "sick of the world and of mankind."

"Another *friend* of yours has been in England," Swainson said. "Mr. Ord . . . has been doing you all the *good* he can: if these are samples of American Naturalists, defend me from ever coming in contact with any of their whole race."

Ord had written to Alexander Lawson—the Philadelphia engraver who'd dismissed Audubon's drawings out of hand—that Audubon was not entitled to the kind of success he was enjoying, and this was beginning to sink in. Ord went on to say that he himself had "long ago predicted this result" and reminded Lawson that he had shared this opinion. Ord was amazed that Audubon could find anyone willing to engrave his drawings, since "no one of taste and knowledge can behold these monstrous engravings without feelings of dissatisfaction, if not of contempt." Lawson's work, meanwhile, was much admired throughout London, Ord said. His recent plates for Bonaparte had caused a stir in London when they had been compared to Audubon's. So simple and elegant were the prints made for the prince, said Ord, that people were reassessing their estimation of Audubon. An uncolored proof of one of Lawson's engravings he had personally presented to the British Museum had been judged better than anything being produced in England, colored or not. Ord said he was now convinced that Audubon's reputation was in steep decline, and that "many of those who have afforded their patronage to the contemptible imposter, will blush to think that they ever made his acquaintance."

Lucy had joined Audubon on his trip to repair the subscription list, which took him north through Birmingham, Leeds, York, and Newcastle. She was thrilled to see England again, and impressed by the industrial advances in evidence everywhere. In Manchester she and Audubon toured a cotton mill seven stories high that employed nine hundred people. Lucy wrote about it to Victor and Johnny, describing an amazing contraption—a "platform" in the middle of the building that rose at a "good speed" when they stood on it, stopping at each floor as it went. The machine conveyed them back down the same way, "rather faster" though not disagreeably so.

In October they arrived in Edinburgh, and to Audubon's delight were able to rent rooms in the very same building on George Street where Audubon had first stayed four years earlier. Audubon continued having some success in restoring subscriptions, in a few cases by promising to replace substandard plates. The latest Numbers, meanwhile, seemed to impress everyone. Havell was preparing to relocate his shop down the block and around the corner. The new location was on Oxford Street, a busy West End avenue, in a narrow, three-story brick building. In addition to engraving, printselling, and publishing, Havell advertised art supplies and an extensive collection of zoological specimens "stuffed & preserved in the highest perfection." Audubon asked Havell to display plates from The Birds of America prominently in the front windows. Satisfied that Havell was again on track and would put the engravings right, Audubon turned to a different task: composing and publishing his ornithological observations.

Alexander Wilson had been an author who taught himself to draw. For Audubon, it was the reverse. He was at ease drawing, but turned into an anxious lump when he sat down to write. Despite years of journal-keeping and nearly manic letter-writing, Audubon recognized the limitations of his vocabulary and the confusing effect of a wobbly syntax that bumped along in everything he wrote. His habit of underlining words he wished to emphasize, seemingly at random, didn't help. Nor did his punctuation—an idiosyncratic spray of dashes, apostrophes, periods, and haphazard or missing commas. The result almost tracked, but usually not quite, as in this excerpt from a letter to Lucy in 1829:

> My letter will be through necessity of interest either in facts or of their nature a short and dull one but I like to write to thee *regularly*—when Sunday comes I have measuring its distance since the one just gone to speak to thee—I have no other pleasures—I live alone and see scarcely anyone besides those belonging to the house I am at—I raise before day, take a walk, return and set to my work untill night fall—

From the beginning of his time in England, Audubon had been working on written descriptions of the birds depicted in the plates for *The Birds of America*. Audubon envisioned these bird "biographies" as the backbone of a multivolume text that would accompany the engraved plates as a separate publication. There were practical considerations behind the division of words and pictures into two distinct works. Audubon, of course, had to pay his engravers, first Lizars and then the Havells, as he went. He had started selling subscriptions as soon as the first Number—only five pictures—was complete. There was no time to prepare a finished text and no way of incorporating one with each Number as it was produced. Unlike Alexander Wilson, whose smaller-scale drawings could be easily bound with text, Audubon had chosen a format for his illustrations—the double-elephant-sized folios—that was impractical for text. Another factor in the decision to separate the words from the pictures was the copyright law in Britain, which required that an author deposit any copyrighted work at no charge with each of nine major public libraries throughout the United Kingdom. This would have been prohibitively expensive if the work included Audubon's plates. No similar provision applied to an uncopyrighted collection of engravings.

Audubon's hesitancy about his writing wasn't only about his command of the language. Audubon confided to Charles-Lucien Bonaparte on a number of occasions that he knew his formal education was inadequate, that he was really no scientist. Scientific descriptions of more than four hundred species of birds would require a sophistication and breadth of knowledge he did not possess. He was particularly uneasy about describing bird morphologies in a rigorous way, and early on he had looked for someone to help him. Audubon had thought initially of William Swainson, and had written to him proposing that he and Lucy should stay with the Swainsons at their country home while they worked together on the bird biographies. Slightly delirious at the prospect of such a comfortable and collegial collaboration, he had made the ridiculous offer to supply wine for himself and Lucy during their stay.

It was an offer Swainson couldn't refuse fast enough. He told Audubon that their coming to stay with him was out of the question. If he still wanted Swainson's help on technical issues in his books, Swainson would supply it—but at a charge of twelve guineas—nearly $60—for each sixteen-page "sheet," plus a stipulation that Audubon credit his contribution with a byline as coauthor. Although Audubon never hid the fact that other people helped with his work and at one time or another hinted that he would be willing to partner with Bonaparte—an idea Bonaparte never encouraged—he was unwilling to have anyone's name next to his. And in any case, he could not afford Swainson's fee.

Havell was starting work on the twentieth Number about the same time the Audubons arrived in Edinburgh. This meant subscribers would soon have the first one hundred engravings—roughly the number Audubon planned to write about in each volume of what he called the letterpress. Determined that publication of the letterpress parallel production of the engravings, Audubon renewed his search for someone to assist him. One of the people he talked to was James Wilson, a naturalist and a contributor to the *Encyclopaedia Britannica*, which was published in Edinburgh. Wilson suggested a man named William MacGillivray.

Eleven years younger than Audubon, MacGillivray was a compact man, with a high, domed forehead and lively eyes. He was born in Aberdeen, but had been raised on the remote, wind-battered coast of South Harris Island in the Outer Hebrides, and he occasionally undertook long, solitary hikes across Britain. MacGillivrary had learned both Greek and Latin at an early age, and had studied various branches of natural history, including geology and botany. But his special passion was ornithology. Like Audubon, MacGillivray was crazy for birds and had spent a fair amount of time shooting and drawing them. He was also plainspoken and rather unrefined—qualities that appealed to Audubon. Unlike Audubon, MacGillivray was a trained taxonomist and a close student of Linnaeus. He was also a meticulous anatomist. As a young man MacGillivray had carefully measured and then dissected a walrus that had been killed on the beach near his home. Another time he shot and dissected a bear, which he later stuffed. When Audubon met him, MacGillivray was between jobs, having most recently worked as a special assistant and specimen curator for Professor Robert Jameson, Audubon's patron at the University of Edinburgh.

Toward the end of 1830, MacGillivray agreed to become Audubon's editor and scientific adviser on the letterpress—for one-sixth the fee Swainson had asked and with no demand for credit. Feeling it was urgent to get started, Audubon at once began to feed copy to MacGillivray, and they soon fell into a work pattern that would continue on and off for the next eight years. Audubon, rising at dawn each day, wrote until dark, sometimes continuing on by candlelight until he was exhausted. MacGillivray matched Audubon's manic pace, though he preferred to do most of his work late at night. This was reassuring to Audubon, who considered nocturnal scribbling the mark of a serious author.

Lucy worked alongside her husband. Prone to rheumatism, Lucy found Edinburgh pretty but disagreeably cold and damp after years of living in the swelter of Louisiana. Audubon, whom she observed was "still fatter" and in the pink of health, supplied her with heavy woolens against the bone-chilling mists and the chattering winds off the North Sea. It was so foggy in Edinburgh, Lucy said, that they often had to light their candles by four in the afternoon. Outside their windows, the streetlamps on George Street illuminated the pale nighttime fogs. After their long and sometimes angry separation, Audubon and Lucy were once again of the same mind and mood in all matters. No doubt Lucy contributed many corrections and amendments to Audubon's composition of the letterpress. More important, she became his deputy in dealing with everything and everyone else in the world as he was more immersed in writing. Anyone having business with Audubon had to get past her. She corresponded with Havell on a regular basis, providing chatty updates on the weather in Edinburgh and what they had seen or done of late—but also to keep the wheels turning in London. She told Mrs. Havell that they were far too busy to go out and rarely accepted invitations from anyone—the implication being that Mr. Havell should be so industrious. Audubon, she said, often wrote until eleven o'clock at night. In the thin gray light of morning, they would shiver and begin again.

In a burst of headlong writing, Audubon and MacGillivray with their steel-nibbed pens and low-burning candles completed the first volume of the letterpress between December 1830 and March 1831. The typeset version ran to over five hundred pages. Audubon titled it *Ornithological Biography*. It would be followed by four more volumes in the same format and tone. Descriptions of bird species followed the order of the birds depicted in the engravings for *The Birds of America*. These descriptions, or "biographies," varied in length and detail, depending on Audubon's familiarity with and fondness for the species. He devoted more than fifteen pages to the first one—his loving account of the turkey. In cases where his observations were limited—or where the descriptions were received entirely from other naturalists whose travels took them places not visited by Audubon—the accounts were as brief as a single short paragraph.

Audubon affected a breezy style, speaking directly to the "kind reader" and including rollicking tales of his exploits in the field. He also carefully described a bird's flight, its song, its feeding and reproductive habits, its nest building and what its eggs look like—as well as where and how he had found it, shot it, and probably ate it. At the conclusion of each account, MacGillivray added a scientific description, including precise measurements, plumage characteristics, and taxonomic designations. Close attention was paid to features distinguishing males from females, and juveniles from adults. In the case of new species, Audubon provided both scientific and common names of his choosing. He named a number of species for friends and colleagues. For known species, the taxonomies of Linnaeus, Wilson, and Bonaparte, among others, were used to identify the bird. Later in the series, MacGillivray—especially after Audubon began supplying him with bird skins from America—also included occasional black-and-white sketches he made of specific body parts and internal organs. In his introduction to Volume I, Audubon stated his debt to MacGillivray:

I feel pleasure here in acknowledging the assistance which I have received from a friend, Mr. William MacGillivray, who being possessed of a liberal education and a strong taste for the study of the Natural Sciences, has aided me, not in drawing the figures of my Illustrations, nor in writing the book now in your hand, although fully competent for both tasks, but in completing the scientific details, and smoothing down the asperities of my Ornithological Biographies.

Audubon planned to sell the *Ornithological Biography* to his subscribers at a nominal additional cost, but he eventually gave it to them free. Nonsubscribers were to pay twenty-five shillings—about $5. For its bird accounts alone, *Ornithological Biography* would have been an amazing document. As a picture of the American wilderness, it was breathtaking. Audubon had nearly doubled Alexander Wilson's inventory of American birds. For some species that would soon be swallowed in the dust of extinction—like the passenger pigeon and the Carolina parakeet— Audubon's descriptions preserved a lost, far richer world.

But Audubon did not limit himself to birds in *Ornithological Biography*. From the time he began to think seriously about the text for *The Birds of*

America, he had imagined something more wide-ranging. For him, the birds were inseparable from their context—from the woods and swamps and river bottoms on the frontier of a boisterous young nation. Audubon wanted to describe the places he had been and the people and things he had seen. And so he interspersed the bird accounts with his own vivid Americana in a series of sidebars, or "delineations of American scenery and manners," as he called them, which eventually numbered more than sixty. Most of these vignettes were highly autobiographical, with Audubon as the featured player and frequent hero. Some of them were even true.

As he had done his whole adult life, Audubon carefully calculated his audience and what it wanted to believe, then blended fact, exaggeration, and outright lies into a mélange of self-promotion. He seemed to take for granted that his subscribers, hungry for tales of derring-do, would accept a larger-than-life version of his experiences in the New World, so that's what he gave them.

In many of the "episodes," as they were later called, Audubon stuck to simple narratives that were almost certainly the truth or close to it. Several gave accounts of his travels on the Ohio and Mississippi Rivers. These included entertaining studies of weather, navigation, pioneer settlement, fishing, and, of course, hunting. Audubon told about his and Lucy's travels between Pennsylvania and Kentucky, as well as the time he lost his portfolio in Natchez. In "Kentucky Barbicue on the Fourth of July," he gave a lively description of raucous pioneers partying on Independence Day. He wrote a devoted remembrance of the mustang Barro. Audubon also reported his encounters with men like Alexander Wilson and Constantine Rafinesque. Although he worried that the clearing of the great forests for farmland would someday reduce bird populations, Audubon was mightily impressed by settlers who scraped out an existence all along the American frontier. He wrote enthusiastically of "squatters" on the move across the continent in search of land and a future. A collector of local lore and myth wherever he went, Audubon also devoted a few of his episodes to tales others had told him. Some were more credible than others. There was a pioneer family's recollection of their harrowing escape from a deadly forest fire, and a man's account of having been lost for forty days in a swamp only a few miles from his home. Then there was the ghastly—and suspiciously well rehearsed—story told by a sailor who'd kept watch through a long night as a mortally injured pirate died from his wounds.

Some of the episodes were meant to shock, especially those dealing with a cruelty to animals that Audubon casually accepted as part of frontier life—savageries in which he was often a willing participant. In "Pitting of Wolves," Audubon told an improbable story in which two young slaves walking through the woods at night were set upon by a pack of wolves, which managed to kill one of them. Audubon then explained a method for dealing with wolves shown to him by a farmer with a special loathing for the animal. The farmer dug pit traps around his property, covering them with brush and baiting them with putrid venison. On the day Audubon visited, the farmer had caught three wolves in one of his pits. Astonished at first and then hugely amused, Audubon watched as the farmer leapt into the pit, where the wolves cowered, ears flattened against their heads. One by one, the farmer grabbed each by the hind feet and with a deft motion of his hunting knife severed the leg tendons at the hamstrings. Climbing back out, the farmer then threw a noose around the neck of one and then another wolf, hauling each bleeding and half-strangled animal out onto the ground, where they were fed to a pack of dogs.

After an entertaining discussion of the lives of bears, Audubon launched into another ugly tale in "Scipio and the Bear." In this episode, Audubon told of being summoned by a neighbor one night to assist in hunting down a group of marauding bears destroying a cornfield. Audubon, the neighbor, and a third friend, assisted by "four stout Negro men, armed with axes and knives," mounted horses, led out a pack of dogs, and surrounded the bears. A warm drizzle was falling. Blowing horns and loosing the dogs, the hunting party advanced noisily toward the center of the field where a number of dead trees stood, flushing the bears ahead of them. There turned out to be five of the animals in the field, an adult and four cubs. Presently, all five were treed.

Two of the cubs were shot at and wounded badly enough to fall from the trees. The dogs finished them off. Now eager to "procure as much sport as possible," the white men directed the slaves to chop down the tree holding the largest of the remaining bears. This took some time, but at last the tree swayed and then crashed to the ground. Audubon could hardly believe that the bear survived the fall, but he was even more surprised when it tore into the dogs, killing several. Just when they were about to shoot the bear, it suddenly charged and seized a horse ridden by a young slave named Scipio. After a brief, violent struggle, the horse was rolled onto the ground. Scipio, however, smoothly stepped off his mount as it went down and with a single blow of his axe crushed the bear's skull.

As dawn approached the rain stopped. The last two small bears were located in one tree. The men gathered brush at the base of the trunk and set it alight. Flames crawled up the tree and choking columns of smoke enveloped the cubs. The panicked bears climbed to the highest limbs that would support them as the tree became a "pillar of flame." Blinded by the smoke and feeling the intense heat rushing up at them, the bears tottered for a few minutes and finally fell in a fiery heap, snapping off burning limbs and branches as they came. Once on the ground, they were left to the dogs. Surveying this scene as daylight came on fully, Audubon noted that the dogs and fires and general mayhem had done far more damage to the cornfield than the bears ever would have managed.

In "The Prairie," Audubon recounted the night he lay awake next to the half-blind Indian as he made ready to defend himself against the crone and the drunken sons determined to kill him for his pocket watch. Who could tell how much was true and how much was embellishment? There was a similar dubious quality to the events Audubon described in an episode called "The Runaway," in which he told of a suffocatingly hot afternoon in a Louisiana swamp. Burdened with his gun and a pack loaded with the carcasses of half a dozen wood ibises, Audubon came to the bank of a narrow, treacherous-looking bayou. Fearing he might sink in the muck if he tried to wade across, Audubon threw his gear to the opposite shore, drew his knife in case of alligators, and gingerly half-waded and half-swam to the other side. His hunting dog, happy to get wet in the heat, swam and frisked by his side. But as Audubon stood up dripping after the crossing, the dog suddenly began to growl. Someone yelled at him to halt. Audubon grabbed his gun, cocked it, and leveled his barrels at a blank wall of vegetation from which the voice had seemed to emanate. Presently, a "tall, firmly built Negro emerged from the bushy underwood." Audubon aimed his gun at the man's chest and nudged his triggers. But on seeing how rusted and dilapidated the other man's gun was, Audubon decided he had little to fear and slowly lowered his own piece.

Audubon's refusal to shoot the man on the spot had an unexpected effect. The black man at once became subservient, addressing Audubon as "master" and inviting him back to his humble camp in the woods. It was getting late, the man said, and Audubon would be welcome to spend the night and to hear his story. Which was this: The man was a runaway slave who had recently been sold from his home plantation, along with his wife and three children, all five of them being sent to different owners. Unable to endure this separation, the man had escaped and stolen away first his wife and then each of the children, taking them deep into the swamp, across murky bayous and through heavy canebrakes. Audubon, who had judged himself physically equal to the black man in the event this was some kind of trick, was at first alarmed when he came into their camp and was surrounded by the whole family. But they were friendly and quite obviously intimidated by him. As the children petted his dog and the wife prepared dinner, the man cleaned and greased Audubon's gun and asked if there was anything to be done for his poor family. Audubon assured him there was. The next day he took them out of the swamp and back to their original owner—with whom Audubon was acquainted. After some discussion Audubon had arranged for the family to be bought back and reunited. Audubon concluded this story on an ambiguous note, saying the family was ever after "rendered happy as slaves generally are in that country," but adding that since the time of this event it had become illegal to involuntarily separate slave families.

Of course, all of this could have been true. Audubon's admission that he was frightened at being outnumbered by a man in company with his wife and three small children feels authentic enough. The happy ending, however, seems dubious—rather like his sudden rescue in "The Prairie." Audubon may have known a few plantation owners in Louisiana, but he was hardly on an equal footing with them at the time. Could an impoverished woodsman married to the local schoolteacher have prevailed on a rich cotton grower in this way?

What seems probable is that Audubon simply took a liberal license in the episodes, steering real events into more dramatic waters. In "The Earthquake" he told of riding over the "barrens of Kentucky" one November day when a "sudden and strange darkness" opened on the western horizon. Thinking a storm was on the way, he gave Barro a boot to bring him to a gallop. But to Audubon's consternation the horse instead slowed and began picking his way over the ground like it was a "sheet of ice." After a little of this, Barro stopped altogether, quivering and splaying all four legs out as if something terrible were about to happen. And something did. As Audubon dismounted, the trees and bushes around him began to sway and the earth itself heaved in successive waves "like the ruffled waters of a lake." Audubon hurried home and was relieved to find his family safe, though for weeks afterward more tremors shook Henderson at intervals, unnerving everyone. This, Audubon said, was all due to the New Madrid earthquake—so named for its epicenter near New Madrid, Missouri, where huge craters formed as the earth sank into itself as the ground pitched wildly and eerie lights played across the sky. Whole islands disappeared, and the course of the Mississippi River was permanently altered.

Audubon without question experienced the New Madrid earthquake—almost everyone then in North America did. Where he was at the time is hard to say and he was wrong about the dates. The New Madrid earthquake was actually three distinct quakes, all connected by resounding aftershocks. The first quake occurred in December of 1811. The second and strongest of the three was in the first week of February 1812. It was the most powerful earthquake to hit North America in recorded history, estimated now to have exceeded 8.0 on the Richter scale. It was felt in every corner of the continent but the far Pacific Coast. Houses rattled, clock pendulums stopped, and chandeliers were set swinging all up and down the Eastern Seaboard. In Richmond, the tremors caused church bells to ring.

At the time of the initial quake in December, Audubon was not in Kentucky. He, Lucy, and Victor were visiting Lucy's family at Fatland Ford just outside of Philadelphia. Leaving his family behind, Audubon had then gone off toward Henderson sometime later that month, reaching Pittsburgh by the first of the year. From there, he and Barro had gone downriver by boat, putting ashore before Cincinnati and riding overland the rest of the way. It's possible that he was still on the road in early February when the big quake hit. But the implication that he then rushed onward to Henderson to see to his family can't be right, since they weren't there. Audubon returned to Philadelphia that same winter and it wasn't until the following summer that he brought Lucy and Victor home to Kentucky.

The minor confusions of dates and places are forgivable. After all, twenty years had gone by. But the other problems with some of Audubon's episodes for *Ornithological Biography* cannot be dismissed as inadvertent mistakes. Audubon did not misremember his interference between a master and a slave, nor did he simply mix up the details of a near-death experience in a frontier cabin. Despite having lived an adventurous life, Audubon apparently decided the simple truth was not exciting enough,

and woven into many of his episodes are exaggerations and invented exploits that he apparently believed were the kind of colorful scenes his
readers expected from the American West. From the moment he'd
stepped off a ship in New York in 1803 with a new name and a blank past,
Audubon had taken liberties with the truth about himself whenever it
suited his purposes. Audubon may not have been a habitual liar, but he
was a chronic fictional character, first as the Louisiana-born son of an admiral and a Southern belle, trained by Jacques-Louis David and given an
American plantation—and now as the main attraction in a kind of serial
autobiography.

Two of Audubon's most memorable episodes concerned his exploits
with America's most famous woodsman, Daniel Boone. "Kentucky
Sports" began with Audubon's rough-and-ready account of the early settlement of Kentucky, as the Western frontier was first opened up by pioneers streaming in from Virginia. Audubon wrote of the hardships of
the wilderness, the bloody perils of Indian attack, and the excitement of
descending the Ohio River by flatboat. Kentucky, he carelessly said, had
"probably been discovered by a daring hunter, the renowned Daniel
Boone."

Audubon continued with a lengthy discussion of the shooting prowess
of Kentucky riflemen that was more myth than fact. Any self-respecting
Kentucky hunter thought nothing of shooting the head off a turkey at a
hundred yards, Audubon said. These same intrepid marksmen also loved
shooting contests. In one such event, riflemen took turns attempting to
drive a nail into a board from around forty paces—at least one hundred
feet. Audubon said it usually took no more than three shots to drive the
nail home. In another test, each shooter attempted to fire a ball through
the flame of a candle from fifty yards without extinguishing it. These
boasts were so much a part of the Kentucky character that Audubon
probably gave little thought to repeating them, even though such sharp-
shooting feats with the primitive rifles then in use would have been beyond remarkable.

The most interesting shooting trick, however, was a hunting technique
Audubon claimed Boone himself had shown him. This happened near the
town of Frankfort, about halfway between Lexington and Louisville, in
the woods along the banks of the Kentucky River. Audubon described

Boone that day as a "stout, hale, and athletic man, dressed in a homespun hunting shirt, bare-legged and mocassined." The acorn mast was heavy that year, and the two hunting companions found the forest full of squirrels. Boone offered to teach Audubon a way of shooting them with a heavy rifle without destroying the meat. He called it "barking off squirrels." Spotting a squirrel sitting motionless on a tree limb, Boone lifted his rifle and took aim. At the "whip-like report" of Boone's gun, Audubon expected to see the squirrel cut in two. Instead, the ball struck the limb just beneath the animal, splintering the bark and creating a concussive explosion that killed the squirrel without harming a hair on its body.

Audubon gave a much fuller description of the great long hunter in an episode titled "Colonel Boon." In this story, Audubon and Boone had spent a day hunting together. After returning home and getting ready for bed, Audubon sized up his friend thus:

> The stature and general appearance of this wanderer of the western forests approached the gigantic. His chest was broad and prominent; his muscular powers displayed themselves in every limb; his countenance gave indication of his great courage, enterprise, and perseverance; and when he spoke, the very motion of his lips brought the impression that whatever he uttered could not be otherwise than strictly true. I undressed, whilst he merely took off his hunting shirt, and arranged a few folds of blankets on the floor, choosing rather to lie there, as he observed, than on the softest bed.

The episode continues on with a bedtime story from Boone about his capture many years before by a band of Indians. In those days, Boone said, he hunted Indians in the wilds of Kentucky in the same way he did "any ravenous animal." Boone told of escaping his captors when they got drunk and passed out. For a moment he considered killing them where they lay, but thought better of it and instead cut a mark on a nearby tree by which to remember the place. Sometime later, Boone's mark was used to settle a land dispute.

The stirring composite portrait of Boone in these two episodes, as well as Audubon's claim of having prowled the Kentucky woods with the great man, was false. Daniel Boone left Kentucky and resettled permanently in Missouri in 1799—while Audubon was still a navel cadet in

France. Although rumors of Boone passing through Kentucky after that occasionally circulated, the family and friends who knew him best insisted that Boone never again set foot in Kentucky. And even if he had, he would have borne no resemblance to the man Audubon described. When Audubon and Lucy first moved to Kentucky in the spring of 1808, Boone was almost seventy-four years old. Aged and increasingly frail, Boone by then was subsisting mostly on mush. No one who met him would have described Boone as "gigantic" at any point in his life. He was fit and trim as a young man, but of modest build—more wiry than powerfully put together. As an old man, Boone appeared gaunt.

The only contact Audubon likely had with Boone was a brief exchange of notes in the summer of 1813, during a trip Audubon made to St. Genevieve. Audubon wrote to Boone, asking if they might meet and go hunting together. Boone, who was by then almost eighty, sent back a curt answer saying his hunting days were over, as he was weak and nearly blind.

It's not hard to imagine the temptation that led Audubon to take liberties with the truth in composing the episodes for *Ornithological Biography*. The contrast between his exquisite drawings and his he-man American persona had proved an intoxicating combination to the British. What's a little harder to conceive is what Lucy's role in crafting some of these stories may have been. Working alongside her husband, she had the chance to compare the Audubon portrayed on paper with the Audubon she knew. Was she a coconspirator? Perhaps, though it's unfair to judge her too harshly in this. There may well have been other, more far-fetched episodes that she talked him out of using. And it's more than likely that Lucy often didn't know what to question because Audubon had spent so much time away from her in his wanderings that she could not have said one way or another when he was telling the truth and when he was not. What can't be questioned is her loyalty to Audubon and to his work. Lucy wrote to Mrs. Havell to say that so much "close writing" was giving Audubon headaches and worry. Audubon was not suited to such fretful, sedentary pursuits. What he really needed, she said, was exercise.

In the fall of 1831, the schooner *Agnes*, fighting contrary winds and climbing steep seas, made her way down the Atlantic coast between South Carolina and Florida. At night the ship pitched wildly in the gale, and by day the frothing gray ocean turned hypnotically blue whenever the sky cleared. Off to starboard the surf crashed against a succession of white beaches. On November 20 the *Agnes* made port at St. Augustine, taking the better part of the day to thread its way through the hidden sandbars and treacherous currents that guarded the entrance to Matanzas Bay. Once ashore, Audubon walked through the town as his stomach settled. It reminded him of "an old French Village" and seemed the poorest place he had ever been to in America. Established in 1565 by the Spanish, St. Augustine was in fact the oldest European settlement in North America. There wasn't much to it. The city was dominated by a crumbling relic of a Spanish fort called Castillo de San Marcos. Constructed of an unusual limestone that was embedded with coquina shells, the fort had walls sixteen feet thick and had taken more than twenty years to build. Its sun-bleached hulk sat on the bay at the north end of a cluster of small, whitewashed houses and shops that huddled along a handful of narrow, sandy streets.

Audubon thought the people here were the laziest he had ever met with, completely unlike the pioneers who had settled the heart of the country with their sweat and blood. The Floridians he met in St. Augustine seemed to do nothing. When they were hungry they fished in the bay, or picked fruit from the orange trees that grew in profusion in the jungly forest that crept up to the backside of the town. There didn't seem to be any real "country" beyond that back border. Audubon, incredulous that this was the same region William Bartram and other naturalists had thought a near paradise, found it a flat, sand-blown, forbidding wasteland tangled with live oak and pine and razor-sharp palmettos. The weather, too, was awful—oppressive heat and humidity alternating with a shocking cold that rode in on powerful northeast winds. One day Audubon explored the long, blinding strand of shoreline on nearby Anastasia Island, where lovely dunes surmounted the beach and the scraggly trees were bent inland by the ocean winds. It was hot. He killed a couple of snakes and saw lots of birds and some butterflies. The next day turned gloomy and the barometer plunged.

All of this made Audubon perversely happy. Even in this forsaken tropical wilderness, it was exhilarating to be hunting and drawing again. With each day, Audubon felt more energized. He wrote a series of cheerful letters to Lucy, who had gone to Louisville, telling her not to be depressed about anything lest her mood affect her health. He admitted that he himself had been concerned again about the fate of *The Birds of America* almost as soon as they'd gotten to America. He even devised a plan by which Victor would go to England to make arrangements for continuing the project in the event that Havell suddenly died. But letters from Havell and some of the subscribers had convinced Audubon that Havell was doing marvelously with the engravings. "Do not despond my Lucy," Audubon wrote, "depend upon it we must yet see better days and I think as I believe in God that *he* will grant me Life and health to enable me to finish my tremendous enterprise and grant us happy Old Life. I feel as young as ever and I now can undertake and bear as much hardship as I have ever done in my Life. Industry and perseverance joined to a sound heart will cary me a great ways."

Back in Edinburgh just months earlier, as Audubon finished correcting the galleys for the *Ornithological Biography*, it had suddenly occurred to him that with Havell now starting on the next twenty Numbers, he could afford to go back to America and resume his old plan of visiting Florida, and perhaps explore other parts of the Gulf of Mexico and the northeast Atlantic coast. He needed more drawings, more bird skins, more chances at finding new or undescribed species, especially water and sea birds. The subscriber list seemed to have leveled off and was holding roughly between 130 and 140. Perhaps there were more to be had in America. Besides, Lucy needed to see the boys. On August 1, 1831, after less than a year in England and Scotland, the Audubons had sailed for New York from Portsmouth.

From New York they had gone to Philadelphia, where four subscribers signed up. The astounding news was that these included the Academy of Natural Sciences and the American Philosophical Society, the city's other great learned institution. Audubon declared, prematurely it turned out, that all his enemies in the city "were going down hill very fast." Victor met his parents at Philadelphia and they continued on down to Baltimore, where Victor and Lucy turned off for Kentucky. Audubon traveled south by steamship down the Chesapeake Bay, then via coach overland to Charleston, South Carolina. He was accompanied again by the painter George Lehman, who was to help with background illustrations and drawings of plants, and also by a young man from England named Henry Ward. Ward was a taxidermist who would prepare the hundreds of bird skins Audubon planned to collect.

Audubon and his companions reached Charleston in mid-October.

Worn out, they checked into an expensive rooming house, heedless of the cost. But the next day, they moved to the home of a most remarkable man Audubon had met on the street. On hearing Audubon's name, the man had jumped off his horse, rushed over, and clasped Audubon's hand, saying how thrilled he was to make his acquaintance. The man's name was Bachman.

The Reverend John Bachman, a Lutheran pastor, was five years younger than Audubon. They had a lot in common, not least a shared enthusiasm for natural history. Bachman was originally from upstate New York, where he had learned about birds and animals from one of his family's slaves. At the age of twelve, Bachman had been sent off to school in Philadelphia, arriving in the city about a year before Audubon. Their paths did not cross there, but Bachman was acquainted with other naturalists who later figured in Audubon's career, including Alexander Wilson and George Ord. Bachman and Wilson had met at William Bartram's gardens. Wilson, in fact, got help from Bachman in learning to identify birds in the field. According to Bachman, he had skinned some jays during a vacation in New York and had given one or two specimens to Wilson on his return. These were apparently the same species that Wilson later claimed to have discovered on his trip to Niagara Falls.

Bachman took an instant liking to Audubon and his work. Whatever allegiance he may have felt to Wilson went unmentioned. Audubon, for his part, thought Bachman wonderfully knowledgeable and hospitable. Bachman lived in a large, three-story house fronted with wide verandas. The busy household hummed with the activities of a big family that included Bachman's wife, Harriet, their daughters Eliza and Maria, plus Harriet's unmarried sister, Maria Martin. Miss Martin, a gifted artist, thought Audubon altogether wonderful. Over time Audubon's friendship with the Bachmans would become the deepest and most enduring he would ever know.

Bachman insisted that Audubon and his companions remain in Charleston as his guests for at least three weeks before heading south to Florida, warning them that until a frost came the insects there would be unbearable. Three weeks sounded conservative, as they were then in the middle of a heat wave. Audubon made good use of his time with Bachman, making fifteen new drawings and killing more than two hundred birds of sixty different species for Ward to skin and stuff. They were well convinced of Bachman's advice about the bugs—Ward was so badly bitten

even in Charleston that his skin began to slough off and for a time he was
sure he would die. While Ward recovered and they waited for a change
in the weather, Audubon got news. Seven years after he'd been blackballed in Philadelphia, word arrived that he had been elected to the Academy of Natural Sciences.

Lucy had reached Louisville at about the same time Audubon got to
Charleston. After her time in England, America seemed a bit rough
around the edges. "This is a wild country compared to yours," she wrote
to Havell. But she was happy that subscribers were signing up for *The
Birds of America* and that Audubon, whose name was turning up with
growing frequency in newspapers and magazines, was at last gaining a
measure of fame. "They make much mention of him in America now,"
she told Havell.

With Audubon in the field, it was left to Lucy to keep track of
Havell's progress. This turned out to be a large and often worrisome
task. No sooner did American subscribers begin receiving their Numbers
than Lucy started hearing complaints. These mainly concerned the same
sloppy or unnaturally bold hand-coloring that had disappointed subscribers in England and Scotland. It also came to Lucy's attention that
Havell had begun offering unauthorized discounts on *The Birds of America*
and had also sold some stray prints individually. Worse, Havell stopped
keeping her informed. Unsure whether his letters were miscarrying and
whether her own letters were in fact reaching him, Lucy launched a vol-
ley of increasingly short-tempered communications back to London.
From November through March—a winter so cold in Louisville that she
scarcely went outside—Lucy sent one scalding letter after another, demanding that Havell correct the coloring problems, refrain from unauthorized transactions of any kind, and please, please begin writing back.
Havell, exasperated, finally did—mainly to say he was sick and tired of
Lucy's badgering.

Overlooked in this long-distance friction was a regrettable decision
Havell apparently made on his own that was much worse than anything
Lucy complained of. Havell was by now quite used to assembling some of
the plates from different drawings supplied by Audubon. These often included different views of male and female birds, and also background
landscapes or botanical features drawn by Audubon's various assistants.

Audubon gave specific instructions about how to assemble these elements—the finished "drawing" was sometimes more of a collage—and
he paid close attention to other aspects of the final engraving, like background colors, that Havell himself was to add. When Havell came to the
plate for the Mississippi kite—a strikingly handsome gray-and-white raptor—he discovered he had only a single drawing of the bird for a composition that clearly required two birds perched together on a tree limb.
Inexplicably, Havell simply appropriated Alexander Wilson's drawing
from *American Ornithology*, which happened to be about the right size.
Carefully copying the image—a male bird that was erroneously labeled a
female in Audubon's plate—Havell flipped the bird over, so that it faced
the other way. When the plate was published, there was no mistaking
where the "female" kite had come from—it was a perfect mirror image
of Wilson's drawing. Whatever Audubon thought or said about this outright theft when he discovered it isn't known. The great work simply
continued on.

Meanwhile, unaware of this transgression, Lucy had written Havell a
somewhat conciliatory letter. "I am sorry any expressions of mine should
have offended you," Lucy wrote innocently. "That was not our intention."
Her point, she went on, was merely to provide a "check" on Havell's
work, which he was perhaps too absorbed in to be fully competent to
evaluate. She said she had never written to him in anger, but only in sorrow. "I assure you Mr. Audubon will thank me for pointing out to you
those things which I have and on which his success and reputation so
much depend," Lucy wrote. "Mr. A and I are of one mind."

The real "check" Lucy provided was in the person of Victor, whom
she dispatched to London a few months later to oversee the engravings
and subscriptions. Meanwhile, oblivious to Havell's protestations that he
was doing his best, Lucy didn't let up. She wrote again to Havell, admonishing him to be quicker about sending the latest Numbers to subscribers in America, who were now twenty-two and counting.

Audubon, Lehman, and Ward spent the balance of November and most
of December exploring the area around St. Augustine. Most days they
were up at dawn and then out into the marshes, first by boat and then
slogging through mud and reeds on foot. Audubon found the birds abundant but wary. He had to paint anything he shot quickly before it spoiled

in the heat. Each evening when the birds returned to their roosts, Audubon and his companions went wearily back to town.

Audubon had begun to talk of his work on *The Birds of America* as if it were a kind of divine mission that had chosen him as much as the other way around. Writing to a friend in Philadelphia, Audubon said he had suffered through a hard life, with many privations. This was the lot of many men, but unlike other men, his work had become inseparable from who he was and what he was put on earth to accomplish: "The life I lead is my vocation, full of smooth and rough paths," Audubon wrote. "My physical constitution has always been good, and the fine flow of spirits I have, has often greatly assisted me in some of the most trying passages of my life. I know that I am engaged in an arduous undertaking; but if I live to complete it, I will offer to my country a beautiful monument of the varied splendour of American nature, and of my devotion to American ornithology."

So far, Audubon had shot and drawn about a dozen species of birds, including a vulturelike bird that seemed to belong to an unknown genus. Audubon, Lehman, and the indefatigable Henry Ward had also managed to stuff nearly four hundred bird skins. Audubon had acquired a telescope, and this proved useful in observing water birds, which were often sighted in hard-to-reach places and tended to fly off before one could get close. Audubon wrote descriptions of everything each night, hoping that these accounts would find their place with little revision in *Ornithological Biography*. Audubon felt he had exhausted the area or soon would. In truth, much of what he saw disappointed him, from the scrubby desolation of the land to the indifferent shooting. If it could be managed, he hoped to travel on foot and by boat all the way down the eastern shore of Florida. The land between the ocean and St. John's River, which ran parallel to the coast for most of the length of the peninsula, was said to be an untouched wilderness of waterways and forests that was home to a great many birds.

In mid-December of 1831, Audubon set out to the south, following the old King's Road, an overgrown remnant of a brief English presence in the area. He was intent on visiting some of the local plantations, which were few in number and mostly quite remote. On Christmas day, about fifty miles below St. Augustine, Audubon and company walked down a long, sand-covered lane beneath a canopy of live oaks that arched high overhead, forming a darkening, moss-draped tunnel that led deep into the forest. The narrow path rose and fell gently, and it seemed to Audubon and his companions that they were passing out of the known world and into the nether reaches of an utterly wild place. As they went, strange sounds, like the workings of heavy machinery, became discernible. After a considerable hike, the forest opened and they came into a glen on the banks of a clear, fast-running stream. On the opposite side of the creek was an expanse of rice fields and salt marshes. Overlooking the fields was a big, airy, two-story frame house that had a veranda encircling the upper floor. Ringing the clearing was a horseshoe of nearly fifty huts that served as slave quarters. Beyond these were fields of sugarcane as far as the eye could see. A few hundred yards into the forest stood the massive stone walls and spires of the largest steam-driven sugar mill in Florida, rising like a cathedral toward the roof of the jungle and belching smoke.

The stream was Bulow Creek, the plantation Bulow Plantation. It was owned by a twenty-five-year-old bachelor planter named John Bulow, who was more than happy to have company. Educated in Paris, Bulow was a worldly, enthusiastic young man who kept one of the best wine cellars in America. Audubon remained there for several weeks. George Lehman, who was finding the Florida landscape more inspiring than Audubon found its birds, made drawings of the plantation, including a magnificent, ground-level view of the primordial salt marsh with the ghostly outlines of palms and moss-draped cypress in the distance that became the background for Audubon's portrait of the tell-tale godwit, or snipe.

Just before New Year's, Bulow provided Audubon with a boat and six slaves for a short expedition. Pushing off from the plantation's landing on Bulow Creek, they made their way to the Halifax River, which was here more like an inland arm of the sea. Audubon thought this was likely to be good brown pelican habitat, and he hoped to shoot as many as twenty-five of the wary birds—one to paint and the rest for skins. On the morning of the second day they traversed a shallow bay so dense with fish that the boat's progress was actually impeded by them. As they rounded a point, Audubon saw a stand of mangroves ahead, in which several hundred pelicans were roosting. Audubon ordered the rowers to backwater and put ashore. Leaping over the side, Audubon bent low and splashed ahead, keeping down behind a curtain of rushes until he got close. When he cautiously straightened up, Audubon saw that the birds were asleep and completely unaware of his presence. He watched them for a few minutes, trying to memorize their features. Finally he brought up his gun and fired.

Two fine specimens dropped. In the excitement, Audubon jammed his gun while reloading and had to content himself with just the two, as the rest of the flock rose into a blindingly blue sky and faded from sight.

As they started back, a northerly wind came up, lashing the river's surface into a frenzy and combining with the outrushing tide to drop the water level alarmingly. Feeling a steely cold coming behind the breeze, Audubon and Bulow implored the crew to pull hard at their oars. But at nightfall they ran aground, some three hundred yards away from a marshy shore that was hardly more solid than the shifting mudflat on which they were stuck. With little chance of moving and none of making a fire, the party wrapped themselves in their thin cloaks and hunkered down in the bottom of the boat, shaking and miserable. Audubon said it was the worst night of his life. The wind stayed up and it got colder and colder. No one could sleep. Every minute, Audubon said, felt like an hour.

When day at last broke, the crew seemed half dead. The wind had kept the tide from refloating the boat and there was nothing to be done but to get into the water and push it off. Audubon and Bulow looked at each other, and went over the side. The crew followed. "Push for your lives!" Bulow yelled. Aiming for a point where they could see a small grove of trees, the men shoved and dragged the boat forward at an agonizing pace. In places the black, oozing bottom of the bay rose to their chests. Audubon said he felt as if he were walking in chains. After more than two brutal hours of this, they reached the point. Two of Bulow's slaves immediately collapsed from hypothermia and exhaustion. They were dragged onto dry ground, where Audubon struck a fire. Most of the men could not even stand. Gradually, everyone warmed up and Audubon made some tea. But he knew they were far from safe. Audubon was certain the wind would not abate now, and that the next night would be colder still.

They got the boat floated and were so happy about it that some of the men stupidly lit the marsh afire. The flames sped off ahead of the wind and small animals poured out of the tall grass. Audubon paid them little attention. He was more worried about the low water in which they still found themselves. Sure enough, they ran aground again and were forced back into the freezing water to push. This happened several more times. Audubon and Bulow huddled. Where was the tide? They did not like their chances of making it home by water. They were too tired and too cold, the boat too heavy. They decided to put ashore and strike out overland for the coast, hoping they could make it to the beach and walk back.

They abandoned the boat, packed Audubon's birds onto the backs of the crew, and began walking east, pushing their way through thickets of palmetto with frozen hands. At last they came to the beach. The ocean, Audubon said, looked "angry," and thundered onto the "desolate and naked" sands. Turning left, the party trudged north, walking straight into the frigid wind. It was horrible. The men were stiff and fading fast. The beach was slanted and soft, forcing them to walk at an awkward gait. With each step, their feet sank far into the sand. Audubon said it felt more like wading than walking. Grim-faced and numb, the party kept on. Even the youthful Bulow appeared done in. Audubon kept one eye on him and the other on the sand beneath his feet, occasionally pausing to bend down to pick up a curious-looking shell. Somehow, they all made it back.

Audubon remained in Florida through early March of 1832, exploring the northeast corner of the state. There was little reason to stay on, but Audubon and his companions lingered. Audubon had convinced the Department of the Treasury to allow his party to travel aboard United States revenue cutters patrolling against smugglers in the region. This unusual permission was an explicit acknowledgment of his growing stature, and Audubon was determined to take advantage of the opportunity. It seemed to confirm what he was now reading about himself, courtesy of the once-dreaded critics. Reviews of The Birds of America, almost universally flattering, now appeared regularly, and the papers up and down the Eastern Seaboard had started to notice Audubon's comings and goings. During his first visit to Charleston, the City Gazette and Daily Commercial Advertiser had carried Bachman's effusive notice of his arrival there. Bachman had called him a "celebrated ornithologist, and the worthy successor of the adventurous and enthusiastic Wilson." In Philadelphia, the short-lived Monthly American Journal of Geology and Natural History published several rave reviews of both The Birds of America and Ornithological Biography, quoting lengthy autobiographical passages from the latter. In February, the Philadelphia Gazette reported that Audubon had collected hundreds of specimens in the South, including some new species—as well as the news from European sources that The Birds of America was "advancing rapidly toward completion."

There were no revenue cutters in St. Augustine at the time, but Audubon used his authorization to board a U.S. man o' war, the schooner *Spark*. The *Spark* conveyed them back up the coast and into the St. John's River, which Audubon and company explored for some distance past Jacksonville. Audubon continued to find the birds and the land disappointing. East Florida, he said, was a barren place, covered over with poor soils and ragged pine forests, the forbidding marshes and swamps the only productive areas. The weather was "unsteady," he added, and the endless flat savannas were "unfit for civilization." William Bartram, who had thought this part of the world a Garden of Eden, had to be excused, Audubon said. He was, after all, a mere botanist.

Audubon had hoped the *Spark* would take him on down the East Coast to the Florida Keys and into the Gulf of Mexico, but bad weather prevented this. Audubon went back to Charleston briefly, where he soon secured passage on the cutter *Marion*, which was to be at his disposal during a two-month deployment to Florida waters. He wrote to Lucy, saying that this expedition would complete his work in Florida and the Audubon family would soon be together again. He now had more than one thousand bird skins. All he needed were the water birds he was sure to find farther south. In April and May Audubon traveled down through the Keys and out to the Dry Tortugas. The islands, which may have reminded him of his distant childhood home at Saint-Domingue, were delightful. They had fine weather—with a few squalls—and he found the birds there much more plentiful than they had been near St. Augustine. He even saw flamingos, though he never did manage to shoot one and eventually had to make his drawing of the bird—to many people today the most recognizable of all Audubon paintings—from a skin shipped to him in England.

In Louisville, Lucy monitored Audubon's southern adventures with growing irritation. She'd had enough of long separations. And with Victor soon headed off to England to take charge of the engravings and subscriptions, she was determined that the family not remain any more scattered than necessary. Although both of the boys had grown into responsible young men, Lucy had been mortified at the modest livings they were eking out in Louisville, barely enough to keep themselves clothed and fed. Johnny, in particular, seemed to be suffering and was often un-

der the weather with minor illnesses Lucy believed were the conse-
quence of too much hard work and too little reward.

Lucy wrote to Audubon, thanking him for the letters he managed to
send her from such a "dismal" place as Florida. But she wanted him
home. "Why are you in that desolate region?" she asked. "When there are
no new birds why remain? Do not let enthusiasm make you quite forget
what is due to yourself, to your family, and depend upon it my love the
World will never repay either your toil, your privation or your expense."

"Do come away," she said.

Lucy was also concerned that their lengthening absence from London
put *The Birds of America* in jeopardy. Subscribers were once again lagging
in payments. Audubon's funds, as Lucy pointedly put it, were "not accumulating." And of all the places in the world to linger while his great
project went on without him, surely Florida was the worst. "Do come
home," Lucy said again, "and put us all at ease. I assure you I regret more
every day that I did not go straight down and resume my labours in the
South; but now I wait most anxiously your replies, or your presence.
How you can think of remaining in the South so late I cannot conceive,
when you reflect that you have been in Europe so long and the South
never agreed with you?"

But Lucy stopped short of an ultimatum. After their reconciliation,
she seemed resigned to pleading with her husband but never insisting.

"If you *cannot* come up," Lucy said, "or if you can write your plans,
your wishes *decidedly* do so and promptly they will be obeyed depend
upon it by your most Affectionate Sons and your true friend, adviser and
affectionate Wife."

Audubon, though not completely insensitive to Lucy's demands, chose
to answer only her concerns about his own health and safety. He told her
not to worry, that travel to the south of Florida aboard a heavily armed
naval vessel was the safest thing in the world. "I will be as prudent as need
be," he said, "and being constantly surrounded by the Sea breeze no harm
can arise."

In fact, a profound change was taking place in Audubon's outlook. He
fretted less about the chances of his success and thought more about the
logistics of completing *The Birds of America*. The idea of living out his life
in Europe, where it once seemed hundreds of subscribers might be had,
was fading. Audubon seemed content at the prospect of merely main-
taining those subscribers he had in Britain. Within the year he would

write to Victor in London, telling his son that he was not there merely to keep watch over *The Birds of America*, but to take full charge of the whole enterprise on that side of the ocean. Audubon would himself work on American subscriptions, which had been steadily increasing. It had taken only a few months to raise the number in America to more than twenty subscribers, and orders from the state legislatures in South Carolina and Louisiana were encouraging of many more. Audubon also gave up the plan of a permanent exhibition of his work in England. Joseph Kidd, who had signed a contract to paint oil reproductions of the first one hundred plates from *The Birds of America*, had fallen behind and was instead making excuses and asking for loans. Audubon left it to Victor to deal with him— and with everything else. "I have nothing to say to you about our Business in Europe," Audubon told Victor. "It is given to you for the benefit of us all and we all feel so proud at knowing that you are all competent that should accidents take place we would feel contented at being assured that no fault can be brought home to you."

Audubon wrote to Havell, urging his engraver to keep his work to the very highest standards, as *The Birds of America* would more and more be measured against itself. "Now my Dear Sir," Audubon said, "*you must be more careful than ever* about this great work of ours. The whole of the United States are on the watch & every plate that is turned out of your shop criticized here with a closeness which is astonishing."

Audubon's growing sense of peace with himself and with the future of his work is most apparent in the drawings he made during his sojourns in South Carolina and Florida. Despite his repeated complaint that birds were scarce and hard to hunt there, the drawings he made from this period would later be seen as among his signature works. In the field, the vigor he felt returning to his bones after years of confinement in Britain seemed to flow into his paintings as well—especially in the magnificent portraits of wading birds, the egrets and herons with their fine long legs and wispy plumages, many of them posed against George Lehman's dreamy landscapes, and all of them exquisitely engraved by Havell. Many of these birds were widely distributed in America, but some were peculiar to the South and a few were quite unlike other birds more commonly seen. The roseate spoonbill, with its pink feathers and preposterous rounded beak, was strange and exotic. So was the brown pelican, which inspired one of Audubon's greatest paintings, a drawing that perhaps more than any other hinted at what Audubon himself thought and felt about his life at the time. Audubon had first worked on the pelican in New Orleans, but the drawing of the bird that became part of *The Birds of America* was probably made while he was in the Florida Keys. Audubon showed the great, awkward-looking bird in a moment of graceful repose, perching on a mangrove limb, its huge beak and pouch resting against its elegantly curved neck and a knowing, satisfied look in its eye.

And now the years flowed by in a steady, mostly uneventful way as *The Birds of America* moved inexorably toward completion. After leaving Florida by way of Charleston and arriving back in Philadelphia, Audubon was rejoined by Lucy and John Woodhouse. In 1833, Audubon and John Woodhouse led an expedition north, along the coast of Labrador. Here Audubon painted seabirds and cliff-dwellers of the colder regions, including puffins and grouse and buntings, though his drawing of the nearly extinct great auk had to be made later from a museum specimen in England.

Later that year, the Audubons went to visit the Bachmans in Charleston, where they remained for several months while Audubon painted and worked on another volume of the *Ornithological Biography*. Audubon wrote to Victor that in the future, he hoped to spend as little time in England as he could manage. With luck, he thought there might be as many as one hundred subscribers to be found in America. This must have made Victor a little crazy, as much of his time was now spent trying to reconcile the confusing accounts of subscriptions that were maintained by himself, by Audubon, and by Havell.

But in 1834 and 1835, the Audubons were back in Britain. Much of their time was spent in Edinburgh, where they worked again with MacGillivray on the letterpress. MacGillivray thought Audubon's prose style much improved, but offered the familiar complaint that Audubon always thought too big. MacGillivray believed *Ornithological Biography* should be shorter and snappier, like other best-selling natural histories. Audubon paid him no attention, and continued to slave away. He wrote to Bachman that he would rather walk through a Florida swamp in mosquito season wearing no shirt than labor as he had "with the pen." He said he looked forward to the not-so-far-off day when he could forget his work and his critics and "retire from the World encased as it were within the circle of a few friends such as yourself." In the meantime, Audubon said, he planned to "write, draw, and finish all I can" before leaving

England again for America. As usual, he was concerned about what would ensue in the event that he died on the Atlantic crossing. Whatever happened, the most important thing now would be the completion of *The Birds of America*. Audubon told Bachman that he was arranging all his affairs such that nothing would stop the production of "my great work."

Audubon returned to America in 1836, leaving Lucy in London with Victor. He managed to get his hands on bird skins collected by a recent government expedition to the Pacific Northwest, thus enabling him to cobble together descriptions and make drawings of a number of Western birds he had never personally seen. The following year he traveled once more, this time making an expedition along the Gulf Coast of Texas. At the same time, the Bachman and Audubon families were becoming permanently entwined. In May 1837 John Woodhouse married the Bachmans' daughter Maria.

Audubon complained about his detractors only rarely, and never engaged in public disputes. Instead, he took solace in his success. Once, when Victor had expressed concern about Charles Waterton's criticism of his father, Audubon advised him to pay such rumors no heed. "I am sorry that you should trouble yourself about the attacks of Mr. Waterton," Audubon wrote, "and more so that you should answer any of these attacks. Depend upon it, the World will Judge for itself." *The Birds of America*, he often said, was the only rebuttal he needed to make to the "academicians" in Philadelphia who had denied him in his own country. Over time, the ranks of those who spoke against him dwindled until they became a small circle who talked among themselves about issues and slights that nobody else cared about. Charles-Lucien Bonaparte called on Audubon several times during Audubon's visits to London, once even waking him up in the night and sitting by Audubon's bedside, prattling about birds. Sometime later, when Bonaparte published another installment of his American bird accounts, Audubon believed it contained many of his own observations that Bonaparte had unfairly appropriated from their private conversations. Audubon vowed never to speak to the prince again. Bonaparte, who was evidently likewise put out with Audubon, began telling people he had firsthand knowledge that Audubon had never studied painting with Jacques-Louis David. Audubon eventually wrote to Bonaparte and offered to forgive and forget their misunderstandings. Bonaparte did not answer, and Audubon never wrote to him again.

In Philadelphia, George Ord kept up his hounding of Audubon, though his only real audience now seemed to be Charles Waterton, the strange British naturalist of caiman-riding fame who was a whole ocean away. Ord must have been desperate to correspond with someone similarly ill-disposed to Audubon, as Waterton was surely Ord's complete opposite number. Rich and eccentric, Waterton struggled with words and with natural history, Ord's specialties. Waterton never used the Linnaean system of binomial nomenclature, relying instead on the less "jaw-breaking" common names for birds and animals. Notoriously accident-prone, Waterton was also known for regularly administering therapeutic bleedings to himself and also for being unafraid of high places. Once, when visiting Rome, Waterton climbed to the top of St. Peter's Basilica and placed his glove atop its lightning rod. Supposedly the pope, convinced this rendered the lightning rod ineffective, ordered the glove taken down—but could find no one willing to make the ascent. Waterton finally obliged, climbing back up and retrieving his glove to the cheers of a crowd that had gathered to watch.

For Ord, however, it was enough that Waterton shared a distaste for Audubon. In a correspondence notable for its attention to minor details, Ord catalogued Audubon's many affronts to science. These included his ridiculous account of the rattlesnake and his picture of the mockingbirds, which in addition to showing a rattlesnake up a tree also showed it with fangs that "recurved" to the front. Actually, Audubon, though he exaggerated the amount of recurve, was correct. Most naturalists at the time simply didn't know that the fangs bent slightly forward at the tips. Audubon never argued the point, nor did he ever explain that the picture in question did not, in fact, depict the snake attacking the mockingbirds. It was the other way around. The birds were harrying the rattler, a much more plausible scene.

On other matters—including Audubon's suspect experiments on the turkey buzzard and his "discovery" of the Bird of Washington—Ord was on firmer ground. As for the drawings—the horrible drawings!—these were the worst things of all in Ord's view. The whole affair was so awful, Ord said, that he could not even bring himself to denounce Audubon publicly. "I have been repeatedly solicited to review Audubon's great work, and his history or biography of our birds," Ord said, carelessly using

Audubon's own terminologies, "but I have forborn, for the sake of peace, as I am confident that I should have a swarm of hornets about my ears, were I to proclaim to the world all that I know of this impudent pretender, and his stupid book. His elephant-folio plates, so far from deserving the encomiums which are daily lavished upon them, are so vile, that I wonder how anyone, possessing the least taste or knowledge in the fine arts, can endure them."

Audubon heard all this, directly or otherwise, and simply ignored it. In 1836, he wrote to a friend that he felt it was his duty on earth to do as much good as he could and more particularly, to do as little harm as possible, "even by words."

"To have enemies is no uncommon thing nowadays," Audubon said. "To deserve them we must ever and anon guard ourselves against."

In the fall of 1839, Audubon donated a complete five-volume set of the *Ornithological Biography* to the Academy of Natural Sciences in Philadelphia. Ord made off with it for an extended personal inspection, eventually bringing it back annotated with penciled comments written in his small, neat hand in the margins. Most of the entries are brief, disputing a small fact here and there, though usually in a nasty, demeaning tone. In a few of the notes, Ord's bitterness verges on a sour black humor. Coming upon Audubon's entry for "Maria's Woodpecker," which he had named for Bachman's sister-in-law, Ord could not restrain himself, writing in the adjacent white space:

> It is a fortunate circumstance for the credit of "American Ornithology" that the author of "Birds of America" had not more frequent opportunities of paying such compliments, or we should have had an introduction to all the old maids of his acquaintance with their pretty names affixed to peckers, cocks, and snipes.

Havell, racing against himself, had promised the final engravings for *The Birds of America* by the close of 1837. In the end, it took only slightly longer. Number 87, the last set of five, was completed on June 20, 1838, bringing the total to 435 double elephant plates. It had taken just under twelve years from the time Lizars traced the first outline of the wild turkey onto copper in Edinburgh. Audubon spent another year finishing the final volume of *Ornithological Biography*, leaving Edinburgh a last time in the fall of 1839 to go home. On his landing in New York, the American press celebrated his triumphant return. In Boston, the *Atlas* proclaimed *The Birds of America* a masterpiece and its author a hero for the ages in decidedly extravagant prose:

> The conclusion has been attained of an undertaking, which, unrivalled for the boldness almost amounting to temerity with which it was commenced, the perseverance and untiring zeal with which it was carried on, and the fidelity, industry, and celerity with which it has been completed, will remain an enduring monument to American enterprise and science.

Just before leaving Edinburgh, Audubon had sat for a portrait by John Woodhouse, who unlike his business-minded brother Victor had inherited his father's aptitude for drawing. The portrait, coming at the conclusion of his epic project, showed a different Audubon from the handsome, muscular huntsman John Syme had painted when Audubon first arrived in Scotland. Gone were the massive dark curls of hair cascading down his back, and gone too were the broad shoulders, the gun, and the hunting clothes. In John Woodhouse's picture, Audubon, appearing almost diminutive, is dressed in a suit coat, vest, and high-collared shirt. He sits stiffly in an overstuffed armchair, his hands folded in his lap. Audubon's hair, still longish, is parted, neatly combed, and mostly gray. His sober expression is made more so by the loss of most of his teeth, which gives him a tight-lipped, slightly downcast look.

Audubon and Bachman had begun contemplating a multivolume illustrated natural history of mammals they planned to call *The Viviparous Quadrupeds of North America*. This was not the quiet, private retirement Audubon had often talked of during the long years he worked on *The Birds of America*. In fact, it was not clear that Audubon had earned enough to retire. *The Birds of America* had made his reputation, but had not made him wealthy. Audubon estimated that his "great work" had cost him upwards of $115,000 to produce, not counting his own time. While there never was a perfect accounting for all of the subscribers, it seemed that somewhere between 170 and 200 subscriptions had been filled at roughly $1,000 each. Almost the instant Havell had completed his work, Audubon decided to publish a smaller version of *The Birds of America*—an admission, of a sort, that there might be a market for a less expensive and cumbersome edition. The "little work," as Audubon called it, was a project for John Woodhouse, who went to work with a publisher and lithographer in Philadelphia, reducing his father's life-size drawings by means of a camera lucida, a temperamental device that employed a system of prisms and lenses to project a scaled-down image onto paper where it could be traced. With skill and patience, the image could be copied over and then transferred to an engraving—in this case onto stone. Audubon had high hopes for the little work.

Although he could not be called rich, Audubon felt he now had the means to provide his family with a comfortable home and to undertake his long-wished-for expedition to the western United States. Audubon still thought he would like to see what was beyond the America he already knew. Bachman, who declined to accompany him, promised to compose the text for the mammal drawings Audubon would make on his trip. In the meantime, Audubon applied for a permit from the mayor of New York to shoot rats in the Battery so he could paint those.

In 1841, the Audubons, who had been living in an apartment in New York, brought a tract of land "in the country." It was a parcel of nearly forty acres on the Hudson River, in the area of upper Manhattan that would come to be known as Washington Heights, between 155th and 158th Streets. The land was wooded and sloped toward the river. Audubon named it "Minnie's Land," after an odd Scottish variant on Lucy's name that he'd picked up in Edinburgh. They built a big, square, two-story house, with ample porches front and back. Forever in love with rivers, Audubon had steps built from the front porch down to a large patio they called the *piazza*, where they could sit and watch the Hudson flowing past. Later on, Victor and John Woodhouse built houses on the property too, and Audubon's grandchildren would one day recall him as a tall, white-haired old gentleman who played with them and taught them to dance in a house by a river.

Audubon, dressed in a "dark frock coat, velvet vest, and blue hunting shirt," left for the West in March of 1843. The expedition, on which he planned to ascend the Missouri River into the Yellowstone country of Montana and possibly beyond, included a wealthy farmer named Ed Harris, whom Audubon had met on his first visit to Philadelphia in 1824 and who had also gone with him to Texas a few years earlier. They took with them an assistant painter, a taxidermist, and one general helper. The party went by train to Baltimore, then via stagecoach to Wheeling, West Virginia, where they caught a steamboat to Louisville. Audubon stayed briefly with Lucy's brother William. They next boarded a filthy, dilapidated steamer named *Gallant* that Audubon rode in stoic misery to St. Louis.

Audubon spent four weeks in St. Louis, making ready to once more leave civilization. Reporters there were struck by his appearance. They described him as "quite an aged man." But while he had "silver locks and weight of years upon him," Audubon seemed to everyone still strong and energetic, thanks, it was assumed, to a sturdy constitution and an active life. Audubon, who'd actually spent the better part of the last seventeen years writing and drawing, was only fifty-seven.

On the morning of April 25, the day before his birthday, Audubon and his fellow expeditioners walked to the levee and boarded the steamboat *Omega*, which was pointing upriver. About a hundred fur trappers, a wretched lot, were also traveling on the boat. Most had gotten drunk the night before, and quite a few were still drunk. While the captain rounded them up, Audubon stood patiently on the deck watching the brown waters of the Mississippi sliding by. Just before noon the *Omega*'s boiler was stoked. Audubon felt the wheels begin to turn as the lines were cast off and the boat angled into the current, where it hung motionless for a long moment before gathering speed and moving away toward the frontier.

16

AFTER

Corvus corax: **The Raven**
There, amid the tall grass of the far-extended prairies of the West, in the solemn forests of the North, on the heights of the midland mountains, by the shores of the boundless ocean, and on the bosom of the vast lakes and magnificent rivers, have I sought to search out the things which have been hidden since the creation of this wondrous world, or seen only by the naked Indian, who has, for ages, dwelt in the gorgeous but melancholy wilderness.   —*Ornithological Biography*

J ohn James Audubon died at his home in New York City on January 27, 1851. He was sixty-five. Near the end he was in pain and paralyzed, but before he became unconscious he opened his eyes and gave a "wistful" look at Lucy, Victor, and John Woodhouse, who were at his bedside. Sometime earlier, Audubon had spoken his last words to Lucy's younger brother, William Bakewell. Bakewell, who had been a boy of five when Audubon first called on his sister at Fatland Ford, had later hunted and tramped the woods with Audubon in Pennsylvania and Kentucky. Now in his fifties, Bakewell had come for a last look at his brother-in-law. Audubon, who hadn't said a lucid thing for some time, suddenly looked intently at Bakewell and exclaimed, "Yes, yes, Billy! You go down that side of Long Pond, and I'll go this side and we'll get some ducks."

Audubon's addition to the taxonomic inventory of American birds was substantial. No firm count of the number of species he discovered or even depicted is possible because species are even today continually reclassified. But *The Birds of America* was a great leap forward. Alexander Wilson had drawn about 250 species. Audubon—by a fair estimate— represented more than 440 species. He happily named many of his newly discovered birds for friends and colleagues: Bonaparte's Flycatcher, the Rathbone Warbler, Bartram's Vireo, Swainson's Warbler, MacGillivray's

Warbler, Bachman's Sparrow. There was an Audubon's Warbler and an Audubon's Shearwater, though both seemed to have been named for the artist himself and not for Lucy. Audubon paid tribute to her in a quite different way, instructing Havell to engrave in the caption for Plate CLXXV, the swamp sparrow, the words "Drawn from Nature by Mrs. Lucy Audubon" in place of his own usual credit. The drawing was, of course, by Audubon.

Audubon was fifty-four when he completed *The Birds of America* and *Ornithological Biography*. The mental strain and physical exhaustion he endured before and during their publication took a toll, and in truth he was not the same man after his "great work" was done. His collaboration with John Bachman on *The Viviparous Quadrupeds of North America*, which occupied him for several years, was a mixed success. On the expedition to the West, Audubon and his companions got as far as Fort Union, near the mouth of the Yellowstone River in far western North Dakota. They passed much of their time there hunting buffalo, which they killed in unconscionable numbers, taking only the tongues and leaving the carcasses to the wolves and vultures. Audubon, who uncharacteristically seemed less energetic as the expedition wore on, lingered in camp, writing and drawing. The buffalo slaughter disgusted him, and he seemed not to care to hunt other animals on his own. After eight months, they returned home with what John Bachman said was a meager and disappointing collection of new mammals. Audubon did, however, find fourteen species of birds to add to later editions of *The Birds of America*.

Both Victor and John Woodhouse contributed significantly to *The Viviparous Quadrupeds of North America*, which was initially published between 1845 and 1848 in three volumes at the "imperial" folio size, on pages about twenty-eight by twenty-two inches. Both sons worked on background landscapes, as did Maria Martin down in Charleston. The mammals were not, of course, life-sized, as the birds had been. But Audubon used much the same technique in drawing them, wiring freshly killed specimens into graceful poses and then outlining the figure in pencil before working over the image with watercolors and pastels. The results were often breathtaking, especially the delicate, soft textures Audubon achieved in depicting fur and hair. In one of his plates, for the gray squirrel, Audubon copied the animal he had used in the engraving for the barred owl in *The Birds of America*. For the otter, he went back to his tried-and-true image of the snarling animal caught in a trap—minus the trap. Audubon did not see *The Viviparous Quadrupeds of North America* through to completion. In the end, about half the animals were painted by John Woodhouse, a number of them from specimens he studied in museum collections in England.

Audubon declined noticeably after his return from the Western expedition. His eyesight dimmed and he started to drink to excess from time to time. By 1846 he had stopped working. A year later he wrote his last letters. In the spring of 1848, John Bachman visited the Audubons at Minnie's Land and was shocked at Audubon's condition. Writing home to Maria Martin, Bachman said Audubon was no longer himself. "Alas, my poor friend Audubon, the outlines of his countenance and his form are there," said Bachman, "but his noble mind is all in ruins."

The cause of this precipitous collapse is not certain. Audubon may have suffered one or more small strokes. In 1833, while staying in Boston, Audubon had suffered a brief paralysis that was almost certainly what is known today as a transient ischemic attack, a mini-stroke. These not-uncommon events are caused by the temporary clogging of a small artery in the brain by either a tiny blood clot or a speck of plaque breaking loose from a vein. The symptoms, though alarming, are short-lived and do no lasting damage to the brain. But they can be indicative of a predisposition to a more severe stroke at a later time.

Audubon seemed to age at an accelerated rate. His hair turned white and his once-handsome features collapsed, his toothless mouth sinking into his chin in a perpetual grimace. By the time he was in his early sixties, Audubon looked at least twenty years older than he was. A hard-to-characterize dementia accompanied his physical breakdown. It may have been Alzheimer's disease. Audubon became less communicative, though his craziness was often expressed in childish pranks—hiding things or ringing the dinner bell at odd times. Audubon would not go to bed at night without kisses from all the women in the house, and he insisted on being sung to in French as he went to sleep. Any of these symptoms could simply have resulted from early senility following a hard life.

It's also possible that some of Audubon's health problems were related to his frequent exposure to arsenic, which he had used throughout his career as a preservative for bird skins. He also endured lesser exposures to mercury, which was used in taxidermy, and to the toxic compounds present in oil paints. Chronic exposure to such toxins can cause symptoms not unlike Audubon's—including the premature loss of teeth, though poor hygiene could well have been the cause of both Audubon and Lucy's dental problems. Like most naturalists and painters of the time, Audubon knew instinctively that some of substances he handled were toxic. He complained, for example, of the ill effects he experienced when grinding his own oil paints. But he assumed that these effects were short-lived—comparable to the experience he once had in trying to kill an eagle with carbon monoxide. The charcoal that Audubon burned in a small room for nearly two days in an unsuccessful attempt to euthanize the bird instead nearly asphyxiated the naturalist himself.

In the spring of 1845, not long before his mind clouded over forever, Audubon went to Philadelphia on business. He called on one of his subscribers there, the American Philosophical Society, which had been in arrears on its payments for a number of years.

The Philosophical Society, formed in 1743 by Benjamin Franklin, was the oldest learned institution in the country. It was housed in a handsome old two-and-a-half-story brick building on Second Street, adjacent to Independence Hall. When Audubon got there, the official on duty was one of the many members who also belonged to the Academy of Natural Sciences. It was George Ord. Twenty-one years had passed since their last meeting. Apparently the unexpected encounter was cordial enough. Ord, abashed at being confronted by the still formidable woodsman, listened politely as Audubon explained his ongoing project with the quadrupeds. Ord thought him hopeless, a fool who should have known by then that such expensive projects were doomed. But, as Ord later said, "you can do nothing with an enthusiast."

After their meeting, Ord wrote to Waterton with the surprising news that he had recently been in civil conversation with Audubon, the effect of which had been quite remarkable. Ord found that he felt a grudging admiration for Audubon. He was still certain that Audubon's many scientific errors would cause his work to disappear from the history of ornithology over time. But in the end, Ord could not so easily dismiss Audubon's dogged determination, or the imposing man himself.

"The old gentleman has a very venerable look," Ord wrote, "and appears, from his robust frame and agile step, to be yet capable of enduring fatigue. The industry he displayed in prosecuting to completion his great work is certainly worthy of all praise. If the fidelity of his narratives had corresponded with his perseverance, his fame would repose on a basis which time would not diminish."

The linkage between the Audubon and Bachman families grew deep and tragic. In 1839, two years after John Woodhouse married Maria Bachman, Victor married Maria's sister Eliza. By 1841, both sisters were dead of tuberculosis. In 1846 John Bachman's wife, Harriet, also died. His own health declining, Bachman married his sister-in-law, Maria Martin.

Victor Audubon injured his spine while disembarking from a railcar in 1856. His condition worsened, and within a year he was an invalid. He died on August 18, 1860, at the age of fifty-one. John Woodhouse, always the more sensitive of the brothers, made a series of terrible business decisions, including an ill-fated trip to join in the California Gold Rush. In 1858, he invested in a project to reproduce his father's double elephant folios by means of chromolithography. By 1860, more than one hundred stunningly beautiful plates were completed. But the outbreak of the Civil War devastated the publishing business and erased many hoped-for subscriptions. Exhausted, his fragile nerves in ruins, John Woodhouse fell ill just after the first of the year in 1862 and died within a month. He was forty-nine.

Lucy lived on. She had survived her husband and her children, and would soon outlast the meager residue of their lives together. In 1863, awash in debt, Lucy sold Minnie's Land. That same year she also sold Audubon's watercolor originals for The Birds of America to the New-York Historical Society, which paid her just over $4,000 for the collection. The committee organized for this purpose congratulated themselves on having raised such a generous sum while the country was divided in wartime. Two years after the purchase, Audubon's granddaughter Maria visited the society and found a handful of the paintings cheaply framed and indifferently hung on bare walls in a dingy room.

For a time, Lucy lived by herself in a boardinghouse in Washington Heights. Spending most of her time alone, Lucy worked on a superficial, sanitized biography of Audubon adapted from his journals. It was eventually published in London in 1869, though Lucy was correct in her expectation that she would never make any money from it. She said she seemed to herself "a stranger in the world." Writing to a relative, Lucy bitterly measured her unhappy circumstances, as if she had lived a long dream and awoken in the hard light of a remorseless day: "It does seem to me," she wrote, "as if we were a doomed family for all of us are in pecuniary difficulty more or less. As to myself I find it hard to look back patiently upon my great ignorance of business and the want of a wise adviser."

In her eighties and in waning health, Lucy moved to Louisville to live with relatives. She went by train, sitting and watching the countryside pass by. The train clattered along the hillsides and streams that she and Audubon had once galloped over on horseback. She thought rail travel pleasant enough, more comfortable anyway than the flatboat that had long ago brought a young English girl and her handsome husband down a beautiful wild river and into the West.

Feeble and nearly blind, Lucy died near Louisville at her brother William's home in Shelbyville in June of 1874, at the age of eighty-seven. Her body was taken back East, traveling one last time over the mountains. Lucy's ashes were buried next to Audubon in Trinity Cemetery in New York City.

In 1839, just a year after completing *The Birds of America*, Robert Havell Jr. retired and moved to America. He settled in upstate New York, where he painted and lived quietly until his death in 1878 at the age of eighty-five. Before leaving England, Havell had complied with Audubon's request that he be sent the copper plates for *The Birds of America*. According to one story, the vessel carrying them sank alongside the dock shortly after arriving in New York City, and the coppers sat at the bottom of the harbor for several months before being salvaged. Somewhat corroded, they were recovered, a few "disappeared," and the rest were stored in a Manhattan warehouse, where a fire in 1845 destroyed or badly damaged many of the plates. Audubon had the surviving coppers removed to Minnie's Land, where for years they gathered dust in a shed. Lucy eventually attempted to auction them off. Failing at that, she apparently sold them for scrap. The coppers ended up at the Ansonia Brass and Copper Company in Connecticut, where they were being fed into a furnace one day when the plant manager's teenage son realized what they were and saved as many as he could.

Fewer than eighty of the original coppers are known to still exist. In 2002, the John James Audubon State Park Museum in Henderson, Kentucky, which owns one, cleaned it up and struck two hundred and fifty uncolored prints from it. It's plate CCCVIII, the tell-tale godwit, or snipe, which Havell engraved in 1836. In the drawing, two birds stand on the marshy fringe of Bulow Creek in east Florida. As the prints were lifted from the copper the birds reappeared after 166 years, a little scratched and blurred, like ghosts.

No one knows with certainty how many complete sets of the original double elephant folio of *The Birds of America* were produced. It was almost surely fewer than two hundred, although lapsed subscriptions and individual prints that were sold out of Havell's shop mean that there are more copies of some of the plates. Victor maintained that there were about 175 finished sets altogether, roughly 80 of which were purchased in the United States. George Ord, who in so many ways saw through Audubon without being able to see what he had accomplished, was wrong in his belief that the prints would be worthless and fade from memory. *The Birds of America* is one of the most revered and highly valued of American artworks. The last time a complete set of the double elephant folio was sold at auction, it fetched $8.8 million. The new owner was Sheik Hamad bin-Khalifa Al Thani of Qatar.

ACKNOWLEDGMENTS

I needed help bringing Mr. Audubon back to life. I got it from the librarians and archivists who guided me through the words and images he left behind. I am grateful for their assistance and their eagerness to find an answer for any question. A good librarian is hard to stump.

A collective thanks to the staffs at the Beinecke Rare Book and Manuscript Library, Yale University; the Filson Club Historical Society in Louisville; the Ewell Sale Stewart Library and Archives at the Academy of Natural Sciences of Philadelphia; the Houghton Library, Harvard University; the Rare Books & Special Collections department of Princeton University Library; the New-York Historical Society; the Free Library of Philadelphia; the Historical Society of Pennsylvania; the St. Paul Public Library; the Guildhall Library in London; and the Royal Society Library in London.

Specific thanks to Earle Spamer, archivist at the Academy of Natural Sciences, for providing access to materials and a place to work during the early stages of my research. Likewise I want to thank Robert Peck, fellow of the academy, for his wise perspective on Audubon and the other naturalists of his day. Special thanks to Nate Rice, manager of the ornithology collection at the academy and birdman extraordinaire. When he wasn't in some far-off corner of the world collecting specimens, Nate answered my questions about birds and on one pretty morning in Philadelphia spent a couple of hours showing me how to skin a duck.

At the American Philosophical Society, also in Philadelphia, I got able and enthusiastic assistance from Rob Cox and Valerie-Anne Lutz. My deepest thanks to them both. Thank you to Nathalie Andrews and Carol Ely of the Portland Museum in Louisville, who provided unique insights into Audubon's character and business acumen. And thanks also to Linda Boice and Alan Gehret, both at the Audubon Wildlife Sanctuary at Mill Grove, for help during my visit to Audubon's first American home.

Thank you to Alisa Gallant, at the United States Geological Survey EROS Data Center in Sioux Falls, for researching North American bamboo distribution. Thanks also to Phoebe Lloyd, of the Art History Department at Texas Tech University in Lubbock, for her perspective on arsenic and heavy-metal toxicity. And thanks to Cole Rogers, artistic director at the Highpoint Center for Printmaking, in Minneapolis, for a personal tutorial on the art of engraving.

Warmest thanks to my friends Paul Lombino and Leslie Schultz, of Somerville, Massachusetts, for their hospitality and good company while I was working at Harvard.

In London, Gina Douglas made me welcome at the Linnaean Society's splendidly musty old library. In Edinburgh, Tricia Boyd helped at the Edinburgh University Library. A special thank-you, as well, to John Chalmers, also of Edinburgh, for his gracious sharing of information. Dr. Chalmers, a retired surgeon and a student of Audubon's sojourn in Scotland, is the author of his own fine book, *Audubon in Edinburgh*.

It is believed that about 120 complete sets of the original double elephant folio still exist. I had the enviable task of inspecting several of them, and I want to express my gratitude to the people who made that possible. Thanks to Leslie Morris at the Houghton Library, and to Daniel Wong and John Rathe of the Rare Books Division of the New York Public Library. Many thanks also to Don Luce and Susan Stekel Rippley, at the James Ford Bell Museum and Library at the University of Minnesota in Minneapolis, who granted my odd request to measure several eagles on Audubon's original plates.

Roy Goodman, at the American Philosophical Society, allowed me to spend time with their folio. A true gentleman scholar, Roy's encyclopedic knowledge of America in its formative years and his ability to recall the most obscure sources of historical information helped me time and again.

I doubt that anyone knows more about Audubon than does Don Boarman, museum curator at John James Audubon State Park in Henderson, Kentucky. Don's generosity in opening the museum's collection to me, in loaning materials, and in sharing his own inexhaustible knowledge is much appreciated.

I owe more than thanks to Charlotte Porter of the Florida Museum of Natural History in Gainesville. Dr. Porter's Ph.D. thesis, completed at Harvard University, helped clarify my thinking on the relationship between Audubon and Wilson, and between the two of them and the Academy of Natural Sciences of Philadelphia. Her book, *The Eagle's Nest*, which expanded on her thesis, added immeasurably to my understanding of the struggle by American naturalists to free themselves from European domination. In a conversation we had under the Florida sun one late autumn day, she also reminded me of how brave and how lucky these men were— and of how fortunate we are to have the work they left behind. I am deeply in her debt.

Somebody had to keep track of me and my stuff. Thanks to Liza Bolitzer, formerly of Carlisle & Company. Special thanks to Stacia Decker of North Point Press for her tireless help in preparing the manuscript and tending to permissions.

Christy Fletcher, my agent, sent me off in search of a story about American naturalists. When the road led to Audubon, she was unstinting in her enthusiasm and sound advice. Thank you, Christy, for being right about so many things. And thanks, also, to Becky Saletan, my editor at North Point, who understood this story from the beginning and who shared my fascination with Audubon and his times. Becky has a knack for always knowing what it is I am trying to say, so she must know how much I appreciate her help and friendship.

They say that writing is a lonely, quiet life. Not at my house. I owe the biggest thanks of all to my wife, Susan, and to our four children, to whom this book is dedicated. Sometimes they left me alone to work. Mostly they didn't. For the hectic freight of everyday life they surround me with—the now that makes the past worth revisiting—I am lucky indeed. Whenever I aimlessly imagined myself drifting toward the early nineteenth century to walk a field or wade a slough with Audubon, I was abruptly hauled back to the present to cook a meal or find a dog or go to a soccer game. I don't often thank my family just for being there for me. But I should.

NOTES

John James Audubon had a limited education. He also spoke and wrote in a language he did not learn until he was a young man. But he nonetheless left a lengthy paper trail. Letters, journals, real estate transactions, legal pleadings, shop ledgers, and other Audubon documents survive—including his extensive published works. These, along with similar materials relating to Alexander Wilson, have been the primary sources for my research.

Wherever possible, I relied on original documents (or facsimiles of them). Many of these, of course, have been included or edited in previously copyrighted works. These, too, I have consulted and made use of, and in the interest of fairness I have attempted to cite both the physical location of original materials and any published reference as seems appropriate.

For a variety of reasons—notably Audubon's own unreliable accounts of himself, as well as the sanitized versions offered by his heirs—some sources are better than others. Lucy's biography, adapted from Audubon's journals and edited by Robert Buchanan, contains a wealth of presumably authentic detail but cannot be trusted as a single authority on substantive issues. The same is true of the journals bowdlerized and published by Audubon's granddaughter, Maria. They depict an Audubon often at variance with the real person.

Audubon's own words also required careful evaluation. His letters and two of the journals that escaped recrafting by Lucy and Maria—one from 1820–1821 and the other from 1826—were invaluable. But many of his other writings, especially in *Ornithological Biography*, demanded a skeptical eye. The "facts" of Audubon's life were not always as he presented them. To the extent that I could manage it, I relied on multiple sources—and common sense—in assembling a composite picture of Audubon that I hope gets as close to the truth as possible.

I depended heavily on two biographies of Audubon for the general outline and chronology of Audubon's life. These were *Audubon the Naturalist*, the seminal, two-volume biography published in 1917 by Francis Hobart Herrick; and *John James Audubon*, from 1964, by the foremost Audubon scholar, Alice Ford. Likewise, I owe much to Clark

Hunter's *The Life and Letters of Alexander Wilson*, from 1983; and to Robert Cantwell's *Alexander Wilson: Naturalist and Pioneer*, from 1961.

Owing to the large volume of correspondence held at the Houghton Library at Harvard and the Beinecke Rare Book and Manuscript Library at Yale, I have used the following shorthand to indicate those locations: (Houghton) and (Beinecke). A substantial selection of these letters was edited by Howard Corning and published in a limited, two-volume edition in 1930 by the Club of Odd Volumes.

1. PHILADELPHIA

3 *On a fine spring afternoon*   Audubon, *Ornithological Biography*, vol. I, page X, and Witmer, "The Old Turnpike."

3 *The stage rumbled over a wooden bridge*   Weigley et al., *Philadelphia: A 300-year History*, page 231.

3 *He was an imposing figure*   Burstein, *The Passions of Andrew Jackson*, page 154. Audubon's height and build can be guessed at given that he once served as a body double for a portrait of Andrew Jackson—whom Burstein describes as being "about six feet high, slender in form, long and straight in limb." However, this may be well wide of the truth. In one of the journals edited by Audubon's granddaughter Maria, Audubon describes himself flatteringly as "about five feet ten inches, erect, and with muscles of steel." This, too, seems perhaps a little larger than life. It turns out that Audubon had at least one passport. It was discovered by Francis James Dallett and published in *The Princeton University Library Chronicle* in 1959. According to the passport, Audubon was five feet, eight and one half inches tall—that last half inch suggesting a rather accurate measurement. Intriguingly, this passport was issued to Audubon in the spring of 1830, after he told Lucy he had grown an inch taller during his first long trip to Great Britain.

3 *—his wedding anniversary*   Ford, *John James Audubon*, page 73.

4 *A waxing moon hung low*   *Poulson's Daily Advertiser*, April 5, 1824.

4 *In one dispute, Audubon had lost*   Ford, *John James Audubon*, pages 103–5.

5 *By 1823, Audubon felt his time*   Ibid., page 138.

5 *Two daughters had died*   Ibid., pages 93, 111.

5 *He may have envisioned some kind of book*   Audubon, *Ornithological Biography*, vol I, page X. Audubon repeatedly claimed that he never thought of publishing his drawings before his visit to Philadelphia in the spring of 1824. However, journal entries some years earlier indicate otherwise, and it is reasonable to conclude that his purpose in going to Philadelphia was to publish the drawings.

5 *He left New Orleans*   Audubon, *Ornithological Biography*, vol. III, pages 371–75. Audubon's journey north with Victor is recounted in the episode titled "A Tough Walk for a Youth."

7 *Rooms were cramped but cheap*   Lathrop, *Early American Inns and Taverns*.

7 *He also felt his curling locks*   Ford, *John James Audubon*, page 141.

7 *Mease was a prominent physician*   Wilson (ed.), *1825 Philadelphia Directory and Strangers Guide*.

8 *Awed by Audubon's paintings*   Herrick, *Audubon the Naturalist*, vol. I, pages 327–28.

8 *Only twenty-one years old*   Stroud, *The Emperor of Nature*, pages 34–45.

8 *Bonaparte had been welcomed*   Ibid., pages 46–48.

8 *The academy, formed only eleven years earlier*   Phillips, "The Academy of Natural Sciences of Philadelphia," *Transactions of the American Philosophical Society.*

9 *In January 1824, Bonaparte submitted*   Minutes of the Academy of Natural Sciences of Philadelphia, 1824.

9 *Bonaparte had wealth and a title*   Ford, *John James Audubon*, page 142.

9 *When Mease took Audubon*   Herrick, *Audubon the Naturalist*, vol. I, pages 329–30.

9 *Bonaparte may have allowed himself to hope*   Stroud, *The Emperor of Nature*, page 49. From the moment of his arrival in the United States, Bonaparte was determined to "correct" American ornithological studies, principally Alexander Wilson's.

10 *It is unclear at which meeting*   Minutes of the Academy of Natural Sciences of Philadelphia, 1824. Audubon was formally nominated for membership at the meeting on July 27. Three members—Charles-Alexandre Lesueur, Reuben Haines, and Isaiah Lukens—proposed him for membership. Neither George Ord nor Charles-Lucien Bonaparte was in attendance that evening, which argues that Audubon's visit must have occurred prior to his nomination. Assuming that all five members—Bonaparte, Ord, Lesueur, Haines, and Lukens would have been present, the meetings Audubon could have gone to would have been May 11, June 29, or July 20.

10 *In his brief time in the city*   Herrick, *Audubon the Naturalist*, vol. I, page 328.

10 *With Bonaparte as his patron*   Ibid., page 330.

11 *Audubon was on safe ground*   Ford, *John James Audubon*, page 142.

11 *Beginning with Thomas Jefferson*   Waldstreicher (ed.), *Notes on the State of Virginia*, page 127.

11 *But Audubon threatened the legacy of*   Ford, *John James Audubon*, pages 143–45.

12 *It was almost sure to cost him*   Hunter, *The Life and Letters of Alexander Wilson*, page 80.

12 *When he died suddenly in 1813*   Cantwell, *Alexander Wilson*, page 258.

12 *At the Academy of Natural Sciences*   Porter, *The Eagle's Nest*, pages 41–51.

12 *He may have alluded to his later claim*   Audubon, *Ornithological Biography*, vol. I, pages 438–40. Audubon wrote of his encounter with Wilson in an episode titled "Louisville in Kentucky."

12 *All of this—the sketchy story*   Ford, *John James Audubon*, page 143.

12 *They walked down a sidewalk*   Phillips, "The Academy of Natural Sciences of Philadelphia," *Transactions of the American Philosophical Society.* A drawing of the academy building and grounds as they appeared in 1824, owned by the Historical Society of Pennsylvania, is published in this article.

13 *Although the members of the academy*   Ford, *John James Audubon*, pages 143–48.

13 *The son of a rich ship chandler*   Rhoads, "George Ord," *Cassinia: Proceedings of the Delaware Valley Ornithological Club.*

13 *His only serious attempt at field research*   Porter, "Following Bartram's 'Track.'"

13 *What Ord had that Audubon didn't*   Rhoads, "George Ord," *Cassinia: Proceedings of the Delaware Valley Ornithological Club.*

13 *Ord had been a close friend*   Alexander Wilson's will, dated August 16, 1813, American Philosophical Society.

13 *He'd completed Wilson's unfinished*   Ford, *John James Audubon*, page 143.

13 *Ord dismissed Audubon's drawings*   Herrick, *Audubon the Naturalist*, vol. I, page 329.

13 *In the weeks following*   Ford, *John James Audubon*, page 144.

13 *Ord was delighted*   Ibid., page 146.

14 *Bonaparte hinted at a future partnership*   Herrick, *Audubon the Naturalist*, vol. 1, pages 329–30; and Ford, *John James Audubon*, page 144. The interactions between Audubon, Bonaparte, and Ord during Audubon's 1824 visit to Philadelphia aren't precisely known. But over the course of the years following their first meetings, it became apparent that Ord's hostility toward Audubon was deep and instantaneous. Bonaparte and Audubon shared an on-again, off-again friendship in which occasional offers of assistance from one to the other never materialized into a full collaboration.

14 *But he was already engaged in*   *Minutes of the Academy of Natural Sciences of Philadelphia, 1824.*

14 *Jacques-Louis David, Audubon's supposed teacher*   Stroud, *The Emperor of Nature*, page 27.

14 *Bonaparte's father had negotiated*   Ibid., page 6.

14 *He took Audubon to see*   Herrick, *Audubon the Naturalist*, pages 330–31.

15 *"You may buy them," Lawson said*   Quoted in Ford, *John James Audubon*, page 145.

15 *Charles-Alexandre Lesueur, a fellow French*   Ibid., page 143.

15 *Admission to the academy*   *Minutes of the Academy of Natural Sciences of Philadelphia, 1824.* Audubon was the only person nominated but not elected that year.

15 *When the vote for Audubon*   Ibid. The academy still has in its archives a voting box, into which members dropped either a white (for) or black (against) marble in balloting for membership. Thus, being *blackballed* was a literal expression.

15 *Audubon was, by then*   Ford, *John James Audubon*, pages 147–48. Evidently, Audubon anticipated his rejection in Philadelphia well ahead of its actuality, heading off for New York nearly a full month before he was denied membership in the academy when the vote took place on August 31.

15 *His work was so admired there*   Ibid., page 148.

15 *But he continued to feel uncomfortable*   Buchanan, *The Life and Adventures of John James Audubon*, page 90.

15 *Audubon entertained the contradictory thought*   Ibid.

15 *He took his time*   Ford, *John James Audubon*, pages 149–50.

16 *Unshaven and wearing moccasins*   Ibid., pages 153–54.

16 *On the long way back*   Audubon, *Ornithological Biography*, vol. I, page XI.

16 *Audubon began to imagine*   Ibid.

2. COMING ACROSS

18 *At the end of the eighteenth century*   Stoddard, *The French Revolution in San Domingo*, pages 1–5.

18 *On April 26, 1785*   Ford, *John James Audubon*, page 14.

19 *Audubon's mulatto housekeeper*   Ibid., pages 13–15.

19 *They called the little boy*   Ibid., pages 14–17.

19 *Young Jean's eyes*   Ibid., page 17.

19 *Pelicans, sandpipers, frigate birds*   Wetmore and Lincoln, "Additional Notes on the Birds of Haiti and the Dominican Republic," pages 13–14.

19 *In winter months they were joined*   Personal communication with Nate Rice, Academy of Natural Sciences of Philadelphia, January 22, 2003.

19 *Jean Audubon continued* Ford, *John James Audubon*, page 4.

19 *Seeking his fortune* Ibid., pages 4–9.

19 *In the spring of 1789* Ibid., pages 18–19.

20 *With only 35,000 French colonists* Stoddard, *The French Revolution in San Domingo*, pages 21, 50.

20 *They blamed the sudden instability* Ibid., page 82.

20 *Those who didn't leave* Ibid., pages 349–50.

20 *Finally, he arranged passage* Ford, *John James Audubon*, pages 22–23.

20 *Three years later* Ibid., page 29.

20 *He was sent to school* Herrick, *Audubon the Naturalist*, pages 93–96.

20 *In March 1803* Ford, *John James Audubon*, page 36.

20 *Audubon dispatched an agent* Ibid., pages 36–37.

21 *When he walked down* Ibid., page 37.

21 *Despite a modest first printing* Burns, *Poems in Scots and English* (Introduction by Donald A. Low), pages xix–xxxi.

21 *One of them was* Cantwell, *Alexander Wilson*, page 15.

21 *It seemed that everyone in Paisley* Hunter, *The Life and Letters of Alexander Wilson*, page 31.

21 *Now a suburb of Glasgow* Cantwell, *Alexander Wilson*, pages 15–16.

21 *It was also a hub* Ibid.

21 *As much as half the tea* Ibid., page 34.

21 *But it was cloth making* Hunter, *The Life and Letters of Alexander Wilson*, pages 16–17.

21 *Many of them belonged to* Cantwell, *Alexander Wilson*, page 16.

22 *As a boy, Wilson was called Sandy* Ibid., pages 15–16.

22 *He was thin, but grew tall* Ibid., pages 16–17.

22 *The Wilson family fortunes* Ibid., pages 23–24.

22 *Young Sandy, who was bright* Ibid., page 21.

22 *His father quickly remarried* Ibid., page 27.

22 *He much preferred reading* Ibid.

22 *At thirteen, Wilson accepted* Ibid., page 28.

22 *When his father renewed* Ibid., pages 28–29.

22 *Nobody knew for sure* Ibid., page 30.

22 *Wilson visited his family* Ibid., page 29.

22 *He took up hunting* Ibid., page 31.

22 *He developed a love of poetry* Hunter, *The Life and Letters of Alexander Wilson*, pages 29–31; and Cantwell, *Alexander Wilson*, page 43.

22 *He took a job in a weaving shop* Cantwell, *Alexander Wilson*, page 44.

22 *When business was good* Ibid., page 45.

23 *Respected Sir* Wilson to David Brodie, December 31, 1788. In Hunter, *The Life and Letters of Alexander Wilson*, pages 123–25. As is true of much of the Wilson and Audubon correspondence, this letter begat numerous subsequent reproductions. The original is in the Paisley Museum and Art Galleries in Scotland. A transcription is in the Houghton Library at Harvard. In addition to Clark Hunter's published version, cited here, there is also Alexander Grosart's in *The Poems and Literary Prose of Alexander Wilson*, from 1876. Infrequent discrepancies, mostly minor adjustments to spelling and punctuation, exist among the various forms of all the letters I ex-

amined from Wilson, Audubon, and others. Hunter also reports that the transcript of this letter at Harvard, which I did not look at, is missing the second verse. However, such a notable error strikes me as unusual. In direct comparisons of hundreds of original documents alongside their published counterparts, I found the different versions scarcely different at all.

23 *When Wilson was broke* Cantwell, *Alexander Wilson*, page 45.

23 *Wilson was an eager sightseer* Ibid.

24 *The Wintry West extends his blast* Burns, "Winter, A Dirge," *Poems in Scots and English*, page 89.

24 *Unlike Burns, his vocabulary* Cantwell, *Alexander Wilson*, page 46.

24 *The way a drop of water* Wilson to David Brodie, December 31, 1788. In Hunter, *The Life and Letters of Alexander Wilson*, pages 123–25.

24 *He fell in love with a woman* Cantwell, *Alexander Wilson*, pages 52–53.

24 *In Wilson's mind* Ibid., page 59.

25 *Encouraged to publish* Ibid., pages 57–58.

25 *Wilson had to beg forgiveness* Ibid., page 58.

25 *But he complained* Wilson to David Brodie, January 5, 1791. In Hunter, *The Life and Letters of Alexander Wilson*.

25 *He fell ill* Cantwell, *Alexander Wilson*, page 60.

25 *Weavers in Scotland were beginning* Ibid., page 65.

25 *One of these poems resulted in* Ibid.

25 *He placed second in a speech contest* Ibid., page 63.

25 *Wilson then did something* Ibid., pages 64–72. This peculiar episode, including the clumsiness of Wilson's attempted extortion and the murky details of his subsequent imprisonments, has puzzled Wilson scholars for two centuries. But Alexander Grosart—along with George Ord, a sympathetic Wilson biographer—argued that Wilson was neither a blackmailer nor a seditionist, but was instead guilty only of living in politically charged times. Brushing aside Wilson's admission of extortion, Grosart insisted that Wilson's satirical attacks on Paisley loom owners were entirely justified, as the lot of them were "local self-importances and petty tyrants," whose exploitation of their workers warranted exposure. Wilson, he said, had merely given voice to "truisms of civil and religious freedom" that were held then to be threats to the monarchy.

26 *Over the course of many months* Hunter, *The Life and Letters of Alexander Wilson*, pages 53–60.

26 *Ironically, it was at this time* Cantwell, *Alexander Wilson*, page 75.

26 *Jail, he said* Wilson to David Brodie, May 21, 1793. In Hunter, *The Life and Letters of Alexander Wilson*, page 147.

27 *During one of his releases* Ibid., pages 59–61.

27 *"I must get out of my mind"* Quoted in Cantwell, *Alexander Wilson*, page 79.

27 *They'd gone first to Belfast* Wilson to his parents, July 25, 1794. In Hunter, *The Life and Letters of Alexander Wilson*. This long, action-packed letter was written home shortly after Wilson's arrival in Philadelphia. It proclaimed, emphatically, the start of a new life in the New World.

27 *After fifty days at sea* Ibid.

28 *Mulling what to do next* Ibid.

28 *One day he shot several cardinals*   Ibid. At least I believe they must have been cardinals. Wilson said only that he shot some "red birds." When he wrote the natural history of the cardinal some years later, the species had been exported to Europe and
was becoming known on the other side of the ocean. Oddly, Cantwell insists that
the birds Wilson killed on this occasion were red-headed woodpeckers—a tri-col-
ored species that even the most careless observer would not likely describe as a
"red bird."

3. A NAME FOR EVERY LIVING THING

29 *Most of the country's*   Scordato, *The New York Public Library Desk Reference*, page 866.
29 *Thomas Jefferson's purchase of*   Ibid.
30 *European naturalists, disinclined to let*   Porter, *The Eagle's Nest*, pages 1–11.
30 *Inevitably, the same principles*   Ibid.
30 *Linnaeus, the father of modern taxonomy*   Koerner, *Linnaeus*, page 15.
30 *A man of wide interests*   Ibid., pages 121–22. Linnaeus's conviction that Mediter-
ranean and even tropical flora could thrive in the near-arctic environment of Sweden was largely premised on a naïve assumption that the harshness of the Northern
winter was offset by the long periods of daylight that occur in the summer at high
latitudes. He was wrong. Linnaeus, and his worshipful students, believed plants
could be "fooled" into adapting to different climatic conditions. But since Linnaeus
did not believe in evolution, and only grudgingly accepted the principle of hy-
bridization, he could never explain exactly how such adaptations would occur. Like
so many frustrated pre-Darwinian naturalists, Linnaeus, by the end of his life, had
begun to suspect that nature was more changeable than prevailing religious and scientific doctrine supposed.
30 *In the Linnaean system*   Ibid., pages 15–16.
30 *A thousand years before Linnaeus*   Barnes (ed.), *The Complete Works of Aristotle*, vol. I,
page 774.
30 *He emphasized the importance*   Ibid.
30 *A close observer of animal behavior*   Ibid., page 781.
31 *"[W]e must take animals species by species"*   Ibid.
31 *For several decades*   Porter, *The Eagle's Nest*, page 15.
31 *"The thing is"*   Koerner, *Linnaeus*, page 45.
31 *He estimated the total*   Ibid.
31 *There are something like*   Tudge, *The Variety of Life*, pages 6–7.
31 *Current guesses put the number*   Ibid., page 7.
31 *Beetles alone make up*   Ibid., page 304.
32 *As new species turned up*   Charlotte Porter, personal communication, November 21,
2002.
32 *In Linnaeus's day*   Ibid. The emphasis on species as the primary units of biology in
the eighteenth and early nineteenth centuries is roughly analogous to the way we
think today about the importance of genes. Identifying species was then fundamental to understanding the living world. The irony, of course, is that close study of
species would one day lead to the concept of evolution. In her book, *The Eagle's
Nest*, and in her interview with me, Dr. Porter argues that American naturalists like

Wilson and Audubon—who gave unprecedented weight to direct field observation in classifying species—were nudging science forward in a direction that would eventually undermine the belief that all of life on earth was determined at the moment of biblical Creation.

32 *"We count so many species"* Koerner, *Linnaeus*, page 44.

32 *Linnaeus was sure these processes* Ibid.

32 *The presence of plant and animal shapes* Prothero, *Bringing Fossils to Life*, page 1.

33 *It was believed by some* Ibid., pages 1–2.

33 *Speculation during the Middle Ages* Ibid.

33 *Aristotle believed such fossils* Ibid.

33 *Leonardo da Vinci thought* Ibid., page 2.

33 *Linnaeus took a pragmatic view* Ibid., page 4.

33 *All of this would have to be rethought* Porter, "The Excursive Naturalists," pages 11–14.

33 *Born in 1707 to a middle-class family* Roger, *Buffon*, pages 3–43.

33 *In 1739, King Louis XV* Ibid., pages 45–47.

33 *It was actually a well-organized academy* Ibid., page 51.

33 *This work morphed into* Ibid., page 79.

34 *Buffon endeavored to explain* Porter, *The Eagle's Nest*, page 15.

34 *Buffon thought the Linnaean system* Roger, *Buffon*, pages 312–13.

34 *Nature, Buffon insisted* Ibid., page 312.

34 *A species, Buffon decided* Ibid., page 314.

34 *"The ass resembles the horse"* Ibid.

34 *A species, Buffon said* Ibid.

34 Buffon's Natural History *was massive* Porter, *The Eagle's Nest*, page 15.

34 *Prior to writing the* Natural History Roger, *Buffon*, pages 15–58.

35 *Intrigued by the story of Archimedes* Ibid., pages 52–53.

35 *He believed the earth was much older* Ibid., pages 106–15; and Porter, *The Eagle's Nest*, page 16.

35 *Anticipating Darwinian evolution* Porter, *The Eagle's Nest*, page 16.

35 *European horticulturalists saw the botanical wealth* Porter, "The Excursive Naturalists," page 2.

35 *Buffon supposed that America* Roger, *Buffon*, page 305.

36 *What was most remarkable to Buffon* Ibid.

36 *The differences between* Ibid.

36 *In the New World* Quoted in Kastner, *A Species of Eternity*, page 122.

36 *"The air and the earth"* Ibid.

36 *"These changes are made only slowly"* Roger, *Buffon*, page 307.

36 *Buffon argued that* Ibid., page 305.

37 *Although the savage* Quoted in Waldstreicher (ed.), *Notes on the State of Virginia by Thomas Jefferson*, page 120.

37 *In 1705, a farmer mucking about* Semonin, *American Monster*, page 15.

38 *It was sent to the Royal Society* Ibid.

38 *Its president at the time* Ibid., page 16.

38 *Cotton Mather, the influential Boston cleric* Ibid., pages 27–40.

38 *Perhaps they came from large sea creatures* Ibid., pages 42–43.

38 *Elephants, believed to have been* Ibid., page 44.

38 *Even Isaac Newton still believed* Ibid., page 60.
38 *There was growing interest in* Ibid., page 62.
38 *In America it was dubbed* Ibid., pages 62–63.
39 *One possible explanation* Waldstreicher (ed.), *Notes on the State of Virginia by Thomas Jefferson*, pages 109–11.
39 *Meanwhile, a new term* Ibid., pages 62–70.
39 *In 1739, a French military expedition* Semonin, *American Monster*, page 87.
39 *Great herds of bison and deer and elk* Ibid., page 109.
39 *They soon returned laden with* Ibid., page 87.
39 *Benjamin Franklin, serving as* Ibid., page 143.
40 *Interest in the fossils remained so high* Ibid., pages 176–78.
40 *It was just before the end of the war* Waldstreicher (ed.), *Notes on the State of Virginia by Thomas Jefferson*, page 16.
40 *In his book* Ibid., pages 79–208. (Specific references can be found in Waldstreicher's contents, pages viii–ix.)
40 *In his discussion of the people* Ibid., pages 121–25.
40 *Emerging from revolution* Ibid., pages 18–19.
40 *America, he believed* Ibid., pages 20–21.
41 *Like other adherents* Ibid.
41 *"Such is the economy of nature"* Ibid., page 116.
41 *Mammoth remains hinted at* Ibid., page 109.
42 *Jefferson thought there was only one* Ibid., page 110.
42 *Jefferson was well versed in* Ibid., pages 107–108.
42 *Some years later* Kastner, *A Species of Eternity*, page 120.
42 *But to whatever animal we ascribe* Waldstreicher (ed.), *Notes on the State of Virginia by Thomas Jefferson*, pages 110–11. Jefferson's wonderful little book, considered *in toto*, was more than an enumeration of America's natural riches and a defense against Buffon. Taking the long view, Jefferson argued that America—young, vital, and big—was in merely the early stages of its ascendancy, and that Europe, which was by contrast old and growing feeble, was in decline, even if nobody on the other side of the ocean could yet believe it.
43 *Jefferson prevailed on the governor* Kastner, *A Species of Eternity*, page 125.
43 *He denounced Buffon's* Waldstreicher (ed.), *Notes on the State of Virginia by Thomas Jefferson*, page 121.
43 *This argument, especially* Ibid., pages 175–81.
44 *Listing more than 120 species* Ibid., page 127.
44 *Twenty years after* Wilson to Thomas Jefferson, March 18, 1805. In Hunter, *The Life and Letters of Alexander Wilson*, pages 232–33.

4. LESSONS

45 *Only months before* Cantwell, *Alexander Wilson*, page 120.
45 *Wilson acknowledged that* Wilson to Thomas Jefferson, March 18, 1805. In Hunter, *The Life and Letters of Alexander Wilson*, pages 232–33. (The drawing at issue is reproduced in Kastner, *A Species of Eternity*, page 167.)
45 *The president was impressed* Thomas Jefferson to Wilson, April 7, 1805. Ibid.

46 *As for the bird that so beguiled* Wilson to William Bartram, July 2, 1805. Ibid.

46 *With the dawn* Wilson, *American Ornithology*, vol. II, page 107.

47 *In the summer of 1803* Wilson to Thomas Crichton, June 1, 1803. In Hunter, *The Life and Letters of Alexander Wilson*, page 203.

47 *In the summer of 1794* Weigley et al., *Philadelphia*, pages 190–91.

47 *The fever was a terrifying* Ibid., page 180.

47 *Many who left did so* Ibid., page 182.

48 *Rush thought that a great load of ruined coffee* Ibid., pages 180–81.

48 *In reeking hospitals the dying and the dead* Simon, "Houses and Early Life in Philadelphia." Simon quotes at length from the diary account of Elizabeth Drinker, a Philadelphia resident who lived through the epidemic. Drinker, like everyone else in the city, was horrified by conditions at an estate called Bush Hill, which had been turned into a temporary hospital and which soon became a "great slaughter house." Anyone even mildly ill who was taken to Bush Hill regarded this as "the seal of death." Ironically, Bush Hill was eventually cleaned up and turned into a model of proper sanitation and more effective treatments for the fever.

48 *The sky itself turned black* Ibid.

48 *Rush adhered to an old-fashioned* Weigley et al., *Philadelphia*, pages 184–85.

48 *A few doctors who were more familiar with tropical diseases* Ibid., pages 185–87.

48 *But the disease ran rampant* Ibid., pages 187–88.

49 *When he couldn't find work as a weaver* Hunter, *The Life and Letters of Alexander Wilson*, page 64.

49 *Philadelphia was then* Weigley et al., *Philadelphia*, page 208.

49 *Built on an orderly grid* Ibid., pages 208–21.

49 *It was twice as wide* de Montule, *Travels in America*, page 25.

49 *Every inn and hotel in the city* Ibid., page 24.

49 *By day the streets were clean* Weigley et al., *Philadelphia*, page 220.

49 *Wilson said that coming to America* Wilson to an anonymous Paisley friend, 1796. In Hunter, *The Life and Letters of Alexander Wilson*, page 152.

49 *No matter what a man's occupation* Wilson to an anonymous Paisley friend, probably in 1795. Ibid.

49 *"When I look round me here"* Wilson to an anonymous Paisley friend, 1796. Ibid.

50 *After a few months* Hunter, *The Life and Letters of Alexander Wilson*, page 64.

50 *Having little education* Ibid., pages 65–66.

50 *He found his neighbors pleasant and honest* Wilson to his father, August 22, 1798. Ibid., pages 153–58. A sharp observer of odd habits and sour moods in others, Wilson's own depressive personality was rarely far below the surface. He closed this letter home as follows: "May providence continue to bless you with Health, Peace, and Content, and when the Tragic-Comic scene of Life is over, may all meet in regions of Bliss and Immortality. I am, till Death, Dear Father, Your truly affectionate son."

50 *Mallards, redheads, teal* Cantwell, *Alexander Wilson*, pages 94–95.

51 *It began with blue-winged teal* Wilson, *American Ornithology*, vol. III, page 205.

51 *Although the birds were wary* Ibid.

51 *Canada geese—which were shot* Ibid., pages 175–81.

51 *Hunters had to conceal themselves* Ibid.

51 *The duck waters around Philadelphia* Ibid., pages 219–25.

51 *As early as 1727* Miller, *Early American Waterfowling*, page 79.

52 *On moonlit nights* Wilson, *American Ornithology*, vol. III, pages 219–25.

52 *The hunter—also dressed in white* Miller, *Early American Waterfowling*, page 101.

52 *The method that most intrigued Wilson* Wilson, *American Ornithology*, vol. III, pages 219–25.

52 *The great thing about letter-writing* Wilson to Charles Orr, July 21, 1800. In Hunter, *The Life and Letters of Alexander Wilson*, pages 170–72.

52 *William Duncan moved to upstate New York* Wilson to his father, November 1798. Ibid., pages 158–60. This letter was evidently composed over a period of time that month.

53 *In 1798, Philadelphia was again gripped* Ibid.

53 *Wilson could scarcely believe* Ibid.

53 *It was possible* Ibid.

53 *At one point he even resigned* Cantwell, *Alexander Wilson*, page 102.

53 *In one letter, Wilson suggested* Wilson to Charles Orr, July 21, 1800. In Hunter, *The Life and Letters of Alexander Wilson*, pages 170–72.

53 *I, for my part, have many things* Ibid.

53 *A few days later* Wilson to Charles Orr, July 23, 1800. Ibid.

55 *Although he still felt he was* Cantwell, *Alexander Wilson*, pages 103–4.

55 *In May, only months after* Wilson to Charles Orr, May 1, 1801. In Hunter, *The Life and Letters of Alexander Wilson*. As with most of the Orr correspondence, the original of this letter is in the National Library of Scotland.

55 *Orr found Wilson in a miserable state* Cantwell, *Alexander Wilson*, page 105.

56 *At one point he asked Orr* Wilson to Charles Orr, September 14, 1801. In Hunter, *The Life and Letters of Alexander Wilson*, pages 188–89.

56 *In a tortured letter* Wilson to Charles Orr, February 7, 1802. Ibid., pages 189–90.

56 *A week later he wrote* Wilson to Charles Orr, February 14, 1802. Ibid., pages 190–92.

56 *The schoolhouse, a squat, one-room building* Illustrated as Figure 11, Ibid.

56 *The road passed out of the city's busy streets* Cantwell, *Alexander Wilson*, page 113.

57 *He was the son of John Bartram* Harper (ed.), *The Travels of William Bartram*, page xvii.

57 *The elder Bartram had been revered* Cantwell, *Alexander Wilson*, page 119.

57 *William, who from an early age* Harper (ed.), *The Travels of William Bartram*, pages xvii–xviii.

57 *The extensive Alachua savanna is a level, green plain* Ibid., pages 119–20.

58 *In one of his most talked-about escapades* Ibid., pages 169–70. No animal native to North America even comes close to the rattlesnake as a source of fear and fascination to early settlers and explorers, and no self-respecting naturalist failed to include the snake among the living wonders of the New World. Bartram recorded this anecdote in his *Travels*—though it actually occurred on his earlier visit to northeast Florida with his father—as part of a general discussion of the snake and his various encounters with it in different locales. Bartram, showing rather insufficient skepticism for an otherwise careful student of nature, apparently believed in the power of "fascination" that rattlesnakes supposedly used to hypnotize their prey. In debunking this myth several decades later, Audubon would create a controversy

that plagued him for years. In between, Alexander Wilson, after studying with Bartram, told his own rattlesnake story in his epic poem, *The Foresters.*

58 *He reported that Florida swamps* Ibid., page 75.

58 *And he assembled a new list* Ibid., pages 377–78.

59 *Three years after the book* Ibid., page xxvi.

59 *Long devoted to rambling* Cantwell, *Alexander Wilson*, page 120.

59 *But by the spring of 1803* Hunter, *The Life and Letters of Alexander Wilson*, pages 73–74.

59 *In March, he sent* Wilson to William Bartram, March 4, 1803. In Hunter, *The Life and Letters of Alexander Wilson*, page 202.

59 *Wilson worked on images of birds* Wilson to William Bartram, October 30, 1803. Ibid., pages 203–4.

59 *The two-volume book consists almost entirely* Meyers and Pritchard, *Empire's Nature*, pages 2–17.

60 *The bird stands on the limb* Ibid., page 239.

61 *Catesby did his own engraving* McBurney (ed.), *Mark Catesby's Natural History of America*, page 17.

61 *He did this by producing* Ibid.

61 *One uncolored installment* Ibid.

61 *"For the Satisfaction of the CURIOUS"* Ibid.

61 *Linnaeus himself based many* Ibid., page 19.

61 *At the time, there was still much uncertainty* Meyers and Pritchard, *Empire's Nature*, pages 60–61.

61 *Another surprisingly durable theory* Ibid.

61 *Catesby was humbled by* Kastner, *A Species of Eternity*, page 17.

61 *Catesby made all of his drawings* Ibid.

62 *In South Carolina, he lived through* Meyers and Pritchard, *Empire's Nature*, page 74.

62 *After awaking at an inn* Kastner, *A Species of Eternity*, pages 16–17.

62 *He got to know the Philadelphia engraver* Cantwell, *Alexander Wilson*, page 125.

62 *In the spring of 1804* Wilson to Alexander Lawson, March 12, 1804. In Hunter, *The Life and Letters of Alexander Wilson*, pages 206–7.

63 *Wilson had taken lodgings near* Cantwell, *Alexander Wilson*, page 114.

63 *The grove was full of birds* Ibid., page 115.

63 *Wilson was sometimes joined* Hunter, *The Life and Letters of Alexander Wilson*, pages 217–18. The evidence here is a previously unpublished poem from the summer of 1804, titled "The Beechen Bower." In it, Wilson speaks of his "love" for Anna, and of her "fair form." Hunter cautions against any erotic reading of these lines, though it seems natural to suppose some attraction formed between two such companions in the quiet glade. In any event, if Wilson felt strongly about Anna, nothing apparently ever came of it.

63 *Given the more than two hundred birds* Cantwell, *Alexander Wilson*, page 125.

63 *Within two years of his coming to Gray's Ferry* Wilson to William Bartram, March 29, 1804. In Hunter, *The Life and Letters of Alexander Wilson*, pages 207–9.

63 *He received a whole basket of* Wilson to William Bartram, March 31, 1804. Ibid., pages 209–12.

63 *He finally decided to kill*   Ibid.
64 *On one of these walks*   Wilson, *American Ornithology*, vol. I, page xxxiii. The account of this incident is not Wilson's, but that of his friend and earliest biographer, George Ord, who included it in an introduction to a posthumous edition.
64 *"Close application to my profession"*   Wilson to an anonymous friend in Paisley, June 1, 1803. In Hunter, *The Life and Letters of Alexander Wilson*, page 203.

5. A BEAUTIFUL PLANTATION

65 *Yellow fever had broken out*   Ford, *John James Audubon*, page 41. Obviously, Audubon did not contract and develop symptoms of yellow fever on a walk of only a few hours' duration. More likely he contracted it from a mosquito bite while his ship was lying offshore or making way for port.
66 *Audubon's father and Dacosta had*   Herrick, *Audubon the Naturalist*, vol. I, page 113.
66 *To the extent that anybody*   Ibid., page 101.
66 *It was near the confluence*   Audubon, *Ornithological Biography*, vol. I, page ix.
66 *Its shaft was twelve feet*   The description of Mill Grove and its grounds is my own, based on a visit in September 2002.
66 *Recent surveys at Mill Grove*   Ibid.
67 *In the evenings he practiced*   Ibid.
67 *He was always reluctant*   Audubon, *Ornithological Biography*, vol. I, page ix.
67 *In a crevice in the rocks*   Herrick, *Audubon the Naturalist*, page 106.
67 *Curious as to whether*   Ibid., page 107.
67 *Expensive stocks of fancy-bred*   Ford, *John James Audubon*, pages 43–44.
67 *It was said that they had*   Ibid., page 44.
68 *Bakewell was friendly and*   Ibid.
68 *Audubon never forgot that day*   Buchanan (ed.), *The Life and Adventures of John James Audubon*, page 8. This account of Audubon and Lucy's first meeting may or may not be accurate. Certainly, it's the authorized family version of the event, having been first reported in the material supplied by Lucy to Buchanan for his biography.
69 *He got to know all the Bakewells*   Ford, *John James Audubon*, page 46. This seems as good a place as any to state what may be intuitively obvious: There is less certainty about the events of Audubon's youth than there is about his better-documented later life. Elsewhere I have stated my preference for the biographies by Herrick and Ford over the flimsy and often-suspect materials edited by Lucy and by Audubon's granddaughter, Maria. However, both Herrick and Ford relied extensively on those very sources for much of their accounts of Audubon's early days in America. In other words, where the evidence is slim, Audubon's best interpreters accepted significant material from his worst. In between and since, other biographers, including me, have sorted through these reflected versions of what happened, tweaking the story according to our own tastes and suppositions, and to avoid literal copying. The result is an approximation of the truth—at best—that has passed through a kind of fun house hall of mirrors. The important point is that not too much significance should be attached to which source I have elected to cite here, as they are all equally good—and equally dubious.

69 *On another occasion* Ford, *John James Audubon*, page 47.

69 *He foolishly told the Bakewells* Ibid.

69 *It gave William Bakewell pause* Ibid., pages 48–49. Audubon first took Lucy to the grotto above the Perkiomen in the spring of 1804—incredibly at the very same time that Alexander Wilson was communing with Bartram's niece among the birds and beeches not far away.

69 *One afternoon in late winter* Buchanan (ed.), *The Life and Adventures of John James Audubon*, pages 10–11.

70 *In France, as a boy* From the transcript of a manuscript by Audubon titled "My Style of Drawing Birds," in the collection at John James Audubon State Park in Henderson, Kentucky. This essay, written in Scotland, was published in a slightly different form by the *Edinburgh Journal of Science* in 1828 under the title "Method of Drawing Birds." One of Audubon's endearing traits was a lifelong willingness to share his technique.

71 *But when he compared* Ibid.

71 *Audubon later claimed* Ibid.

71 *He marked off the surface* Ibid.

72 *When Audubon got sick* Ford, *John James Audubon*, page 54.

72 *Evidently the two argued* Ibid., pages 51–52.

72 *In truth, Audubon's father had never* Herrick, *Audubon the Naturalist*, vol. I, pages 113–16.

72 *The elder Audubon, having also heard* Jean Audubon to François Dacosta, circa 1804–1805, quoted in Herrick, *Audubon the Naturalist*, vol. I, pages 116–18.

72 *He wrote to Dacosta* Ibid.

72 *In a follow-up letter* Jean Audubon to François Dacosta, March 9, 1805. Ibid., pages 118–19.

73 *He wrote to Dacosta, reassuring him* Ibid.

73 *Only an instant is needed* Ibid.

73 *If this could be accomplished* Ibid.

73 *He demanded funds* Ford, *John James Audubon*, page 55.

73 *After recovering from* Ibid., page 58.

74 *Short of funds, he also* Ibid., page 61.

74 *The elder Audubon, sensing the advantage* Ibid.

74 *In March 1806* "Articles of Association," a formal agreement between Audubon and Rozier respecting their business partnership, was executed on March 23, 1806, in Nantes. Reproduced in Herrick, *Audubon the Naturalist*, vol. II, pages 344–49.

74 *On April 12, 1806* Ford, *John James Audubon*, page 61.

74 *Rozier found work* Ibid., page 65.

74 *Audubon, in a monumental mismatch* Ibid.

75 *I am allways in* Audubon to his father, April 24, 1807, quoted in Herrick, *Audubon the Naturalist*, pages 159–61.

75 *Convinced they would never devise* Ford, *John James Audubon*, page 69.

75 *Rozier, meanwhile, considered* Ibid., page 68.

75 *Audubon encouraged this view* Ibid.

75 *There are discrepancies in the record* Sharp and Sharp, *Between the Gabouri*. This book-

let consists of various sorts of documents, including the above-mentioned "Articles of Association" between Audubon and Rozier. But it mainly concerns itself with the diary Rozier kept during their trip west. Ambiguities about the date apparently arose in some early translation of the diary from French.

75 *At first they made splendid time*   Ibid.

76 *In a place called Walnut Bottom*   Ibid.

76 *Audubon and Rozier spent twelve days*   Ibid.

76 *Despite its captivating location*   Cramer, *The Navigator*, pages 49–72. This extraordinary little book is a great piece of Americana. An indispensable guide to descending the Ohio River and traveling to the frontier, it provided maps, information on settlements, and how-to advice on boats and river travel. First published in 1801, it went through twelve subsequent editions and floated west with countless settlers who pushed off from the Pittsburgh waterfront.

76 *Pittsburgh was already becoming*   Ibid.

76 *The estimated value of all trade*   Ibid.

76 *Audubon and Rozier were elated*   Sharp and Sharp, *Between the Gabouri*.

77 *The two men bought passage*   Ibid.

77 *The boat moved swiftly*   Ibid.

77 *Occasionally the boat careened*   Ibid.

77 *He treated the passengers roughly*   Ibid.

77 *It stood on the slightly elevated south bank*   Cramer, *The Navigator*, page 119.

77 *The "Falls of the Ohio"*   Ibid., page 118.

77 *The town of Louisville had been laid out*   Yater, *Two Hundred Years at the Falls of the Ohio*, pages 2–3.

77 *About twenty families*   Ibid., page 3.

77 *By the time Audubon and Rozier*   Ibid., page 33.

78 *Businessmen—many of them French*   Ibid., page 31.

78 *Some sixty thousand tons of goods*   Ibid., page 32.

78 *There was already talk of building*   Cramer, *The Navigator*, pages 119–20.

78 *Audubon listened excitedly*   Ford, *John James Audubon*, pages 70–71.

78 *The wedding took place on*   Ibid., page 73.

78 *Lucy quietly endured the coarse language*   DeLatte, *Lucy Audubon*, pages 42–44.

78 *A young woman who made the journey*   Dwight, *A Journey to Ohio in 1810*, pages 40–41.

79 *One day, as they climbed a steep*   Ford, *John James Audubon*, pages 73–74.

6. THE FORESTER

80 *A spell of Indian summer came*   This long description of Wilson's trip to Niagara Falls is taken from his epic poem, "The Foresters," in Grosart, *The Poems and Literary Prose of Alexander Wilson*, vol. II, pages 111–73.

82 *Wilson's return from Niagara*   Hunter, *The Life and Letters of Alexander Wilson*, pages 76–77. In the same volume, Hunter includes a letter from Wilson to William Duncan, dated December 24, 1804, pages 226–28, which provides many of the same details of the return trip.

83 *Though in this tour*   Wilson to William Bartram, December 15, 1804. Ibid., pages 225–26.

83 *Both the Schuylkill and the Delaware froze*   Wilson to William Duncan, February 20, 1805. Ibid.

84 *Peale, part naturalist and part showman*   Porter, *The Eagle's Nest*, pages 27–30. The word mastodon had come into general use to distinguish the American species from the Asian mammoth.

84 *Peale's collections were so extensive*   Ibid.

84 *Wilson also sent drawings of twenty-eight birds*   Wilson to William Bartram, July 2, 1805. In Hunter, *The Life and Letters of Alexander Wilson*, pages 243–44.

84 *He also sent more drawings to Thomas Jefferson*   Wilson to Thomas Jefferson, September 30, 1805. Ibid., pages 244–45.

84 *Early in 1806, Wilson suggested*   Wilson to William Bartram, January 27, 1806. Ibid., pages 247–48.

84 *Wilson had recently spoken with*   Ibid.

85 *By chance, just as Wilson*   Wilson to Thomas Jefferson, February 6, 1806. Ibid., pages 249–51.

85 *His eyesight was failing*   Ibid.

85 *In February 1806, Wilson wrote*   Ibid.

85 *In April he quit his job*   Ibid., page 79.

85 *He was freed at last*   Ibid.

86 *When Bradford agreed to finance*   Ibid., page 80.

86 *The prospectus offered*   Ibid., pages 268–72.

86 *When the first volume*   Ibid., page 83.

7. THE EXQUISITE RIVER

87 *Lucy, like other visitors*   Lucy Audubon to Euphemia Gifford, May 27, 1808 (Princeton University Library). Lucy corresponded on a number of occasions with a "Miss Gifford" in Derby, England, whom she addressed as her cousin. It's probable, though not certain, that this was Euphemia Gifford, who was actually a cousin to Lucy's father. Years after this letter was written, according to Alice Ford, Lucy asked Audubon to call on Euphemia when he was in England.

87 *Lucy, in a letter sent*   Ibid.

87 *Without even mentioning*   Ibid.

88 *"As yet they have been light"*   Ibid.

88 *A typical boat large enough*   Bogardus, *Flatboatin' on the Old Ohio*, pages 8–9; and Cramer, *The Navigator*, page 35.

88 *Travelers were advised*   Cramer, *The Navigator*, pages 36–40.

89 *At their final destination*   Bogardus, *Flatboatin' on the Old Ohio*, page 10.

89 *The boat, Lucy reported*   Lucy Audubon to Euphemia Gifford, May 27, 1808 (Princeton University Library).

89 *Lucy packed bread and ham*   Ibid.

89 *Lucy found the dense wall*   Ibid.

89 *The name Ohio*   Cramer, *The Navigator*, page 24.

89 *The Ohio, it was said*   Ibid.

89 *At its head in* Ibid., pages 21–22.

90 *Zadok Cramer, a Pittsburgh bookseller* Ibid., page 13.

90 *The Ohio River's uniform breadth* Ibid., page 24.

90 *The uplands were thick with* Ibid., page 29.

90 *But it was the sycamore* Ibid., page 30.

90 *The summer following* Ibid.

90 *The first serious influx* Harrison and Klotter, *A New History of Kentucky*, pages 18–19, 24–32.

91 *On the lawless frontier* Ibid., pages 251–53.

91 *Audubon, like many people* Audubon, "The Regulators," *Ornithological Biography*, vol. I, pages 105–7.

91 *Kentuckians also had problems* Harrison and Klotter, *A New History of Kentucky*, pages 30–32.

91 *But that still left an abundance* Cramer, *The Navigator*, page 28.

91 *Bear and deer were so common* Ibid.

91 *When the Audubons got to Louisville* Harrison and Klotter, *A New History of Kentucky*, page 99.

92 *The Audubons took lodging at* Ford, *John James Audubon*, page 74.

92 *The ground floor featured a* Yater, *Two Hundred Years at the Falls of the Ohio*, page 31.

92 *Even so, Lucy declared* Lucy Audubon to Euphemia Gifford, May 27, 1808 (Princeton University Library).

92 *"I am very sorry there is no library"* Ibid.

92 *During his more extended absences* Audubon, "Louisville in Kentucky," *Ornithological Biography*, vol. I, pages 437–40.

92 *These years, he said later* Ibid.

92 *By the time he and Lucy left* Ibid.

93 *Victor Gifford Audubon was born* Ford, *John James Audubon*, page 74.

93 *He later said that only his family* Audubon, *Ornithological Biography*, vol. I, page X.

93 *This, Audubon maintained* Ibid.

93 *And probably no bird fascinated him more* Audubon, "The Wild Turkey," *Ornithological Biography*, vol. I, pages 1–17. Audubon's long, detailed, and admiring natural history of the turkey is the basis for this entire section.

97 *One of his fans* Ford, *John James Audubon*, pages 183–84. The wax impression of the turkey is still readily found on seals attached to much of Audubon's correspondence.

97 *He recognized and often speculated* To be fair, it should be said that while Audubon noted and described in some detail the egregious slaughter of certain species such as the passenger pigeon, the Carolina parakeet, and the ivory-billed woodpecker—to name three extinct examples—he was generally dismissive of the suggestion that human predation would ever completely eradicate any of these birds. In fact, he more correctly predicted that habitat loss would play a greater role in the reduction of bird numbers than would hunting.

97 *He sometimes said* Audubon, "Letter from J. J. Audubon," *Monthly American Journal of Geology and Natural History*, vol. 1, no. 9 (1832): 407–14. This rare journal—it was published for only a single year—is in the Ewell Sale Stewart Library at the Academy of Natural Sciences of Philadelphia.

98 *Shotguns in Audubon's time*   Carmichael (ed.), *The Story of American Hunting and Firearms*, pages 119–22.

98 *They typically had two barrels*   Ibid. I also examined and measured Alexander Wilson's gun, which is at the Academy of Natural Sciences of Philadelphia. Additionally, some of the discussion of firearms and wingshooting is based on my own experience.

98 *Care had to be exercised*   Carmichael (ed.), *The Story of American Hunting and Firearms*, pages 119–22.

98 *A more life-threatening*   Ibid.

98 *Around 1825, percussion firing caps*   O'Connor, *The Shotgun Book*, page 4.

99 *Modern ornithologists still collect*   Personal communication, Nate Rice, Academy of Natural Sciences of Philadelphia. I discussed ornithology generally with Rice on several occasions in April and September of 2002.

99 *Although Audubon spent*   Ford, *John James Audubon*, pages 200–201.

99 *In Kentucky, where his technique matured*   Blaugrund and Stebbins (eds.), *John James Audubon*, pages 7–8.

100 *Audubon most likely never used*   Audubon did not write about his field equipment in detail, and this assessment is necessarily somewhat conjectural. He did, however, indicate many times the importance of his wiring technique, and it seems unlikely that the large boards he needed for this purpose would have been carried on routine excursions into the woods.

100 *He liked to sleep in the open*   Audubon, "The Wood Thrush," *Ornithological Biography*, vol. I, page 372. In this lyrical account of one of his favorite birds, Audubon speaks of spending a stormy night in the forest beneath his "slender shed." Whether this was, strictly speaking, a lean-to or some other type of shelter he fashioned for himself, it is clear that Audubon did not indulge himself with elaborate protection from the elements.

100 *Several collections of*   Personal observation, Academy of Natural Sciences of Philadelphia. Nate Rice generously allowed me to examine many of Audubon's specimens in the collection in April and September of 2002.

100 *Methods varied—everyone tended to*   Personal communication, Nate Rice. Academy of Natural Sciences of Philadelphia. Rice invited me to observe him as he skinned a duck and explained the process to me on September 18, 2002.

102 *Once, Audubon and a group of friends*   Clark, *The Rampaging Frontier*, pages 211–12.

102 *In the quiet hours he spent*   Blaugrund and Stebbins (eds.), *The Watercolors for The Birds of America*, pages 3–25. Theodore E. Stebbins Jr.'s superb essay on Audubon's life and art is a definitive study of the evolution of Audubon's drawing style.

102 *Audubon destroyed his*   Ibid., page 3.

102 *A sign of what was to come*   Ibid., pages 7–8.

102 *Later, when Audubon recalled*   Audubon, "Kentucky Barbicue on the Fourth of July." *Ornithological Biography*, vol. II, pages 576–79.

103 *In the spring of 1810*   Herrick, *Audubon the Naturalist*, vol. I, page 198.

103 *Lucy's father, complaining*   Ibid., page 199. Herrick quotes a letter from William Bakewell to Audubon and Rozier, dated April 10, 1810, in which Bakewell discussed the terms of the sale and the disposition of the proceeds. Bakewell went on

to report that a "considerable quantity of ore" had been extracted from the lead mine, but it had yet to produce income—a hint, perhaps, that Lucy's father thought the sale unwise until the true value of the property was known. The mine was eventually purchased by a Philadelphia paint manufacturer, who operated it profitably for many years.

8. MR. WILSON'S DECADE

104 *Wilson told Bartram about*   Wilson to William Bartram, April 8, 1807. In Hunter, *The Life and Letters of Alexander Wilson*, pages 260–61.

104 *In 1807, Samuel Bradford's company*   Cantwell, *Alexander Wilson*, pages 140–41.

105 *One of the species formerly unknown*   Ibid., page 141.

105 *Wilson called on*   Wilson to Samuel Bradford, October 2, 1807. In Hunter, *The Life and Letters of Alexander Wilson*, pages 265–66.

105 *In New York, where he met*   Wilson to Daniel Miller, October 12, 1808. Ibid., pages 275–84.

105 *His reception was not always warm*   Wilson, undated journal fragment. Ibid., pages 291–92. This recovered section of Wilson's travel diary during his tour of the Northeast is short—but chock-full of bitterness and sharp rebukes of the people he called on. One official in a state health office idly thumbed through a few pages of *American Ornithology* and declared the $120 price tag outrageous. Another public official said bluntly that he never bothered with books about "animals, fishes, plants or birds," but that Wilson's work was indeed beautiful. Wilson called the man a "reptile."

105 *He found New York and Boston cramped and dirty*   Wilson to Daniel Miller, October 12, 1808. In Hunter, *The Life and Letters of Alexander Wilson*, pages 275–84.

105 *He was surprised and offended*   Wilson to Daniel Miller, February 22, 1809. Ibid., pages 296–304.

105 *White women stayed out of sight*   Ibid.

105 *It was rare*   Ibid.

105 *The general features of North Carolina*   Ibid.

106 *Wilson didn't care for*   Ibid.

106 *In South Carolina*   Ibid.

106 *But plantation owners were*   Ibid.

106 *Near Wilmington, North Carolina*   Wilson, *American Ornithology*, vol. I, pages 134–35. The alert reader will wonder how it can be that Wilson's account of this bird appears in the first volume of *American Ornithology* when the episode in question occurred while Wilson was on a sales trip with the already-completed first volume under his arm. The answer is that Wilson's species accounts were later rearranged for the text-only 1831 Edinburgh edition cited here.

106 *Wilson's shot only wounded the bird*   Ibid.

107 *There is a charm, a melody*   Wilson to Samuel Bradford, March 8, 1809. In Hunter, *The Life and Letters of Alexander Wilson*, pages 309–12. The original of this letter, which is in the archives at the Academy of Natural Sciences of Philadelphia, does not show an addressee, and while most modern scholars believe—based on the

date and content—that it was to Bradford, Alexander Grosart indicated that it was to William Bartram.

107 *Wilson later calculated the cost*   Wilson to Daniel Miller, March 5, 1809. Ibid., pages 305–7.

107 *He was victimized by innkeepers*   Ibid.

107 *Sometimes he was forced to advertise*   Ibid.

107 *Despite the many difficulties*   Wilson to William Bartram, March 5, 1809. Ibid., pages 307–9.

107 *That same month*   Wilson to Alexander Lawson, February 22, 1810. Ibid., pages 320–25.

108 *Near the town of Carlisle*   Ibid.

108 *Wilson—in one of his moods*   Ibid.

108 *Later that evening*   Ibid.

108 *In Pittsburgh, Wilson was struck*   Ibid.

108 *Wilson sold nineteen subscriptions*   Ibid.

108 *Wilson bought a one-man skiff*   Ibid.

108 *He left near the end of February*   Wilson to Alexander Lawson, April 4, 1810. Ibid., pages 326–39.

108 *When he rowed*   Ibid.

109 *It was as if all these human beings*   Ibid.

109 *It was the breeding time for owls*   Ibid.

109 *On the morning of the seventeenth*   Ibid.

109 *Wilson found a room*   Audubon, "Louisville in Kentucky," *Ornithological Biography*, vol. I, pages 437–40. And here we go. Audubon's account of Wilson's visit—later disputed by Ord and contradicted by the Wilson journal entry Ord produced for the ninth volume of *American Ornithology*—is nonetheless brimming with fascinating and perhaps fabulous details. Audubon wrote that Wilson was a solitary, melancholy figure at the hotel, and that the moody tunes Wilson played on his flute made Audubon sad himself. If Audubon in fact heard Alexander Wilson play the flute, he seems to be the only person who ever said so. On one point, at least, the two naturalists agreed. Wilson *did* stay at the Indian Queen. Since Audubon, Lucy, and Victor were living there at the time, it would seem indisputable that some kind of contact must have occurred.

109 *The dining room at the Indian Queen*   Yater, *Two Hundred Years at the Falls of the Ohio*, page 31.

110 *A day or two after his arrival*   Audubon, "Louisville in Kentucky," *Ornithological Biography*, vol. I, pages 437–40.

110 *Audubon, who claimed Wilson*   Audubon, "The Whooping Crane," *Ornithological Biography*, vol. III, pages 203–4.

111 *In fact, Wilson stated*   Wilson, *American Ornithology*, vol. III, page 25.

111 *A few days later*   Wilson to Alexander Lawson, April 4, 1810. In Hunter, *The Life and Letters of Alexander Wilson*, pages 326–39.

111 *Audubon said that when he compared*   Audubon, "Louisville in Kentucky," *Ornithological Biography*, vol. I, pages 437–40.

111 *Audubon also maintained*   Ibid.

111 *Audubon told these stories*   Ibid.

111 *There was not a single subscriber*   Ibid. To the extent that we can read Audubon's mind long after the fact, his quotation of the offending Wilson journal text, dated March 23, 1810, is, I think, a telling argument in favor of Audubon's version of events. Audubon was famous for rarely offering formal responses to his critics. The fact that he does so here suggests that he felt this was an egregious misrepresentation on Wilson's part—or, more sinisterly, on the part of George Ord, who chose to publish Wilson's alleged comments.

111 *In a journal Wilson kept*   Extracts quoted in Herrick, *Audubon the Naturalist*, vol. I, pages 224–25. It seems George Ord put out a slightly different version of Wilson's Louisville journal entry for each of the various editions of *American Ornithology* published in America and abroad in the years after Wilson's death. In what appears to be the fullest excerpt from the lost journal, Wilson writes that two days after he got to Louisville, he examined "Mr.—'s drawings in crayons—very good. Saw two new birds he had . . ." Then, two days after that, "Went out shooting this afternoon with Mr. A." Herrick believed this fuller excerpt clarified the record and supported Audubon's story. So do I.

111 *There is evidence that Wilson had been alerted*   Ford, *John James Audubon*, page 75. And we might also consider the reverse possibility: Did Audubon know of Wilson before Wilson showed up in Louisville? In his account of the meeting, Audubon suggests that Wilson and his *American Ornithology* were a revelation to him when Wilson walked into the store in March 1810. Theodore E. Stebbins Jr., however, points out that Audubon cited Wilson for the scientific name of the indigo bunting, on a drawing Audubon made of the bird in June 1808. Wilson did, in fact, include the indigo bunting—or "indigo bird" as he called it—in the first volume of *American Ornithology*. But that was not published until September 1808. So Audubon must have added the name some time after he drew the bird. Whether that was before he met Wilson is impossible to say.

111 *And a different version*   Herrick, *Audubon the Naturalist*, vol. I, pages 224–25.

112 *Wilson made drawings*   Wilson to Alexander Lawson, May 18, 1810. In Hunter, *The Life and Letters of Alexander Wilson*, pages 358–70.

112 *Wilson had wounded*   Wilson to Alexander Lawson, April 4, 1810. Ibid., pages 326–39.

112 *Wilson actually met a man*   Wilson to Alexander Lawson, April 28, 1810. Ibid. A number of Wilson's very long and richly detailed letters from the frontier—such as this one of several thousand words—were published in Philadelphia in the journal *The Port Folio*, which had been recently purchased by Samuel Bradford.

112 *In western Tennessee*   Wilson to Alexander Lawson, May 18, 1810. Ibid.

112 *At the end of April*   Ibid.

113 *I was advised by many*   Ibid.

113 *Eleven miles from Nashville*   Ibid.

114 *He later gave a full account*   Ibid.

114 *In the summer of 1811*   Hunter, *The Life and Letters of Alexander Wilson*, page 105. Ord apparently got in touch with Wilson after reading Wilson's plea for information about birds from "gentlemen of leisure" who were interested in natural history, which he published in the Preface to the third volume of *American Ornithology*. Given the outlines of their lives, their seemingly instantaneous part-

nership, the intensity with which Ord continued Wilson's work long after Wilson's death, and Ord's ferocious attacks on Audubon, it is not unreasonable to wonder about the extent of the intimacy between Ord and Wilson. Wilson's intermittent, frustrating connections with women don't tell us much, apart from the fact that he was unlucky in love. So was Ord, who was twice married. His first wife died and his second was confined to a mental hospital for most of her adult life. Ord had two children, a daughter who died in infancy and a son who became an artist. Ord apparently lived as a bachelor.

114 *Two years later, Ord got*   "Minutes of the Academy of Natural Sciences of Philadelphia," June 19, 1813. Although Wilson and his work are both intimately linked with the formative years of the academy, his election to membership came only two months before his death.

114 *Say, a founder of the academy*   Stroud, *Thomas Say*, page 40.

115 *In the end, he colored most*   Hunter, *The Life and Letters of Alexander Wilson*, pages 110–11.

115 *The original run of two hundred copies*   Cantwell, *Alexander Wilson*, page 234. The main problem with subscriptions was that Wilson, already overwhelmed with work on the engravings, could not find time to make collection trips. In the summer of 1812, just a year before he died, Wilson wrote to Sarah Miller—the sister of his friend Daniel—that Bradford was demanding payment and that if he could not make a trip soon to collect money he was owed, he faced "absolute ruin." The confiding tone of this letter is evidence, according to Clark Hunter in *The Life and Times of Alexander Wilson*, that Wilson and Miller were in the early stages of a romance destined never to bloom.

115 *Many of his early subscribers*   Ibid., page 277.

115 *Volumes five and six*   Ibid., page 254.

115 *Wilson had by then*   Hunter, *The Life and Letters of Alexander Wilson*, pages 104–5.

115 *The seventh volume was finished*   Ibid., pages 112–13.

115 *He was now owed by his subscribers*   Cantwell, *Alexander Wilson*, pages 238, 253–54.

115 *His physical condition*   Hunter, *The Life and Letters of Alexander Wilson*, page 113.

115 *George Ord, who'd been away*   A copy of Wilson's will is in the archives at the American Philosophical Society in Philadelphia. The other coexecutor was Daniel Miller. Wilson left any and all other assets to Sarah Miller.

116 *Wilson had crossed the Tennessee River*   Wilson to Alexander Lawson, May 18, 1810. In Hunter, *The Life and Letters of Alexander Wilson*, pages 358–70.

9. AT THE RED BANKS

121 *Ferdinand Rozier wanted to move*   Herrick, *Audubon the Naturalist*, vol. I, page 236. Herrick says merely that the partners, discouraged by their failing business, decided to relocate. Alice Ford, perhaps closer to the truth in *John James Audubon*, speculates that Audubon, happily distracted by the woods and birds, barely realized the desperate situation at the store and only reluctantly agreed to the move.

121 *Henderson's origins predated*   Towles, *Henderson*, page 15.

121 *In the years just before*   Ibid., page 22.

121 *Boone was one of the self-styled*   Faragher, *Daniel Boone*, page 28. As the name im-
plies, "long hunts" were extended shooting and trapping expeditions that lasted
weeks and, often, many months at a time. Boone made his first long hunt in 1750,
through the Blue Ridge Mountains along what later became the Virginia/North
Carolina border, eventually making his way up to Philadelphia, where he sold pelts
from the trip. In the winter of 1767–1768, Boone undertook his first hunting trip
into Kentucky, where he was trapped in a blizzard but also killed his first buffalo.
Faragher states that in 1769, perhaps already secretly employed by Richard Henderson, Boone departed on a hunting trip into Kentucky that lasted two years—
during which he was captured by, and escaped from, Shawnee Indians.

121 *In the summer of 1774*   Towles, *Henderson*, pages 21–22.

122 *Daniel Boone and thirty men*   Ibid., pages 22–23.

122 *These mainly dealt with courts and militia*   Ibid., page 23.

122 *In September of 1775*   Ibid., pages 23–24.

122 *Two years later the Virginia House*   Ibid., page 25.

122 *In the spring of 1797*   Ibid., page 26.

122 *There was a loop in the Ohio*   Ibid., page 17.

122 *The bluff on the Kentucky side*   Ibid. Spring floods of the Ohio were a nearly annual
occurrence, and because these could be mighty inundations, Henderson's elevation was a significant asset. For a time, the Henderson city slogan was "On the
Ohio, not in it."

123 *There were 264 lots*   Ibid., pages 26–27.

123 *A general store operated for a while*   Ibid., page 30.

123 *When Henderson's first saloon*   Ibid.

123 *Concern for law and order was considerable*   Adams, *John James Audubon*, page 113.

123 *Currency was hard to come by*   Towles, *Henderson*, page 32.

123 *The people spread throughout*   Ibid., page 29.

123 *By the time Audubon and Rozier visited*   Ibid.

123 *Even at that, Audubon*   Audubon, "Fishing in the Ohio," *Ornithological Biography*,
vol. III, pages 122–27.

124 *Audubon, sidestepping the whole truth*   Ibid.

124 *The garden they planted*   Ibid.

124 *Lucy even had with her*   DeLatte, *Lucy Audubon*, page 59.

124 *Audubon and Rozier, meanwhile, invested*   Towles, *Henderson*, page 31.

124 *Pope was a dubious asset*   Audubon, "Fishing in the Ohio," *Ornithological Biography*,
vol. III, pages 122–27.

124 *Not long after they got to Henderson*   Ford, *John James Audubon*, page 77.

124 *Her father, Captain James Speed*   Ibid.

124 *Though it was no grand estate*   John James Audubon State Park Museum, Henderson, Kentucky. The museum's photograph of Meadow Brook shows that it was a
dark and rather loose-looking frame house—though by frontier standards it must
have seemed luxurious. It was symmetrical, with stone chimneys on either end.
Originally, the central entrance was an open hallway that bisected the first floor
from one side to the other, so that you could see daylight clear through. The passage was large enough to admit a horse, and this style of home was locally known

as a "dog trot." The Rankins eventually closed up the entrance and fitted it with a standard door and entryway.

124 *Elizabeth, who was impressed* DeLatte, *Lucy Audubon*, pages 60–61.

125 *He wanted to move still farther* Ibid., page 60.

125 *Audubon didn't feel a similar impulse* Ford, *John James Audubon*, page 77.

125 *In early December of 1810* Ibid., pages 77–78.

125 *They went in a keelboat* Ibid., page 78.

125 *The travelers were repeatedly delayed* Ibid., pages 78–79.

125 *Audubon conceded later* Audubon, "Breaking Up of the Ice," *Ornithological Biography*, vol. III, pages 408–10.

125 *His bird drawings entertained them* Buchanan (ed.), *The Life and Adventures of John James Audubon*, page 30.

126 *Audubon was fascinated by* Audubon, "Breaking Up of the Ice," *Ornithological Biography*, vol. III, pages 408–10.

126 *Audubon accepted some cash* Herrick, *Audubon the Naturalist*, vol. I, page 242.

126 *When he arrived back at Meadow Brook* Ford, *John James Audubon*, page 81.

126 *St. Genevieve had more than* Cramer, *The Navigator*, pages 170–71.

126 *Ferdinand Rozier stayed there* Herrick, *Audubon the Naturalist*, pages 245–46.

126 *But he claimed that the only* Audubon, "The Prairie," *Ornithological Biography*, vol. I, pages 81–84.

126 *He was alone, taking his time* Ibid. The record of Audubon's travels between St. Genevieve and Henderson is muddled, and the events that inspired this account could have occurred on a different trip. Since the entire episode is of dubious authenticity, it is doubly hard to say exactly when any of this might have taken place.

128 *He located new space in town* Delatte, *Lucy Audubon*, pages 62–63.

128 *The Audubons were invited to stay* Ibid.

129 *Sometimes they would swim across the Ohio* Ford, *John James Audubon*, page 82.

129 *Audubon bought the once-wild mustang* Audubon, "A Wild Horse," *Ornithological Biography*, vol. III, pages 270–74.

129 *Audubon rode him to Philadelphia* Ibid.

129 *She asked Audubon to take her east* DeLatte, *Lucy Audubon*, page 63.

129 *Audubon rigged a seat* Lucy to Euphemia Gifford, January 5, 1812 (Princeton University Library).

129 *At Louisville, they stopped* Ibid.

129 *It was November of 1811* Ibid.

129 *"I can scarcely believe"* Ibid.

130 *Audubon stayed just long enough* Ford, *John James Audubon*, page 84.

130 *It was on this ride* Audubon, "A Wild Horse," *Ornithological Biography*, vol. III, pages 270–74.

130 *Nolte remembered their introduction differently* Ford, *John James Audubon*, page 85. Ford, clearly, preferred Nolte's version of events, which he recorded in his memoirs. Whichever account is correct, Vincent Nolte was to eventually play a pivotal role in Audubon's life.

130 *But when Audubon reached Henderson* DeLatte, *Lucy Audubon*, page 68.

131 *For some reason he went by boat* Audubon, "A Wild Horse," *Ornithological Biography*, vol. III, pages 270–74.

131 *In April, the Audubons learned*   Ford, *John James Audubon*, page 86.

131 *In a moment of rare candor*   Dallett, "Citizen Audubon: A Documentary Discovery," *Princeton University Library Chronicle*, vol. XXI, nos. 1 and 2 (Autumn 1959 and Winter 1960): 89–93. Audubon's naturalization in 1812 was actually a finalization of an application begun six years earlier, following his return from a visit to France. Audubon had accurately stated his birthplace in that first declaration back in 1806.

10. KENTUCKY HOME

132 *Back down the Ohio*   Audubon, "The Ohio," *Ornithological Biography*, vol. I, pages 29–32.

133 *After a couple of days, Audubon opened the trunk*   Audubon, *Ornithological Biography*, vol. I, pages xiii–xiv.

134 *He'd begun to set his birds*   Blaugrund and Stebbins (eds.), *John James Audubon*, pages 9–10.

134 *Tom Bakewell had arrived*   Ford, *John James Audubon*, page 88. Alice Ford reports that when Bakewell walked in on him, Audubon was busy with a watercolor depicting an otter with its foot caught in a trap. The original was lost, but Audubon repainted the gruesome scene many times in oil while he was in England.

134 *In November, Lucy gave birth*   Ibid.

134 *Audubon, determined at last*   DeLatte, *Lucy Audubon*, page 71.

134 *Audubon bought several adjacent lots*   Ibid., page 74.

134 *The state of Kentucky named the town*   Towles, *Henderson*, page 54.

134 *Audubon found domestic goods*   DeLatte, *Lucy Audubon*, page 74.

134 *Early in 1814, Audubon and Tom Bakewell opened a second store*   Ibid., page 75.

135 *Audubon tried his hand at*   Ibid., page 74.

135 *In a six-year period*   Ibid.

135 *They evidently acquired*   Ibid., page 76.

135 *She sent for her pianoforte*   Ibid.

135 *Fencing wasn't a popular diversion*   Ford, *John James Audubon*, page 96.

135 *Another time, the whole town*   Herrick, *Audubon the Naturalist*, vol. I, page 253.

135 *One of Henderson's leading lights*   DeLatte, *Lucy Audubon*, page 83. There's some conjecture here, but I think DeLatte makes a persuasive case that Lucy's status was defined by Audubon's wealth and physical courage, which made him quite a heroic figure in the community. Audubon could be rough and coarse, but on the frontier these attributes were to his advantage, and he was looked up to in the small town. Lucy's well-appointed house, her friendship with the Rankins, and her husband's appealing blend of artistic sensitivity and pioneer derring-do undoubtedly distanced Lucy from many neighbors not nearly so well off or well-married.

135 *When Audubon found a very young turkey*   Audubon, "The Wild Turkey," *Ornithological Biography*, vol. I, pages 1–17.

136 *Audubon was not fond of swan meat*   Audubon, "Trumpeter Swan," *Ornithological Biography*, vol. IV, pages 536–42.

136 *Knowing the huge white bird*   Ibid.

136 *When Audubon lived in Kentucky*   Personal communication, Nate Rice, Academy of Natural Sciences of Philadelphia, April 17, 2002.

136 *But the brown-headed cowbird* Ibid.
136 *There were no house sparrows* Ibid. See also the species accounts in Sibley, *The Sibley Guide to Birds*, and also in Bull and Farrand, *The Audubon Society Field Guide to North American Birds, Eastern Region*.
136 *Audubon never saw a* Ibid.
137 *He sees advancing from afar* Audubon, "The Green-Winged Teal," *Ornithological Biography*, vol. III, pages 219–25.
138 *Once, while watching mallards* Audubon, "The Mallard," *Ornithological Biography*, vol. III, page 164–72.
139 *Audubon liked to stand on the bank* Audubon, "The American Woodcock," *Ornithological Biography*, vol. III, pages 474–82.
139 *One of his favorite pursuits* Audubon, "Fishing in the Ohio," *Ornithological Biography*, vol. III, pages 122–27.
140 *The form in all the varieties* Ibid.
141 *Audubon was especially interested in* Audubon, "A Flood," *Ornithological Biography*, vol. I, pages 155–59.
141 *One day as Audubon walked along* Audubon, "The Eccentric Naturalist," *Ornithological Biography*, vol. I, pages 455–60.
143 *If you picture to yourself* Ibid.
145 *Rafinesque eventually became a professor* Kastner, *A Species of Eternity*, pages 246–48. Upperclassmen advised younger students not to miss Rafinesque's humorous and wildly entertaining lecture on ants, in which he attributed to the insects many traits of human society.

11. LEGIONS OF THE AIR

146 *The cedar bird—now called the cedar waxwing* Audubon, "The Cedar Bird," *Ornithological Biography*, vol. I, pages 227–31.
146 *Audubon thought goldfinches and purple finches* Audubon, "The American Goldfinch," *Ornithological Biography*, vol. I, pages 172–76.
147 *Everything about the great horned owl* Audubon, "The Great Horned Owl," *Ornithological Biography*, vol. I, pages 313–18.
147 *He discovered that he could get quite close* Ibid.
147 *He thought it ironic that* Audubon, "The Night-Hawk," *Ornithological Biography*, vol. II, pages 273–78.
148 *American white pelicans were numerous* Audubon, "American White Pelican," *Ornithological Biography*, vol. IV, pages 88–102.
150 *The last time anyone saw a Carolina parakeet* Sibley, *The Sibley Guide to Birds*, page 14.
150 *The passenger pigeon had disappeared* Ibid.
150 *Bill white. Iris hazel* Audubon, "The Carolina Parrot," *Ornithological Biography*, vol. I, pages 135–40. Parrot or parakeet? Audubon and Wilson casually switched between both names for this parakeet, which was a member of the parrot family. I've elected to use the currently accepted term—parakeet—except where quoting from another source.
150 *Carolina parakeets, he wrote* Ibid.

152 *In the fall of 1813* Audubon, "The Passenger Pigeon," *Ornithological Biography*, vol. I, pages 319–27.

153 *Some years after seeing* Ibid.

154 *Once, near the Green River* Ibid.

155 *Passenger pigeons in flight, high and untouchable* Ibid.

156 *On a chilly winter day in 1814* Audubon, "The Bird of Washington," *Ornithological Biography*, vol. I, pages 58–65.

157 *It happened again near the Green River* Ibid.

158 *Then, while walking from Henderson* Ibid.

158 *Audubon saw this eagle* Ibid., and Corning (ed.), *Journal of John James Audubon, 1820–1821*, page 28.

159 *That's about 50 percent larger* Sibley, *The Sibley Guide to Birds*, page 127. Sibley gives eighty inches for the wingspan of a bald eagle, a weight of 9½ pounds, and a length of thirty-one inches.

159 *Not even the California condor* Ibid., page 106.

159 *"All circumstances duly considered"* Audubon, "The Bird of Washington," *Ornithological Biography*, vol. I, pages 58–65.

159 *On closer examination* Ord to Charles Waterton, April 23, 1832. American Philosophical Society. George Ord, always foremost among Audubon's detractors, was obsessed with trying to discredit Audubon's account of the Bird of Washington. This ten-page letter, in Ord's minute, precise handwriting, offers perhaps his most detailed analysis, containing extensive tables, measurements, and extrapolations intended to show that the bird simply could not have been as big as Audubon claimed it was. Ord never gave up. Three years later, he was still corresponding with Waterton on the subject. In a letter dated April 15, 1835 (American Philosophical Society), Ord informed Waterton that Titian Peale, the artist who had completed a number of drawings for later editions of the Wilson/Bonaparte *American Ornithology*, was certain the bird was an immature bald eagle.

160 *Canada geese, for example* Personal observation and Sibley, *The Sibley Guide to Birds*, page 74. The size variability of the Canada goose is not typical of most bird species. Sibley notes that the species includes our "largest and nearly our smallest geese," and he gives a weight range of 3½ pounds to over 9 pounds.

160 *A comparison of the three images* Personal observation. To my knowledge, no one has ever bothered to measure Audubon's drawing of the Bird of Washington to see if it corresponds to his statements about its size, or for the purpose of comparing it to his drawings of the adult and juvenile bald eagle. I did exactly that on September 25, 2003, using three drawings that are part of the original double-elephant folio in the library of the James Ford Bell Museum of Natural History at the University of Minnesota in Minneapolis. Laying down sheets of clear acetate to protect the prints, I measured the birds with a yardstick laid directly atop the images. The results are, I believe, convincing evidence that Audubon's Bird of Washington really was as big as he claimed. Although Audubon was often untrustworthy in what he said or wrote, he never varied his basic drafting technique, in which matching grids on his mounting board and drawing paper were used to produce an image that was exactly life-size. And I can think of no reason why,

when making his drawing of this bird many years before it even occurred to him to publish a written description of it, he would have decided to scale up its dimensions. I think instead that Audubon unwittingly provided proof of what he later said about the enormity of the specimen. All of which leaves the major question unanswered. What kind of bird was it? Of the several ornithologists I asked about this, none could conceive that it was a distinct species of native eagle no longer in existence. Nate Rice, of the Academy of Natural Sciences in Philadelphia (personal communication, June 16, 2003), told me it would be unlikely that such an animal existed without having been observed and reported by other naturalists working at the time, and that, lacking a specimen, no evaluation of Audubon's claim is possible. Rice did say that there are occasional sightings of a "melanistic" variant of a species of Pacific sea eagle that is larger than the bald eagle. Rice said a colleague had recently examined a specimen of a "giant black eagle" in Russia that turned out to be a melanistic sea eagle. However, Rice stressed that the species is only thinly distributed in Alaska and is rarely seen in the lower forty-eight states. Finding a doubly rare melanistic variant in the central United States would have thus been mind-bogglingly improbable.

My own, unscientific, feeling is that Audubon lived in Kentucky at a time when a number of species once common in the area—bison, wolves, grizzly bears— were disappearing—so who knows? It seems clear that Audubon shot and drew an unusually large eagle. It seems equally clear that we'll never know for sure what it was.

161 *It was mildly astonishing to the Audubons*   Ford, *John James Audubon*, pages 90–92.
161 *Meanwhile, Audubon and Tom Bakewell*   Ibid., page 90.
162 *When the Audubons' first daughter was born*   Ibid., page 91.
162 *Sick at first, as infants sometimes are*   Ibid., pages 91–93.
162 *By the time little Lucy died*   Ibid., page 92.

12. EVER SINCE A BOY

163 *Almost from the time construction began*   Ford, *John James Audubon*, page 92. It seems that almost from the moment the mill was under construction, Audubon was having second thoughts, and Bakewell—apparently for the first time—realized that demand for lumber in the area was exceedingly small, as was the local wheat crop. They built anyway, in the vain hope that business would come. It never did.

163 *When it was done, the mill was gargantuan*   Personal inspection of several photographs of the mill in later years, notably published in Towles, *Henderson*, and Herrick, *Audubon the Naturalist*, vol.1.

163 *Crumbling remains of its stone footings*   Personal observation. I visited the city park in Henderson in August 2002 and walked among the ruins.

164 *The years following the successful conclusion*   Harrison and Klotter, *A New History of Kentucky*, pages 96–97.

164 *The war's interruption of trade*   Ibid.

164 *The Kentucky Insurance Company*   Ibid., pages 143–44.

164 *In 1818, the Kentucky Insurance Company failed*   Ibid.

164 *In the Panic of 1819*   Ibid., page 97.

164 *When the banks and then the state* Ibid.

165 *Then, in 1818, his father died* Ford, *John James Audubon*, page 97.

165 *After protracted litigation* Ibid., pages 97–98.

165 *At the same time, Tom Bakewell* Ibid., pages 103–4.

165 *In a convoluted exchange of credits* Ibid.

165 *Audubon, rashly it would seem* Herrick, *Audubon the Naturalist*, vol. I, pages 257–59.

166 *Even if he managed to catch up* Ford, *John James Audubon*, pages 105–6. The eventual sale of all their assets for $21,000 not long after this episode left the Audubons still deep in debt.

166 *Because of either a lack of funds* Herrick, *Audubon the Naturalist*, page 259.

166 *It was shortly after his return* Ford, *John James Audubon*, pages 104–5.

166 *A local judge, in dismissing an assault charge* Ibid.

166 *By summer, Bowen was back on his feet* Ibid., page 105.

166 *An old friend in Shippingport bought* Ibid., pages 105–6. The buyout was divided thus: $14,000 for the Audubon interest in the mill and $7,000 for his house, landholdings, and personal property. A note of indenture, dated October 13, 1819, includes a list of the items of personal property that is both heartbreaking and mysterious. Among the items the Audubons sold were Lucy's piano, 150 books—possibly including Wilson's *American Ornithology*—and, shockingly, "all my drawings, crayons, Paints, pencils, drawing paper, silver compasses, rules," etc. Clearly, Audubon retained his essential portfolios of work; any drawings that actually changed hands were quite a bargain.

166 *Adding to this crushing burden* DeLatte, *Lucy Audubon*, page 100.

167 *In Louisville he was arrested* Ford, *John James Audubon*, page 106.

167 *When he asked his hosts to recommend him* Ibid., pages 106–7.

167 *One of his specialties was* Audubon, Maria R., *Audubon and His Journals*, vol. 1, page 36.

167 *After a few weeks of painting* Ford, *John James Audubon*, page 107.

167 *But before they could move* Ibid.

168 *Watching his new daughter nursing* Corning (ed.), *Journal of John James Audubon, 1820–1821*, pages 47–48. Only 225 copies of this remarkable document were published in 1929 by the Club of Odd Volumes in Boston. The original is in the Houghton Library at Harvard University.

168 *Audubon applied and was hired* Ford, *John James Audubon*, page 109.

168 *More significantly, his portfolio of bird drawings* Adams, *John James Audubon*, pages 194–95.

168 *After repeatedly promising him his pay* Ford, *John James Audubon*, page 111.

168 *Lucy, who'd anticipated this* Ibid.

168 *Audubon thought he was* Ibid., page 112.

169 *He was in command of a large flatboat* Corning (ed.), *Journal of John James Audubon, 1820–1821*, page 16. Audubon's opinion of Captain Aumack varied, and not long after the date of this entry he had a falling-out with Aumack. Except as indicated below, the balance of the account of Audubon and Mason's journey downriver and their first year in New Orleans—comprising the bulk of this chapter—is taken from Audubon's journal. Quotations and significant events are individually cited by page number in the Corning edition.

169 *Late in the afternoon of October 12, 1820* Ibid., page 3.

170 *Audubon persuaded Mason* Ibid., page 12.

172 *The meeting of the Two Streams reminds me* Ibid., page 30.

172 *One morning when it was too rainy to hunt* Ibid., pages 42–49.

173 *Ever since a Boy* Ibid.

176 *The sleekest and most deadly* Bull and Farrand, *The Audubon Society Field Guide to North American Birds, Eastern Region*, page 470.

179 *New Orleans was the fifth-largest city* Richard, *Louisiana*, page 49.

179 *The city was also a principal immigration point* Ibid.

179 *Almost incomprehensibly, a few of these free blacks* Ibid.

179 *Quadroon balls were popular events* Ibid., page 48.

180 *The Mississippi River between New Orleans and Natchez* Ibid., page 49.

180 *One bit of gossip hinted* Arthur, *Audubon*, pages 300–304.

181 *He seemed a steadying and cheerful influence* Audubon to Lucy Audubon, May 24–May 31, 1821 (American Philosophical Society). This is the long letter that also included Audubon's journal excerpt regarding the mysterious Ms. Andre.

181 *But sour feelings were never* Corning (ed.), *Journal of John James Audubon, 1820–1821*, page 116.

181 *One day as he walked down a back alley* Audubon to Lucy Audubon, May 24–May 31, 1821 (American Philosophical Society).

183 *In a long letter to Lucy* Ibid.

183 *Weary and losing weight* Ibid. Audubon was, among other things, attempting to respond to a series of complaining letters he'd received from Lucy that spring.

183 *Her father had recently died* Lucy to Euphemia Gifford, April 1, 1821 (Princeton University Library).

184 *"[F]or the last year"* Ibid.

184 *That same spring, Lucy was writing* Audubon to Lucy Audubon, May 24–May 31, 1821 (American Philosophical Society).

184 *Her letters, he wrote in his journal* Corning (ed.), *Journal of John James Audubon, 1820–1821*, page 120.

185 *"Wert thou not to give me hints"* Audubon to Lucy Audubon, May 24–May 31, 1821 (American Philosophical Society).

185 *In June of 1821* Corning (ed.), *Journal of John James Audubon, 1820–1821*, page 159.

187 *Audubon and Mason went back downriver* Ibid., pages 197, 200.

188 *After weeks of meeting one boat, then another* Ibid., page 223.

188 *Lucy got work as a governess* Ford, *John James Audubon*, page 134.

188 *Lucy and the boys joined him at Natchez* Ibid., page 135.

189 *Audubon gave Mason some paper and chalks* Herrick, *Audubon the Naturalist*, vol. I, page 321.

189 *The woman, Jane Percy, lived on a plantation* Ford, *John James Audubon*, pages 136–38.

189 *In better days, when business was good* Personal communication, Don Boarman, museum curator at John James Audubon State Park, Henderson, Kentucky. The museum holds all eight volumes of *American Ornithology* owned by Audubon. The first six were evidently purchased on a trading trip in the south, and bear the inscription "1816 Louisiana."

189 *Audubon attributed this unwillingness*   Corning (ed.), *Journal of John James Audubon, 1820–1821*, page 122.

189 *When George Ord was elected to*   Rhoads, "George Ord." *Cassinia: Proceedings of the Delaware Valley Ornithological Club*, No. XII, 1908.

190 *In New York, to which he'd fled*   Ford, *John James Audubon*, page 148.

191 *After a slow bird-watching detour*   Ibid., pages 149–52.

191 *A skiff delivered him ashore*   Herrick, *Audubon the Naturalist*, vol. I, pages 345–46. Herrick, along with virtually all of Audubon's subsequent biographers, accepts this early journal account of Audubon losing his way in the woods as a description of his return to Lucy in 1825, after his long visit to Philadelphia. Alice Ford, however, believes this is instead the story of his return to Lucy after his nearly three-year absence in England and Scotland several years later. Ford cites Maria Audubon's bowdlerized version of the journals as the main authority on this point, and I will grant that she may be right in doing so. However, Lucy changed employers during Audubon's British sojourn, and when he returned she had moved to a new house, the location of which would have been vague to Audubon if he knew it at all. The fact that he struck out at night, thinking he would find his way home in the rain and darkness, I think, argues that this was his earlier return from Pennsylvania, when he was going back to Beech Woods. Suffice it to say that, in both homecomings, Audubon's long absence made him eager to complete his journey and that husband and wife greeted one another each time with profound emotion.

191 *Audubon was astonished to learn*   Ford, *John James Audubon*, page 154.

191 *One evening, he instructed a class*   Buchanan, *The Life and Adventures of John James Audubon*, pages 98–99.

192 *On hot afternoons, the Audubons would ride together*   Streshinsky, *Audubon*, page 155. Audubon discreetly recalled his happiness at watching Lucy bathe her "gentle form."

192 *Some field notes that Audubon had mailed*   Audubon to Charles-Lucien Bonaparte, January 12, 1825 (American Philosophical Society). (The society has a collection of microfilm copies of Bonaparte's correspondence. The originals are in the Bibliothèque, Museum Nationale d'Histoire Naturelle in Paris.)

192 *Thinking he was speaking confidentially*   Ford, *John James Audubon*, page 158.

192 *Haines—rather stupidly, the prince said*   Ibid.

192 *Visiting a nearby pond*   Audubon, "Observations on the Natural History of the Alligator."

192 *Audubon had an equally dicey experience*   Ford, *John James Audubon*, page 155.

193 *In the spring of 1826*   Ibid., page 159.

193 *Lucy, supportive but perhaps irked*   Ibid.

193 *Having some time before the ship was ready*   Ford (ed.), *The 1826 Journal of John James Audubon*, page 16.

193 *He got in to see the governor*   Ibid., page 17.

193 *Audubon had seen Nolte on the street*   Corning (ed.), *Journal of John James Audubon, 1820–1821*, page 158.

193 *By far the more valuable of the two*   Ford (ed.), *The 1826 Journal of John James Audubon*, page 18.

193 *On May 17, 1826*   Ibid., page 20.
194 *Once clear of land*   Ibid.
194 *While he stayed up on deck*   Ibid., page 21.

13. EDINBURGH

195 *It was raining when Audubon stepped onto the wharf*   Ford (ed.), *The 1826 Journal of John James Audubon*, page 81. As in the preceding chapter, a surviving Audubon journal is the principle source for much of the material in this chapter. Except where indicated otherwise, the story related here is from the 1826 journal, but I have provided selective individual citations to it for significant quotations and important episodes. Rightly skeptical readers will note many instances in which I have characterized Audubon's thoughts and feelings. This is possible because the 1826 journal—a remarkable document—is highly revealing as to Audubon's state of mind. Depressed and alone in a strange country, Audubon confided his innermost emotions to his journal, a record that, if anything, is more dramatic and subjective than any representation I have made of its content.

197 *Several times as he walked through town*   Ibid., page 85.
198 *The Rathbones, both Richard and William*   Ibid., page 82. This information is not, strictly speaking, part of Audubon's journal. Rather it comes from one of the many invaluable biographical notes supplied by Alice Ford throughout the text of the journal.

199 *One of these was William Roscoe*   Ibid., page 96.
199 *On Monday, July 31*   Ibid., page 111. Among the throngs in attendance at the exhibition were some critics, a title Audubon said possessed a "savage" aspect.

200 *Edward Stanley—Lord Stanley—was in a few years*   Fisher (ed.), *A Passsion for Natural History*, pages 45–51.
200 *As a young man he had studied Buffon's work*   Ibid.
200 *When Stanley was introduced and led into the room*   Ford (ed.), *The 1826 Journal of John James Audubon*, page 121. Audubon said that, given the quantity of hair he possessed, this effect was truly startling.

203 *As he walked along the banks*   Ibid., pages 157–58.
204 *Suddenly Audubon put down his pen*   Ibid., page 147.
205 *Still, he was disappointed*   Ibid., page 169.
205 *He wrote to Victor, who was still in Louisville*   Audubon to Victor Audubon, September 1, 1826 (Beinecke). Two large collections of the letters Audubon wrote from 1826 onward are in the archives of the Houghton Library at Harvard University and the Beinecke Rare Book and Manuscript Library at Yale University. A substantial selection—but not all—of these same letters was published in a limited, two-volume set edited by Howard Corning for the Club of Odd Volumes in 1930.

205 *In a letter to Lucy*   Audubon to Lucy Audubon, September 1, 1826 (Beinecke)
206 *Manchester was much more crowded*   Ford, *The 1826 Journal of John James Audubon*, pages 192–93.
206 *Now he was much relieved*   Ibid., page 199. Audubon, elated at finally getting mail from home, said that however "dull" Manchester was, it now contained "at least one happy individual."

206 *The actual plan, which had taken some time to coalesce* Ibid., pages 205–8. This portion of the journal was actually a copy of a letter to Lucy, dated September 17, 1826, which Audubon presumably sent. According to Alice Ford, letters such as this, which she has interspersed in chronological order throughout the text, were copied into Audubon's journal by a scrivener he hired for that purpose.

206 *Recognizing that this last undertaking implied* Ibid.

207 *If, for some reason, she could not come* Ibid. This odd suggestion that Lucy might not join him in England—and that he was prepared to support her wherever she wanted to live—seems to have come out of the blue. Perhaps they had discussed the possibility of separation previously, but the subject had never come up in Audubon's journal entries or letters until now. It would remain an often unstated subtext of their communication for the next couple of years.

208 *A book made from his life-sized paintings* Ibid., pages 232–34. Audubon wrote in his journal that he planned to follow Bohn's advice. As Alice Ford notes, parenthetically, Audubon in the end pretty much ignored Bohn's advice. Bohn was certainly correct that Audubon's drawings, if bound into volumes at full size, would be enormous books. A standard, leather-bound volume of the original double-elephant folio stands nearly four feet tall, is over two and a half feet wide, a couple of inches thick, and weighs in at around fifty pounds. Bohn's worry that such volumes would, as he put it, "encumber the table" proved groundless, as many owners had special cabinets build to house *The Birds of America*.

210 *Edinburgh, Audubon declared, was* Ibid., pages 301–5.

210 *The city was arranged on two parallel hilltops* Personal observation. In March 2003, I visited Edinburgh to conduct research on Audubon's time there, and to explore the city itself, which is not very much altered in its general appearance from the 1820s. At the special collections department of Edinburgh University Library, I photocopied an 1831 map of the city—produced for the Post Office and engraved on steel by William Home Lizars—which proved perfectly serviceable for navigating the streets of Edinburgh today.

210 *Home to artists and architects* Cosh, *Edinburgh*, pages 56–57.

210 *The origins of the modern age* Ford (ed.), *The 1826 Journal of John James Audubon*, page 301. Audubon said that as his coach passed near Scott's home, he strained for a glimpse of it.

210 *He had breakfast at ten* Ibid., pages 303–4. The boardinghouse on George Street, operated by Mrs. Dickie, was a four-story stone building that stood on the corner of the square. This location is now occupied by a modern building housing the Bank of Scotland.

211 *He hinted darkly that he now and then worried* Ibid., pages 305–6.

211 *Named for Jameson's mentor* From *Minutes of the Wernerian Society*, vol. I

212 *Audubon got a brusque reception* Ford (ed.), *The 1826 Journal of John James Audubon*, page 304.

212 *The "Sir" was William Jardine* "Note." *Dover Pictorial Series: 286 Full-Color Animal Illustrations from Jardine's "Naturalist's Library,"* page iii.

212 *He wrote to Victor at Louisville, telling him how fine* Ford (ed.), *The 1826 Journal of John James Audubon*, pages 319–23. Another letter, this one dated October 29, 1826, was recorded in the journal by Audubon and presumably copied and sent.

In it, Audubon reasserts his contention that Edinburgh is the most beautiful city in the world.

213 *He'd even had two of his paintings exhibited*   Bryan, *Bryan's Dictionary of Painters and Engravers*, vol. II.

213 *But his father's death a year later*   Ibid.

213 *Lizars had a thriving business*   Mr. [?] Greville to William Jardine, January 6, 1829 (Edinburgh University Library, Special Collections).

215 *One of the people who called that day*   Ford (ed.), *The 1826 Journal of John James Audubon*, pages 335–36.

216 *There was again discussion as to how big*   Ibid., page 347. Another journal letter, this one to William Rathbone in Liverpool, dated November 24, 1826.

216 *Set in the middle of the enormous sheets*   Audubon to Lucy Audubon, December 21, 1826 (Beinecke).

216 *The Birds of America, it stated*   Herrick, *Audubon the Naturalist*, vol. II, pages 386–88. Audubon issued several versions of the prospectus as the project moved forward over the years. But these essential elements were featured in each one. Herrick here reproduces the 1828 prospectus.

217 *The way his luxurious hair was pulled back*   A portion of Syme's portrait appears on the cover of this book.

217 *One who was then popular was*   "Charles Waterton: Naturalist," pages 1–40. This pamphlet, from 1880, was written by James Simson, and is at the Edinburgh University Library Special Collections department.

218 *Instead, he wrote about the turkey buzzard*   "Minutes of the Wernerian Society," December 16, 1826 (Edinburgh University Library Special Collections department).

218 *It faced the street*   Personal observation. It was still called "Edinburgh College" when Audubon visited. Today, Edinburgh University sprawls well south of the original building, now commonly referred to as "The Old College."

219 *The Wernerians met in a long room*   Ford (ed.), *The 1826 Journal of John James Audubon*, page 396.

219 *When Audubon walked in*   Ibid.

219 *It was substantial, occupying thirteen typeset pages*   Audubon, "Account of the Habits of the Turkey Buzzard."

219 *While it is the case that most bird species*   Sibley, *The Sibley Guide to Bird Life and Behavior*, page 36.

220 *The minutes from the meeting instead*   "Minutes of the Wernerian Society," December 16, 1826 (Edinburgh University Library Special Collections department).

220 *At the conclusion of the session*   Ibid.

220 *Just before Christmas of 1826*   Audubon to Lucy Audubon, December 21, 1826 (Beinecke).

221 *Audubon thought the boys would benefit*   Ibid.

221 *Instead, he asked her to tell him*   Ibid. Who can read between these lines? Audubon suggested to Lucy that she talk the matter over with friends or even with Victor, and to then assess her own feelings and convey them to him. Whatever Lucy was saying in her letters at this time—they are long lost—Audubon clearly got the idea that she was reluctant to join him.

221 *In late November she'd written her cousin* Lucy to Euphemia Gifford, November 29, 1826 (Beinecke).

222 *Audubon continued to attend meetings* "Minutes of the Wernerian Society," January 13, 27, 1827; and February 10, 24, 1827 (Edinburgh University Library Special Collections department).

222 *The discussions at these sessions* Ibid.

222 *On January 13, "John James Audubon Esquire of Louisiana"* "Minutes of the Wernerian Society," January 13, 1827 (Edinburgh University Library Special Collections department).

222 *At the same meeting, Audubon delivered* Ibid.

222 *The group found the paper* Ibid.

222 *But two weeks later* "Minutes of the Wernerian Society," January 27, 1827 (Edinburgh University Library Special Collections department).

222 *Two more weeks after that* "Minutes of the Wernerian Society," February 10, 1827 (Edinburgh University Library Special Collections department).

222 *He started off by suggesting* Audubon, "Notes on the Rattlesnake."

224 *Almost everything in Audubon's account* Klauber, *Rattlesnakes: Their Habits, Life Histories, and Influence on Mankind*, vol. 1, pages 454–63. Although nearly forty years old, Klauber's book is regarded as an authoritative classic.

224 *Rattlesnakes can climb trees* Ibid. Additionally, I am indebted to Dr. Harry W. Greene, professor of ecology and evolutionary biology, Cornell University, who confirmed the numerous errors in Audubon's account.

224 *The Wernerians were oblivious* Ibid.

224 *It was suggested then* Ibid. Klauber reports this conjecture and also tacitly endorses it. But, for the reasons given in the text, I simply cannot believe that this was a case of mixed-up field notes. With or without notes, no one having spent as much time in close field observations of wildlife as Audubon had would have misremembered this episode. Whatever the case, it is ironic that so much enmity toward Audubon was focused on the very animal that engendered so much fear and so many fanciful notions.

224 *For one thing, Audubon also reported* Audubon, "Notes on the Rattlesnake."

225 *Audubon had gotten word that Charles-Lucien Bonaparte* Ford (ed.), *The 1826 Journal of John James Audubon*, page 376.

225 *In late December, he'd finally received a letter* Audubon to Lucy Audubon, December 22, 1826 (Beinecke). This letter was actually appended to the one dated just one day earlier.

225 *Audubon, always concerned that he remain* Ibid.

225 *He'd written to Bonaparte as soon as* Audubon to Charles-Lucien Bonaparte, August 31, 1826 (American Philosophical Society [Bibliothèque Nationale de Museum d'Histoire Naturelle]).

225 *Audubon wrote again in early December* Audubon to Charles-Lucien Bonaparte, December 9, 1826 (American Philosophical Society [Bibliothèque Nationale de Museum d'Histoire Naturelle]).

225 *He reiterated that he had sent* Ibid.

225 *One of these letters came from* Ford, *John James Audubon*, page 206.

225 *Apparently Scott wasn't much impressed* Ibid.

225 *When the coach halted in front of Dalmahoy* Ford (ed.), *The 1826 Journal of John James Audubon*, page 419.

226 *In Edinburgh, Audubon also met* Ibid., page 354.

226 *By May he had signed up* Audubon to Lucy Audubon, May 16, 1827 (Beinecke).

14. DEAREST FRIEND

227 *London, one of the great cities* Audubon to Lucy Audubon, August 6, 1827 (Beinecke).

227 *In fact, most of its almost 2 million residents* Weinreb and Hibbert, *The London Encyclopedia*, rev. edition.

227 *Frustrated, he put the letters in the mail* Herrick, *Audubon the Naturalist*, vol. I, pages 377–78.

227 *Audubon stayed briefly at an inn* Ibid., page 377.

227 *He'd asked Lucy to show her copy* Audubon to Lucy Audubon, March 24, 1827 (Beinecke).

228 *Audubon had spent April 5* Ford, *John James Audubon*, page 209.

228 *Departing Edinburgh, Audubon had traveled* Audubon to Lucy Audubon, May 1, 1827 (Beinecke).

228 *Three subscribers had even signed up* Ibid.

228 *Bonaparte was enthusiastic about* Ford, *John James Audubon*, page 216.

228 *Altogether, Audubon had landed* Audubon to Lucy Audubon, May 16, 1827 (Beinecke).

228 *This was important, Audubon explained* Ibid.

229 *If he could secure two hundred subscribers* Ibid.

229 *Perhaps all of this was on Audubon's mind* Audubon to Lucy Audubon, March 24, 1827 (Beinecke).

229 *While he was at Leeds* Audubon to Lucy Audubon, May 1, 1827 (Beinecke).

229 *Reports of storms and shipwrecks* Audubon to Lucy Audubon, March 24, 1827 (Beinecke).

229 *Lucy had written to say* Ford, *John James Audubon*, page 208.

229 *Audubon wrote back saying she should wear her hair* Audubon to Lucy Audubon, May 1, 1827 (Beinecke).

230 *In March, addressing her as* Audubon to Lucy Audubon, March 24, 1827 (Beinecke).

230 *Audubon told Lucy she must wait* Audubon to Lucy Audubon, May 16, 1827 (Beinecke).

231 *One of the first persons he'd met on his arrival* Ford, *John James Audubon*, page 211.

231 *He invited Audubon to show his drawings* Ibid., page 212.

231 *A proper gentleman, Children* Ibid.

231 *On May 24, Audubon and Children made their way* "List of Visitors," Royal Society Library.

231 *The doorway to the society* Personal observation. I visited Somerset House in March 2003. The society is no longer located there, but its chiseled name still appears above the door and directly beneath a bust of Sir Isaac Newton.

231 *The Royal Society, organized informally*   "About the Foundation of the Royal Society,"
     a brief précis available to society visitors.
231 *The society took an interest in*   "Seapower, Science & Splendour: The Royal Navy at
     Somerset House," a brief précis available to Somerset visitors.
231 *The society had nearly seven hundred members*   "Record of the Royal Society," (1830).
231 *As the meeting progressed, Audubon listened*   "Minutes," *Journal Book of the Royal Soci-*
     ety, vol. XLV (1827–1830).
232 *He may have relaxed a little*   "List of Visitors," Royal Society Library.
232 *In mid-June, Lizars informed him*   William Lizars to Audubon, June 16, 1827 (Bei-
     necke).
232 *Lizars confided that all this was partly because*   Ibid.
232 *Lizars pleaded with Audubon*   Ibid.
232 *In one letter, Audubon said he had no doubt*   Audubon to Lucy Audubon, June 20,
     1827 (Princeton University Library).
232 *Here in such a "Civilized Country," he wrote*   Audubon to Lucy Audubon, May 15,
     1827 (Princeton University Library).
232 *Audubon asked Lizars to send down*   Audubon to Lucy Audubon, August 6, 1827
     (Beinecke).
233 *A questionable version of what happened next*   Herrick, *Audubon the Naturalist*, vol. I,
     pages 382–84. The story of Audubon reuniting the estranged Havells evidently
     originated with an account written by George Alfred Williams for *The Print-*
     Collector's Quarterly in 1916. Herrick, who published his biography of Audubon the
     following year, acknowledged Williams as the source of this information. Alice
     Ford repeated the same facts. Shirley Streshinsky toned it down considerably, dis-
     pensing with the reunion of the Havells altogether—but adding a dubious scene in
     which Audubon supposedly kissed both Havells on the cheeks. Frankly, any of this
     could be true. But for me, it seems too precious by half, and the contradicting evi-
     dence is hard to ignore. Suzanne M. Low, in her superb book, *A Guide to Audubon's*
     Birds of America, states categorically that while two versions of the prothonotary
     warbler were made, both were by Lizars. Herrick, too, had questioned this part of
     the tale. Then there is the matter of Robert Havell & Son existing as a going concern
     as early as 1823. While this doesn't rule out the possibility of a rift prior to
     Audubon's arrival, it undermines the claim that the partnership was first forged in
     Audubon's presence. Finally, common sense is against the legend. If the elder
     Havell's insistence that his son pursue some other line of work was so powerful
     that they had parted ways over it, then why would the elder Havell have changed
     in mind on the spot so that his son could take up an engraving project that might
     take ten or even fifteen years to complete? If he wanted the kid out of the busi-
     ness, this was no way to accomplish it. (See also the six notes directly following.)
233 *For years he'd worked in partnership*   Williams, "Robert Havell, Junior."
233 *Aquatinting was a refinement of the engraving process*   Low, *A Guide to Audubon's* Birds
     of America, pages 9–13. Low's description of the aquatinting process—heavily re-
     lied on here—is by far the best I've come across. Low also nicely explains how dif-
     ferent versions of the first ten plates from Lizars, some of which were retouched
     by the Havells, led to some confusion as to what was done by whom. What sepa-

rates the Havells from Lizars is aquatinting, which Lizars did not use. Alice Ford often writes of Lizars making "aquatints" of Audubon's plates, but she was mistaken—or perhaps only using this specific term as casually and inaccurately as the term "engraving" is also used in the same context.

234 *He was fifty-eight, he said*   Herrick, *Audubon the Naturalist*, vol. I, page 383.

234 *Supposedly, Havell suggested that they visit*   Ibid., pages 382–84.

234 *The firm of Robert Havell & Son was listed*   The firm appears in the *London & Provincial Directory for 1823–1824.*

234 *Similarly, there's no evidence that*   Low, *A Guide to Audubon's* Birds of America, pages 29–30.

235 *Because Havell Junior would have help*   Audubon to Lucy Audubon, August 6, 1827 (Beinecke).

235 *The Havells also had more ready access to*   Ibid.

235 *Amazingly, the Havells sweetened the deal*   Ibid.

235 *In early August he wrote to Lucy*   Ibid.

235 *Audubon now told Lucy he imagined*   Ibid.

235 *Meanwhile, he repeatedly insisted*   Ibid. Audubon reminded Lucy of this in other letters as well.

235 *Early that fall, Audubon wrote to Victor*   Audubon to Victor Audubon, August 25, 1827 (Beinecke).

236 *In late September, Audubon again wrote to Lucy*   Audubon to Lucy Audubon, September 20, 1827 (Beinecke). Apparently, Lucy had recently written to accept Audubon's proposal that she join him around New Year's. In this response, Audubon repeats, as always, his eagerness to be with Lucy again—but now he tells her to make no move until she hears from him with instructions.

236 *By the middle of November*   Audubon to Lucy Audubon, November 12, 1827, and November 25, 1827 (Beinecke).

236 *He said the Scottish people's reputation*   Audubon to Lucy Audubon, November 25, 1827 (Beinecke).

237 *Perhaps less certain of himself*   Ibid.

237 *Audubon reported that his health was fine*   Ibid.

237 *He admitted that he was a hopeless*   Ibid.

237 *Audubon signed off saying he was due*   Ibid.

238 *Back in London*   Audubon to Lucy Audubon, February 24, 1828 (Beinecke).

238 *He did mention that he was thinking of going*   Audubon to Lucy Audubon, March 17, 1828 (Beinecke).

238 *Evidently Lucy worried that*   Ibid.

238 *In another letter a few days later*   Audubon to Lucy Audubon, March 22, 1828 (Beinecke).

238 *In August he wrote to say*   Audubon to Lucy Audubon, August 8, 1828 (Beinecke).

238 *Once again, he told his "dearest friend"*   Ibid.

238 *But instead of contemplating a return*   Ibid.

239 *In June she'd written to Victor*   Lucy Audubon to Victor Audubon, June 15, 1828 (Beinecke).

239 *"What he really means I cannot tell"*   Ibid.

239 *He heard that he was being made fun of*   Ford, *John James Audubon*, pages 216, 219–20.

239 *Feeling especially low one day*   Ibid., page 222.

239 *They'd met after Audubon was approached*   Ibid., page 224.

240 *Swainson bluntly told Audubon*   William Swainson to Audubon, April 9, 1828 (Linnaean Society Archives).

240 *"I assure you my dear sir"*   Audubon to William Swainson, Ibid.

240 *Audubon, who still suffered*   Audubon to William Swainson, April 18, 1828 (Linnaean Society Archives).

240 *He hoped someday that he and Lucy*   Audubon to William Swainson, June 16, 1828 (Linnaean Society Archives).

240 *At the beginning of July*   Audubon to William Swainson, July 1, 1828 (Linnaean Society Archives).

241 *She informed him that she had borrowed some money*   Ford, *John James Audubon*, page 229.

241 *He told Swainson that thoughts of suicide*   Audubon to William Swainson, August 9, 1828 (Linnaean Society Archives).

241 *Then, out of the blue, he asked Swainson*   Ibid.

241 *Audubon spent the next few weeks*   Audubon wrote a series of notes to Swainson during the balance of August, outlining itineraries, ports of departure, etc. (Linnaean Society Archives).

241 *Audubon, accompanied by William Swainson*   Ford, *John James Audubon*, page 231.

241 *He wrote back to say that he was happy*   Audubon to Victor Audubon, November 10, 1828, and December 22, 1828 (Beinecke).

241 *Audubon had learned that Lucy was disappointed*   Ford, *John James Audubon*, page 241.

241 *In fact, the rooms above the Havells' shop*   Audubon to Victor Audubon, December 22, 1828 (Beinecke).

242 *He continually pored over*   Ibid.

242 *Just before Christmas*   Audubon to William Swainson, December 20, 1828 (Linnaean Society Archives).

242 *Audubon had to decline the Swainsons' suggestion*   Audubon to William Swainson, December 25, 1828 (Linnaean Society Archives).

242 *And he was angry enough when*   Ibid.

242 *Sometime after the first of the year*   Audubon to Lucy Audubon, January 20, 1829 (Beinecke).

242 *Lucy, devastated by Audubon's recent letters*   Lucy Audubon to Victor Audubon, January 19, 1829 (Princeton University Library). It's ironic, to say the least, that within one day of each other—essentially at the same instant after more than two years apart—Audubon and Lucy each decided to cross an ocean to join the other.

242 *In mid-January of 1829, Lucy wrote to Victor*   Ibid.

243 *At virtually the same moment*   Audubon to Lucy Audubon, January 20, 1829 (Beinecke).

244 *Audubon was also seriously worried about*   Audubon to Lucy Audubon, February 1, 1829 (Beinecke).

244 *The mail was so slow*   Lucy Audubon to Audubon, February 8, 1829 (Princeton University Library).

244 *Unsure if he was getting her letters*   Ibid.

245 *But he told her it was really the only way*   Audubon to Lucy Audubon, February 1, 1829 (Beinecke).

15. MY GREAT WORK

246 *Audubon, now in his mid-forties* Ford, *John James Audubon*, page 245.

246 *On April 25, 1830* Herrick, *Audubon the Naturalist*, vol. I, page 437. Herrick has the Audubons departing New York on April 1, and this is one of the two possible embarkation dates Audubon had mentioned in a letter to Havell several months earlier. Alice Ford states that the Audubons arrived in Liverpool on April 2, 1830, but this can't be. They were still in Louisville as late as March 2, when Audubon wrote out his will and sent it to Victor. They could not have gotten to England—with stops in Washington, D.C., and New York—by the beginning of April. Everyone agrees that it must have been a rough crossing that lasted twenty-five days, which is what Audubon said in a note to Swainson shortly after their arrival. (Audubon to William Swainson, May 5, 1830 [Linnaean Society Archives].)

246 *Rather than rush to Bayou Sara* Audubon to Lucy Audubon, May 10, 1829, and Audubon to Victor Audubon, July 18, 1829 (Beinecke).

246 *Apparently still convinced* Audubon to Lucy Audubon, May 10, 1829 (Beinecke).

246 *In an odd, quasi-legal plea* Ibid.

247 *Audubon again turned to Victor* Audubon to Victor Audubon, July 18, 1829 (Beinecke).

247 *Apparently there had been something like* Ibid.

247 *When Havell wrote a troubled letter* Audubon to Robert Havell Jr., July 7, 1829 (Houghton).

247 *Bonaparte was certainly good for the money* Ibid.

247 *Audubon's friend Dr. Richard Harlan* Ford, *John James Audubon*, page 257.

248 *He passed most of the month of August* Audubon to Victor Audubon, August 25, 1829 (Beinecke).

248 *By October, though he'd found not a single* Audubon to Robert Havell Jr., October 24, 1829 (Houghton).

248 *He'd also found a new partner* Audubon to Lucy Audubon, October 11, 1829 (Beinecke).

248 *Audubon said he would be at Louisville* Ibid.

248 *Although she had begun packing* Lucy Audubon to Audubon, August 29, 1829 (Beinecke).

248 *Lucy said that if she remained* Lucy Audubon to Audubon September 27, 1829 (Beinecke).

248 *"You must choose what I shall do"* Ibid.

248 *Lucy added that her savings* Ibid.

249 *"I thought that I would feel sufficiently settled"* Audubon to Lucy Audubon, February 6, 1828 (Beinecke).

249 *"I do not look to anything like labour"* Lucy Audubon to Audubon, August 29, 1829 (Beinecke).

249 *Lucy still hoped Audubon might come* Lucy Audubon to Audubon, October 11, 1829 (Beinecke).

249 *When Audubon told her he'd cut his hair* Lucy Audubon to Audubon, June 12, 1829 (Beinecke).

249 *In fact, she'd grown older* Lucy Audubon to Audubon, March 27, 1829 (Beinecke).

249 *"I live, and regulate all concerns"* Ibid.

250 *"I am gray quite," she said* Lucy Audubon to Audubon, June 12, 1829 (Beinecke).

250 *"You say you must not speak"* Lucy Audubon to Audubon, February 2, 1829 (Beinecke).

250 *Instead he collected his gun and dog* Audubon to Robert Havell Jr., October 27, 1829 (Houghton).

250 *Victor was so much taller and more mature-looking* Buchanan (ed.), *The Life and Adventures of John James Audubon*, page 169.

250 *At dawn he walked in on her* Ibid. Again, contrary to this account, Alice Ford states that it was on this occasion, and not on his earlier return from Philadelphia, that Audubon found Bayou Sara deserted due to a yellow fever outbreak, borrowed a horse, and lost his way in the night before finally getting home. Audubon and Lucy both mention the presence of yellow fever at Bayou Sara in their letters at this time, though for the reasons stated earlier I prefer the version I've given here. Either way it is a small matter, and seems to depend on which of two mangled versions of Audubon's journals you choose to believe. The more compelling question—which unfortunately is answered nowhere in the record—is how Audubon and Lucy patched things up when he finally came home after an absence of more than three years.

250 *One of the subscriptions he'd managed to sell* Ibid., page 170.

250 *Before leaving Victor and Johnny in Louisville* Audubon to Victor Audubon, March 2, 1830 (Beinecke).

251 *Children had written to say* John George Children to Audubon, November 23, 1829 (Beinecke).

251 *Audubon wrote to Havell* Audubon to Robert Havell Jr., January 29, 1830 (Houghton).

251 *After they got to England* Audubon to Lucy Audubon, April 30, 1830 (Beinecke), and Audubon to Robert Havell Jr., June 7, 1830 (Houghton).

251 *When the Audubons finally got to London* "Chronological Register of Fellows," Royal Society Archives. Audubon was elected to membership on March 18, 1830.

251 *He went to a meeting and paid his dues* Ford, *John James Audubon*, page 265.

251 *George Ord, who had been conveniently abroad* "List of Visitors," Royal Society Archives. Ord stopped by the society on June 18, 1829.

251 *He immediately directed Havell* Audubon, *The Birds of America*.

251 *A short while later, Dr. Harlan* Richard Harlan to Audubon, August 19, 1830 (Beinecke).

252 *Havell sent Audubon a note updating him* Robert Havell Jr. to Audubon, June 2, 1830 (Houghton).

252 *The paper itself—heavy linen stock* Personal observation. Of the various original double elephant folios I've looked at, none appeared the worse for wear because of any frailty of the paper, which really is extraordinary. On many pages of most sets, the pressing together of the prints under the great weight of the bound volumes has caused the images to transfer faintly onto the backs of the adjacent prints. But the prints are sturdy. In fact, they appear to have held up in some cases to careless handling. One print I saw bore the smudged tracks of a house cat across its face.

252 *Worst of all was a scathing letter*   Ford, *John James Audubon*, page 269.

252 *Enraged, Audubon wrote to Havell*   Audubon to Robert Havell Jr., June 29, 1830 (Houghton).

252 *Chagrined at not having caught*   Ibid.

252 *He warned Havell that if*   Ibid.

252 *Stung, Havell fired back*   Robert Havell Jr. to Audubon, June 30, 1830 (Houghton).

253 *Swainson sent Audubon a sarcastic note*   William Swainson to Audubon, May 1 [10?], 1830. Quoted in Herrick, *Audubon the Naturalist*, vol. II, pages 97–99.

253 *Ord had written to Alexander Lawson*   George Ord to Alexander Lawson, circa 1830 (Houghton). Only a fragment of this biting and bitter letter survives. I wonder about the date, as it seems more likely to have been written during Ord's visit the year before.

253 *Lucy wrote about it to Victor and Johnny*   Lucy Audubon to Victor and John Woodhouse Audubon, August 30, 1830 (Beinecke).

254 *In October they arrived in Edinburgh*   Buchanan (ed.), *The Life and Adventures of John James Audubon*, page 171.

254 *In addition to engraving, printselling, and publishing*   Printed advertisement, circa 1830 (Ewell Sale Stewart Library and Archives).

254 *Audubon asked Havell to display*   Audubon to Robert Havell Jr., January 16, 1831 (Houghton).

254 *My letter will be through necessity*   Audubon to Lucy Audubon, October 11, 1829 (Beinecke).

255 *Another factor in the decision*   Fries, *The Double Elephant Folio*, page 47.

255 *Audubon confided to Charles-Lucien Bonaparte*   Audubon to Bonaparte, July 14, 1830. Quoted in Ford, *John James Audubon*, pages 269–70. Audubon had been telling this to Bonaparte since they had first met in Philadelphia six years earlier. In this letter, he put it bluntly, saying that he was "not a learned naturalist" but only a "practical one."

255 *Audubon had thought initially of William Swainson*   Audubon to William Swainson, August 22, 1830 (Linnaean Society Archives).

255 *He told Audubon that their coming to stay with him*   William Swainson to Audubon, between August 24 and August 28, 1830. Quoted in Herrick, *Audubon the Naturalist*, vol. II, pages 103–5.

256 *One of the people he talked to was*   Ralph, *William MacGillivray*, page 35.

256 *Eleven years younger than Audubon*   Ibid., pages 1–35. The physical description is from the frontispiece likeness of MacGillivray in Ralph's book.

256 *When Audubon met him*   Ibid., pages 29–32.

256 *Toward the end of 1830*   Ibid., page 35. A few months later, MacGillivray apparently regretted not asking for credit as a coauthor, and complained of it in a letter—Willliam MacGillivray to Audubon, May 7, 1831 (Beinecke).

256 *Audubon, rising at dawn*   Buchanan (ed.), *The Life and Adventures of John James Audubon*, page 172.

257 *MacGillivray matched Audubon's manic pace*   Ibid.

257 *Prone to rheumatism, Lucy found Edinburgh*   Lucy to Robert Havell Jr., December 2, 1830 (Houghton).

257 *Audubon, whom she observed* Ibid.

257 *It was so foggy in Edinburgh* Ibid.

257 *Anyone having business with Audubon* Ibid. Lucy's correspondence on behalf of Audubon commenced in Edinburgh and would continue, as needed when "Mr. Audubon" was "particularly engaged," for many years.

257 *She told Mrs. Havell that they were far too busy* Lucy Audubon to Mrs. Havell, February 27, 1831 (Houghton).

257 *In a burst of headlong writing* Buchanan (ed.), *The Life and Adventures of John James Audubon*, page 172. Apparently the book was typeset as the copy was produced, as it was ready to ship within weeks of Audubon and MacGillivray completing their draft.

257 *The typeset version ran to* Audubon, *Ornithological Biography*, vol. I.

258 *I feel pleasure here in acknowledging* Ibid., pages xviii–xix.

258 *Audubon planned to sell* Fries, *The Double Elephant Folio*, page 50.

259 *And so he interspersed the bird accounts* Audubon, title page, *Ornithological Biography*, vol. I.

259 *In "Kentucky Barbicue"* Audubon, "Kentucky Barbicue on the Fourth of July," *Ornithological Biography*, vol. II, pages 576–79.

259 *He wrote a devoted remembrance* Audubon, "A Wild Horse," *Ornithological Biography*, vol. III, pages 270–74.

259 *He wrote enthusiastically of* Audubon, "The Squatters of the Mississippi," *Ornithological Biography*, vol. II, pages 131–34.

259 *There was a pioneer family's recollection* Audubon, "The Burning of the Forests," *Ornithological Biography*, vol. II, pages 397–402; and "The Lost One," *Ornithological Biography*, vol. II, pages 69–73.

259 *Then there was the ghastly* Audubon, "The Death of a Pirate," *Ornithological Biography*, vol. II, pages 185–89.

260 *In "Pitting of Wolves," Audubon told* Audubon, "Pitting of Wolves," *Ornithological Biography*, vol. III, pages 338–41.

260 *After an entertaining discussion* Audubon, "Scipio and the Bear," *Ornithological Biography*, vol. I, pages 479–82.

261 *In "The Prairie," Audubon recounted* Audubon, "The Prairie," *Ornithological Biography*, vol. I, pages 81–84.

261 *There was a similar dubious quality* Audubon, "The Runaway," *Ornithological Biography*, vol. II, pages 27–32.

262 *In "The Earthquake" he told of riding* Audubon, "The Earthquake," *Ornithological Biography*, vol. I, pages 239–41.

263 *Audubon without question experienced* Walker, *Earthquake*, pages 112–13.

263 *At the time of the initial quake* Lucy Audubon to Euphemia Gifford, January 5, 1812 (Princeton University Library).

264 *"Kentucky Sports" began with* Audubon, "Kentucky Sports," *Ornithological Biography*, vol. I, pages 290–95.

265 *Audubon gave a much fuller description* Audubon, "Colonel Boon," *Ornithological Biography*, vol. I, pages 503–6.

265 *The stature and general appearance of this wanderer* Ibid.

265 *Daniel Boone left Kentucky* Faragher, *Daniel Boone*, pages 308–9.

266 *Boone, who was by then almost eighty* Ford, *John James Audubon*, page 88.

266 *Lucy wrote to Mrs. Havell to say that so much* Lucy Audubon to Mrs. Havell, February 27, 1831 (Houghton).

266 *In the fall of 1831* Audubon to Lucy Audubon, November 23, 1831 (Beinecke).

267 *Off to starboard the surf crashed* Personal observation. I have family in this part of the world, and have spent much time on the same beautiful and often wild stretch of ocean.

267 *On November 20 the Agnes made port* Audubon to Lucy Audubon, November 13, 1831, and November 23, 1831. The arrival date is derived from Audubon's plan to leave Charleston "the day after tomorrow" stated in his November 13 letter, and the duration of the passage, stated as five days in the letter of November 23 (Beinecke).

267 *It reminded him of "an old French Village"* Audubon to Lucy Audubon, November 23, 1831 (Beinecke).

267 *Established in 1565 by the Spanish* Gannon, *The New History of Florida*, page 44.

267 *Audubon thought the people here were the laziest* Audubon to Lucy Audubon, November 29, 1831 (Beinecke).

267 *The weather, too, was awful* Ibid.

267 *One day Audubon explored* Audubon to Lucy Audubon, November 23, 1831 (Beinecke).

267 *He wrote a series of cheerful letters to Lucy* Audubon to Lucy Audubon, December 5, 1831 (Beinecke). Audubon said being once again in the wilds of America had made him feel "as young as ever." Lucy, he advised, should be "gay" and "happy."

268 *He even devised a plan* Ibid.

268 *But letters from Havell* Ibid.

268 *"Do not despond my Lucy"* Ibid.

268 *The subscriber list seemed to have leveled off* Ford, *John James Audubon*, page 281.

268 *On August 1, 1831* Audubon to Robert Havell Jr., July 31, 1831 (Houghton).

268 *From New York they had gone to* Audubon to Robert Havell Jr., September 20, 1831 (Houghton). Although Audubon mentions only three subscribers in this letter, he got a fourth—the Academy of Natural Sciences of Philadelphia—as Lucy reported in a letter to Mrs. Havell twelve days later—Lucy Audubon to Mrs. Havell, October 2, 1831 (Houghton). A month after this Richard Harlan wrote to Audubon about the arrival and condition of the academy's copy of *The Birds of America*.

268 *Audubon declared, prematurely it turned out* Audubon to Robert Havell Jr., September 20, 1831 (Houghton).

268 *Victor met his parents* Audubon to Lucy Audubon, October 9, 1831; October 13, 1831; and October 23, 1831 (Beinecke).

268 *He was accompanied again* Audubon to Lucy Audubon, October 23, 1831 (Beinecke).

268 *Audubon and his companions* Ibid.

269 *The Reverend John Bachman* Shuler, *Had I the Wings*, pages 18–23.

269 *Bachman lived in a large, three-story* Description from a photograph in Herrick, *Audubon the Naturalist*, vol. II, page 6.

269 *The busy household hummed*   Audubon to Lucy Audubon, October 23, 1831 (Beinecke).

269 *Bachman insisted that Audubon*   Ibid.

269 *Audubon made good use*   Audubon to Lucy Audubon, November 7, 1831 (Beinecke).

269 *They were well convinced of*   Ibid.

270 *Seven years after he'd been blackballed*   Thomas McEwan to Audubon, October 25, 1831 (Beinecke). McEwan was the corresponding secretary of the academy. Ironically, William MacGillivray had been elected a member a few weeks earlier.

270 *"This is a wild country"*   Lucy Audubon to Robert Havell Jr., November 1, 1831 (Houghton).

270 *From November through March*   Lucy Audubon to Robert Havell Jr., November 30, 1831 (Houghton). This letter was typical of a number that Lucy fired off to Havell that winter. In it, she insists that he cease selling individual prints and pay closer attention to the coloring and finishing of the plates: "Excuse my urging at Mr. Audubon's request your most particular attention to the work in all points for there are ever ready persons disposed to find every objection possible."

270 *Havell, exasperated, finally did*   Actually, it may have been that Havell had been writing all along, but that his letters were delayed. Audubon got several in December, while he was in Florida, and Lucy heard from Havell in February—Lucy Audubon to Robert Havell Jr., February 20, 1832 (Houghton).

271 *Audubon gave specific instructions*   Personal observation. At Mill Grove, I examined Audubon's notations on a proof that Havell was to use in making a finished print.

271 *Inexplicably, Havell simply appropriated*   Personal observation. This famous theft has been well documented elsewhere, but just to make sure I measured and examined both Wilson's and Audubon's kites at the Houghton Library. The reversed images are identical.

271 *Meanwhile, unaware of this transgression*   Lucy Audubon to Robert Havell Jr., March 22, 1832 (Houghton).

271 *"Mr. A and I are"*   Ibid.

271 *The real "check" Lucy provided*   Victor Audubon to Robert Havell Jr., July 21, 1832 (Houghton). Victor informed Havell that he would sail for England by the beginning of October. Prior to this decision, Audubon and Lucy debated how best to involve Victor in the project, with Audubon initially arguing that his son could best be used to solicit subscriptions in America. Audubon eventually acquiesced to this plan and was glad of it.

271 *She wrote again to Havell, admonishing him*   Lucy Audubon to Robert Havell Jr., June 24, 1832 (Houghton).

271 *Audubon, Lehman, and Ward*   Audubon to Lucy Audubon, November 29, 1831 (Beinecke). In this letter, Audubon said his transition from "Idleness to hard Labour" was having a tonic effect—energizing him like an "electric fluid," and helping him to set aside many of the concerns that had occupied his thoughts for so long. Only a week before, he had confessed to Lucy that he feared Havell might have died. But he was growing confident that anything—even a disaster such as his engraver's untimely demise—could be overcome. Havell, meanwhile, was fine.

The daily routine described here, including Audubon's practice of quickly drawing the outlines of birds before the heat spoiled the specimens, is from "Letter from Audubon to the Editor," *Monthly American Journal of Geology and Natural History*, vol. I, no. 8 (1832), 358–63.

272 *Writing to a friend in Philadelphia* "Letter from Audubon to the Editor," *Monthly American Journal of Geology and Natural History*, vol. I, no. 8 (1832), 358–63.

272 *This was the lot of many men* Ibid.

272 *So far, Audubon had shot and drawn* Audubon to Lucy Audubon, November 29, 1831 (Beinecke). Audubon gave conflicting assessments of the avian bounty in northeastern Florida. Though he frequently complained of having trouble finding new species, he seems to have kept himself busy drawing and on other occasions noted the abundance of birds in the area. Presumably, he saw birds everywhere and all the time, but was sometimes frustrated by their wariness or by the fact that many were already well-known to him.

272 *Audubon had acquired a telescope* Audubon to Lucy Audubon, December 8, 1831 (Beinecke). It's generally thought that Audubon did not use optics in his fieldwork. This is the only reference I'm aware of that mentions either a telescope or binoculars.

272 *The land between the ocean and* Ibid.

272 *In mid-December of 1831* Audubon to Lucy Audubon, January 4, 1832 (Beinecke).

272 *On Christmas day, about fifty miles below St. Augustine* "Letter from Audubon to the Editor," *Monthly American Journal of Geology and Natural History*, vol. I, no. 12 (1832), 529–37. The description of the approach to Bulow Plantation is a personal observation from my visit there in November 2002. The long, sandy road was empty and quiet, and the overarching live oaks seemed to close behind me as I drove slowly in, coming at last to the opening in the forest where Bulow's house and the slave quarters once stood. A way off from this compound, in a jungly clearing, the black, hulking ruins of the sugar mill looked out of place—a fantastic mistake. Down by the creek, the clear current swept by silently, and now and then a bird called from an unseen perch in the forest.

273 *Audubon remained there for several weeks* Audubon to Lucy Audubon, January 16, 1832 (Beinecke).

273 *Just before New Year's* "Letter from J. J. Audubon to the Editor," *Monthly American Journal of Geology and Natural History*, vol. I, no. 9 (1832), 407–14.

275 *There was little reason to stay on* Audubon to Lucy Audubon, January 16, 1832 (Beinecke).

275 *During his first visit to Charleston* The report is quoted in Shuler, *Had I the Wings*, page 7.

275 *In Philadelphia, the short-lived* "Audubon." *Monthly American Journal of Geology and Natural History*, vol I, no. 10 (1832), 456–68.

275 *In February, the* Philadelphia Gazette *reported that* Philadelphia Gazette, Feb. 11, 1832.

276 *There were no revenue cutters* Audubon to Lucy Audubon, January 16, 1832 (Beinecke).

276 *East Florida, he said, was a barren place* "Letter from Audubon to the Editor," *Monthly American Journal of Geology and Natural History*, vol. I, no. 12 (1832), 529–37.

276 *William Bartram, who had thought* Ibid.

276 *Audubon had hoped the* Spark *would take him* Audubon to Lucy Audubon, January 16, 1832 (Beinecke).

276 *Audubon went back to Charleston briefly* Audubon to Lucy Audubon, April 15, 1832 (Beinecke).

276 *He wrote to Lucy, saying that this expedition* Ibid.

276 *In April and May Audubon traveled* Proby, *Audubon in Florida*, page 4.

276 *He even saw flamingos* Audubon, "American Flamingo," *Ornithological Biography*, vol. V, pages 255–64.

276 *Although both of the boys had grown* Lucy Audubon to Audubon, March 19, 1832 (Beinecke).

277 *Lucy wrote to Audubon, thanking him* Ibid.

277 *Audubon's funds, as Lucy pointedly put it* Ibid.

277 *"Do not come home"* Ibid.

277 *"If you* cannot *come up"* Ibid.

277 *"I will be as prudent as need be"* Audubon to Lucy Audubon, April 15, 1832 (Beinecke).

277 *Within the year he would write to Victor* Audubon to Victor Audubon, February 24, 1833 (Beinecke).

278 *Joseph Kidd, who had signed a contract* Joseph Kidd to Victor Audubon, April 3, 1833 (Houghton).

278 *"I have nothing to say to you"* Audubon to Victor Audubon, February 24, 1833 (Beinecke).

278 *"Now my Dear Sir"* Audubon to Robert Havell Jr., April 20, 1833 (Houghton).

279 *Audubon showed the great, awkward-looking bird* Audubon, *The Birds of America*, Plate CCCCXXIII.

279 *In 1833, Audubon and John Woodhouse* Audubon to Victor Audubon, May 31, 1833 (Beinecke).

279 *Here Audubon painted seabirds* Audubon to Victor Audubon, September 9, 1833 (Beinecke).

279 *Later that year, the Audubons went to visit* Audubon to Victor Audubon, November 4, 1833 (Beinecke).

279 *Audubon wrote to Victor that in the future* Ibid.

279 *But in 1834 and 1835* Audubon to Robert Havell Jr., January 19, 1834 (Houghton).

279 *MacGillivray thought Audubon's prose style* William MacGillivray to Audubon, July 18, 1835 (Beinecke).

279 *He wrote to Bachman that he would rather* Audubon to John Bachman, November 19, 1834 (Houghton).

280 *Audubon told Bachman that he was arranging* Ibid.

280 *Audubon returned to America* Audubon to John Bachman, July 9, 1836 (Houghton).

280 *He managed to get his hands on* Audubon to John Bachman, October 2, 1836 (Houghton).

280 *The following year he traveled once more* Audubon to [no name], February 13, 1837 (Beinecke). This letter, bearing the salutation "My Dearest Friends," was almost

certainly to the Havells, judging by its many references to drawings shipped and instructions concerning Victor's oversight of their reproduction.

280 *In May 1837 John Woodhouse married* Ford, *John James Audubon*, page 428.

280 *Once, when Victor had expressed concern* Audubon to Victor Audubon, November 4, 1833 (Beinecke).

280 *Charles-Lucien Bonaparte called on Audubon* Ford, *John James Audubon*, page 348. In a letter, Audubon to John Bachman, December 20, 1837 (Houghton), Audubon spoke derisively of Bonaparte, calling the prince "Charley," and saying he knew far less about birds than he pretended.

280 *Sometime later, when Bonaparte published* Ford, *John James Audubon*, page 351.

280 *Bonaparte, who was evidently* Ford, *John James Audubon*, page 374. Ford quotes from a letter Waterton wrote to Ord, informing Audubon's archenemy that the prince had told him directly that Audubon had not studied with David.

280 *Audubon eventually wrote to Bonaparte* Audubon to Charles-Lucien Bonaparte, February 26, 1843 (American Philosophical Society [Bibliothèque Nationale de Museum d'Histoire Naturelle]).

281 *Bonaparte did not answer* Stroud, *The Emperor of Nature*, page 198.

281 *Rich and eccentric, Waterton struggled* Simson, "Charles Waterton: Naturalist," a forty-page biographical pamphlet prepared in 1880 and published in Edinburgh by James Miller.

281 *These included his ridiculous account* George Ord to Charles Waterton, April 23, 1832 (American Philosophical Society). This detailed letter runs fully ten pages in Ord's tiny, impeccable script.

281 *Actually, Audubon, though he exaggerated* Klauber, *Rattlesnakes*, vol. I, page 462. Klauber states that Audubon's enhancement of the curvature is pretty significant, and that the mockingbird plate does little to "enhance Audubon's reputation for accuracy of detail." But he grants the all-important point that rattlesnakes can, and sometimes do climb trees, and that the image of a rattler invading a mockingbird nest is not implausible.

281 *The birds were harrying the rattler* Audubon's prospectus for *The Birds of America* at one point included William Swainson's 1828 review, in which a number of the engravings are discussed in some detail. Swainson—who was in effect collaborating with Audubon on the review and presumably discussed the images with their author—referred to the infamous Plate XXI as "Mocking Birds defending their Nest from a Rattlesnake." In Swainson's interpretation, the mother bird's alarm has attracted a small flock of defenders.

281 *"I have been repeatedly solicited to review"* George Ord to Charles Waterton, April 23, 1832 (American Philosophical Society).

282 *In 1836, he wrote to a friend* Audubon to Richard Harlan, April 28, 1836 (Beinecke).

282 *"To have enemies is no uncommon thing"* Ibid.

282 *In the fall of 1839, Audubon donated* Audubon's inscription is in the first volume in the Wolf Reading Room of the academy's Ewell Sale Stewart Library.

282 *Ord made off with it* Personal observation. That is to say, I did not see Ord do this with my own eyes, but I did examine the marginalia that resulted.

282 *It is a fortunate circumstance*   Ord marginalia in *Ornithological Biography*, vol. V, page 181 (Wolf Reading Room, Ewell Sale Stewart Library, Academy of Natural Sciences of Philadelphia).

282 *Havell, racing against himself*   Audubon to John Bachman, August 14, 1837 (Houghton).

282 *Number 87, the last set of five*   Herrick, *Audubon the Naturalist*, vol. II, page 177.

282 *Audubon spent another year finishing*   Audubon to Robert Havell Jr., June 30, 1839 (Houghton).

283 *The conclusion has been attained*   From "Chronicle," *Niles National Register*, August 17, 1839.

283 *Audubon and Bachman had begun contemplating*   Audubon to John Bachman, January 2, 1840 (Houghton). In this letter, Audubon formally proposes their collaboration, which has been under discussion, even though both men are getting old. In fact, Audubon was thinking about and drawing mammals long before he met Bachman. In 1831, he'd mentioned such a project to Charles-Lucien Bonaparte. He incorporated many mammals in the plates for *The Birds of America*, and there was, of course, the example of his beloved and oft-painted "Otter in a Trap."

283 *Audubon estimated that his "great work" had cost him*   Fries, *The Double Elephant Folio*, page 114.

283 *While there never was a perfect accounting*   Low, *A Guide to Audubon's* Birds of America, page 3. Victor, who spent years trying to reconcile the various subscriber lists, estimated the total at 175.

284 *The "little work," as Audubon called it*   Fries, *The Double Elephant Folio*, page 353.

284 *In the meantime, Audubon applied for a permit*   Ford, *John James Audubon*, page 380. Permission was granted by the mayor, who stipulated that Audubon conduct his shooting expeditions "early in the morning" in order to minimize the danger to local residents.

284 *In 1841, the Audubons, who had been living*   Herrick, *Audubon the Naturalist*, vol. II, pages 234–35.

284 *Audubon named it "Minnie's Land"*   Ibid., page 235.

284 *Forever in love with rivers*   Based on a lithograph and a later photograph of Minnie's Land in Herrick, *Audubon the Naturalist*, vol. II.

284 *Later on, Victor and John Woodhouse*   Maria Audubon to Unknown Recipient, possibly Francis Herrick, June 19, 1925. Maria, quite old at the time, said, "I remember my grandfather perfectly, with his beautiful, long white hair and he taught us all to dance." (Audubon Museum, John James Audubon State Park, Henderson, Kentucky.)

284 *Audubon, dressed in a*   Ford, *John James Audubon*, page 389.

284 *The expedition, on which he planned*   Ibid., pages 388–89.

285 *The party went by train to Baltimore*   Ibid., page 392.

285 *They next boarded a filthy, dilapidated steamer*   Ibid., page 393.

285 *Audubon spent four weeks*   Ibid., page 394.

285 *They described him as*   Ibid.

285 *On the morning of April 25*   Audubon, Maria (ed.), *Audubon and His Journals*, vol I, pages 455–56.

16. AFTER

286 *John James Audubon died*   Ford, *John James Audubon*, page 422.

286 *Near the end he was in pain*   Ibid.

286 *"You go down that side of Long Pond"*   Ibid.

286 *Audubon—by a fair estimate*   Low, *A Guide to Audubon's* Birds of America, page 16.

287 *Audubon paid tribute to her*   Audubon, *The Birds of America*, Plate CLXXV.

287 *On the expedition to the West*   Boehme (ed.), *John James Audubon in the West*, page 60.

287 *The buffalo slaughter disgusted him*   Ford, *John James Audubon*, pages 400–401.

287 *Both Victor and John Woodhouse*   Boehme (ed.), *John James Audubon in the West*, page 148.

287 *Both sons worked on background landscapes*   Ford, *John James Audubon*, pages 409–10.

287 *But Audubon used much the same technique*   Boehme, *John James Audubon in the West*, pages 29–30.

288 *In the end, about half the animals*   Ibid., page 26.

288 *His eyesight dimmed and he started to drink*   Victor Audubon to John Bachman, March 27, 1846 (Beinecke). Victor in this letter mentions his father's failing eyesight. The excessive drinking—apparently sporadic—was duly noted by Bachman during Audubon's visit to Charleston in the spring of 1840—John Bachman to Victor Audubon, June 25, 1840.

288 *By 1846 he had stopped*   Ford, *John James Audubon*, page 414.

288 *A year later he wrote his last*   Herrick, *Audubon the Naturalist*, vol. II, page 288.

288 *Writing home to Maria Martin*   Quoted in Ibid., page 289.

288 *Audubon may have suffered one or more small strokes*   Ford, *John James Audubon*, page 429.

288 *In 1833, while staying in Boston*   Audubon to Richard Harlan, March 20, 1833. Audubon told Harlan that his right hand and his mouth had been paralyzed for about one hour, rendering him unable to speak and scaring the wits out of Lucy. I wish to thank Dr. John Chalmers, of Edinburgh, who is both a medical expert and an Audubon scholar, for suggesting that these symptoms are consistent with a transient ischemic attack. However, the supposition that this is, in fact, what happened is my own and Dr. Chalmers is blameless if I am in error.

288 *His hair turned white*   Based on his appearance in a daguerreotype made circa 1850 in Herrick, *Audubon the Naturalist*, vol. II.

288 *Audubon became less communicative*   Streshinsky, *Audubon: Life and Art in the American Wilderness*, page 361.

288 *Chronic exposure to such toxins*   Lloyd and Bendersky, "Arsenic, An Old Case." Audubon's final illness cannot be diagnosed, though as the estimable Dr. Lloyd says, history can be almost as instructive as a postmortem. In the case of Raphaelle Peale—one of Charles Willson Peale's painting sons, he also prepared specimens for his father's Philadelphia museum—Lloyd and her colleague Gordon Bendersky make a persuasive argument that long, chronic exposure to arsenic and mercury solutions used in taxidermy produced goutlike suffering, loss of teeth and bones in the jaw, and a stumbling aphasia that caused people to think Peale was often drunk. Audubon's exposure to the same toxins—presumably less severe than Peale's—could not have done him any good, and perhaps played a part in his physical and mental deterioration.

289 *But he assumed that these effects were short-lived* Audubon, "The Golden Eagle," *Or-nithological Biography*, vol. II, pages 464–70.

289 *He called on one of his subscribers* George Ord to Charles Waterton, June 22, 1845 (American Philosophical Society). Victor had been corresponding with the society for a period of time in an attempt to collect the outstanding balance.

289 *The Philosophical Society, formed in 1743* Lingelbach, "Philosophical Hall."

289 *It was housed in a handsome old* Ibid. Philosophical Hall is still there and still lovely. Much of the society's business is now conducted across the street, in its library building.

289 *It was George Ord* George Ord to Charles Waterton, June 22, 1845 (American Philosophical Society).

289 *Ord thought him hopeless, a fool* Ibid.

289 *But, as Ord later said* Ibid.

289 *After their meeting, Ord wrote to Waterton* Ibid.

289 *"The old gentleman has a very venerable look"* Ibid.

290 *In 1839, two years after* Ford, *John James Audubon*, page 428.

290 *By 1841, both sisters were dead* Ibid., pages 370, 429. Ford states that Eliza developed a terrible cough almost immediately following Maria's death.

290 *In 1846 John Bachman's wife* Shuler, *Had I the Wings*, page 203.

290 *His own health declining* Ford, *John James Audubon*, page 419.

290 *Victor Audubon injured his spine* Herrick, *Audubon the Naturalist*, vol. II, page 295. A different version has it that Victor—who at the age of two had ridden from Henderson, Kentucky, to Philadelphia sitting on a saddle in front of his father—hurt his back falling into a basement window well.

290 *He died on August 18, 1860* Ibid.

290 *John Woodhouse, always the more sensitive of the brothers* Ford, *John James Audubon*, pages 419–21.

290 *In 1858, he invested in a project* Herrick, *Audubon the Naturalist*, vol. II, page 296.

290 *But the outbreak of the Civil War* Ibid.

290 *Exhausted, his fragile nerves in ruins* Ibid., page 297.

290 *In 1863, awash in debt* DeLatte, *Lucy Audubon*, page 227.

290 *That same year she also sold* Blaugrund and Stebbins (eds.), *John James Audubon*, page viii.

290 *The committee organized for this purpose* Ibid. The exact purchase price was $4,230, or about $9 a drawing.

290 *Two years after the purchase* Ibid.

290 *For a time, Lucy lived by herself* DeLatte, *Lucy Audubon*, page 227.

290 *Spending most of her time alone* Buchanan, *The Life and Adventures of John James Audubon*, page v. In his preface, Robert Buchanan states that the manuscript was delivered to him in 1867, and that it consisted "chiefly of extracts" from Audubon's journals. He said Lucy had had some help with the text—Herrick states that it was from a friend, the Reverend Charles Coffin Adams—but that it was overlong and in desperate need of revision.

290 *She said she seemed to herself* Lucy Audubon to an unnamed relative, July 11, 1865. Quoted in Herrick, *Audubon the Naturalist*, vol. II, pages 301–2.

290 *"It does seem to me"* Ibid.

291 *She went by train, sitting and watching* DeLatte, *Lucy Audubon*, page 229.

291 *She thought rail travel pleasant enough* Ibid.

291 *Feeble and nearly blind* Ibid.

291 *Lucy's ashes were buried* From a transcript of Lucy Audubon's eulogy. (John James Audubon State Park Museum, Henderson, Kentucky.)

291 *In 1839, just a year after completing* Williams, "Robert Havell, Junior."

291 *Before leaving England* Fries, *The Double Elephant Folio*, page 390.

291 *According to one story* Ibid., pages 390–91.

291 *Somewhat corroded, they were recovered* Ibid. The part about the fire, at least, was true. (Herrick, *Audubon the Naturalist*, vol. II, page 267.)

291 *Audubon had the surviving coppers removed* Herrick, *Audubon the Naturalist*, vol. II, page 268. Herrick's photograph of John Woodhouse's home on the Minnie's Land compound shows the shed where the coppers were stored.

291 *The coppers ended up at* Ibid., pages 307–8.

291 *Fewer than eighty of the original coppers* Fries, *The Double Elephant Folio*, page 394.

292 *As the prints were lifted* Personal observation.

292 *It was almost surely fewer than two hundred* Fries, *The Double Elephant Folio*, page 140.

292 *Victor maintained that there were* Ibid.

292 *The new owner was* From my friend Don Boarman, curator of the John James Audubon State Park Museum in Henderson, Kentucky.

BIBLIOGRAPHY

MANUSCRIPT COLLECTIONS

American Philosophical Society, Philadelphia
Audubon Wildlife Sanctuary at Mill Grove, Audubon, Pennsylvania
Beinecke Rare Book and Manuscript Library, Yale University, New Haven, Connecticut
Edinburgh University Library Special Collections, Edinburgh, Scotland
Ewell Sale Stewart Library and Archives, Academy of Natural Sciences, Philadelphia
Filson Club Historical Society, Louisville
Free Library of Philadelphia
Guildhall Library, London
Historical Society of Pennsylvania
Houghton Library, Harvard University, Cambridge
John James Audubon State Park and Museum, Henderson, Kentucky
Linnaean Society, Archives, London
Museum of Arts and Sciences, Center for Florida History, Daytona Beach
New-York Historical Society, New York City
Princeton University Library, Rare Books and Special Collections Department, Princeton
Royal Society Library, London
St. Paul Public Library, St. Paul, Minnesota

BOOKS AND PERIODICALS

Adams, Alexander B. *John James Audubon: A Biography.* New York: G. P. Putnam's Sons, 1966.
Amadon, Dean. *American Bird Engravings: All 103 Plates from* American Ornithology, *by Alexander Wilson.* New York: Dover Publications, 1975.
Arthur, Stanley Clisby. *Audubon: An Intimate Life of the American Woodsman.* Gretna, La.: Firebird Press, 1937 (2000 reprint).

Audubon, John James. "Account of the Habits of the Turkey Buzzard (Vultur aura)." *Edinburgh New Philosophical Journal* 2 (1826–27): 172–184.

————. "Observations on the Natural History of the Alligator." *Edinburgh New Philosophical Journal* 2 (1826–27): 270–280.

————. "Notes on the Rattlesnake (Crotalus horridus)." *Edinburgh New Philosophical Journal* 3 (1827): 21–30.

————. *Ornithological Biography, Or an Account of the Habits of the Birds of the United States of America; Accompanied by Descriptions of the Objects Represented in the Work Entitled* The Birds of America, *and Interspersed with Delineations of American Scenery and Manners.* 5 vols. Edinburgh: Adam Black, 1831–1839.

————. *The Complete Audubon.* 5 vols. Kent, Oh.: Volair Books for the National Audubon Society, 1978.

Audubon, Maria R. *Audubon and His Journals.* 2 vols. New York: Dover Publications, 1897 (1986 reprint).

Barnes, Jonathan, ed. *The Complete Works of Aristotle: The Revised Oxford Translation.* 2 vols. Princeton: Princeton University Press, 1984.

Bell Jr., Whitfield J. "A Box of Old Bones: A Note on the Identification of the Mastadon, 1766–1806." *Proceedings of the American Philosophical Society* 93, no. 2 (1949): 169–177.

Benton, Michael, and David Harper. *Basic Paleontology.* Essex, U.K.: Pearson Education Limited, 1997.

Blaugrund, Annette, and Theodore E. Stebbins Jr., eds. *John James Audubon: The Watercolors for* The Birds of America. New York: Villard Books / The New-York Historical Society, 1993.

Boehme, Sarah E., ed. *John James Audubon in the West: The Last Expedition, Mammals of North America.* New York: Harry N. Abrams, 2000.

Bogardus, Carl R. *Flatboatin' on the Old Ohio.* Warsaw, Ky.: The Gallatin Historical Society, 1984.

Bogart, W. H. *Daniel Boone and the Hunters of Kentucky.* Boston: Lee and Shepard, 1870.

Buchanan, Robert, ed. *The Life and Adventures of John James Audubon, The Naturalist.* London: Sampson Low, Son & Marston, 1869.

Bull, John, and John Farrand Jr. *The Audubon Society Field Guide to North American Birds, Eastern Region.* New York: Alfred A. Knopf, 1977.

Burns, Robert. *Poems in Scots and English.* London and Rutland, Vt.: Everyman / Charles E. Tuttle Co., 1996.

————. *Selected Poems.* New York: Penguin Books, 1993.

Burstein, Andrew. *The Passions of Andrew Jackson.* New York: Alfred A. Knopf, 2003.

Cantwell, Robert. *Alexander Wilson: Naturalist and Pioneer.* Philadelphia and New York: J. B. Lipincott Company, 1961.

Carmichael, Jim, ed. *The Story of American Hunting and Firearms.* New York: Outdoor Life / E. P. Dutton & Company, 1959 (1976 revised).

Chalmers, John. "Audubon in Edinburgh." *Archives of Natural History* 20, no. 2 (1993): 157–166.

Chancellor, John. *Audubon: A Biography.* New York: The Viking Press, 1978.

Clark, Thomas D. *The Rampaging Frontier.* New York: Bobbs-Merrill Company, 1939.

Corning, Howard, ed. *Journal of John James Audubon, Made During His Trip to New Orleans in 1820–1821*. Boston: The Club of Odd Volumes, 1929.

———. *Journal of John James Audubon, Made While Obtaining Subscriptions to His Birds of America 1840–1843*. Boston: The Club of Odd Volumes, 1929.

———. *The Letters of John James Audubon 1826–1840*. 2 vols. Boston: The Club of Odd Volumes, 1930.

Cosh, Mary. *Edinburgh: The Golden Age*. Edinburgh: John Donald Publishers, 2003.

Cramer, Zadok. *The Navigator*, 8th ed. Pittsburgh: Cramer, Spear and Eichbaum, 1814 (1966 Readex Microprint reprint).

Dallett, Francis James. "Citizen Audubon: A Documentary Discovery," *The Princeton University Library Chronicle*, vol. XXI, nos. 1 and 2 (Autumn 1959 and Winter 1960): 89–93.

Deak, Gloria-Gilda. *American Views: Prospects and Vistas*. New York: Viking Press/New York Public Library, 1976.

DeLatte, Carolyn. *Lucy Audubon: A Biography*. Baton Rouge: Louisiana State University Press, 1982.

Donovan, Frank. *River Boats of America: From Flatboats to Floating Palaces, From the Cotton Blossom to the Staten Island Ferry*. New York: Thomas Y. Crowell Company, 1966.

Drepperd, Carl W. *Pioneer America: Its First Three Centuries*. Garden City, N.Y.: Doubleday & Company, 1949.

Durant, Mary, and Michael Harwood. *On the Road with John James Audubon*. New York: Dodd, Mead & Company, 1980.

Dwight, Margaret Van Horn. *A Journey to Ohio in 1810*. New Haven, Conn.: Yale University Press, 1912 (1991 Bison Book reprint).

Dyche, Russell. *The Wilderness Road—And Other Early Trails and Roads through the Wilderness to Kentucky*. Frankfort: The Register of the Kentucky State Historical Society, 1946.

Earle, Alice Morse. *Stage Coach and Tavern Days*. New York: Macmillan Company, 1900.

Elman, Robert. *America's Pioneering Naturalists: Their lives and times, exploits and adventures*. Tulsa, Okla.: Winchester Press, 1982.

Engeman, Thomas S., ed. *Thomas Jefferson and the Politics of Nature*. Notre Dame: University of Notre Dame Press, 2000.

Faragher, John Mack. *Daniel Boone: The Life and Legend of an American Pioneer*. New York: Henry Holt and Company, 1992.

Fisher, Clemency. *A Passion for Natural History: The Life and Legacy of the 13th Earl of Derby*. Liverpool, U.K.: Bluecoat Press, 2002.

Ford, Alice. *John James Audubon*. Norman: University of Oklahoma Press, 1964.

Ford, Alice, ed. *The 1826 Journal of John James Audubon*. New York: Abbeville Press, 1967.

———. *Audubon, By Himself*. Garden City, N.Y.: The Natural History Press, 1969.

Fries, Waldemar H. *The Double Elephant Folio: The Story of Audubon's Birds of America*. Chicago: American Library Association, 1973.

Funkhouser, William Delbert. *Wild Life in Kentucky: The Reptiles, Birds, and Mammals of the Commonwealth, with a Discussion of Their Appearance, Habits and Economic Importance*. Frankfort: The Kentucky Geological Survey, 1925.

Gannon, Michael. *The New History of Florida*. Gainesville: The University Press of Florida, 1996.

Graustein, Jeannette E. *Thomas Nuttall, Naturalist: Explorations in America 1808–1841.* Cambridge: Harvard University Press, 1967.

Grosart, Alexander B. *The Poems and Literary Prose of Alexander Wilson, The American Ornithologist.* 2 vols. Paisley, Scotland: Alex. Gardner, 1876.

Haites, Erik F.; James Mak; and Gary M. Walton, et al. *Western River Transportation: The Era of Early Internal Development, 1810–1860.* Baltimore: Johns Hopkins University Press, 1975.

Harper, Francis, ed. *The Travels of William Bartram: Naturalist Edition.* Athens: University of Georgia Press, 1998.

Harrison, Lowell H., and James C. Klotter. *A New History of Kentucky.* Lexington: University of Kentucky Press, 1997.

Henderson, Archibald. *The Transylvania Company and the Founding of Henderson, Ky.* (Pamphlet), 1829.

———. *The Significance of the Transylvania Company in American History.* (Pamphlet), 1835.

Herrick, Francis Hobart. *Audubon the Naturalist: A History of His Life and Times.* 2 vols. New York: D. Appleton and Company, 1917.

Hunter, Clark. *The Life and Letters of Alexander Wilson.* Philadelphia: American Philosophical Society, 1983.

Huston, McCready. "Poet with Fowling Piece." *Frontiers* (October 1943): 6–10.

Illick, Joseph S. "Pennsylvania Trees." *Bulletin, Pennsylvania Department of Forestry* 11, 4th ed. (1923): 11–20.

Imlay, Gilbert. *A Topographical Description of the Western Territory of North America.* 3rd ed., 1797. New York: Augustus M. Kelley, 1969. (Reprint).

Irmscher, Christoph. *The Poetics of Natural History: From John Bartram to William James.* New Brunswick, N.J.: Rutgers University Press, 1999.

Kastner, Joseph. *A Species of Eternity.* New York: Alfred A. Knopf, 1977.

King, Gail. *A Flatboat Hornbook.* Henderson, Ky.: Gleaner Print Shop, 1975.

Klauber, Laurence M. *Rattlesnakes: Their Habits, Life Histories, and Influence on Mankind.* 2 vols. Berkeley and Los Angeles: University of California Press, 1956.

Koerner, Lisbet. *Linnaeus: Nature and Nation.* Cambridge: Harvard University Press, 1999.

Lingelbach, William E. "Philosophical Hall: The Home of the American Philosophical Society." *Transactions of the American Philosophical Society* 43, no. 1 (1953): 43–69.

Lloyd, Phoebe. "Philadelphia Story." *Art in America* November (1988): 155–203.

———. "Invisible Killers: Heavy Metals, Saturnine Envy, and the Tragic Death of Raphaelle Peale." *Transactions & Studies of the College of Physicians of Philadelphia* Series V, Vol. XVI (1994): 83–99.

Lloyd, Phoebe, and Gordon Bendersky. "Arsenic, An Old Case: The Chronic Heavy Metal Poisoning of Raphaelle Peale (1774–1825)." *Perspectives in Biology and Medicine* 36, no. 4 (1993): 654–664.

Low, Susanne M. *A Guide to Audubon's Birds of America.* New Haven and New York: William Reese Company & Donald A. Heald, 2002.

McBurney, Henrietta, ed. *Mark Catesby's Natural History of America: The Watercolors from the Royal Library, Windsor Castle.* Houston: The Museum of Fine Arts, Houston/London: Merrell Holberton Publishers, 1997.

McDermott, John Francis, ed. *Up the Missouri with Audubon: The Journal of Edward Harris.* Norman: University of Oklahoma Press, 1951.

————. *Before Mark Twain: A Sampler of Old, Old Times on the Mississippi.* Carbondale and Edwardsville: Southern Illinois University Press, 1968.

Meyers, Amy R. W., and Margaret Beck Pritchard. *Empire's Nature: Mark Catesby's New World Vision.* Chapel Hill: University of North Carolina Press, 1998.

Michaux, F. Andrew. *Travels to the Westward of the Allegany Mountains.* Philadelphia: Richard Phillips, 1805.

————. *The North American Sylva; or A Description of the Forest Trees of The United States, Canada, and Nova Scotia.* Vol. III. Philadelphia: A. N. Hart, 1856.

Miller, Charles A. *Jefferson and Nature: An Interpretation.* Baltimore: Johns Hopkins University Press, 1988.

Miller, Stephen M. *Early American Waterfowling 1700s–1930.* Piscataway, N.Y.: New Century Publishers, 1986.

Monthly American Journal of Geology and Natural History, vol. 1 (1832).

de Montule, Edouard. *Travels in America 1816–1817.* Translated from the 1821 French edition by Edward D. Seeber. New York: Kraus Reprint Co., 1969.

O'Connor, Jack. *The Shotgun Book.* 2nd ed. New York: Alfred A. Knopf, 1986.

Oleson, Alexander, and Sanborn C. Brown, eds. *The Pursuit of Knowledge in the Early American Republic: American Scientific and Learned Societies from Colonial Times to the Civil War.* Baltimore: Johns Hopkins University Press, 1976.

Peattie, Donald Culross. *Audubon's America: The Narratives and Experiences of John James Audubon.* Cambridge, Mass.: The Riverside Press, 1940.

Phillips, John C. *A Bibliography of American Sporting Books.* Boston: Edward Morrill and Son, 1930.

Phillips, Maurice E. "The Academy of Natural Sciences of Philadelphia." *Transactions of the American Philosophical Society* 43, no. 1 (1953): 266–274.

Porter, Charlotte M. "The Excursive Naturalists, or The Development of American Taxonomy at the Philadelphia Academy of Natural Sciences 1812–1842." Cambridge: Harvard University, 1976 (Thesis).

————. "Following Bartram's 'Track': Titian Ramsay Peale's Florida Journey." *Florida Historical Quarterly* April 1983: 431–444.

————. *The Eagle's Nest: Natural History and American Ideas, 1812–1842.* University of Alabama: University of Alabama Press, 1986.

Proby, Kathryn Hall. *Audubon in Florida, with Selections from the Writings of John James Audubon.* Coral Gables: University of Miami Press, 1974.

Prothero, Donald R. *Bringing Fossils to Life: An Introduction of Paleobiology.* New York: WCB/McGraw-Hill, 1998.

Rafinesque, C. S. *On Botany.* Frankfort, Ky.: The Whippoorwill Press, 1993.

Ralph, Robert. *William MacGillivray.* London: HMSO, 1993.

Rhoads, Samuel N. "George Ord." *Cassinia: Proceedings of the Delaward Valley Ornithological Club*, no. XII (1908): 1–8.

Richard, C. E. *Louisiana: An Ilustrated History.* Baton Rouge: The Foundation for Excellence in Louisiana Public Broadcasting, 2003.

Roger, Jacques. *Buffon: A Life in Natural History.* Translated by Sara Lucille Bonnefoi. Ithaca, N.Y.: Cornell University Press, 1997.

Rourke, Constance. *Audubon.* New York: Harcourt, Brace and Company, 1936.

Rudwick, Martin J. S. *Georges Cuvier, Fossil Bones, and Geological Catastrophes: New Transla-*

tions & Interpretations of the Primary Texts. Chicago: University of Chicago Press, 1997.

Scordato, Ellen, ed. *The New York Public Library Desk Reference,* 4th Ed. New York: Hyperion, 2002.

Semonin, Paul. *American Monster: How the Nation's First Prehistoric Creature Became a Symbol of National Identity.* New York: New York University Press, 2000.

Sharp, Mary Rozier, and Louis J. Sharp III. *Between the Gabouri: A History of Ferdinand Rozier and 'Nearly' All His Descendents.* Ste. Genevieve, Mo.: Histoire de Rozier, 1981.

Shuler, Jay. *Had I the Wings: The Friendship of Bachman & Audubon.* Athens: University of Georgia Press, 1995.

Sibley, David Allen. *The Sibley Guide to Birds.* New York: Alfred A. Knopf, 2000.

———. *The Sibley Guide to Bird Life & Behavior.* New York: Alfred A. Knopf, 2001.

Simon, Grant Miles. "Houses and Early Life in Philadelphia." *Transactions of the American Philosophical Society* 43, no. 1 (1953): 280–299.

Spamer, Earle. "The legacy of 'friends of natural science': A systematic look at the scientific publications of the Academy of Natural Sciences of Philadelphia, 1817–2000." *Proceedings of the Academy of Natural Sciences of Philadelphia* 150 (2000): 3–13.

Speed, Thomas. *The Wilderness Road: A Description of the Routes of Travel by which the Pioneers and Early Settlers First Came to Kentucky.* Louisville: The Filson Club, 1886.

Starling, Edmund L. *History of Henderson County, Kentucky.* Henderson: NP, 1887.

Stoddard, T. Lothrop. *The French Revolution in San Domingo.* Boston: NP, 1914.

Streshinsky, Shirley. *Audubon: Life and Art in the American Wilderness.* New York: Villard Books, 1993.

Stroud, Patricia Tyson. *Thomas Say: New World Naturalist.* Philadelphia: University of Pennsylvania Press, 1992.

———. *The Emperor of Nature.* Philadelphia: University of Pennsylvania Press, 2000.

Towles, Susan Starling. *Henderson: Home of Audubon.* American Guide Series. Compiled by the Workers of the Writers' Program of the Work Projects Administration in the State of Kentucky. New York: Bacon, Percy & Daggett, 1941.

Townsend, John Kirk. "Description of Twelve New Species of Birds, Chiefly from the Vicinity of the Columbia River." *Journal of the Academy of Natural Sciences of Philadelphia* VII (1837): 187–193.

Tudge, Colin. *The Variety of Life: A Survey and a Celebration of All the Creatures that Have Ever Lived.* Oxford, U.K.: Oxford University Press, 2000.

Wade, Richard C. *The Urban Frontier: Pioneer Life in Early Pittsburgh, Cincinnati, Lexington, Louisville, and St. Louis.* Chicago: University of Chicago Press, 1964.

Waldstreicher, David, ed. *Notes on the State of Virginia by Thomas Jefferson, with Related Documents.* New York: Palgrave, 2002.

Walker, Bryce. *Earthquake.* New York: Time-Life Books, 1982.

Wall, Bennett H., et al. *Louisiana, A History.* 4th ed. Wheeling, Il.: Harlan Davidson, 2002.

Weigley, Russell F., et al. *Philadelphia: A 300-Year History.* New York: W. W. Norton & Company, 1982.

Weinreb, Ben, and Christopher Hibbert, eds. *The London Encyclopedia,* Revised Edition. London: Papermac, 1993.

Wetmore, Alexander, and Frederick C. Lincoln. "Additional Notes on the Birds of Haiti and the Dominican Republic." *Proceedings of the United States National Museum* 82, Art. 25, pages 1–68. Washington, D.C.: Smithsonian Institution, 1933.

Williams, George Alfred. "Robert Havell, Junior, Engraver of Audubon's 'The Birds of America.'" *The Print-Collector's Quarterly* 6 (1916): 226–255.

———. "Portraits of Robert Havell, Junior, Engraver of Audubon's 'The Birds of America.'" *The Print-Collector's Quarterly* 7 (1917): 298–304.

Wilson, Alexander, and Charles-Lucien Bonaparte. *American Ornithology, or The Natural History of the Birds of the United States.* 4 vols. Edinburgh: Constable and Co., 1831.

Witmer, A. E. "The Old Turnpike." *Papers Read before the Lancaster County Historical Society* II, no. 3 (1897): 67–86.

Yater, George H. *Two Hundred Years at the Falls of the Ohio: A History of Louisville and Jefferson County.* Louisville: The Heritage Corporation, 1979.

Yochelson, Ellis L. "Mr. Peale and His Mammoth Museum." *Proceedings of the American Philosophical Society* 136, no. 4 (1992): 487–505.

INDEX